International African Library 32
General Editors: J. D. Y. Peel, Colin Murray and Suzette Heald

ISLAM AND THE PRAYER ECONOMY

The *International African Library* is a major monograph series from the International African Institute and complements its quarterly periodical *Africa*, the premier journal in the field of African studies. Theoretically informed ethnographies, studies of social relations 'on the ground' which are sensitive to local cultural forms, have long been central to the Institute's publications programme. The *IAL* maintains this strength but extends it into new areas of contemporary concern, both practical and intellectual. It includes works focused on problems of development, especially on the linkages between the local and national levels of society; studies along the interface between the social and environmental sciences; and historical studies, especially those of a social, cultural or interdisciplinary character.

International African Library

General Editors

J. D. Y. Peel, Colin Murray *and* Suzette Heald

ISLAM AND THE PRAYER ECONOMY

HISTORY AND AUTHORITY IN A MALIAN TOWN

BENJAMIN F. SOARES

EDINBURGH UNIVERSITY PRESS
for the International African Institute, London

© Benjamin F. Soares, 2005

Edinburgh University Press Ltd
22 George Square, Edinburgh

Typeset in Plantin
by Koinonia, Bury, and
printed and bound in Great Britain
by The Cromwell Press, Trowbridge, Wilts

A CIP record for this book is available
from the British Library

ISBN 0 7486 2285 3 (hardback)
ISBN 0 7486 2358 2 (paperback)

For other publications of the International
African Institute, please visit their web site at
www.iaionthe.net

CONTENTS

LIST OF FIGURES

ACKNOWLEDGEMENTS

Various parts of the research for this study were made possible through financial support from Fulbright-Hays (the US Department of Education), the Fulbright Program of USIA through the West African Research Association/Center, the Wenner-Gren Foundation for Anthropological Research, and Northwestern University. The NIMH Program on Culture and Mental Health Behavior, the Committee on Human Development, the University of Chicago, and the National Science Foundation-NATO provided funds in the form of postdoctoral fellowships for the writing. A term of paid leave from the University of Sussex allowed me to work on revisions of the manuscript.

I am grateful to the Institut des Sciences Humaines in Bamako and the USIS staff of the US Embassy in Bamako for facilitating my research in Mali. Many individuals in West Africa and especially in Nioro du Sahel helped make the research possible. While it is not possible to thank them all individually, I want to express my deepest gratitude to Nioro's most eminent religious leaders (in alphabetical order): the late Sadikou Diakité, Mohamédou Ould Cheikh Hamallah, and Tierno Hady Tall. I am also deeply indebted to the late Sidy Modibo Kane of Dilly. At the risk of oversight, I have decided not to single out the countless others who helped me during fieldwork in Nioro and beyond with the following exceptions: Mohamed Aliou Sow, Mamadou Diarra, M'Péné Diarra, and Modibo Tiambel Guimbayara. Much of what follows is only possible because of their help, guidance, friendship and good humour.

This study began as a PhD dissertation at Northwestern University, which proved to be a most welcoming place for me to pursue my interests in anthropology, history, Islam and Africa. I owe the greatest of debts to Robert Launay, the chair of my dissertation committee, for his advice, encouragement and support. I would also like to thank my teachers, Karen Tranberg Hansen, John O. Hunwick, David William Cohen, Brinkley Messick, Richard Parmentier and Judith Irvine, whose ideas have influenced what follows. This book in its present form took shape and was rewritten as I have moved from Chicago to Paris, then back to Chicago, before moving to Brighton, England, and now to the Netherlands where I completed the final revisions at the African Studies Centre.

Some of the many people who have helped along the way include: the late Moustapha Kane, Abdoulaye Sall, and Oumar Watt in Dakar; Jean-Loup Amselle, Corinne Fortier, Constant Hamès, Danièle Hervieu-Léger, Ibrahima-Abou Sall, Jean Schmitz and Jean-Louis Triaud in France; Salman Tamboura, Moussa Djiré, Isaie Dougnon and Shaka Bagayoko in Bamako; and Louis Brenner, Bertram Cohler, Mamadou Diawara, Micaela di Leonardo, James Fairhead, Jane Goodman, Hudita Mustafa, Maria Grosz-Ngaté, Jane Guyer, Rosalind Hackett, John Hanson, Gil Herdt, Abdullahi Ali Ibrahim, Gregory Mann, Adeline Masquelier, Caroline Osella, Filippo Osella, Richard Roberts, Armando Salvatore, Boukary Savadogo, Rüdiger Seesemann, Rebecca Shereikis, Richard Shweder, Rosalind Shaw, Eric Silla, Mette Shayne, Diana Stone, Niels Teunis and Theo van der Meer. Ralph Austen, Jean Comaroff, Hudita Mustafa, Armando Salvatore, Rüdiger Seesemann, and Rebecca Shereikis all read and commented on various chapters or parts of chapters, sometimes at short notice, and for this I am grateful. I owe special thanks to Murray Last for the idea of the prayer economy that I have developed here.

I am also pleased to be able to thank a most generous group of readers, who reviewed the book. John Bowen, one of the reviewers of the first draft, provided excellent advice on how to revise the manuscript, as well as words of encouragement. The subsequent reviewers for the International African Institute (IAI), Louis Brenner, David Robinson and the editor, John Peel, offered much constructive criticism, which I have tried to incorporate into this final version. The usual disclaimers apply.

I would like to thank my mother, as well as a group of friends, Zeynep Erim, Jacalyn Harden, Elise Levin, John Maguire and William Mar, who have been there throughout a project that has taken much longer to complete than expected. Above all, I thank John Edward Harrelson.

Some of the material in Chapter 3 appeared as 'Notes on the Tijaniyya Hamawiyya in Nioro du Sahel after the second exile of its shaykh' in J.-L. Triaud and D. Robinson (eds), *La Tijâniyya*, Paris: Karthala, 2000, pp. 357–65, and is used here with the permission of Karthala; parts of Chapter 6 appeared as 'Muslim saints in the age of neoliberalism' in Brad Weiss (ed.), *Producing African Futures: Ritual and Reproduction in a Neoliberal Age*, Leiden: Brill, 2004, pp. 79–105, and are used here with the permission of Brill; and portions of Chapter 8 and several passages in the Conclusion appeared in 'Islam and public piety in Mali' in A.Salvatore and D. F. Eickelman (eds), *Public Islam and the Common Good*, Leiden: Brill, 2004, pp. 205–26, and are used here with the permission of Brill.

NOTES ON ORTHOGRAPHY
AND TRANSLATION

Place names are written as they appear on maps – thus, Ségou rather than Segu. For personal names, I have generally followed orthographic self-representation rather than use other more recently adopted orthographic conventions – thus, Seydou rather than Seedu and Tall rather than Taal. In a few cases, I have used newer orthographic conventions to aid readers with pronunciation – thus, Cerno and Jakhite, rather than Tierno (or Thierno) and Diakhité. In other cases, I have opted for commonly used orthographies that also more closely approximate pronunciation of local names – thus, Hamallah rather than Hamahoullah or other such variants. For transliteration of words from Bambara, Fulfulde and Soninke, I have, when possible, followed orthographic conventions used by the DNAFLA, Direction nationale d'alphabétisation fonctionnelle et de la linguistique appliquée, in Mali. For transliteration of words from the Arabic, I have used a simplified system with plurals sometimes indicated by adding an 's' to the transliterated word, for example, *muqaddam* (s.) and *muqaddams* (pl.). Finally, for certain personal names from the Arabic, I have followed the standard transliteration system from Arabic, though I have altered them slightly to more closely approximate local pronunciations – thus, Umar and Amadu, rather than 'Umar and Ahmad.

All translations are my own, except when otherwise noted.

ABBREVIATIONS

ANM	Archives Nationales du Mali, Koulouba, Mali
ANS	Archives Nationales du Sénégal, Dakar, Senegal
AOF	Afrique occidentale française (French West Africa)
CAOM	Centre des Archives d'Outre-Mer, Archives Nationales, Aix-en-Provence, France
CARAN	Centre d'Accueil et de Recherche des Archives Nationales, Paris, France
CHEAM	Centre des Hautes Etudes Administratives sur l'Afrique et l'Asie Modernes, Paris, France
EI	*Encyclopaedia of Islam*, (new edition), Leiden, 1960–2002
HSN	Haut-Sénégal et Niger (Upper Senegal and Niger)
IFAN	Institut Fondamental d'Afrique noire, Dakar, Senegal (formerly Institut français d'Afrique noire)
SEI	Gibb, H. A. R. and J. H. Kramers (eds) (1974), *Shorter Encyclopaedia of Islam*, Leiden.

GLOSSARY

bamanaya (Bambara) – expert knowledge of the Bambara, including medico-religious knowledge, understood as non-Muslim

baraji (Bambara, Pulaar, Soninke; from the Arabic *bara'a*) – divine recompense

bay'a (Arabic) – act of allegiance

bid'a (Arabic) – unlawful innovation

boli (or *basi*) (Bambara) – 'power object' or 'fetish' in the colonial lexicon

cerno (Pulaar) – Muslim religious leader; term roughly equivalent to *shaykh* (Arabic)

doma (Bambara) – healer

du'a (Arabic; *duwaw* in Bambara, Pulaar, Soninke) – blessings or petitionary prayers

hadaya (Bambara, Pulaar, Soninke, from the Arabic *hadiyya*; pl. *hadaya*) – literally 'gift', though the term designates gifts to elevated Muslim religious leaders

hadith (Arabic) – traditions reporting the actions and statements of the Prophet Muhammad

hajj (Arabic) – pilgrimage to Mecca

Hamawi – member of the Hamawiyya, a branch of the Tijaniyya Sufi order, whose spiritual leader is Shaykh Hamallah

hijab (Arabic, from the root meaning to conceal or hide) – amulet

hijra (Arabic; Pulaar, *fergo*) – literally 'flight' from non-Muslim rule

ijaza (Arabic) – diploma or licence

jihad (Arabic) – literally 'struggle', including against non-Muslims

jine-don (Bambara) – literally, 'the dance of the spirits (*jinns*)'; spirit possession cult or society.

kafir (Arabic) – non-Muslim

khalifa (Arabic) – person authorised to name *muqaddam*s of a Sufi order

madrasa (Arabic; in French, médersa) – Islamic educational institution

Mahdi (Arabic) – the divinely guided one, expected at the end of the world

marabout (French from the Arabic) – Muslim religious specialist, in the French colonial lexicon

mawlud or *mawlid* (Arabic) – the date marking the birth of the Prophet Muhammad

muqaddam (Arabic) – 'deputy', person authorised to initiate others into a Sufi order

nyamakala (Bambara, Soninke; Pulaar, *nyeenybe*) – 'caste'; a hereditary social category of occupational specialisation, including bard, blacksmith and leather- and wood-worker

Qadiri (Arabic) – member of the Qadiriyya, the Sufi order founded by 'Abd al-Qadir al-Jilani (d. twelfth century)

qutb (Arabic) – literally 'pole'; highest ranking Muslim saint

sadaqa (Arabic) – alms

sharif (Arabic; pl. *shurfa*) – descendant of the Prophet Muhammad

shaykh (Arabic) – Muslim religious leader; title generally reserved for select few

shirk (Arabic) – 'idolatry', associationism

siru (Bambara, Pulaar, Soninke; Arabic, *sirr*, pl. *asrar*) – secret(s)

Sunna (Arabic) – authoritative practice of the Prophet Muhammad

tariqa (Arabic) – literally 'path', Sufi order

Tijani (Arabic) – member of the Tijaniyya, the Sufi order founded by Ahmad al-Tijani (d. 1815) in North Africa

Wahhabi (Arabic) – term widely used to designate 'reformist' Muslims in West Africa who are sometimes erroneously said to follow the teachings of Muhammad b. Abd al-Wahhab (d. 1791) from Arabia

wali (Arabic) – Muslim saint

wird (Arabic) – special litany of prayers that members of a Sufi order recite

zakat (Arabic) – obligatory alms

zawiya (Arabic) – literally 'corner'; place where those associated with a Sufi order gather for prayer, socialising, and so forth

ziyara (Arabic) – literally 'visit'; a visit to a living or deceased Muslim religious leader and his family

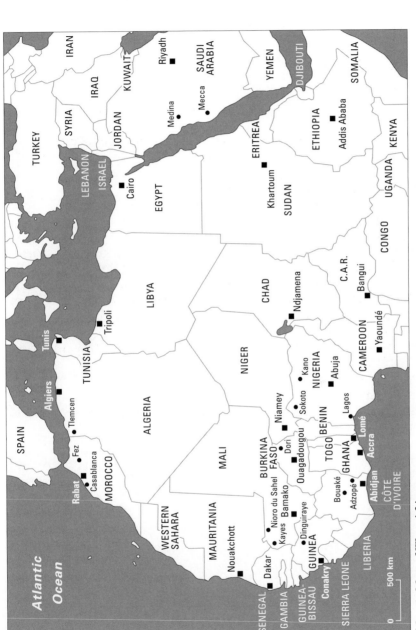

Map 1 Map of West Africa

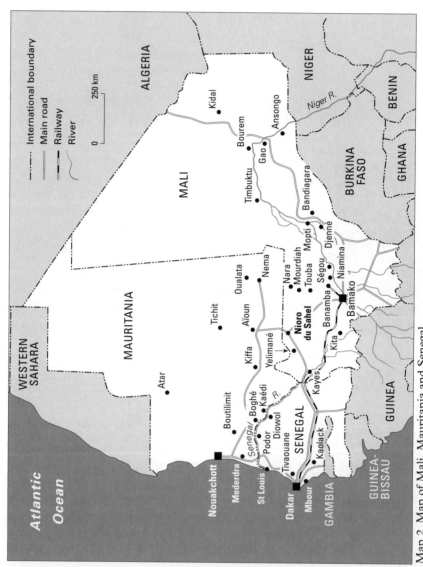

Map 2 Map of Mali, Mauritania and Senegal

INTRODUCTION

In a cemetery in Montluçon, a town in central France not far from Vichy, there is a grave that many take to be that of Shaykh Hamallah, one of the most renowned Muslim religious figures in twentieth-century West Africa and head of a branch of the Tijaniyya Sufi order or brotherhood – the Hamawiyya – that bears his name.[1] In the first half of the twentieth century, many living under French colonial rule in West Africa recognised Hamallah not only as a living Muslim saint or *wali* (Arabic), but also as the highest-ranking saint of the day. Hamallah attracted a wide range of followers and admirers from all sectors of society, including Muslim scholars, colonial civil servants, the newly urbanised, and recent converts to Islam from throughout French West Africa (Afrique Occidentale Française, hereafter AOF). His appeal was so great that he seemed poised to supplant those Muslim clerics favoured by the French, or so the colonial authorities and some of Hamallah's African detractors thought. It is perhaps no coincidence that members of the French colonial administration suspected Hamallah of anti-colonial and 'xenophobic' proclivities. Indeed, the administration eventually accused Hamallah and some of his followers of subversive intent.

In 1941 on a day remembered as Black Thursday, the French colonial administration – under pro-Vichy control – arrested Hamallah and forced him into exile, ostensibly for a ten-year period.[2] Hamallah's arrest came after violent attacks on a group of Muslims in the region of the Sahel. Although Hamallah took no part in these attacks, he was held ultimately responsible for them. Two of his sons who did take part in the attacks were tried and executed along with more than two dozen others, and many of Hamallah's followers in West Africa were subsequently persecuted. Hamallah was eventually taken to France and interned in a concentration camp[3] where his health deteriorated. After his death and burial in Montluçon at the beginning of 1943, the French colonial administration kept his death secret until after the war, not least because of the fear that the news might have caused unrest among his followers in West Africa.[4]

In the mid-1940s, when the French colonial administration in West Africa circulated the news of Hamallah's death, many refused to accept this news as true. At that time, many insisted that Hamallah had instructed his followers he would leave Nioro but would eventually return. As early as

1944, a West African soldier stationed in France sought official permission to go to Montluçon to visit Hamallah's grave, though permission does not seem to have been granted.[5] By the late 1940s, other West Africans had learned from the metropolitan French government where Hamallah had allegedly died in France, and some had even begun to make 'pilgrimages' to Montluçon.[6] In the 1950s, other West Africans petitioned the French government to recognise Hamallah and his followers officially as 'victims of Vichy', something which the government never publicly conceded.[7] Over the past several decades, a steady stream of West Africans and others – visitors to and residents of France – have travelled to Montluçon to visit the presumed grave of Hamallah. Such people are continuing the longstanding religious practice of visiting the tombs of Muslim saints in order to pay respects to the deceased and, in many cases, to seek such a saint's intercession with God.

To the present day, there is almost an enforced silence surrounding Hamallah's death in Nioro du Sahel, the town – in what is present-day Mali – from which Hamallah came. While some in the town admit privately that he is dead, a vocal contingent, including some recently affiliated to the Hamawiyya, insist that he will return. For many such people, it is patently false that Hamallah is dead, let alone that he could have a grave in France. However, many of these people are aware of the visits that some (even from the town) have made to the grave in Montluçon and the repeated claims made about Hamallah's death in a series of publications in French that have appeared over the years. Almost defiantly, these people hold on to the hope that Hamallah will return.

At the time of my fieldwork in the 1990s, the absent Shaykh Hamallah still had a hold on the social imagination, and not only the social imagination, of those who consider themselves his followers. The situation in Nioro with its silences about Hamallah only constitutes one part of the broader conversations, discussions, and debates about Hamallah, his ultimate fate, and Islam more generally. Hamallah's treatment by the French has been so widely recognised as unjust that many elevated him to an African anti-colonial resistance figure and a specifically Muslim one. This does not, however, resolve the issue of his fate, which is a matter of concern to his followers, admirers and sometimes even his detractors. More than a half-century after his exile, many ordinary people – in and outside Nioro – still wonder what happened to him. On several occasions, I listened to followers of Hamallah as they pondered what Hamallah could possibly have meant when he said he would return. Once when I was in a crowded shared taxi in Bamako, the capital of Mali, a friend drew my attention to two men sitting across from us who were discussing rather intensely whether Hamallah was in fact dead. Such discussions are very much alive in other places in Mali and beyond, though they are certainly more muted in the town of Nioro itself where Hamallah's descendants and followers are to be found in great numbers, thereby helping to guarantee that discussions of his fate are discreet.

The conversations about Hamallah, the grave in France, the refusal by many people to accept his death, and so forth, are usually also discussions about Islam, and they highlight some of the central concerns of this study. The analytical focus is on the changing ideas about and practices of Islam and the shifts in authority in the town of Nioro du Sahel, which has been an important Islamic religious centre since the mid-nineteenth century. I consider some of the complexities of the re-valuing of religion within the context of French colonialism and within an officially secular or 'laïc' postcolonial state that frequently associates itself with public expressions of Islam.

ISLAM AND MUSLIM SOCIETIES AS OBJECTS OF STUDY

I have written this study in part in relation to the ever-expanding literature, anthropological and otherwise, that has been concerned with the role of religion in the contemporary world and with Islam and Muslim societies in particular. The grand narratives of modern social theory that come from Marx, Durkheim and Weber have usually taken the presumed trajectory of the modern West as the model for understanding processes of change elsewhere in the world. For a long time, social theorists claimed that so-called Third World societies would replicate the presumed historical processes and trajectory of the West, including 'modernisation' and 'rationalisation.' In many of the dominant social theories about modernity, religion was expected to undergo 'modern' processes of 'secularisation', that is, either to decline in importance or, at the very least, to become more privatised and removed from the public arena. Many theorists also expected that, through processes of differentiation, the state and the economy would eventually be largely free from religion. Moreover, many theorists have posited that the rationalisation accompanying the spread of education, urbanisation and other signs of the modern necessarily leads to a decline of 'traditional' religious practices (cf. Weber 1978). That is, many have assumed that there will be a withering away of 'traditional' and possibly not 'rational' religious and 'magical' beliefs and practices.[8] Although 'modern-isation' theories have been largely discredited, such ideas about religion continue to have a hold – a very strong hold – on the social imagination and have been widely held in and out of the academy. However, a number of developments, generally characterised as forms of religious 'fundamentalism' or 'resurgence' – most notably, the Iranian revolution, the establishment of an Islamic republic in that country, and the persistence of 'de-privatised' religion in the US, among other places (Casanova 1994) – have challenged social theorists to re-evaluate their assumptions about religion and social change in the modern world.

Given that religion has obviously not receded in many places in the world, a major focus in the recent social scientific study of contemporary societies has been on so-called religious renewal or resurgence and the various 'fundamentalisms' in the world religions. This interest in 'funda-mentalism' has been perhaps furthest developed in the study of 'Islamic fundamentalism' and, more recently, Islamism and 'political Islam', particularly by political scientists and policy makers concerned with the Middle East. Such terms of analysis – resurgence, Islamic fundamentalism and political Islam – have become privileged analytical frames for under-standing Muslim societies and their historical development. Indeed, they have come to dominate many of the discussions of Islam and contemporary Muslim societies. However appealing such analytical frames might seem at first glance, it is a central premise of this study that they are ultimately too restrictive for understanding Muslim societies, past and present. After outlining some of the inherent problems with such research, I consider more closely the specific contribution and relevance of anthropology and this study in particular to our understanding of Islam and Muslim societies.

I have sometimes been rather surprised at how pervasive the analytical frames of Islamic fundamentalism and political Islam can be. On several occasions, I have been criticised for not focusing more explicitly in my research on those Islamists and Muslim fundamentalists that are presumed to exist almost *a priori* in all Muslim societies.[9] Although I have taught American Muslim college students who self-consciously embrace the appellations 'Islamist' and 'fundamentalist', I can state that such Islamists or Muslim fundamentalists are rather thin on the ground in contemporary Mali. This is not to deny that there are any self-styled Islamists in Mali. However, if one were to follow some press coverage of Mali, even before 11 September 2001, one would be led to believe that there is a rising tide of Islamism and political Islam in Mali that mirrors developments elsewhere in the Muslim world.[10] While Islamism, fundamentalism and political Islam have become increasingly popular analytical frames, finding perhaps some of their crudest expressions in journalism and in policy circles, I want to argue that they are not only unhelpful, but they are also seriously misleading for understanding contemporary Mali, not to mention further afield.

One of the serious problems with approaches that focus on funda-mentalism and political Islam is the monolithic Islam they assume. This monolithic Islam – manifest in both popular and scholarly ideas of Islamic 'fundamentalism' – is usually dependent upon teleological narratives of progressive Islamisation to which many Orientalists and social scientists have long subscribed. Some commentators have asserted that Muslim societies will not, and simply cannot, undergo processes of secularisation and/or the privatisation of religion presumed for the modern West. Instead, there is often the assumption that all Muslim societies will necessarily undergo similar processes of Islamisation. Such processes are assumed to come in the form of revival and reform, which in 'radical' guises or 'resurgence' might entail *jihad* (Ar., struggle), attempts to seize control of the state and to Islamise the society and the polity. Relying upon such notions of a monolithic and essentially unchanging Islam and 'Islamic civilization', political scientist and policy advisor Samuel Huntington has written about the coming 'clash of civilizations' between the West and its Others, including its Muslim Others (Huntington 1996). While it is generally political scientists who produce much of this research on fundamentalism and resurgence, examples can be found in all of the social sciences and in religious studies.[11] The irony is that such approaches often reproduce somewhat uncritically the discourse of certain twentieth-century self-styled Islamists who articulate their own views of Islamism and the future and inevitable triumph of Islam. For that matter, they are not unlike other commentators' views of contemporary political Islam that also treat it as having a particular telos, unfolding along a linear path that some analysts see as eventually doomed to failure (cf. Roy 1994; Kepel 2002). This is, of course, not to deny the importance of such 'political' notions as *jihad* for Muslims in various times and places. In fact, I will demonstrate how *jihad* is just one of the key concepts some Muslims have debated, discussed and used over time in the region of my research.

It is in relation to the often influential literature about political Islam and Muslim fundamentalism that one must consider the work of anthropologists who have long had much to say about Muslim societies in the postcolonial period.[12] Beginning in the 1960s, anthropologists began to publish a series of texts that focused on various Muslim societies in the newly independent nations in Africa and in Asia. In the wake of decolonisation and with nationalism ascendant, this was a time of great social upheaval in the world, including Third World liberation struggles and revolution, and the heyday of modernisation theory in both its Marxist and liberal variants. This was the context in which British and American anthropologists began to offer views on Islam and Muslim societies from which we can still draw lessons today.

In a series of important essays, the British anthropologist Ernest Gellner began to advance ideas about how to study Islam and Muslim societies that drew initially from his fieldwork in 'tribal' Morocco. His basic argument was that forms of Islam can be read from the social structure in Muslim society (which he intentionally referred to in the singular).[13] In his view, rural tribal Muslims practise Islam in ways that are charismatic, ecstatic, and heterodox – in short, 'traditional'. For their part, urban-dwelling Muslims practise Islam in ways that are generally more sober, puritanical, and orthodox – in short, 'modern'. Important to Gellner's argument is the claim that with modernity and its trappings, such as the 'modern' state, 'traditional' practices will necessarily decline in the face of 'reformist' Muslims, those more 'modern', textually-oriented Muslims with knowledge of 'high' culture (Gellner 1981: *passim*). What set Gellner's perspective apart from many other contemporary theorists was his idea that Muslim society could, indeed would, modernise, though in ways that were different from the modern West. According to Gellner, Islam, unlike Christianity, resists secularisation, but it is able to modernise through rational puritanism. In contrast to Weber (1978; cf. Turner 1974), Gellner was arguing not only that Muslim society can modernise, but also that modernity is inevitable.

It was around the same time that Clifford Geertz began to discuss Islam in both Indonesia and Morocco, two countries at opposite ends of the Muslim world where he had conducted fieldwork. While Gellner emphasised social structure as the key to understanding Muslim society, in characteristically American fashion Geertz pointed to the importance of 'culture' in his 1968 book, *Islam Observed*. In this comparative study, Geertz shows how one religion, Islam, differs in Morocco and Indonesia. While it is certainly laudatory to draw such a comparison, as many commentators would later note, Geertz reified and homogenised centuries of Moroccan and Indonesian history into cultural styles, what he calls 'maraboutism' or the cult of saints in the case of Morocco and a Hindu-Buddhist 'illumina-tionism' in the case of Indonesia. A key element of Geertz's argument is that with the advent of 'modernity', secularism and Islamic 'reform' – what he calls Islamic scripturalism – present challenges to the classical religious styles in both countries. This, he argued, was fleeting, merely an 'interlude', since the overall cultural or 'traditional' styles in Morocco and Indonesia would be enduring.

Despite the obvious differences between Gellner and Geertz, their approaches to Islam and Muslim societies as objects of study are actually remarkably similar.[14] Faced with the challenge of making sense of the obvious diversity and complexity within and between Muslim societies across space and time, both Gellner and Geertz employ what has been the most common device to analyse such diversity and complexity. This is the distinction between orthodox and unorthodox or heterodox Islam borrowed from the discipline of Orientalism. Scholars working within the Orientalist tradition have tended to focus their attention on the 'normative' tradition of Islam that is thought to be embodied in 'orthodox' doctrines, texts and rites. Robert Redfield's (1956) understanding of 'great' and 'little traditions' has heavily influenced the anthropological approach to the study of Islam (and other 'scriptural' religions). This has been used to create the dichotomy of urban, scripturalist Islam and rural, popular Islam. The unofficial division of labour between Orientalists and anthropologists was long such that the former studied the written 'great traditions', while anthropologists tended to focus on the local, popular and traditional aspects of religion.[15] That is, they usually studied the kinds of phenomena one expected anthropologists to find living in small communities of one sort or another and that Orientalists might ignore or possibly even denigrate as unorthodox.

Many anthropologists, who have studied Muslim societies, have focused closely in their studies on the local and popular in Geertzian fashion such that Islam as an object of study has often been treated as a plural phenomenon.[16] Thus, many scholars have attached ethnic and geographic qualifiers to Islam and have described various Islams around the world. However, a serious problem with treating Islam as a plural phenomenon – Indonesian, Moroccan, African, and so forth – is that this is theologically questionable from the point of view of most Muslims who assert that Islam is unitary, all the while acknowledging the diversity within and between Muslim societies (Launay 1992). Moreover, as John Bowen has noted, one writes about 'distinct local "Islams" only at the risk of overlooking ... the historic connections across different Muslim societies (1993: 7).' Indeed, such an approach fails to deal with Islam as a world religion in Weber's sense.

Much recent work in the anthropology of Islam and Muslim societies has questioned this dominant interpretive frame, that is, the use of the dichotomy of orthodox and unorthodox or high and low Islam to discuss Islamic discourses and practices that many now recognise as interrelated and not separable analytically (Bowen 1993; Holy 1991; cf. Asad 1986). At the same time, a number of anthropologists have begun to make important contributions to the study of Islamic education, law, courts, preaching, sermons and public argument in Muslim societies (for example Eickelman 1985; Rosen 1984; Antoun 1989; Asad 1993; Gaffney 1994; Messick 1993; Launay 1997b; Peletz 2002; Hirschkind 2001) – that is, all areas assumed in earlier times to have been the preserve of Orientalists with their textual expertise. However, anthropologists with very few exceptions (for example Fischer and Abedi 1990; Launay 1992; Bowen 1993; Blank 2001; Werbner 2003; cf. Gilsenan 1982) have not embraced the challenge to study areas that cut across the false dichotomy of orthodox and un-orthodox Islam. In fact, it is striking that much recent anthropological work about Muslim societies has tended to focus on those putatively 'modern' forms of Islam and seems quite unwilling or unable to consider those practices that used to be studied as forms of 'popular' Islam.

While such a trend may partly relate to the increased attention to larger social formations and other important topics such as globalisation, transnationalism, and even Islamic 'revival', I suspect that it is also the effect of lingering assumptions about religion in the modern world. In a considerable body of anthropological literature, the argument is advanced that, in the face of increased education, urbanisation, and the rise of a middle class, the 'traditional' practices of Muslims will become less socially relevant, being confined to the 'popular' segments or the socially marginal in Muslim societies (for example Crapanzano 1973; Eickelman 1976; Gilsenan 1973, 1982; cf. Ewing 1983; Hoffman 1995), and eventually replaced by 'orthodox', scripturalist Islam (for example Gaffney 1994; Lambek 1993). Such approaches are still best exemplified in the work of Gellner who asserts that, with 'the coming of modernity', those quintessen-tially traditional religious figures, Muslim saints, 'are seen to retain some of their [inherited] perks but to perform little or no social function' (Gellner 1981: 56–7). According to Gellner, the religious authority of saints will necessarily decline in the face of 'reformist' Muslims, those more 'modern', sober, textually-oriented Muslims, effectively Weberian puritans – read fundamentalists – who question the legitimacy of saints and their 'traditional' practices (see Gellner 1981, 1992, 1994).

Such perspectives are also apparent in some of the recent and best social science literature about Muslim societies. For example, in *Muslim Politics* (1996), Eickelman and Piscatori directly challenge the reigning preoccu-pations with Islamic fundamentalism, as well as ideas about the clash of civilisations. Attempting to assess the complexity of changes occurring within and between various contemporary Muslim societies, they do not consider the continuing importance of those practices in certain Muslim societies that might at earlier times be considered popular, 'traditional', and so forth. Thus, those 'traditions' or 'traditional' practices that Gellner claimed would go away when faced with the conditions of modernity, and other anthropologists thought to be enduring, perhaps in the form of 'resistance', are not receiving adequate attention.

In order to avoid such traps as focusing solely on the putatively 'modern', in this study, I follow Talal Asad (1986), who has made the compelling case for treating Islam as a discursive tradition: 'one should begin, as Muslims do, from the concept of a discursive tradition that includes and relates itself to the founding texts of the Qur'an and the Hadith' (Asad 1986: 14). In approaching Islam as a discursive tradition, one considers Islam in relation to those discourses 'that seek to instruct practitioners regarding the correct form and purpose of a given practice' (ibid.). In this way, Asad emphasises the importance of orthodoxy. However, his understanding of orthodoxy is not the prevailing sense of orthodoxy as set doctrines in Islam that one finds in much Orientalist scholarship and in the approaches of anthropologists like Gellner. Rather, it is orthodoxy in the sense of what is deemed correct practice. It follows, as Asad rightly notes, that such orthodoxy always entails a relationship of power. From such a perspective, one can focus on discourses, which include what is taken for granted and what is debated and discussed in both oral and written forms of communication. In other words, one can consider questions of argument and conflict over practices (what is or is not correct) and the ways in which orthodoxy might change over time.

Studying discourses in this way allows one to understand different ways of being Muslim that often emphasise different ideas about Islam, religious practice and authority.

My approach also takes its inspiration from Weber, particularly his insights on the relationship between social groups, their ideas, and the conditions allowing for their transformation over time (Weber 1978; cf. Asad 1993). It also draws on recent work that has sought to explore the conditions for the emergence of one or another kind of authority in specifically Muslim societies (cf. Geertz 1968; Gellner 1981; Munson 1993; Hammoudi 1997; Brenner 2001). Taking the lead from my informants and friends in Mali, I try to understand how they see themselves as Muslims and how they relate what they and others do to Islam. No areas will necessarily be privileged as modern, traditional or popular and, therefore, presumably more or less authentic, orthodox, and so forth. Nor will any teleology be assumed. Rather, I will study Islamic discourses and practices at the inter-section of the local, the supralocal, and the translocal, including the broader scriptural traditions of Islam. Such an approach allows one to understand which discourses or understandings of Islam have been valued over others, as well as to identify the carriers of authoritative discourses and those who might be excluded. Moreover, such an approach allows one to consider the conditions that allow for the emergence of new discourses and their carriers.

I explore the development of different Islamic discourses, practices and institutions in the town of Nioro, the religious centre in Mali and home of the absent shaykh, Hamallah. My objective is to trace the transformations in ideas about Islam and authority and some of the conventions of religious practice, including ritual, prayer and gift-giving, from the pre-colonial period, through French colonial rule, and in the postcolonial period. While all of the Muslims here consider themselves Sunnis – that is, followers of the *sunna*, the authoritative practice of the Prophet Muhammad – there are basically three understandings or traditions of Islam here that place emphasis on different ideas about Islam and authority. However, I want to bring attention to the fact that the different traditions of Islam, which I treat rather like ideal types, cannot be neatly separated into such categories as 'traditionalist' (read conservative and unchanging) and 'modernist' (read changing). The first of these traditions places great emphasis on the Sufi orders (Ar., *tariqa*, pl. *turuq*, 'path'), their leaders, institutional structures, and associated practices.[17] Hierarchy and charisma are among the central defining characteristics of this understanding of Islam. Shaykh Hamallah, the absent shaykh, is just one of the most prominent of those associated with this tradition in Nioro. As shorthand, I will refer to this as the Sufi tradition. The second understanding – variously called 'reformist', Salafi, or 'Wahhabi' – calls much about the first tradition into question and seeks to change the way Islam has long been practised in West Africa. Rejecting existing hierarchies and claims to charismatic authority, those who support this tradition often want to bring the practice of Islam in line with what are deemed more 'correct' practices, modelled on the presumed centre of the Islamic world, the Arab Middle East. I will refer to this as the reformist tradition. The third, incipient tradition is a vision of what it means to be Muslim that partakes of both of these other traditions – Sufi and reformist. This is an increasingly widespread, though hardly uniform, way of being Muslim and it is a commitment to Islam as a religion which allows Muslims to identify with a more supralocal Islamic community. As I will argue, this understanding of Islam has appeared in the context of an expanded public sphere in the postcolonial period. For lack of a better term, I will refer to this as the postcolonial tradition.

However, as Asad also reminds us, different 'Islamic traditions are related to one another formally, through common founding texts, and temporally, through diverging authoritative interpreters' (1993: 236, n. 60). In this study, I will attempt to understand the different understandings of Islam in relation to each other and their interpreters, but also in relation to other sources of power and authority. Thus, I will consider certain practices, such as spirit possession, often deemed as un-Islamic, in relation to the different understandings of Islam. Moreover, I will argue that the changes in ideas about and practices of Islam and these other practices, as well as shifts in authority, can only be understood in relation to the specific colonial encounter in French West Africa and colonial policies towards Islam and Muslims there. I will show how the colonial and postcolonial state has invariably been involved in one way or another in the debates, struggles and transformations in religious discourses and practices, Islamic or otherwise.

My approach to the study of different and sometimes competing discourses is fundamentally historical. Working loosely within a Weberian problematic, I trace two particularly important sets of related historical developments. First, I outline some of the implications of the French colonial presence for the practice of Islam. With the reorganisation of the social landscape came the unprecedented spread of Islam among non-Muslims, the rise of new charismatic religious personalities like Shaykh Hamallah, the mass appeal and widespread affiliation to certain Sufi orders, and the subsequent spread of 'reformist' ideas about Islam. At the same time, there were processes of the standardisation and rationalisation of Islamic religious practice, most importantly, in the spread of a set of standardised ritual norms for ostensibly all Muslims – in short, a more uniform way of being Muslim. It was the expansion of a new colonial sphere and, then, the public sphere in which such developments took place.

Second, I trace some of the differences between Muslims that continue to be important despite such processes of standardisation and rationalisation. This has been the case for some of the practices that have been denounced as either un-Islamic or incompatible with Islam. While some of the practices have been abandoned, others are being transformed. This is in response to critics with their more uniform way of being Muslim, as well as in relation to the public sphere in which religious messages have come to be dominated by Islam.

Such differences between Muslims are perhaps most apparent in what I call, following Murray Last (1988), the prayer economy in the town of Nioro. Although today Nioro is a relatively small and economically marginal town in Mali, it has special significance as an important centre of Islamic religious activity – both past and present. As one of the capitals of the large state Umar Tall, founded in the nineteenth century, Nioro became a major pilgrimage centre for Muslims in the twentieth century. Each year thousands of people travel to this town to seek blessings, offer gifts, and pay homage to the absent religious leader and his descendants. However, this small provincial town is unusual, if not unique, as the home of a prominent rival Sufi centre of the Tijaniyya and its celebrated leader who is a direct descendant of Umar Tall. Together these two Sufi orders, their leaders and followers influence nearly all areas of the town's social life. The prayer economy in this town is an economy of religious practice in which substantial gifts are exchanged for blessings, prayers and intercession with God. In fact, religious authority has been personalised in certain religious leaders with hereditary charisma and reputations as living Muslim saints, who have followers as prominent as African heads of state and high-ranking government officials. The existence of such saints of course raises questions about the nature of charisma and authority and the perennial problems of succession and segmentation – that is, the instability of charisma and authority – that all such Muslim religious leaders and lineages face.

It is precisely in the realm of the prayer economy, where the world of commodities intersects with religious practice, that this project engages with recent work on the postcolonial state, postcoloniality and modernity. In recent years, much has been written about 'sorcery', 'witchcraft', 'occult economies' and the state in postcolonial Africa.[18] None of this literature, however, deals in any explicit way with Islam and Islamic religious practice and how they might relate to the state, authority and changes in political economy. I show how a consideration of Islam and the practices of Muslims can contribute significantly to the understanding of the interrelationships of religion, power and modernity in postcolonial Africa.

Today, religious discourses and practices in the Malian religious centre of Nioro du Sahel are clearly unlike what they were at the time of the French conquest or even during the colonial period. I explore some of the various ways that people in this town – nearly all of whom consider themselves Muslims – have responded to the conditions of French colonialism and postcoloniality, and how such responses have helped in shaping different ways of being modern, that is, alternative visions of modernity (Comaroff and Comaroff 1993; cf. Appadurai 1996). From the colonial period to the present, different groups of Muslims have attached different meanings to Islamic discourses and practices, and these different meanings have been debated and struggled over, sometimes violently so.

I focus on the continuing importance of Islam for people whose lives are increasingly associated with urban living, modern economic activities, greater mobility and education. For many such people, certain practices closely tied to the Sufi orders and their leaders – veneration of certain Muslim religious leaders, the esoteric sciences, and so forth – remain central to what it means to be Muslim. Many other Malian Muslims, who might be less attached to such Islamic religious practices, do not, however, necessarily embrace secularist principles. When confronted with local and translocal modernising and secularising actors and discourses, some are involved in such purportedly un-Islamic 'traditions' as spirit possession. But there are others with their own visions of modernity who advocate different understandings of Islam and seek to change the way Islam is practised locally. These people have opposed the aforementioned visions of modernity largely within the terms erected during the colonial period. Informed by supralocal reformist movements and intellectual currents elsewhere in the world, particularly in the Middle East, they have denounced many of the practices associated with Sufi orders and their leaders as backward and 'traditional'. Still yet others consider themselves Muslim but want to avoid involvement in these kinds of debates.

The exploration of such different and often competing Islamic discourses, practices and institutions, which are also sometimes alternative visions of modernity, helps to illuminate some of the complexity of the processes by which religion has been affirmed and revalued in contemporary Muslim West Africa – a context in which the opposition between secular and fundamentalist is simply not relevant (cf. Marty and Appleby 1991). While such processes are of course not peculiar to Muslim West Africa, the trajectories are, it seems, specific to the kinds of local and regional contexts that are the focus of this study. At the same time, such a study of plural Islamic discourses is important for the study of other religious traditions where the predicaments of religion and modernity have been equally challenging to social analysts.

THE SETTING AND THE RESEARCH

The setting for my research is the area in and around Nioro du Sahel, located in a relatively remote and inaccessible region of northwestern Mali (see Map 2). During the colonial period, Nioro was part of the French colony, which at different times was called Soudan Français (French Soudan) and Haut-Sénégal et Niger (Upper Senegal and Niger, hereafter HSN), and included within Afrique Occidentale Française, the Federation of French West Africa, that lasted from 1904 until it was formally dissolved in 1959. In 1960, the Republic of Mali was founded after the demise of the short-lived Federation of Mali between Senegal and Soudan.

Today Nioro and its environs are home for many descendants and followers of Umar Tall, the eminent leader of the Tijaniyya whose nineteenth-century *jihad* led to the creation of a state, which at one point extended across large parts of what is present-day Mali. Many of the participants in the *jihad* came from the areas of the Senegal River valley. After the French conquest, many of these people and their kin returned to their places of origin, either through expulsion by the French or through their own accord. In any case, many others stayed behind, and their descendants, as well as many of those descended from some of the more unwilling participants in the *jihad*, particularly those of servile status, presently populate the areas in and around Nioro.

The town is also the birthplace of the Hamawiyya, so-called Hamallism in the colonial and scholarly literatures, the Sufi order that emerged early in the twentieth century under French colonialism around Hamallah. One of the initial reasons for my interest in Nioro was to understand the institutional form and social movement around this religious leader as well as recent Islamic discourses and practices in this setting.

At the time of my fieldwork, the population of Nioro and the few surrounding villages that together make up the administrative unit, the commune of Nioro, was about 22,000. The town of Nioro is the seat for the administrative unit, the *cercle*, which is part of the larger unit, the First Region, the capital of which is in the neighbouring city of Kayes. Nioro is ethnically heterogeneous, as is the surrounding area. Most inhabitants in the town and the immediate area consider themselves Soninke, Fulbe, Futanke, Jawambe, Bambara (Bamana), Jakhanke or Bidan ('Moors'). None of these groups could claim to be a majority in the town and vicinity, though the Soninke as a group are the most numerous in the immediate broader region.

A significant dimension of social complexity in the town and broader region is hereditary social status – 'caste' (Bamanakan/Bambara, *nyamakala*), 'free', or 'servile'. Despite the formal abolition of slavery early in the twentieth century and the fact that many members of a 'caste' might never engage in the hereditary occupations – bard, leather-worker, and so forth – particular to their 'caste', such hereditary distinctions continue to be an extremely important feature of the region's social organisation. Because Nioro remains in many ways like a small face-to-face community, most people are aware of the hereditary social status of others in the town. Over time, these groups have been largely endogamous.

People in contemporary Nioro frequently point out that many of the town's inhabitants are descendants of slaves and former slaves. It is even possible that more than half of the region's population is of hereditary servile status, descendants of those who were slaves in the pre-colonial and colonial periods (cf. Chapter 2 below). Muslim religious specialists almost always issue from certain 'free' lineages that have largely maintained a monopoly on Islamic religious knowledge, education and instruction from the pre-colonial period. While it is not possible to identify a one-to-one relationship between such hereditary status – caste, servile, or free – and contemporary political economic status, most people in the town agree that those of servile status are generally much poorer than the other groups, including the religious specialists.

As this suggests, there is considerable economic stratification in contemporary Nioro, a subject about which there is much discussion in the town. Outward displays of wealth and consumption abound, but only by a small number of residents and visitors to the town. Most conspicuous perhaps are the numerous luxury cars seen throughout the town, the lavish homes illuminated at night by electricity from private generators, and satellite dishes visible on the horizon. These commodities, as well as the many other kinds of wealth in this town, can be linked directly or indirectly to the town's most important religious leaders and a number of well-to-do merchants. In contrast to these people, the vast majority in the broader region has had difficulty meeting subsistence needs, especially after years of recurring drought in the 1970s and 1980s.

In close proximity to the border with Mauritania, Nioro has long been a major transit point in the movement of goods and people – migrant labourers, traders, former slaves, students, and scholars – to and from areas in the north. There have long been ties between those in Nioro and people and places across what are now international borders with Mauritania and Senegal. The town's major religious leaders trace their own roots to areas in Senegal and Mauritania and maintain ties with kin and followers in those places. Many other more ordinary people in the town and region also have social, economic or educational ties that connect them across these international borders.

Although the area around Nioro is not rich agriculturally and agricultural output has suffered after years of drought, agriculture is still very important to the economy of the immediate region. Most men who are urban dwellers disparage agricultural labour and seem to avoid it at all costs. They tend to see such labour as unreliable in its profitability and also demeaning. Although many of the prominent lineages in the town have agricultural fields for grain production in the surrounding area, adult men from these lineages almost never engage in agricultural labour. In some cases, they pay others to work the land for them. In other cases, people work the land under a sharecropping system in which the owners of the land receive a portion of the harvest. In contrast, the agricultural cycle and agricultural labour are central to the lives of many of those living in villages near Nioro. Moreover, many urban-dwelling women work their own fields in which they grow vegetables and peanuts for household consumption or sale on the local market.

The raising of livestock – primarily cattle, sheep and goats – is also important to the local economy. Indeed, all but the poorest households would have at least one livestock animal. The enormous herds raised here are ordinarily sold in some of the neighbouring regions in Mali, as well as in Senegal and Mauritania. As in other places in the Sahel, a few wealthy individuals – almost always men, though in a few notable cases women – have some of the largest livestock holdings.

Since early in the colonial period, the region of Nioro has had high rates of migration to areas of greater economic activity. Such migration has long played an important role in local social life and the political economy. In the postcolonial period, with continuing economic difficulties, the movement of persons from this area has only increased. Over the past few decades, vast numbers of Malians have gone as migrant labourers to southern towns in Mali, to more prosperous countries such as Côte d'Ivoire or to Central Africa, not to mention the long-term Malian, and especially Soninke, migration to France and much further afield. Much of this migration, now less seasonal in nature than it once was, is by people who continue to maintain ties with urban- and rural-based kin. Such migration is so pervasive that it is nearly impossible to find anyone who does not have kin or neighbours involved in migration in some way. Although the remittances of such migrants are difficult to quantify, they are undeniably central to the local economy. It is even possible that they are the most important form of investment in the local economy, though local and regional trade is also critical.

Commerce is the preferred occupation for many of the urban dwellers who eschew agricultural labour. This is especially the case for those without other sources of income such as a civil service salary. There are many merchants and traders, ranging from small-scale retail traders to major importers of goods – foodstuffs and consumer goods – who hail from Nioro. A fair number of these merchants – based in Nioro, other Malian towns and cities, neighbouring countries, and Europe – have become considerably wealthy in the postcolonial period. It seems, however, that the vast majority of such merchants are not getting rich, and many operate with very low margins of profit.

This research project was particularly difficult for a variety of reasons, and here I want to raise some of the major challenges in the archival and field research and ethnography. I do this not to dismiss them in order to assert my own 'ethnographic authority', but rather to point to some of the limitations of the study. The theoretical and methodological issues around field and ethnographic research are particularly thorny for research on Islam, given dominant Western notions of Islam as monolithic, which are widely held within and out of the academy, not to mention the resistance by some Muslims to having their religion studied. It is now a platitude that research about Islam by a non-Muslim Westerner at this point in history can only be political and problematical. For this project, I had set out to conduct research on the way that Islam was practised in this town. Given what I knew about colonial history, this was an enormously sensitive topic. The town's two rival Sufi orders' supporters had clashed, sometimes physically, during the colonial period, and one of the two Sufi orders was the object of harsh repressive measures, especially in the 1940s. The archival collections I consulted in Mali, Senegal and France all have huge gaps in the documentation that relates to such events. While much documentation never seems to have been made available to researchers, considerable documentation seems to have been removed from archival collections and, in some cases, made into private collections.

Such limits to archival research were not the only challenges. Before going to Nioro, several Malians warned me not to make mention of Hamallah's death. A few people told me that to do so could be the end of my research in the town. Given such warnings as well as the sensitive nature of the topic, I anticipated having problems. Indeed, I fully expected some people to be wary of me and my questions. In a few cases, my presence was enough to make certain people ill at ease. For example, there was one particular man who had been very close to Hamallah. Several people urged me to have him recount some of his vivid memories of the *shaykh*. After several visits, I realised that his reluctance to speak with me would simply not go away. Some who knew him noted that as a Westerner I most certainly reminded him of the mistreatment he had suffered during his imprisonment in the 1940s for having been a 'dangerous' follower of Shaykh Hamallah. Later, when I encountered this man's son, who had not only a reputation for 'madness', but notoriety as the sole adult male in the town to have ever converted to Christianity, I thought I understood his wariness toward me even better.

Such reactions toward me as a researcher were, however, the exception. On the whole, many people tended to be open to me and my interest in their lives. This openness came, quite frankly, as a surprise to me, as well as to some people in the town. One friend in Nioro told me that at first even he could not understand why people in Nioro made themselves so accessible to me. He said that after reflection it began to make sense to him. I largely concur with what he said. This interest in Hamallah and the Hamawiyya by people from very far away, of which I was but one representative, was for many people further proof that Hamallah and his followers had been right all along and the enemies of Hamallah – both African and French – so terribly wrong. I venture to say that one senses this even among some of those whose parents and grandparents were staunch opponents of Hamallah.

Over the last few decades, a number of North Americans and Europeans have lived in the town. Some of these people have been involved in international development and aid while others have been there as Christian missionaries or church personnel. After independence, the Catholic church opened a parish that has been largely staffed by French White Fathers and, since the 1980s, Protestant missionaries primarily from northern Europe have had a presence in the area. Given this presence of foreign development workers and missionaries, it took some time before certain people in the town stopped automatically associating me with these people and their activities. For many in the town, I was a curious oddity: the first American many had encountered, who also happened to be interested in the study of Islam.

While I conducted the fieldwork, including participant-observation, I neither pretended to be a Muslim nor did I knowingly lead anyone to believe that I was. I invariably presented myself as a scholar interested in the study of religion and Islam in particular. Many saw this as an opening to convince me to convert to Islam, asking why I would learn about Islam unless I wanted to embrace the religion. Despite all my explanations to the contrary, a few people imputed sinister motives, with one person openly accusing me of trying to subvert Islam. Several people pointed out that only the lavish resources of the West and the United States in particular could allow someone to travel half way around the world to study religion in a small West African town, a statement not very easy to dismiss.

Perhaps the greatest difficulties of the research stemmed from my interest in studying the different religious groups in the town. Over the course of the project, I developed close relationships with people associated with both of the town's Sufi orders. On several occasions, I was asked when I was going to choose between the two Sufi orders or at least to choose one of the town's religious leaders as my guide. Some people saw me as an aspirant – though I dispelled such a view whenever it was suggested – and found it troubling that I was unable or unwilling to choose between the different orders. From this way of thinking, by visiting with all kinds of religious leaders I was acting contrary to acceptable religious practice and perhaps even doctrine. I also spent quite a bit of time with some reformist Muslims, who sometimes gave me the impression that they thought I was entirely too favourably disposed to the Sufi orders, their leaders and followers. Most of those who learned about my interest in practices, such as spirit possession, that they considered either un-Islamic or in contradiction with Islam actively discouraged my study of such phenomena.

So as not to be too closely identified with any one group in the town, I decided at the outset that I would rent a house, rather than join a particular household. I lived in one of the many houses in the town ordinarily rented by civil servants from elsewhere in the country. Although I was initially reluctant to hire domestic help, I was expected to and eventually did so. A woman from a neighbouring village who had worked for several years for international development workers in the town convinced me to hire her to do my cooking and cleaning.

Another area of the research fraught with difficulties was my inquiry into esoteric practices or sciences that are usually secret and often deemed dangerous. Since people ordinarily employ these practices to deal with individual personal problems and concerns, many were reluctant to discuss these subjects on more than a general level. Some people only wanted to discuss them with me in order to criticise the engagement of others in what are said to be sinister or socially inappropriate uses of these sciences. Still others wanted to discuss them with me because they thought I might have esoteric things to share or exchange with them.

Another challenge to me as a fieldworker was the fact that so many people were on the move. Many people were travelling, often to make money, sometimes for educational purposes, medical attention, or visits with kin also on the move. In many cases, the distances covered were astounding, at least to me. I met people in Nioro who had been living and working over the past few years in places as far away as Israel, South Africa, Hong Kong and various places in the US Midwest. Others spoke to me about kin and friends in such disparate places as Oman, Thailand and Germany. I was also able to meet people visiting the town's religious leaders who came from nearly every country with which Mali shares borders. Such mobility of course compelled me to see how 'dispersive' discourses could be, even necessarily would be. At the same time, such mobility certainly had its drawbacks for my research. On a number of occasions, I developed relationships with people who I assumed were going to be very important to my understanding of the place, but their often sudden comings and goings hampered sustained interactions and exchanges.

The fact that the broader society is segregated by gender almost guaranteed that most of my informants would be men. In most cases, it would have been inappropriate for me to spend time with women whose male relatives I did not know. A limited number of my important informants were women, all of whom were either the relatives of my male informants and friends and/or widowed, divorced or considerably advanced in age. There is consequently much less information that relates to women and the subject of religion than I would have liked.

Finally, I want to note that some of the field research was conducted during a time of considerable social and political upheaval in Mali. After the overthrow of the regime of President Moussa Traoré in 1991, many had been optimistic about Mali's future. But by the end of 1993, people were much more pessimistic about the country's economic outlook, not to mention political stability (see Fay 1995). Such pessimism seemed to increase with ongoing student protests, especially in the capital, and after the devaluation of the African franc in relation to the French franc in 1994. During much of the time of my research, there were also questions of insecurity in the north and east of Mali related to the long-running rebellion by Tuareg and 'Moors' that certainly had an impact on the town. Although the last reported attack by 'rebels' anywhere near Nioro was in a neighbouring village right before my first visit to the town in the summer of 1992, there were times in 1993–4 when people in Nioro were particularly anxious. For a while in 1994, rumours circulated about impending attacks that never came. At such times, the considerable anxiety in the town and region was certainly spurred by reports on the radio – Malian national radio, Radio France Internationale, among others – of attacks on civilians elsewhere in Mali. Not long after the long period of my fieldwork was completed, the Malian government and 'rebel' groups reached agreement.

While my interest in contemporary and recent historical Islamic religious practices were important in my choice of a site for my fieldwork, language also played a role. I decided to select an area in which I could use the two African languages, Fulfulde/Pulaar and Hassaniyya (the dialect of Arabic widely spoken in Mauritania), which I learned to speak with considerable ease during two years as a Peace Corps volunteer in Mauritania. These languages are two of the four linguae francae of Nioro du Sahel and the broader region. The other two linguae francae are Soninke and Bambara/Bamana, the latter of which is increasingly the country's main lingua franca and therefore widely spoken by civil servants and their kin from other parts of Mali. Such language competence certainly opened doors for me, though it was at times distressing to some of my friends and acquaintances in Nioro that I was never able to learn to speak Soninke and Bambara with any measure of fluency. This problem was mitigated by the fact that many residents of Nioro speak the town's four linguae francae. I was therefore able to speak with many in either of the two African languages I speak or in French – the official language of Mali – which many, especially men, speak.

The study is based on approximately twenty-four months of field and archival research in Mali, Senegal and France. A good deal of the time was spent in and around Nioro du Sahel, which I first visited for several weeks in 1992 to see if the project was feasible. I returned to Mali in August 1993 and left at the end of December 1994. My research in Mali was broken up by archival research in Dakar, Senegal for about five weeks and about one month in France. In 1996, 1998–9 and 2003, I conducted additional archival research in France. Between December 1998 and January 1999, I returned to Mali and Nioro du Sahel for one month of follow-up research.

Between December 2003 and January 2004, I conducted fieldwork on a related project in Mali, worked again in the archives, and made a brief visit to Nioro.

In the text, I have decided to use the names of historical figures and living persons in those limited cases where it would have been misleading not to do so.

OUTLINE

Some of the chapters that follow are historical, or more aptly historical anthropological, as they read back and forth from archival materials, Arabic texts and documents, ethnography and interviews, while other parts are more along the lines of ethnographic description and analysis. I want to emphasise that I am interested less in writing social history than in providing the basis from which to analyse the transformations in ideas about Islam and authority and some of the conventions of religious practice from the pre-colonial period, through French colonial rule, and in the postcolonial period. The book is divided into two parts: I, History, and II, Authority. However, the ordering of the material presented is not strictly chronological.

I begin Part I with a discussion of the history of this region of West Africa. In Chapter 1, I elucidate the social and cultural foundations for the way in which Islam has historically been practised in this region of West Africa and the relationship of different understandings of Islam to ideas about power and authority before the onset of French colonial rule. I focus on notions of hierarchy and charisma in particular and emphasise the centrality of exceptional charismatic leaders, Muslim saints, and the relationship of such figures to Sufism here.

In Chapter 2, I discuss Nioro as a socio-political and religious space in the aftermath of the French conquest, the development of colonial policies toward Islam and Muslims (*la politique musulmane*), and some of the major political economic changes associated with colonial rule. Changes in understandings of Islam and its practices in this setting can only be understood in relation to some of the complex social transformations that began under colonial rule and have continued in the postcolonial period.

In the following two chapters, I present in rather synthetic form the social history of the two main Sufi orders, the Hamawiyya and the Tijaniyya, that are the dominant institutional forms through which Islam has been practised in the region for more than a century. In Chapter 3, I trace the emergence of the Hamawiyya under French colonialism, the appeal of and opposition to Shaykh Hamallah, his persecution, and the repression of his followers. By looking at the Sufi order in the postcolonial period, I focus on what I call an economy of martyrdom around this religious community that largely defines itself in relation to its absent leader and in opposition to other Muslims. In Chapter 4, I consider the decline in influence of the Tijaniyya and its revitalisation, particularly among the Futanke of the region, through the efforts of one of Umar Tall's most prominent descendants in the postcolonial period.

In Part II, I build on the historical discussion in Part I to offer an analysis of the shifts in authority and the contemporary configuration of religious practice in Nioro. In order to do so, I draw more heavily upon ethnography, though historical considerations are no less important to my discussion. In Chapter 5, I focus on one of the most important sources of religious authority in contemporary Nioro, the disparate esoteric practices that together I call the Islamic esoteric sciences. Considering the sociology of the knowledge and use of such practices, I show how they are absolutely central to understandings of Islam here and, therefore, constitute an orthodoxy that has not gone uncontested. In Chapter 6, I discuss the development of the prayer economy, whereby gifts are exchanged for blessings, prayers and intercession with God. I argue that certain processes of commodification have been central to the personalisation of religious authority in the figures of certain Muslim religious leaders with reputations as saints, who have become more privatised religious figures.

In Chapter 7, I look at so-called religious reform, particularly the activities and influence of Muslim reformists, their discourses and efforts to change the way Islam is practised in the town. I consider some of the ways in which reformists and those within the Sufi tradition they criticise have certain shared objectives and values. At the same time, I point to the influence of reformist discourses on the Sufi tradition. In Chapter 8, I consider the importance of the secular state and the development of the public sphere, as well as the impact of these on Nioro as a social and religious space at the end of the twentieth century. Returning to the question of the Hamawiyya and its absent *shaykh*, I discuss the development of a new incipient tradition of Islam that allows some to bypass some of the debates between Muslims in this religious centre.

In the concluding chapter, I return to the question of changing ideas about and practices of Islam, and some of the ongoing tensions around Islam and authority in Mali and particularly in Nioro as a profoundly transformed Islamic religious centre.

PART I

HISTORY

1

ISLAM AND AUTHORITY BEFORE THE COLONIAL PERIOD

INTRODUCTION

My objective in this chapter is to discuss some of the culture and history of the broader region of West Africa where the town and religious centre Nioro du Sahel is located. Although my larger objective in this study is to trace the transformations in ideas about Islam and authority and conventions of religious practice from the pre-colonial period, through French colonial rule, and in the postcolonial period, I begin in this chapter with an overview of such ideas and conventions in the period before the colonial period. I intend this discussion to serve as the backdrop for understanding the onset of colonial rule and its implications (discussed in the following three chapters), particularly shifts in power and authority and transformations in religious practice in Nioro during the colonial and postcolonial periods (see Part II).

I begin by considering the history of Islam in the region in general terms before discussing the variable relationship between Islam and political rule prior to the French conquest. As I will argue, one must look through the lens of regionally salient notions of hierarchy and charisma in order to understand the configurations of power, authority and religious practice here. Such a perspective will be useful for trying to understand the rise of important charismatic figures such as Shaykh Hamallah, shifts in the organisation of religious practice, including the spread of Islam and the standardisation of religious practice, as well as the development of the prayer economy in the postcolonial period.

ISLAM IN HISTORY

In order to understand Nioro du Sahel as a social landscape in the twentieth century, it is crucial to look to the past, particularly the history of Islam, its relationship to political rule, and the organisation of religious practice in the broader region. Although Islam has been present in West Africa for more than a millennium, it was only in the twentieth century that the population of what is present-day Mali became overwhelmingly Muslim. In pre-colonial Muslim West Africa, religious practices generally corresponded with membership of hereditary social and economic categories.[1] That is, whether people called themselves Muslims, whether they practised Islam, and the way in which they did so usually related to their hereditary social status and economic activities as merchants, clerics, warriors or slaves. On the whole, certain lineages were known as Muslims, who historically had control over Islamic religious knowledge, education, scholarship and sometimes trade. Muslim lineages usually corresponded with hereditary social and economic categories whose members shared an identification with the religion of Islam.[2]

Before the colonial period and even during the early colonial period, that is, until at least the first decades of the twentieth century (see Chapter 2), the organisation of religious practice was such that members of Muslim lineages were generally those who performed the ritual daily prayers (Ar., *salât*), fasted during the month of Ramadan, and, as was sometimes the case, paid and redistributed the alms tax or *zakat*. Some individuals did undertake the long, arduous and often dangerous journey overland to perform the *hajj* (or might have had an ancestor who had done so). In short, members of Muslim lineages exhibited some of the outward signs of the practice of Islam.[3] The members of such lineages, who specialised in religious activities and conformed to such norms, were those the French glossed as *marabouts*.

Other lineages – including various 'caste' groups with occupational specialisations (such as bard, wood-, leather- and metal-worker) and those of hereditary slave status, and sometimes even members of the political/ military elite, who may have called themselves Muslims – generally did not adhere to such standards of Islamic religious practice. In some cases, they were not expected to and may even have been discouraged from doing so. In fact, 'warriors' sometimes exhibited behaviour that explicitly contravened such norms. If the colonial view of such a situation – no doubt receiving inspiration from Orientalist tropes – was to assert that such people were 'lax' or 'lukewarm' Muslims or impartially or barely Islamised 'animists', pagans or 'fetishists', matters were considerably more complex. Many 'warriors', even some of those who considered themselves Muslims, drank alcoholic beverages, and they sometimes had reputations for drinking to excess. Moreover, such warriors engaged in other questionable activities, most notably, raiding and pillaging, or, to use the French colonial terminology, the *razzia*. This involved the raiding and the pillaging of individuals and groups, sometimes Muslims, the killing of persons and/or their enslavement. From the perspective of many Muslim clerics, these activities were not only reprehensible, they were a sign of the general state of insecurity or anarchy (Ar., *fitna*). Furthermore, such activities were quite possibly unlawful, particularly when they affected free-born Muslims and their belongings. This is not to suggest, however, that there was no equivocation. To the contrary, Muslim traders regularly received goods for trade, and Muslim clerics received gifts whose provenance was unclear.

It is important to emphasise that the categories of Muslim and non-Muslim and even Islamic religious practice for that matter were not rigid and unchanging. On the contrary, over time the status of members of lineages (and sometimes even entire lineages) might change along with their social and economic activities, for example, when they took up (or abandoned) Islamic education, scholarship or trade. Non-Muslims – Bambara or others – might convert to Islam, which may also have included the taking-up of commercial activities, and, in doing so, they became Soninke, Dyula, and so forth. Over time, certain individuals and groups abandoned warfare to specialise in religious and trading activities and were incorporated into such categories.[4] Certain Bidan groups known for their clerical and trading activities, such as al-Aghlal and Kunta, might sometimes bear arms and engage in military activities, becoming 'marabouts guerriers' in French colonial parlance. Former slaves and members of 'castes' might also take up new economic and social activities. When they did so, they too might conform to standards of Islamic religious practice that included regular prayer, fasting during Ramadan, and so forth. In many such cases, a change in patronym accompanied the change in social and economic activities, thereby indexing the new identification with Islam.

ISLAM AND POLITICAL RULE

Over time, the relationship between Islam and political rule has been subject to considerable variation in this region of West Africa.[5] Before the onset of French rule, Muslims had sometimes lived as the majority in certain urban areas, most notably, in such longstanding centres of trade and Islamic learning as Timbuktu and Djenné. In those cities and in a number of other smaller urban centres, Muslims – scholars and traders – frequently dominated the affairs of the city, including economic activities and political life. Muslims have also lived as the majority in such places as the Senegal River valley since the eighteenth century when Muslims seized power and founded a ruling regime, the Almamate. In other places in West Africa, Muslims lived as a minority among non-Muslims. In many cases, they were part of the vast network of Muslim traders that extended across large parts of West Africa. Prior to colonial rule, much of the long-distance trade in gold, salt, slaves and other commodities (such as grain, kola, gum Arabic, textiles, weapons, horses, livestock) had been a monopoly of such Muslim traders and their networks. Muslim clerical networks that were parallel to, and sometimes overlapping with, the network of Muslim traders also existed across West Africa.[6] For example, the Marka or Soninke and the Dyula engaged in both trading and religious activities while living for centuries as a Muslim minority among non-Muslims within and between various political formations in West Africa.

The rulers of the empire of Mali adopted Islam as the religion of state in the thirteenth century, and many of the rulers of successor states in the region such as Songhay – which reached its apogee in the sixteenth century – were Muslims. However, in many places in the region, Muslim traders and clerics did not claim political sovereignty nor did they seek it, especially if their activities went unhindered (Roberts 1987: 84f.). Rather, they were interdependent with various ruling groups or individuals – whether or not they considered themselves Muslims – and exchanged services with them. In return for safe passage, protection and the payment of tolls or taxes, Muslim merchants and clerics provided politically powerful ruling groups (or those who aspired to rule) with various commodities, as well as counsel and 'supernatural' protection. To take the example of the Bidan, lineages of Muslim clerics and traders called *zawaya*, who were generally not armed, were subordinate to warrior groups called *hassan* from whom they sought protection. As payment for their services, Muslim clerics and traders received various forms of patronage and valuable commodities, such as slaves, from politically powerful groups. In some cases, Muslim traders and clerics also contracted important alliances with non-Muslim ruling groups. They occasionally married the daughters of non-Muslim rulers, and clerical groups were sometimes even responsible for the education of the sons of non-Muslim rulers and notables. This was a pattern that could be found across large parts of West Africa.

If Muslims have had a presence for centuries as merchants and clerics in this region, they were clearly not always the rulers in the various political units – 'states', 'kingdoms' and 'chiefdoms' – that existed in the broader region before French colonial rule. Be that as it may, the general position of Muslims vis-à-vis political power and the position of certain lineages of Muslim clerics in particular would change dramatically as *jihad* (Ar., struggle) movements identified with various charismatic leaders spread in the region, beginning particularly in the eighteenth century. By the nineteenth century, Muslims would come to control some of the largest and most important political formations in the broader region, and on the eve of the French conquest some of the most vociferous opponents to French expansion were the Muslim rulers of some of these polities.

One particularly important development was that many of these new rulers were not only Muslims, but also Muslim clerics and scholars, who had taken up arms to seize political power either from non-Muslims or Muslims whose practice of Islam they called into question. In the Senegal River valley, Muslim clerics ruled over the Almamate regime, and Muslims were also the rulers of the state of Bundu to the east. In the early nineteenth century, a Fulbe Muslim cleric, Amadu Lobbo, and his supporters seized power from the ruling Fulbe chiefs in Macina (in central Mali) and refused to continue to pay tribute to the rulers of the allegedly 'pagan' Bambara state in Ségou. The new ruling elite was comprised of a group of Muslim clerics, who founded a state, ostensibly based on the principles of Islam, that they called the Dina with its capital at Hamdallaye.[7] From this capital, the rulers brought various groups – Muslim and non-Muslim – under their control and sought to Islamise them. Various individuals and groups formally accepted the authority of the rulers through the mechanism of an act of allegiance called the *bay'a* (Arabic). This was explicitly modelled after the act of allegiance that those accepting the Prophet Muhammad's authority are reported to have made in seventh-century Arabia.

In the mid-nineteenth century, one of the most important proponents of *jihad* in the region of Nioro was Umar Tall (d. 1864), the Muslim cleric who hailed from Futa Toro, one of the provinces of the Almamate in the Senegal River valley. After returning from extensive travels that took him to the Hijaz, Sokoto and Macina, among other places, Umar Tall was living with a community of followers and dependants in Futa Djallon in Guinea.[8] After a neighbouring non-Muslim ruler attacked Umar Tall's community, he led a *jihad* against non-Muslims. Recruiting followers, particularly from his natal region, he took up arms and began to build a state or empire that spread eastward into large parts of what is present-day Mali.[9] In the region of Karta, Umar Tall challenged and eventually defeated the non-Muslim Bambara Massassi rulers and then the Bambara of Ségou. Over the course of the *jihad*, various individuals and entire groups – Muslim and non-Muslim – recognised Umar Tall's authority and formally submitted to him through the act of allegiance, the *bay'a*. However, many Muslims in the region, including the rulers of Hamdallaye, refused to accept Umar Tall's authority and actively opposed his expansionist objectives. In some cases, Umar Tall declared his Muslim opponents to have apostatised and subsequently waged *jihad* against them, as he did in the case of the Muslim rulers of Hamdallaye. After a series of violent campaigns, Umar Tall overthrew the rulers of Hamdallaye, though he eventually perished during an uprising organised by the supporters of the rulers of Hamdallaye.

In the long history of Islam in this region and even during the era of *jihads* in the eighteenth and nineteenth centuries, some Muslims remained opposed in principle to the very notion of *jihad*. There is, for example, the case of the Jakhanke Muslim clerics living in various places in West Africa, who, with a few notable exceptions (see Chapter 2), categorically refused *jihad*, as well as political rule.[10] Indeed, these prominent Muslim clerics were not alone in expressing such a view. In the words of al-Bakkay (d. 1865), the eminent Kunta Muslim cleric in Timbuktu, who was one of Umar Tall's staunchest critics and eventually an armed opponent to his expansion in the Middle Niger: '*jihad* leads to kingship and kingship to oppression; our present situation is better for us than *jihad*, and safe from the error to which *jihad* leads' (quoted in Robinson 1985: 44).

Despite such opposition to *jihad*, many who sought to rule in the region in the decades after Umar Tall's death also invoked Islam as the basis for their authority. These included Umar Tall's successors, including several of his sons, as well as Muhammad al-Amin Drame (d. 1887) and his son Shuaybu.[11] The latter two also waged *jihad* in areas close to Nioro and eventually clashed with Umar Tall's successors. At the time of the French conquest, various groups of Muslims specifically invoked Islam as one of the bases for their opposition to the expansion of French rule. In the late nineteenth century, Umar Tall's oldest son, Amadu, and his supporters were among those who offered considerable resistance to the French conquest under the banner of Islam.

On the eve of the French conquest at the end of the nineteenth century, Muslims – often Muslim clerics, scholars and some of their direct descendants – were the rulers of some of the largest and most powerful political formations in the region. Although they commanded considerable authority, they also faced opposition from various individuals and groups, both Muslims and non-Muslims. In fact, many other Muslims in the region, including merchants, clerics and scholars, were opposed to their rule and did not recognise these Muslim rulers' claims to authority.

MUSLIM RELIGIOUS SPECIALISTS

I have tried to emphasise the way in which religious practice has often corresponded to membership in hereditary social and economic categories as well as the variable relationship between Islam and political rule in the pre-colonial period. I now want to consider more closely some of the bases of authority, the key element of charisma and the hierarchical structure of authority. I want to begin by considering the diversity of Muslim social actors and, more specifically, Muslim religious specialists.

Historically, there has been a considerable diversity of Muslim religious specialists in this region of West Africa. Those the French called *marabouts* in colonial French West Africa were usually members of the Muslim lineages discussed above who were also clerics. These clerics ranged from the relatively obscure to the well-known and included urban and rural imams or prayer leaders, teachers, scholars, preachers, saints and Sufis, not to mention confectioners of amulets and diviners, among others. Although at one level it is analytically useful to group such Muslim clerics together, it is perhaps even more important to consider the differences that have existed between them.

The authority and, by extension, the status of a Muslim social actor and a leader, in particular, in this context have historically been based on a number of complex and interconnected factors. As elsewhere in the Muslim world, the status of a Muslim leader has been based at least in part on the person's reputation, whether for scholarship, piety, prodigious powers or miracles, among other things.[12] Given the historically close relationship between hereditary social status and Islamic religious practice, it is not surprising that descent has been very important here. Thus, prior to French rule, Muslim religious specialists were generally restricted to those who were first and foremost members of the lineages of religious specialists and, sometimes, the founders of new such lineages, who sometimes migrated (or claimed to have migrated) to the region from North Africa or elsewhere.

However, various hierarchies of descent have been operative here, and these hierarchies have sometimes changed in significant ways over time. The great respect for – even veneration of – the family of the Prophet Muhammad and his descendants through his daughter Fatima and son-in-law Ali that is so widespread elsewhere in the Muslim world has also been very important in Muslim West Africa. Indeed, sharifian descent, that is, descent from the Prophet Muhammad, has long been a highly significant factor in determining status.[13] Ideas about the nobility, the exemplarity, even infallibility of the Prophet and his descendants have long been commonplace here. Historically, those claiming sharifian descent have frequently found themselves the beneficiaries of important social privileges and prerogatives, such as the ability to circulate relatively freely, as well as the receipt of gifts in honour of their status. There is evidence to suggest that West Africans have long accorded such privileges to *sharif*s.[14] In both the colonial and postcolonial periods, sharifian descent has been a factor in the rise to prominence of certain Muslim religious leaders. This was, most notably, the case for Shaykh Hamallah (see Chapter 3). However, claims of sharifian descent have sometimes been contested.

Since the mid-nineteenth century, descent from Umar Tall has also played a highly significant role, particularly in areas where his descendants settled during and after the *jihad*, including Nioro, Kayes, Ségou, and Bandiagara. Those who can claim such descent have also been accorded a whole host of privileges, not unlike those accorded to descendants of the Prophet Muhammad in the region (see Chapter 4). Descent from some of the other locally and regionally known lineages of Muslim religious special-ists, particularly some of those associated with the *jihad* of Umar Tall and the rule of some of his successors, has also been important here, though somewhat less so. Nevertheless, descent from Muslims, particularly free-born Muslims of long standing, has generally been valued above descent from those of hereditary marginal social status, that is, of 'caste' or servile status, whether or not they are Muslims.

Scholarship and teaching have also been important factors in the making of reputation.[15] Indeed, there is a many-centuries-long tradition of Islamic education and scholarship in this region.[16] If many members of Muslim lineages and men in particular acquired some knowledge of the Quran and the *sunna* (the code of behaviour modelled on the Prophet Muhammad as recounted in the collections of *hadith*), there has long been a small, educated scholarly elite of diverse origins for whom Arabic was a language of written and sometimes oral communication. Members of this elite were those Muslim scholars who, after studying the Quran, sometimes studied some of the other branches of knowledge, the exoteric sciences, such as juris-prudence (Ar., *fiqh*), and the Maliki school in particular. Such advanced studies, which culminated in a diploma or licence (Ar., *ijaza*), often involved travel to scholars who might be able to provide instruction in a particular branch of knowledge. There were long traditions of men travelling for education to various centres of scholarship and learning such as Timbuktu, Tichit, places in Futa Toro and Futa Djallon and elsewhere, and even to quite distant places, such as North Africa and the Hijaz where they might also have performed the *hajj*.

Muslim scholars in this setting had considerable social capital that stemmed in no small part from the notion that the Quran is a divinely revealed text. Given the difficulties involved in acquiring thorough know-ledge of Islamic texts and becoming a scholar, many deemed efforts to acquire such knowledge particularly meritorious. Those who made the transition from learning to imparting such knowledge to others, whether as teachers, jurists, or counsels, acquired even more social capital. Certain scholars with intimate knowledge of Islamic texts developed widespread reputations. Some scholars in the region were treated not only with respect, but also with awe and trepidation, and the most respected of these people also had reputations for piety. Nioro and its environs were in the past, and continue to be in the present, the home of a number of prominent Muslim scholars, all known among other things for their erudition, and some of these scholars are protagonists in the following chapters.

Before the colonial period, some of these Muslim scholars had or claimed such titles as imam, *qadi*, *shaykh*, or 'ruler', for example, *amir* or *khalifa*.[17] One can find examples of the use of such titles – sometimes with variations in meaning – throughout the region over the past few centuries. In many places, there was generally an imam, the person designated to lead the canonical prayers, whose position may have been transmitted hereditarily. In certain areas with sufficient Muslims, a *qadi* (judge) may have provided opinions and advice to rulers and other Muslims. Although anyone who taught another person might be called a *shaykh*, the title of *shaykh*, meaning 'leader', had more restricted use and was applied to very few individuals. If many people recognised Umar Tall as a *shaykh*, he also claimed for himself other, even more elevated titles, such as *khalifa*, a person authorised to name deputies (Ar., *muqaddams*), and *amir al-mu'munin*, literally, the leader or commander of the believers or faithful. After Umar Tall's death, his son, Amadu, also claimed such lofty titles for himself.

ON POWER AND AUTHORITY

If there has historically been this diversity of Muslim religious specialists in West Africa, it is important to consider how individual Muslims have made various claims to authority. Although much of the anthropological literature dealing with Muslim societies has focused on *baraka*, usually glossed as blessing or 'grace', I want to use a Weberian understanding of charisma here that cannot be reduced merely to such a notion of *baraka*.[18] Following Weber, '*charisma* is a general term which simply refers to any belief in extraordinary, superhuman powers residing in people or objects' (Riesebrodt 1999: 12; cf. Weber 1978). It is such a notion of charisma that can be useful for understanding the differences that have existed between Muslim religious leaders, how individual Muslims might be distinguished by way of unusual characteristics or attributes, the rise of exceptional Muslim religious specialists, and their sometimes quite varied careers. If some readings of Weber have stressed the importance of social crisis for charisma and the success of charismatic authority (for example Geertz 1968; O'Brien and Coulon 1988), it is my contention that charisma is an ever-present potentiality even without any such crisis conditions. As I will argue, this can be seen most clearly in the long-reported expectations of leadership and, specifically, that of exceptional Muslim leadership that we know about from this region.

The notion of charisma as the potentiality for extraordinary power must be understood in relation to the 'esoteric *episteme*', which Louis Brenner has argued quite persuasively was dominant in pre-colonial Muslim West Africa (Brenner 2001). In this 'esoteric *episteme*', most forms of knowledge are thought to be hierarchical. Clearly, the idea that the Quran is a divinely-revealed text has been important to the development of the notion of knowledge as esoteric. In this esoteric episteme, access to knowledge at higher levels in the hierarchy is restricted, and the hierarchical structure of knowledge is 'replicated in a hierarchy of religious specialists' (ibid.). Because of the esoteric nature of knowledge, those who transmit knowledge to others are thought to be in a relationship of teacher (*shaykh*) or guide (Ar., *murshid*) to student, or 'master' to 'disciple'. However, it is important to recognise that this organisation of knowledge and such hierarchies have not in any way been limited to Muslims or to areas of knowledge narrowly-defined as 'religious' in West Africa. Rather, they extend to non-Muslim forms of 'religious' knowledge, and also to many areas of knowledge that outsiders might deem secular knowledge, such as technical know-how, where the 'master'-'disciple' hierarchy is also replicated.

Although there has been a close association between Muslims and the practices of Sufism and the Sufi orders over the past few centuries in West Africa, the esoteric episteme and its hierarchical structure embodied in understandings of the 'master'-'disciple' relationship clearly predate the rise in importance of Sufi orders here (Brenner 2001; cf. Hammoudi 1997).

One of the key elements of this esoteric episteme and, indeed, a central defining component to charisma has been a notion of secrets. In my view, a notion of secrets has permeated this social landscape to such an extent that secrets and secrecy are among its most central defining characteristics.

Indeed, secrets are among the most important components or bases of authority – spiritual or religious as well as political – in this predominantly Muslim setting, not to mention elsewhere in West Africa (for example Ferme 2001). It is a regionally salient notion of secret or secrets (Ar., *sirr*) that informs conceptions of power and authority here. Secrets are associated with that which is concealed or hidden (Ar., *al-batin*), and the term is used to refer to things deemed Islamic as well as non-Islamic. At the time of my fieldwork, many laypersons used the term secrets to refer to the diversity of knowledge and practices that can be grouped under the heading of the Islamic esoteric sciences (see below and Chapter 5) or *maraboutage* in the French colonial lexicon. If the disparate practices of the Islamic esoteric sciences are central to the authority of at least some, if not all, Muslim religious specialists in postcolonial Mali, it is this notion of secrets that is key to understandings of power and authority.

In this region of West Africa, some people are thought to have special 'power', with power conceived here as force in its spiritual and material senses, suggesting authority in Weberian formulations (cf. Weber 1978). Moreover, power in all its forms – spiritual, social, political and economic – is often said to be tied to the possession of some secret knowledge, practice, or even object that assures or guarantees this power, and, in some cases, is the very condition of this power. Here, the conception of power *is* as a resource to possess and to wield, and, in this way, is similar to Weberian conceptions of power (cf. Weber 1978; Foucault 1978). Moreover, it is not unlike Nietzschian views of power as an attribute of individuals (cf. Nietzsche 1968).

If such ideas about secrets and power have long been extremely important for Muslims and non-Muslims alike in West Africa (cf. Monteil 1924), they must be understood in relation to the broader history of Islam and the ideas and debates about such matters. There is in fact a very developed notion of secrets that has been central to the traditions of Islam from the earliest centuries of Islam (see, for example, Hamès 1993, 1997b; Lory 1996). Take, for example, the much discussed understanding that God has many names. That is, there are different ways of referring to or addressing God. In fact, there are ninety-nine of these so-called 'names of God' that are readily knowable.[19] These names include some of the names of God Muslims around the world ordinarily invoke in their regular prayers, such as God 'the Compassionate' (*al-rahman*) and 'the Merciful' (*al-rahim*), or God 'the Powerful' (*al-qadir*). There is an additional, 100th and 'greatest name' or 'most exalted name' of God (Ar., *ism Allah al-a'zam*), the final and secret name. *Hadith* collections state quite unambiguously that knowledge of this greatest name guarantees effusions of divine grace, even access to paradise.[20] For many Muslims, there could be no greater secret than this.

The notion of 'secret' knowledge within Islam is so widespread that it has been important to the development of various kinds of practices, including the Islamic esoteric sciences, for the purposes of protection against misfortune, healing, and so forth, in various places throughout the Muslim world, including West Africa. Many, if not all, of these practices, such as forms of mystical retreat, divination and amulet-confection, make use of Arabic literacy and, frequently, the text of the Quran. While many Muslims (and outside observers, including social scientists) have taken the position that these practices are either unorthodox or not part of Islam, this decidedly 'modernist' view of such phenomena fails to deal with the fact that many Muslims in West Africa do not see them in contradiction with Islam. In fact, they are an important part of what constitutes orthodoxy for many Muslims.

Many people in West Africa have thought that it was impossible to rule without some kind of secret. For this reason, those pursuing power have sought out secrets or people willing to transmit or employ a secret on their behalf. While many such secrets have been associated with the religion of Islam, its revealed texts and religious figures, non-Muslims have secrets of their own. In Mali, the secrets of non-Muslims are often understood in relation to the knowledge of the 'Bambara' – *bamanaya* – or the knowledge of other groups, which is thought to be un-Islamic. Such knowledge includes various practices involving blood sacrifice and the use of 'power objects' or 'fetishes' to use the colonial lexicon, as well as medico-religious knowledge and practices that can be employed defensively or offensively.[21] Such allegedly un-Islamic secrets might encompass a range of knowledge and practices, which are very much like the Islamic esoteric sciences, in that they might be for purposes of divination, accumulation, protection against misfortune, defeating a rival or seizing political power.

As some people explained to me, non-Muslim rule, conceived in general terms, necessarily entails the possession of such power objects or secrets. In this way of thinking, non-Muslim rule in the past and the existence of powerful non-Muslims in the present confirm this fact. I want to emphasise that I am not simply projecting a view from the present onto the past. On the contrary, there is considerable evidence to suggest that such a view of secrets and power was applicable to both Muslims and non-Muslims in the pre-colonial past. In fact, ideas linking political rule and power to secrets have long been part of the social imagination in this region of West Africa. For example, it is widely reported that the non-Muslim rulers of the Bambara state of Ségou kept and acquired an array of un-Islamic 'power objects' (Monteil 1924; Tyam 1935), including some that may have incorporated some of the signs of Islam. It is also striking that the Bidan who are Muslims use the name of the ruling non-Muslim Bambara who were their neighbours in the nineteenth century – Massassi – to refer to witch or vampire in their language, Hassaniyya. That the witch whose nefarious, secret practices are said to involve eating people from the inside, should be so designated is revealing. But such ideas about secrets and power can also be seen in a whole range of historical traditions from this part of West Africa. In the story of Wagadu (or Ghana), as reported by Maurice Delafosse, succession to office is contingent upon the possession of the *'talisman des rois'* (Delafosse 1913: 295).[22] Similarly, in the traditions about the founding of the kingdom of Jara, Mamadu, the son of Daman Gille, used a *'hijab'* (Ar., amulet) when he shook the hand of his rival (Mana Makhan Nyakhate) in order to defeat him (ibid.: 304).[23]

The notion that the possession of secrets is necessary to rule also informs many Muslims' conceptions about their own self-rule. For this reason, there is much discussion in the present in Nioro about the secret sources of past rulers' political power. Among the Futanke, who are descendants of participants in the nineteenth-century *jihad* led by Umar Tall and his successors, it is widely held that the success of their ancestors' invading armies was due in no small part to Umar's possession of secret knowledge that he employed in the time leading up to and during the conduct of war. This is clearly in agreement with Umar Tall's self-presentation in his book, the *Rimah*,[24] where he outlines his knowledge of the esoteric sciences and practices, as well as 'secrets'. Moreover, Umar explains that his title of *khalifa* was confirmed through revelations from the Prophet Muhammad.[25] There are also several extant accounts of his use of various esoteric practices such as *khalwa*, or mystical retreat, before making decisions to undertake action during the conduct of the *jihad*.[26]

Similarly, some descendants of non-Futanke allies of Umar Tall who live in Nioro frequently point to their ancestor Alfa Umar Kaba Jakhite, whose use of secret knowledge, they maintain, assured the success of Umar Tall's *jihad* in western Mali (cf. Adam 1903–4). Some claim that upon return from his sojourn in the Hijaz, Umar Tall specifically sought out Alfa Umar in Bundu for his knowledge of the esoteric sciences to employ in the pursuit of *jihad* (cf. Dramé 1988; Chapter 3 below). Such examples could of course be multiplied many times for various people and places in Muslim West Africa (see, for example, Sanneh 1989).

Since power is thought to be sometimes rather precarious, there is a suggestion that a secret revealed or destroyed indexes the loss of power. This is clearly reminiscent of some versions of the epic of Sunjata, the mythical founder of the Malian empire, in which the loss of power by Sunjata's rival is tied to the revealing of his secrets that are represented as un-Islamic in nature (see Bird and Kendall 1980). The rulers of pre-colonial states in the region – and not just Muslim-led states – often destroyed the 'power' objects in the territories they brought under their rule (see Bazin 1986). This seems to have been the case for the non-Muslim Ségou Bambara state in the nineteenth century, as it was for Umar Tall and other Muslim rulers such as Samory who were known for their destruction of what chroniclers called 'idols'. However, certain non-Muslim rulers in the region actually incorporated the 'power' objects of the vanquished into their own repertoires of such objects (Bazin 1986).

SUFISM AND SUFIS

Sufism, the mystical tradition in Islam, *tasawwuf* in Arabic, involves various kinds of practices – special litanies of prayer and techniques of invoking or reciting God's name – that are ostensibly ways for those who employ them to approach God. The notion of secrets has been central to the practice of Sufism in that mystical practice is, by definition, reserved for the initiated, and therefore, restricted and secret in nature. While Sufi practices have a long history elsewhere in the Muslim world, it is not clear when such practices first arrived in West Africa. We do know, however, that beginning in the eighteenth century, the organised Sufi orders gained in importance in West Africa, as they did elsewhere in the Muslim world (Brenner 1988; Levtzion and Voll 1987; cf. O'Fahey and Radtke 1993). Moreover, the development of specific Sufi doctrines and practices, esoteric practices in particular, and their association with the organised Sufi orders have helped to animate ideas about Islam and secrets even further in West Africa. In general, those higher up in the hierarchy of a Sufi order are assumed to have various kinds of secrets, such as knowledge about how to advance to even higher spiritual states, which they might transmit, if they so wish, to others.

The earliest and most important of the Sufi orders in West Africa was the Qadiriyya, which takes its name from 'Abd al-Qadir al-Jilani of Baghdad who died in the twelfth century. Some sources claim that the renowned North African scholar al-Maghili (d. c. 1504) was the first to introduce the Qadiriyya in Africa south of the Sahara.[27] In any case, this Sufi order began to spread among Muslim scholarly elites in West Africa perhaps as early as the sixteenth century (cf. Norris 1986; Hiskett 1984). Central to member-ship of or affiliation with the Sufi order was the special litany of prayers, often called the *dhikr*, literally, remembrance, or, as it is often called in West Africa, the *wird*, the litany of prayers that one must recite. Such a litany of prayers is usually recited on a daily basis in addition to the obligatory ritual daily prayers that Muslims ordinarily perform. People, usually adult men, were formally initiated into the Sufi order by agreeing to perform the special litany of prayers, as well as abiding by certain rules of the Sufi order, such as rules for the proper recitation of the prayers.

Affiliation to a Sufi order such as the Qadiriyya was for long periods largely a private matter in West Africa. It was also restricted to Muslim scholarly elites who did not in any way form a corporate group. Membership in the Qadiriyya eventually became quite widespread across the networks of Muslim clerics in West Africa, and some of the most celebrated Muslim scholars in eighteenth- and nineteenth-century West Africa are known to have been affiliated to the Qadiriyya. These included Sidi al-Mukhtar al-Kunti (d. 1811), the founder of perhaps the most important branch of the Qadiriyya in West Africa (and ancestor of al-Bakkay mentioned above), and Muhammad al-Fadil (d. 1869), the eponymous head of another branch of the Qadiriyya, the Fadiliyya. The Fulbe rulers of the Muslim state in Macina were also members of the Qadiriyya, as was Amadu Bamba, the founder of the Mouride Sufi order in Senegal. In fact, the Mourides form another branch of the Qadiriyya.

From at least the middle of the nineteenth century, another Sufi order, the Tijaniyya that had been founded in North Africa began to spread throughout West Africa. Ahmad al-Tijani (d. 1815), the founder of the Tijaniyya, who died and was buried in Fez in Morocco, claimed to have received the dispensation for the Sufi order that bears his name directly from the Prophet Muhammad (see Abun-Nasr 1965). In addition to this not uncontroversial claim, Ahmad al-Tijani stated that the Tijaniyya was superior to all other Sufi affiliations, and that membership and adherence to its rules, including regular recitation of its special litany of prayers, could guarantee access to paradise. Affiliation to Tijaniyya was to be a lifelong commitment. Indeed, it was explicitly stated that leaving the order or failing to uphold its rules was to invite divine retribution (Abun-Nasr 1965: 39). Ahmad al-Tijani instructed members of the Tijaniyya to renounce all other affiliations and, moreover, not to frequent religious leaders other than one's own (Abun-Nasr 1965). This doctrine of the exclusiveness of affiliation to the Tijaniyya was certainly new, given that until this time Muslims frequently had multiple affiliations, that is, affiliations with more than one Sufi order at the same time. At least initially, affiliation to the Tijaniyya in West Africa – much like the Qadiriyya – remained largely an affair of the small, educated Muslim scholarly elite. Although there are reports of prominent Muslim clerics in West Africa being affiliated with the Tijaniyya along with other Sufi orders such as the Qadiriyya, that is, in direct contravention of Tijani doctrine, practice eventually came to reflect more closely the Tijani doctrine of exclusivity of affiliation. Thus, by the 1930s, those affiliated to another Sufi order, would be expected to renounce such an affiliation prior to initiation into the Tijaniyya.

If the Tijaniyya was present in West Africa during Ahmad al-Tijani's lifetime (Ould Abdellah 2000), its spectacular spread in the nineteenth century and in the twentieth century to become the most important Sufi order in West Africa today relates to the fact that Umar Tall was a recognised leader of this Sufi order. In the late 1820s, one of Ahmad al-Tijani's followers had named Umar Tall a *khalifa* (Ar., deputy) of the Tijaniyya during his sojourn in the Hijaz.[28] In the *Rimah*, Umar Tall reveals that as a *khalifa* he was authorised to appoint a fixed number of *muqaddams*, those able to initiate people formally into the Tijaniyya.[29] After Umar Tall's return to West Africa, the Tijaniyya became closely associated with his activities, including the *jihad* that he led and the state that he organised. Given the geographic area in which he, his followers, and successors operated, the Tijaniyya spread far and wide both during and after his death. On the eve of the French conquest, the Tijaniyya had become very important in the region, and many of the Tijani *muqaddams* throughout West Africa would trace their initiation into the Sufi order through chains of initiation that led to Umar Tall.[30] It was not, however, until colonial rule that there would be mass affiliation to Sufi orders, including the Tijaniyya and the branch associated with Shaykh Hamallah.

Since their rise in importance, Sufi orders and their associated practices have been crucial in helping to determine the status of particular Muslim religious leaders and their claims to authority in this part of West Africa. Members of Sufi orders in West Africa and sometimes from beyond the region have used these institutions to authorise, elevate or distinguish particular religious leaders, for example, by appointing them to important positions such as *muqaddam* or *khalifa*. In some cases, those with such supralocal sources of religious authority have been able to influence the shape of the social landscape and the career trajectories of particular individuals by, in turn, appointing them to important positions with the Sufi orders. If Umar Tall is a good example from the pre-colonial period, I will explore in later chapters how Sufism and its associated practices provided viable paths for some to achieve reputations as religious leaders in the colonial and postcolonial periods.

From around the middle of the nineteenth century, the organised Sufi orders, particularly the Qadiriyya and the Tijaniyya, became one of the primary institutional forms for Islamic religious practice in this part of the West Africa, though mass affiliation only came under colonial rule. The hierarchical structure of authority that characterises these Sufi orders is such that one is enjoined to follow a religious leader or *shaykh*, who acts as a guide for other Muslims. Given how widespread these Sufi orders became, such a leader has usually come from within the existing Sufi order structure or in new branches or even in new orders that have arisen. In theory, all adult Muslims have been expected to have a relationship with a religious leader higher up in what we might call a spiritual hierarchy that leads from humans to God. I now want to turn to the Muslim saints who are thought to be at the highest point in this hierarchy of Muslims before God.

SAINTS

Verily, the Friends of God [saints] have nothing to fear, nor are they
sad. (Quran x, 62)

As I have suggested, over time Sufism and its institutional forms became
increasingly important factors in the careers of Muslim religious specialists
in West Africa. Although I have discussed the diversity of Muslim religious
specialists, their reputations, and bases of authority in some detail, I want to
consider those persons considered to be truly exceptional. Historically,
particular Muslim religious specialists have overshadowed others, and these
persons have generally been considered Muslim saints. Although the term
saint is borrowed from Christianity, it is preferable to some of the other
possible options – such as *marabout* in French or *shaykh* in Arabic – which
are too vague for the exceptional Muslim religious figures here. By saint, I
am referring to the term *wali* in Arabic that is actually a loan word in many
languages spoken in West Africa.[31] Understandings of saints in West Africa
are heavily indebted to the notion of sainthood (Ar., *walâya*) that al-
Tirmidhi (d. 9th century) developed and the celebrated thirteenth-century
Sufi, Ibn 'Arabi (d. 13th century) later elaborated.[32] Only the most exceptional Muslim religious leaders are considered saints. A whole host of possibly
intersecting circumstances – attracting many followers or developing a
reputation for learning, piety, generosity or prodigious powers, such as
mystical insight or miracles – may lead some people to consider a religious
leader exceptional and, possibly, even a saint.

As I noted earlier, many West Africans stress that some people have
special 'power' and equate power with force in both its material and non-
material senses. Such notions of power are also used in relation to exceptional Muslim religious leaders. When people talk about such leaders, they
frequently make reference to their 'power'. In this context, power is meant
to indicate God's favour, for which there is no single term, but instead a
whole host of related notions in the region's vernaculars, such as 'gifts of
God', as well as *baraka, hurma* (Ar., sanctity), and *ni'ma* (Ar., prosperity),
to name only a few words of Arabic origin that people readily invoked in the
region's vernaculars. These are also some of the terms one finds in Arabic
texts – chronicles, biographical writings and poetry – about such exceptional
persons. There is a general sense that power emanates from God who
bestows his favour on whomever he wants (cf. Denny 1988). Broadly
conceived, God's favour is indexed by all that people might want: wealth,
good health, power, progeny, good fortune, social prestige, and so forth.

The truly exceptional, even more so than those with 'power', are thought
to be saints.[33] Usually men, though in some cases women, saints may be
living or deceased. People presume that saints are actually closer than
ordinary Muslims to God, as well as to the Prophet Muhammad. That is,

saints are said to be foremost in the hierarchy of authority that leads from humans ultimately to God. They are thought to have special power, knowledge, and favour from God. Their knowledge of the secrets, even the greatest of secrets, including the 100th name of God, is widely assumed, indeed, taken for granted. In the one passage ostensibly about saints in the Quran, it is stated that such 'friends of God' have 'nothing to fear, nor are they sad'. As some of my Malian informants explained, this indicates in no uncertain terms that the access of God's friends – who are none other than his saints – to paradise is assured.

Malian Muslims also talk about saints as leading exemplary lives in the sense that they follow very closely the life of the Prophet Muhammad, who was known as 'the Perfect Man' (Ar., *al-insan al-kamil*). This notion that Muhammad was the most perfect man has been developed in the scholarly literature of Sufism; it is also widely understood by Muslims from broad sectors of society in this part of West Africa.[34] By association with the Prophet Muhammad, his exemplary life, and maybe even his genealogy (in the case of *sharif*s), saints embody a certain kind of morality. Like the Prophet Muhammad, they are generally known for their piety and devotion to God and other positively valued qualities, all of which are thought to surpass that of ordinary Muslims. Like many Muslims elsewhere in the world, Muslims in West Africa acknowledge that it is God who confers sainthood or the state of being a saint upon whomsoever he chooses. If one's associates may proclaim one to be a saint, one, at least in the contemporary context, almost never declares oneself to be a saint. This contrasts, for example, with Ibn 'Arabi (Chodkiewicz 1986), or more directly relevant here, Ahmad al-Tijani, the founder of the Tijaniyya, both of whom are reported to have proclaimed themselves to be living saints.

Although one may be a saint without oneself or others being aware of it, there are certain reported signs of sainthood. For example, when a Muslim religious figure has had many people around him as followers, clients and/or associates, many have taken this as a sign that the person is special or favoured by God in some way. In many cases, such 'wealth in people' (Guyer 1993) is taken to be a sign from God that the person is a saint. More importantly, perhaps, is the association of presumed saints with miracles – *karamat* in Arabic. It is also widely reported in Mali and much further afield that God will answer the supplicatory or petitionary prayers (Ar., *du'a*) of a saint or at least it is more likely that God will answer such prayers. This relates to the idea that saints have special access to God and his favour. For this reason, many have sought out saints to ask them to intercede on their behalf with God. This understanding of intercession (Ar., *wasila*), the saint's ability to intercede with God or to petition God on behalf of another, has no doubt contributed to the saint's power in the world. If the saint can possibly intercede, he also has the ability to curse. Thus, many have feared and continue to fear saints either for their curse or the divine favour accorded to them. There is a reported saying of the Prophet Muhammad that God said: 'He who hurts a saint (*wali*) has allowed himself to make war on Me' (quoted in al-Hujwiri 1936: 212). Such statements attributed to the Prophet Muhammad have been learned by many Muslims in the region through the study of scholarly texts.

If West Africans have acknowledged the existence of a hierarchy of believers before God, like many Muslims elsewhere they also recognise that there is a hierarchy of saints. Among the many saints thought to exist in the past and in the present, certain saints are thought to have more power and authority than other saints and to have different ranks. In fact, people point to the *qutb* (Ar., 'pole' or 'axis'), the supreme saint, who is characterised as the highest ranking saint of the age. Even above the supreme saint would be 'the Mahdi', the divinely guided one, who is expected at the end of time.

We know quite a lot about certain Muslims from this region of West Africa with reputations as saints, particularly some of those who lived during the eighteenth and nineteenth centuries. These include some of the eminent Muslim religious leaders mentioned above, including Sidi al-Mukhtar al-Kunti, Umar Tall, Muhammad al-Fadil, Alfa Umar Kaba Jakhite, the rulers of Macina, and others. This is a considerably diverse group of Muslim saints. What unites all of them, however, is that they were all noted scholars and teachers. In fact, it seems virtually impossible for a saint, at least in this historical context, to be illiterate.[35] These Muslims also had followers who took them as important saints, and, in some cases, even as the most important saints of the age. In other words, they were thought to be at the pinnacle of the hierarchy of authority during their lives. The reputation for sainthood of each of these saints also related to his reputation as a Sufi, which often included activities within a particular Sufi order and the development and propagation of that Sufi order. The saints also usually had considerable wealth that they often received in the form of gifts from their many followers, and this wealth was thought to be perfectly licit.[36] While some (perhaps most) did not hold political power, Umar Tall and the rulers of Macina were saints who ruled over polities and sought to spread Islam and their rule through armed *jihad*.

The existing hierarchical organisational structure of Islamic religious practice in the broader region is such that many ordinary Muslims have looked to other, presumably more exceptional Muslims for leadership. In fact, Muslims in the region have often been actively seeking new leaders or guides. Such expectations of Muslim leadership – even exceptional Muslim leadership – have even been commonplace. Indeed, at various times and places, many have thought that certain presumed saints were potential leaders with pre-ordained missions. One companion of Umar Tall wrote that the expected Mahdi would be a member of the Tijaniyya.[37] It is striking that some of Umar Tall's followers refused to acknowledge the death of their saintly leader and even talked about his ultimate return to West Africa.[38] This motif about the most charismatic leader of the day is reminiscent of the legend of Sunjata, who is also said not to have died, but to have disappeared. It is also of course the same motif about Shaykh Hamallah's absence.

Over the course of several centuries before the twentieth century, chroniclers from the region identified and documented quite a number of people as *shaykhs*, saints, and even supreme saints, in addition to some of those listed above.[39] In at least one case, it is recorded that some recognised one Muslim religious leader from the Tinwajiyu,[40] a Bidan group of Muslim religious specialists who claim descent from the Prophet Muhammad, as even more exceptional than a saint. This was Shaykh al-Mahdi (d. 1907) who, as his name indicates, some people took during his lifetime to be the Mahdi 'expected at the end of the world'.[41] If the chronicler suggests that such a view did not last very long, such expectations of exceptional Muslim leadership did endure. At the turn of the twentieth century and before the French conquest, prominent Muslim clerics in places such as Oualata and Tichit looked to Muhammad al-Fadil's son, Ma' al-'Aynayn (d. 1910), who actively opposed French expansion, as another exceptional religious leader to whom they turned for guidance and leadership.[42] Such a pattern would continue under French rule, though with certain important changes.

If such expectations of exceptional Muslim leadership, that is, charismatic leadership were widespread in West Africa, it is important to recognise that there have always been discussions, debates and doubts about the status of any particular leader, saintly or otherwise, and that leader's charisma. This relates of course to the instability and impermanence of authority and charisma, the precariousness of authority of individual saints, indeed anyone who might purport to lead or rule, and the problems of succession and segmentation every saint and saintly lineage face. These are some of the themes I will address in some of the following chapters where I confront the complexity of the social transformations within the new colonial order and some of their lasting effects.

2

COLONIALISM AND AFTER

Although French colonial rule was clearly not the first or only rupture with the past that the region of Nioro du Sahel has experienced, it was, in many ways, deeply transformative. Indeed, the French conquest of what was to become the Soudan français in the last decade of the nineteenth century ushered in a variety of profound social transformations in this region. While the full complexity of such transformations is beyond the scope of this study, I focus here on some of those transformations associated with the colonial project that helped to shape Nioro as a social, political and religious space. In doing so, I want to stress the importance of understanding colonialism not only as a political and economic project, but also as a social and cultural one (cf. Dirks 1992) that also must be understood in comparative perspective.

As I will show, some of the transformations outlined here are similar to those that occurred in other colonial contexts, including other Muslim societies and North Africa in particular. However, I will suggest that some of these changes have been specific to the colonial encounter in French West Africa and the colonial policies towards Islam and Muslims there. Early in the twentieth century, Nioro was the setting for the development of a new Islamic institutional form, the Hamawiyya, a branch of the Tijaniyya that flourished under colonial rule. Although the history of the Hamawiyya will be discussed in detail in the next chapter, here I consider some of the general changes, some subtle and others not so subtle, associated with the colonial conquest, colonial rule, and political economy that have left their mark on Nioro. I highlight some of the intended and unintended consequences of colonial rule and policies, the perceptions and misperceptions on the part of the coloniser and colonised, and the reactions of both groups to each other in what was, and is, a socially and ethnically heterogeneous town. Such a discussion points to some of the ambiguities and contingencies of colonial rule, and sets the backdrop for the rise of the Hamawiyya and the later expansion of the public sphere (see Chapter 8).

THE FRENCH CONQUEST AND ITS AFTERMATH

The town of Nioro du Sahel is located in Karta, the region of the western Sahel that is contiguous with the areas of Kingi to the south and the Hodh to the north in present-day Mauritania. These areas are part of a broader region that has long served as a meeting place for different ethnic and linguistic groups and as a crossroads in the extensive trading between the desert and the savanna. Indeed, the town of Nioro was a major trade entrepôt on the fringes of the Sahara where persons, objects and ideas from north, south, east and west met. Over the course of the nineteenth century, this region was peopled by different groups who considered themselves Jawara, Soninke, Jakhanke, Bambara/Bamana, Fulbe, Futanke ('Toucouleurs'), Jawambe, Bidan ('Moors') and Wolof, among others, not to mention the sizeable servile-status population of diverse origins, living within and between a number of different political units ('states', 'chiefdoms') in the region.

I can only allude here to the complex shifting alliances and coalitions between individuals, groups and political units in the period leading up to the French conquest. But one of the most important developments in the nineteenth century was the period of more than three decades during which those participating in the *jihad* and the subsequent state or empire-building of Umar Tall (d. 1864) and his successors moved into the region, including Karta, that the Bambara Massassi had controlled until that time. They made Nioro, the former Massassi capital, one of the main centres of the new Islamic state.[1] The migrants were for the most part 'Toucouleurs' or Futanke, as they called themselves, many of whom came originally from Futa Toro in the Senegal River valley. They called their movement into the area the *fergo* (Pulaar, migration; Ar., *hijra*) that was explicitly modelled after the Prophet Muhammad's move away from his enemies in Mecca. This migration was a process of *de facto* colonisation of the region. Accompanying such colonisation was the political reorganisation of the landscape from the time of the *jihad* campaigns in Karta in the 1850s. Until the French conquest, the Futanke migrants as a group, regardless of the diversity of their origins, were eventually so great in number that they came to dominate the affairs of the state and its economy, generally at the expense of many of those they found living in the region.

Over a period of more than two decades prior to the French conquest, the region was also the setting for protracted disputes between different sons of Umar Tall and their respective supporters and allies from within the ranks of the Futanke and disparate groups in the Sahel.[2] The conflict between Amadu, the oldest son of Umar Tall, who ruled as his father's successor in Ségou, claiming the title of *amir al-mu'minin* (Ar., commander of the faithful), and Muntaga, whom Amadu removed from power in Nioro, contributed to the already considerable instability that reigned in Karta. From the time of the arrival of the first Futanke, there had been opposition to their presence. Some of those living in the areas in and around Karta resisted the rule of Umar Tall's sons and the heavy taxation they imposed.[3]

When the French under the command of Colonel Archinard finally engaged the Futanke in armed conflict in 1890, certain groups, most notably some Soninke and Khassonke, joined the French in the campaigns (Hanson 1996: 151–2).

The French conquest of the Nioro region came in 1890 and 1891 after a series of military defeats for Amadu and his followers.[4] After the French took the town of Nioro in January of 1891, a small group fled along with Amadu to Bandiagara, the other Umarian centre to the east, and after the French conquest of that town in 1893 on *hijra*, with some eventually reaching the Hijaz.[5] Other groups who stayed behind quickly submitted to the French. In the Nioro area, the French expressed extreme hostility toward the Futanke whom they identified as among the most persistent challengers to their rule.[6] Considerable repression of the defeated Futanke immediately followed. While many Futanke returned to the Senegal River valley willingly, many more were driven in forced marches back to the regions from which they or their ancestors had migrated to support the *jihad* and Futanke state.[7] In total, approximately 20,000 Futanke settlers and their kin left the region between 1891 and 1893 (Hanson 1989: 289–91). The departure of so many Futanke, the region's erstwhile leaders, left them seriously weakened as a group. Nonetheless, many Futanke did settle in the Nioro region, including some who were able to do so by a process of dis-simulation; they claimed not to be from Futa Toro, settling among groups who had submitted earlier to the French.[8] However, French hostility toward the Futanke continued through the first decades of colonial rule (see Robinson 1997).

After the conquest, questions of order and stability were of utmost concern to the French. In large measure, order and stability were means to an end, that is, the economic exploitation of the colonies at the least possible cost to the metropole. The main areas that the French planned to exploit in Nioro were agriculture, livestock raising, and commerce.[9] But the difficulties the French faced in the region were considerable. Given Nioro's relatively remote location in the Sahel, logistical problems were daunting to colonial officials in what was initially at least a major administrative centre as the regional capital of the vast Sahelian region. At the same time, Nioro was relatively close to large parts of the Sahel and the Sahara that remained outside French control until after 1910. It was not until 1911 that the French brought the important commercial town of Tichit under their control and, in the following year, Oualata.

Before the end of the First World War, 'pacification' of the Sahel could hardly have been considered complete. Prior to this time, there was a long period that some have characterised as *le temps des 'bandits'*, when many in the Sahel engaged in openly rebellious activities against the French and those living under their rule (Bernus et al. 1993). Indeed, during the first decades of colonial rule, some living in the Sahel declared war against the French. For example, to the north of Nioro the Idaw'ish warned other Bidan against dealing with the French and called for unity in the struggle against the French, a strategy that ultimately failed.[10] Around this same time, the most prominent adversary of the French was Ma' al-'Aynayn (c. 1831–1910), the religious leader known for his ties with Morocco who eventually made claims to the Moroccan throne. The French feared his influence extended to the region, given that some of his extended family lived in the area to the north of Nioro.[11] In the end, it took more than two decades before the effects of the *paix française* could be felt, as populations within French-controlled areas near Nioro were vulnerable to raids and pillaging from groups in the Sahel. Moreover, the French faced enormous difficulties in their attempt to levy taxes on those groups coming from the north in caravans to trade and/or to bring their animals to pasture on lands under their control.

The system of colonial administration that the French implemented for governing this part of the Soudan was distinctive. With the displacement of the Futanke rulers in Nioro, the French assumed direct political control unlike in most other places in their West African colonies at this time (Kanya-Forstner 1969: 196). The ensuing political reorganisation of the region that followed was dramatic. Perhaps most importantly, the French did not allow the Futanke to return to Nioro, the place that had served as the administrative and political centre of their state in Karta. Instead, the French invited some Soninke groups to settle in the town. They did this, so it seems, because they considered the Soninke as a group more tractable than others living in the Sahel.[12] According to the French, the Soninke were peaceful, while others, especially the 'Toucouleurs' or Futanke, were belligerent. Colonial commentators asserted this, all the while ignoring evidence of the widespread support that various Soninke groups in the region had given to Muhammad al-Amin (d. 1887) and his son when they waged war in areas not far from Nioro.

In keeping with the idea that Nioro contribute to the colonial economy, the French identified the Soninke as devoted merchants or traders and, therefore, not inclined to raid and to pillage, as many of the 'Moors' living in the Sahel were imagined to do. Given which particular families were selected, it is clear that French actions were also an attempt to exacerbate divisions between groups whom they perceived to be antagonistic or rivalrous. The Soninke who moved to Nioro were under the leadership of the Kaba Jakhite, or, as they are often called, the Kabalanke, a very prominent lineage of Muslim religious specialists, long established in this part of West Africa, whose genealogical claims link them in the distant past to the uncle of the Prophet Muhammad.[13] The Kabalanke in Nioro were all descendants of Alfa Umar Kaba Jakhite, a Muslim scholar, who had come from

N'Dioum in Bundu and had been among Umar Tall's closest advisors.[14] Alfa Umar was one of the religious leaders – if not the principal leader – with ties to the myriad of groups already living in the region upon whom Umar Tall and his successors relied as an intermediary in order for their campaigns to succeed (Adam 1903–4; Dramé 1988). After Alfa Umar's death in 1865, members of his family were in conflict with Futanke in Nioro who may have resented their influence in the region, exiling them to a small village near Nioro (Dramé 1988). In February 1893, Archinard 'reinstalled' one of Alfa Umar's sons, Fode Bajiri (a.k.a. Kisma) (d. 1906), not only as *chef* (chief or head) of the Soninke (de Lartigue 1898b: 81), but also as *qadi* (Ar., judge) and 'official imam of the town' (Marty 1920: 213) – the person who leads communal prayer.[15]

Along with the Kabalanke came those referred to as 'the baggage of Kaba', including other families of Muslim religious specialists, such as the Sylla and the Maguiraga, with whom the Kabalanke have been associated.[16] In addition, some Jakhanke who had joined Umar Tall in the *jihad* also moved to Nioro and named the part of the town where they settled Diakha after the place where they and their more remote ancestors trace their origins.[17] A small group of 'Moors', for the most part traders, also settled in the town, and their numbers soon grew. Fulbe from Dianvely, a village on the outskirts of Nioro, founded a neighbourhood on the edge of the town. Hereditary 'caste' members and slaves or former slaves also accompanied each of these groups to Nioro. Finally, soon after the French conquest, many slaves and former slaves took advantage of French control and sought refuge in the town. The French also resettled some Bambara Massassi from Ségou in areas very close to Nioro. But of all these groups, the Soninke made up a clear majority of the town's new inhabitants.[18] As for those living outside the town, particularly the Futanke who had been expelled, they settled in a number of villages around Nioro, including some only a few kilometres from the town.

Towards the goal of administering these people, the French set out to identify the various 'ethnies' living in the area and map out their respective places of residence. After identification, each different 'ethnie' was generally administered as a 'canton', a smaller administrative unit of the larger *cercle* or district. Thus, those Fulbe said to have originated from a particular region, for example Bundu, were grouped together and administered as a unit.[19] In a very socially and culturally complex region, such units were perhaps inevitably artificial, that is, creations of ethnic fictions, since disparate groups of people made up each unit. As for the Futanke, the former rulers of the region, one of the main objectives of these units was to prevent any unity among them. The desired effect of this political restructuring was to marginalise the Futanke as much as possible and was explicitly stated as such in colonial policy pronouncements.[20]

Designed for more efficient administration, the cantons were some of the techniques of rule that had broader objectives. They served not only to monitor local people but also to assist in such highly burdensome colonial policies as labour recruitment and tax collection. In the domain of tax collection in particular, the new colonial state differed considerably from its predecessor. Indeed, the large Futanke state does not seem to have had completely organised administrative institutions. It relied heavily upon predation and raiding for its material base, thereby contributing to the widespread resistance against its rule (Roberts 1987). In contrast, the French administrative system that was erected permeated the landscape with elaborate bureaucratic structures for direct and indirect taxation in addition to the increasingly perfected measures for the recruitment of labour for colonial projects and armies (Suret-Canale 1971). The local chiefs of each 'canton' were paid and ranked as civil servants. They eventually became among the most important African actors in this administrative system, with most of their functions centred around tax collection and labour recruitment – areas with considerable room for graft and corruption.

Under the colonial administration, faced with the repression discussed above, many, if not all, Futanke were initially very wary of the French. They were excluded for the most part from those areas in which any measure of power could be exercised in the town of Nioro. In contrast, the French promoted certain Fulbe from the surrounding areas who were seen as more tractable than the Futanke. In particular, members of the Sy family who traced their origins to Bundu and the Babalanke, the family of Baba Wolibo Ba, one of the military commanders in the pre-colonial state, benefitted early on from the colonial presence through appointments, colonial service and largesse.

Similarly, in the urban setting, early colonial appointments and active involvement in the colonial order were to have lasting consequences. In a significant break with the past, the Kabalanke, a family of Muslim 'clerics' with no recent history of political leadership, obtained hereditary control of a political unit, the local *chefferie* in Nioro. In this way, they gained a measure of power in the new colonial system as it was developing, however limited such power might have been given the circumstances of colonial rule. In addition, ever since the French appointed Kisma Kaba Jakhite as imam, the Kabalanke have retained control of the imamate of the only Friday mosque in the town.[21] The mosque over which this family presides is no ordinary mosque, constructed as it was under the orders of Umar Tall in the nineteenth century (see Figure 2.1). Treated by many as a symbol of Umar Tall's *jihad* and state, the mosque has remained in its original form. Control over such an important symbol has given this family and its associates a strong position in matters of religion and religious authority that, as we will see, has not gone uncontested.

2.1 Mosque, Nioro du Sahel   *Photographer*: Benjamin F. Soares

Early in the colonial period, many, if not all, of the employees of the colonial judicial system, such as judges and clerks,[22] in the immediate area were selected from the most prominent lineages of Muslim religious specialists, the Kabalanke, the Sylla and the Semega among the Soninke, and from several Bidan lineages for the 'Moors' in Nioro. Such people had access to the most important positions available to Africans, however limited in number such positions were. And those from the town who joined the nascent colonial civil service as scribes, messengers, and interpreters – jobs that might entail instruction in French-organised schools – often came from these same families, their kin and associates. While only a few Muslim clerics were made into civil servants or what we might call quasi-civil servants, their kin and associates were drawn into the colonial order. Such activities allowed for the accumulation of social capital that could be deployed in various ways under the new colonial regime, including long-distance trade and labour migration. Largely excluded from the affairs of the town and wary of the new colonial regime, the Futanke were, at least initially, not within the ranks of those directed toward colonial civil service and, therefore, unable to accumulate such newly available forms of social capital.

LA POLITIQUE MUSULMANE

I find it very awkward to speak about 'la politique musulmane', because I suppose that like many other kinds of policies – I could say, if I dared, like policy *tout court* – it is much more an affair of tact and circumstance than a question that can be settled following immutable principles and translated into precise formulas. (Governor Clozel 1913: 60)

Although during French colonial rule, some African Muslims migrated for politico-religious (not to mention economic) reasons to areas beyond French control, and argued that other Muslims should also do so, most did not. In fact, after the First World War, most Muslims in AOF eventually came to accept the fact that they were living under non-Muslim rule and did not deem flight or migration (Ar., *hijra*) necessary or possible. Acceptance of non-Muslim – specifically French – rule had occasionally come enthusiastically and, at other times, much more reluctantly. However, as the decades of French rule passed, those Muslims least enthusiastic about the French presence were resigned to, if not accepting, of non-Muslim rule. This was more or less the case until the 1950s, that is, the decade leading up to independence (see Chapter 7).

Nearly at the outset of colonial rule in Nioro, as noted above, the French selected the imam for the mosque in Nioro. In the aftermath of colonial conquest and the military defeat of the Futanke rulers, this direct intervention by the French was in no small part designed to marginalise the former rulers. The assault on the Futanke was also, at least initially, an assault on the spread of Islam.[23] Even if these assaults did not accomplish the desired results, the colonial administration came to see such attacks on Islam as futile. Most African intermediaries – chiefs, clerks, and translators – from the region of Nioro were eventually, however, Muslims, reflecting, among other things, a recognition on the part of the French of the longstanding Muslim presence here, as well as a practical need for literate intermediaries. Interventions like the selection of the imam in Nioro would be repeated in countless places throughout the colonies of AOF in the following decades. Indeed, after the First World War, colonial administrators in AOF were to be deeply involved in many, if not most, successions to indigenous offices, including prestigious Islamic religious positions, such as imam and leadership posts in Sufi orders.[24] Although such involvement often created or exacerbated local and regional tensions within the interconnected realms of politics and religion, they nonetheless helped to ensure that the French were able to monitor, if not actually control, local affairs through intermediaries. Concerned with order when uncertainty was an ever-present factor, administrators sought to search out and diffuse potential disruptions to colonial rule.

Such colonial practices were intimately tied to the development of *la politique musulmane*, which was also broadly directed toward maintaining order.[25] Although French interactions with Muslims in West Africa were hardly consistent over time and subject to changing circumstances, as the opening quote suggests,[26] one can say that in the early twentieth century such interactions were frequently marked by the mistrust of Muslims on the part of the French (not to mention the mistrust of the French on the part of Muslims). In their development in the twentieth century, French colonial policies toward Islam and Muslims were fuelled by a complex mixture of anxiety and fear of Islam and Muslims, what constituted in effect a 'fascination' with Islam and Muslims (Rodinson 1980) as the potential locus of challenge to French rule. Although anti-clericalist sentiments within the French colonial administration undoubtedly helped to nurture and sustain such attitudes toward Islam and its 'clerics', prior experiences in both West and North Africa of conflict with individuals and groups whose opposition to French rule came, or was imagined to come, under the banner of Islam certainly fed this uneasiness.

After French law formally separated religion and state in 1905, the French colonial state expressed its commitment to *laïcité*, that is, laicism or secularism, which meant that the state should not intervene in religious matters (Triaud 1974: 551).[27] In theory, French law guaranteed *liberté religieuse* (freedom of religion), conceived of as private and confessional. In practice, however, freedom of religion was only guaranteed to the extent that those professing a particular religious faith did not themselves overstep the private religious or spiritual domain and engage in politics, the realm that was to remain the preserve of the public or the laity.[28] For *la politique musulmane*, the issues were rather obtrusive given the ambiguity of the separation of religion and politics in Islam and endless speculation about this subject on the part of the French. Consequently, colonial authorities in French West Africa intervened not infrequently against certain religious figures and groups, claiming that they were meddling in politics. Indeed, state intervention in religious matters could always be justified in the interest of maintaining the separation of religion and politics and/or public order (*l'ordre public*).

At different historical moments, the considerable anxiety about Islam and Muslim populations under French rule varied, though the fear of the spread of 'pan-Islamism' remained fairly constant from the late nineteenth century to the eve of independence. This 'pan-Islamism' meant different things over time but the French extended it to include 'any attempt at inter-territorial communication for religious purposes' (O'Brien 1967: 309). Thus, any and all communication related to Islam, written and oral, across colonial boundaries was to be hindered, if not subverted (cf. O'Brien 1967: 309). When France was at war with a Muslim power – the Ottoman empire, during the First World War – anxieties were particularly high about 'pan-Islamism' (read pan-Islamic movements) that might arise in defence of the Ottomans and be subject to manipulation by Berlin (Triaud 1992: 152). Concerned about the loyalty of Muslims, the central administration ordered that declarations of loyalty be collected from prominent Muslim religious leaders.[29] Similarly, developments elsewhere in the Muslim world, such as growing nationalist movements in the Arab world and that other colonial obsession, 'pan-Arabism', were cause for considerable anxiety to colonial authorities (Harrison 1988; Triaud 1974). After the First World War, this fear of Islam was joined with the dread of Bolshevism, not least because of the vast numbers of Muslims living under Moscow's rule.[30]

It is important to note that much of what became *la politique musulmane* in AOF was formulated after the long French colonial encounter with Muslims in North Africa. Not only had some of the key actors involved in developing *la politique* in AOF served as administrators in North Africa (O'Brien 1967: 306), but some of the policies were also analogous to those in North Africa. Increasingly after the 1910s, French colonial policies sought to foster and, at times, to support openly what were seen to be local Islamic traditions, distinct from those elsewhere in the Muslim world. This was part of a broader *politique des races* identified most closely with William Ponty, Governor-General of AOF (1908–15), who promulgated the idea that each 'race', recognised as having its own 'particular mentality', should be freed from 'the religious and political influence of neighbouring groups.'[31] This worked more generally to promote the idea of ethnic particularism and was quite similar to French colonial policies in North Africa that sought to keep Berbers free from Arab influence. In West Africa, the administration wanted to keep the many Africans who were not Muslims – animists or fetishists in the colonial lexicon – free of Muslim influence. However, as the French were to observe, a particular 'race' in West Africa such as 'the Bambara' might actually comprise both Muslims and non-Muslims. Moreover, the category Muslim transcended the very 'racial' boundaries – Bambara, Soninke, and so forth – the French imagined to exist, and potentially linked Muslims in West Africa with those beyond.

In AOF, a whole cadre of French scholar-administrators, including Maurice Delafosse and Paul Marty, drew on such ideas, paving the way for the colonial administration to emphasise 'African' Islam and its particularities (Harrison 1988: 91ff.). This is best exemplified in the *Islam noir* or Black Islam of the colonial imagination, the idea that Islam in West Africa was different from Islam, as found in the north and east in the Muslim world. From this perspective, *Islam noir* was a more debased form than that of other purportedly 'White' forms of Islam because of African 'animist' accretions such as 'magic'.[32] However, colonial administrators perceived this 'African Islam' to be potentially more controllable than those other

non-African forms of Islam and other pan-Islamic traditions and movements (Harrison 1988: 29). Those Muslim religious specialists – *marabouts*
in colonial parlance – to whom ordinary African Muslims were assumed to
owe allegiance were to be the central focus of colonial efforts to ensure that
this 'African Islam' remained under their control.

If, in theory, *la politique musulmane* was concerned with order and
stability – in short the loyalty of Muslim subjects to 'the French cause', as it
was often described – in practice it was to take a variety of forms. For the
most part, as administrative practice it centred largely on efforts to monitor
and to restrict the activities of Muslims and, ultimately, ideas. Over time,
this was achieved by a range of activities carried out by various parts of the
evolving administrative structure, including the following measures and
policies vis-à-vis Muslim religious specialists: (1) their identification and
surveillance, (2) restrictions on their movement and activities, and (3)
alliance formation and the elevation of a Muslim 'establishment'.

Prompted in part by events in the Muslim world such as the Italian-
Sanusi war and the rise of nationalism in the Middle East,[33] the French
attempted to identify in a systematic way all Muslim religious personalities
in AOF whom they glossed as *marabouts*, a process that got fully underway
by the early 1910s.[34] These *marabouts* ranged from the renowned to the
relatively unknown and included village imams, Quranic school teachers
and scholars, as well as amulet makers. Following colonial experiences in
North Africa, the French concentrated a significant part of their surveillance
efforts on the Sufi orders and the religious leaders associated with them.[35]
Each Muslim religious leader's 'ethnie', level of education, library holdings,
lineage, relations with the French and sphere of influence were carefully
recorded on survey forms. In these reports, considerable attention was
devoted to outlining each Muslim religious leader's role(s) within the Sufi
orders, as these were seen as possible arenas for political activities. Such
information was gathered along with other 'intelligence' at the local levels
through administrators as well as spies, with the principal goal of identifying
potential 'friends' and 'enemies' among Muslims. The latter were assumed
to be those who did not accept French rule and might even try to resist such
rule through violent means. Thus, spies and administrators were on the
constant lookout for signs of impending *jihad* or the rise of Mahdis. Such
research about Muslims eventually provided the basis for many of the
voluminous writings on Muslims in colonial West Africa. Indeed, it was the
kind of information which Marty synthesised in his numerous regionally
focused publications of the 1910s and the 1920s that examine Muslim
religious leaders and the Sufi orders in AOF fairly comprehensively.[36] In any
case, these published accounts were in part the culmination of a vast
administrative undertaking, a preoccupation that lasted at least until
independence.

Once notable Muslims and their spheres of influence, were identified, the French sought to ensure that order and regularity as identified by the French themselves were maintained. This translated directly into some of the restrictions on the movement of religious leaders, their income-generating activities, and teaching that began to be implemented around the same time. From early in the colonial period, there had been a constant concern about the circulation of 'foreign' Muslims, whether from North Africa, neighbouring colonies or elsewhere, who might influence Muslim subjects in AOF. With the *paix française* and increased security, there was the possibility of mobility over greater distances and by more people. In the years immediately following the French conquest, many people identified as Muslim religious leaders circulated widely in the French colonies and beyond, and considerable effort was subsequently expended in restricting such movement.

As early as 1909, in efforts to curb what he thought was the undue influence of Muslim religious leaders, Governor-General Ponty ordered restrictions on the freedom of movement of *marabouts* (Harrison et al. 1987: 501). In Nioro, for instance, there were numerous cases of peripatetic *marabouts* and preachers apprehended for being outside their home areas. Often, these men were identified as 'charlatans' and 'vagabonds' by the French and imprisoned for various periods of time or forced to return to their homes under the *indigénat* (summary administrative justice).[37] Such Muslims were usually described in terms that suggested that they were the absolute antitheses of those religious leaders – very often members of the existing Sufi orders – who were 'friendly' and 'loyal' to France. However, the contempt that colonial administrators reserved for those said-to-be illiterate Muslims who preyed on ignorant Africans reflects the prevailing anti-clericalism of the time. Throughout the colonial period, efforts to control the movement of persons and ideas continued, especially as such movement related to Muslims whose loyalty was suspect, not to mention the various restrictions on the *hajj*.

Such restrictions on movement went hand in hand with efforts to restrict the economic activities of religious leaders, not only those deemed disloyal. Because revenue collection had become the prerogative of the colonial administration and its agents, the French sought to control alms collection by religious leaders. At the local level, Muslim religious leaders in some places were prevented from collecting alms taxes or other kinds of tribute that had been their prerogative in the past.[38] In 1912, Ponty issued a directive that Muslim religious leaders should be prevented from 'extorting gifts' from people under the 'pretext' of religion (Triaud 1974: 556). Although colonial authorities usually asserted that they wanted to protect Africans from exploitation by 'charlatans', they were concerned that such gifts to Muslim religious leaders would diminish the resources Africans had to pay colonial taxes. While it seems that Muslim religious leaders were generally allowed to receive money and/or gifts from people from within their immediate area, the French forbade most (though not all) Muslims from travelling on what they called *tournées de quête* in which they collected gifts or offerings from people. Those religious leaders who received substantial gifts invariably attracted the attention of the colonial authorities.

Finally, over time there was increased regulation of, and actual French colonial engagement in, Quranic and Islamic education for Muslims in AOF.[39] For example, the construction of mosques and the opening of Quranic schools were only allowed after obtaining permission from colonial authorities, and, in many cases, such permission was not granted. Those acting without permission faced fines and imprisonment under the *indigénat*. From the French perspective, such restrictions and monitoring of Muslims and their activities were essential to the task of thwarting any and all possible threats to their authority.

In 1922, one colonial administrator summed up the policy toward Muslims in the Sahelian region of the Soudan as it was developing:

> The policy to follow with regard to Muslims is simple. It can be summed up in a few words. No useless harassment of *marabouts* [Muslim religious leaders] who prove to be correct, but severe repression of all subversive propaganda.[40]

According to Harrison, *la politique musulmane* by this time was such that 'Within Muslim areas, where the French had nothing to fear from Islam, the French task was principally of forging alliances with Muslim leaders' (Harrison 1988: 136). Many of these Muslim leaders with whom ties would be forged were those whom Marty (and his local sources) had identified in the comprehensive studies. They then came to treat these leaders and Sufi orders with which they were associated as the cornerstones of *la politique musulmane*, that is, the foundations of order. The colonial experience with Sufi orders and their leaders elsewhere certainly influenced the evolution of such policy in the Soudan. In addition to the colonial encounter with Sufi orders in North Africa, the French also had considerable experience with the Mourides and other Sufi orders in Senegal. Over time, the colonial administration increasingly sought to support the existing Sufi orders throughout AOF (Harrison 1988: 181). The support that the French gave to these organisations and their leaders in AOF varied considerably but included such things as cash, land and public recognition, in 'exchange for services' such as the assistance in labour recruitment and tax collection that some Muslim religious leaders provided.[41]

Those Muslim leaders with whom the French colonial administration worked became what might be called a Muslim 'establishment' that the French elevated and promoted as the guardians of orthodoxy. This establishment was comprised of influential Muslims who did not seem to manifest any objections to French rule and included the heads of Sufi orders, imams and teachers authorised by the colonial state. After the first few decades of colonial rule in AOF, there was a working relationship between this establishment and the French.[42] One colonial administrator offered a glimpse of how this alliance formation and elevation of a Muslim establishment occurred:

> In fact, the loyalty of Muslim religious leaders has been channeled and, in some ways, was 'inevitable' given the respect we lavished upon them, the honors they received, and the trend of making them into civil servants – something they did not know how to avoid. We appealed to self-interest, and this has not been in vain. (d'Arbaumont 1941: 26)

If in North Africa some Sufi orders and their leaders, most notably some associated with the Tijaniyya, were eventually discredited for their 'collaboration' with the French colonial authorities (see Abun-Nasr 1965), this was not the case for many leaders of Sufi orders in AOF.

The Muslim establishment and its constituent parts in West Africa were in important ways products of the colonial encounter, if not exactly outright colonial constructions. Although some African Muslims might have already had a corporate sense of being Tijani or Qadiri, the identification with different Sufi orders would increase over time. While the colonial administration sought to identify this Muslim establishment – usually designated by Sufi order and/or 'race' – with its leaders and presumed followers and spheres of influence, various African Muslims presented themselves as the legitimate and rightful leaders of the emergent establishment. Although one can read about the elements of the Muslim establishment in various colonial archival sources, it is in some of Marty's writings between the mid-1910s and 1920s that this establishment takes its most tangible form. If this Muslim establishment included a part that was Qadiri, comprised of members of different branches of the Qadiriyya, there was also an authorised Tijani establishment after the initial colonial hostility toward the Futanke had lessened. In his work on Islam in Mauritania and Senegal, published in 1915–16, one finds some of the first published references to the Tijani part of the Muslim establishment and the 'Umarian Tijaniyya' in particular, that is, those Tijanis assumed to trace their initiation into the Tijaniyya through Umar Tall.[43]

While the colonial administration sought to restrict the activities of Muslim religious leaders, it also facilitated the activities of certain 'loyal' Muslims from the establishment in a number of ways. They sometimes gave funds to clerics for the purchase of books at a time when published books in Arabic were quite rare commodities. They approved and sometimes even financed the *hajj* for favoured individuals and facilitated their visits to major centres of the Tijaniyya in North Africa, particularly in Fez. They even allowed some Muslims to travel to collect funds from followers or potential followers. For instance, the colonial administration sometimes financed or subsidised the trips of certain prominent Muslim religious leaders within and between colonies. Most notably, members of a high-profile lineage of religious specialists, the Ahl Shaykh Sidiyya of Boutlimit in Mauritania, travelled, often at the expense of the colony, to neighbouring colonies, usually Senegal and Soudan, to collect gifts from their followers and to recruit new followers.[44] More importantly for Nioro was the case of Seydou Nourou Tall, the grandson of Umar Tall who travelled widely throughout the colonies on behalf of the French, providing them with innumerable services.[45] Obtained directly or indirectly from the French, such benefits – those economic and symbolic benefits associated with exposure to countless numbers of people across AOF – allowed such figures to be elevated in stature. Although they gained power and authority, such gains were not without risks, not least of which was the resentment of rivals who did not approve of such colonial-sanctioned authority.

While this discussion of *la politique musulmane* has thus far been rather general, it is important to note the distinctive ways in which it was implemented in Nioro. In contrast to most areas of AOF that the French deemed to be only nominally Muslim, the French had recognised Nioro as a longstanding Islamic religious centre. Indeed, Marty described Nioro as '*le boulevard de l'islam noir dans la région du Haut-Sénégal*' and '*le pôle de l'islam soudanais*' from Saint-Louis to Niger (Marty 1920: 210–11). Moreover, colonial administrators emphasised ties that Nioro historically had with the north, regions where they believed the practice of Islam to be more pure. At the same time, in the colonial imagination, Nioro was a special case, as is apparent from a description of Nioro (and Timbuktu) that predates Marty's comments:

> Nioro and Timbuktu are the two poles of Sudanic [read African or Black] Islamism [*l'islamisme soudanais*]. The two towns are in an analogous position as far as contact between Berbero-Semites, on the one hand, and Blacks, on the other.[46]

Not only are both towns commercial centres important to the trans-Saharan trade, but they are said to be at the crossroads of two 'civilizations', 'Islamism' and 'fetishism':

> They have also become religious capitals at the intersection of two civilizations, one of which, Islam with tendencies toward occupation, has placed its outposts on the edge of animist [*fétichistes*] lands.[47]

Such ideas relate of course to the *Islam noir* of the colonial imagination. In Nioro, the French faced what they thought were special problems because colonial control had never been easy over what various administrators called the 'anarchistic tribes of Nioro', the Bidan.[48] Thus, in the colonial imagination, even though empirical reality could not be so neatly separated into Black and White, Nioro was singled out for special attention because it was here that the unruly 'White' tribes of the Sahel came in contact with 'Black' Africans bordering on areas of 'fetishism'. This empirical messiness, so to speak, along with the perceived orthodoxy of the Islam of the majority in the area made *la politique musulmane* somewhat different than, say, in Senegal. In Nioro, instead of fostering a strictly local tradition, most efforts were concentrated on creating alliances with the local religious leaders, whose influence was identified and appraised, who would act as bulwarks against pan-Islamic influences, as well as help to temper the assumed instability of groups in the region. However, it is apparent from both oral sources and colonial administrative reports that relations between the French and local Muslim religious leaders, even some of those whom the French considered among the most loyal, were not always smooth, especially in the early colonial period.

In general, the overall effect of *la politique musulmane* – whether it was in practice the effort to foster local traditions of Islam and/or to build alliances with local Muslim leaders – seems to have been to attempt to 'freeze' Muslim religious leaders in their spheres of influence in AOF, that is, a process quite similar to what has been reported for the Moroccan protectorate (Eickelman 1976: 181).[49] Through *la politique musulmane*, the colonial monitoring of Muslims and their activities and the elevation and sanctioning of a Muslim establishment became in effect a disciplinary regime. French colonial policies aimed to restrict Muslim religious personalities within particular spheres of influence and to set limits to what was deemed acceptable activity. Muslims monitored themselves and their own actions as well as the actions of other Muslims.

Eventually, the French colonial administration associated with certain Muslim religious leaders and even with certain public expressions of Islam that they or the Muslim establishment promoted. Over time, the administration came to see certain kinds of public expressions of Islam, including public ritual, as acceptable and others as unacceptable. For this reason, the administration sometimes became involved, wittingly or unwittingly, in trying to decide what was 'true' or legitimate Islam. On Islamic holidays, the head of the colony regularly attended prayers that colonial-authorised *marabouts* led at the mosque. In times of crisis, colonial administrators would not only seek loyalty oaths from such religious leaders, but they would even ask them to pray for French victory. There were restrictions on preaching and the building of new mosques and schools, and even sometimes objections to the way that certain Muslims practised Islam. When a particular Muslim religious leader was deemed suspect, that person's practice of Islam – even in its public ritual form – sometimes became a matter of interest and concern to the colonial administration. However, attempts to be the arbiter of Islamic orthodoxy would almost always be fraught with difficulties. This was even more so the case when attempts to decide what was orthodoxy came from the colonial administration.

French policies, it seems, left them rather unprepared for any sort of change, especially in the realm of religious practice and organisation. When faced with such changes, policies toward Islam and Muslims had to be adjusted. These, it must be stressed, were sometimes fitful adjustments. When a new charismatic leader like Hamallah seemed to challenge the authority of existing Sufi orders and particularly the colonial-authorised Muslim establishment, he, his followers and even some of their ritual practices were treated as disruptive or potentially disruptive of order. Similarly, in the 1950s, the colonial administration focussed on new perceived threats, 'reformists' and members of the so-called Wahhabiyya (see Chapter 7).

In short, the French were fearful of the disruptive potential of Muslims and those united behind the banner of Islam in their colonies and beyond. There was a constant effort to be vigilant against any potential challenges that might come in the form of religious 'fanaticism'. Efforts at maintaining order and stability, not only in the case of Nioro, concentrated on alliances with Muslim religious leaders who were often part of the existing leadership of the Sufi orders. This attempt to freeze religious leaders in place was such that it left them unprepared for the emergence of new leaders and changes in the religious practices of Muslims. This was especially the case when such changes extended beyond what they had identified as the locus of order, at least in large parts of AOF – the existing Muslim religious leadership and the Sufi orders with which they were often associated. The emergence of Hamallah with his many followers was just such a change.

A CHANGING POLITICAL ECONOMY AND THE NEW COLONIAL SPHERE

Before concluding this chapter, I want to present a brief overview of some of the important changes in the political economy of Nioro and the broader region during the early part of the colonial period, some of which have been alluded to above. Most importantly, I will suggest that the French colonial presence allowed for the expansion of a new sphere of activity in which the practice of Islam could be different than in the past. This discussion sets the context for the following two chapters where I consider the two Sufi orders that were the dominant institutional forms through which Islam was practised in the town in the twentieth century.

As indicated above, French colonial rule and the ensuing *paix française* had profound and lasting effects. It is not an overstatement that the effects of the new kinds of communication and travel made available by French colonialism were unprecedented. The colonial economy and the elaborate communications and transport systems that developed during the colonial period were to be key factors in some of the transformations of the social landscape.[50] As production, consumption and exchange were reordered under the colonial political economy, Africans – colonial civil servants, recruits for military service, forced labourers, merchants, labour migrants and students in colonial schools and Islamic education – circulated in great numbers and as never before.

Although Nioro was never on a colonial railway line, its close proximity to Kayes, the major colonial town and commercial centre to the east that was the capital of the colony from 1892 until 1907 and was within reach of river transport on the Senegal river, helped to draw the region and its inhabitants directly into the colonial economy, including working as forced labourers in road construction and other public works projects.[51] In 1904, when the railway connected Kayes with Bamako, Nioro was linked even more closely to the colonial economy. The town's location, together with the fact that some in the region had difficulty in meeting subsistence needs and paying their taxes, helped make Nioro a major sending area for labour migration as the free market in labour developed.[52] Many went to work in the peanut basins to the east in Senegal and to areas of greater economic activity to the south in the Soudan, as well as to neighbouring French and British colonies, often returning to the region after periodic absences.

If, in the nineteenth and early twentieth centuries, Nioro was important in trans-Saharan trade, new colonial commercial centres such as Kayes, Kita and Bamako became more central to the colonial economy. While for some time the French commercial houses bought gum and kapok in Nioro for export, the role of such products in trade declined as cheaper substitutes were found.[53] The trade of salt that came in caravans from the north to Nioro continued to be important but not, however, to the overall colonial economy. Nioro remained a prominent regional commercial centre for trade in foodstuffs, especially the millet with which groups in the Sahel provisioned themselves, and the sale of goods – sugar, guinea cloth, European cloth, and so forth – by the European trading houses, all of which had offices or representatives in the town. With the waning of the trans-Saharan trade, merchants worked new trading routes opened up during the colonial period. They were also able to travel in greater numbers and much further distances to places from which they had been excluded in the past because of insecurity or trade monopolies (Launay 1982). Paradoxically, this lessening of the constraints on movement for most people was happening at precisely the same time that the restrictions on the movements and activities of at least some Muslim religious leaders were being implemented.

Nearly from the onset of colonial rule, such dramatic political economic changes were underway. The effects of such changes on the social landscape were considerably more ambiguous than might appear on the surface. From the time of conquest, if not earlier, socio-political and economic relations between social groups in the Sahel and the Sahara were being transformed. On the one hand, involvement in the colonial economy, including new trading opportunities with the French and income-generating opportunities, facilitated some of the transformations. On the other hand, compulsory engagement with the colonial economy, particularly through forced labour, military conscription and taxation, facilitated other transformations. For example, during colonial rule, some groups of Bidan in the Sahel were eager to trade directly with the French in Nioro and, by doing so, were able to break loose from those to whom they had historically paid tribute. Other groups merely sought to escape their 'traditional' tributary obligations through submission to the French. With the *paix française*, various groups of Bidan warriors eventually became ex-warriors. In this way, more direct engagement with the French helped to reorganise relations within and between some of these groups of Bidan. But such changes were by no means limited to the Bidan. Indeed, across the broader region, all sorts of such complex changes were underway.[54]

Within nearly all the groups in the broader region, there are hereditary social distinctions that concern status, indicating whether a person is 'free', 'servile' or a member of a 'caste', groups with occupational specialisations. Some of the most profound changes in this region during the colonial period relate to the distinctions between 'free' and 'servile' that were occasioned by the end of slavery as it had been practised historically.[55] Estimates of the servile-status population in the Nioro region range between 40 and 60 per cent of the total population in some places.[56] After the colonial conquest, the renegotiation of relations between 'slave' and 'free' clearly accelerated. Indeed, such processes are still incomplete today. While in the past, it was not uncommon for female slaves to be integrated into 'free' lineages through concubinage, this almost completely ended shortly after the turn of the twentieth century. For instance, nearly all lineages of religious specialists in Nioro acknowledge that women slaves were integrated into their lineages in the past. Prior to the mass exodus of slaves reported in the first decade of this century, many servile-status persons left their masters.[57] While some simply left when their owners were unable to provide for them during difficult times, others fled. In many such cases, slave owners tried to prevent slaves from leaving. Certain Muslim religious leaders, some of whom were undoubtedly slave owners themselves, were particularly active in trying to halt such changes. Colonial records indicate that Shaykh Sidi Muhammad al-Akhdar, the religious figure from North Africa who appointed Shaykh Hamallah as his successor in Nioro, was arrested in 1906 and sent to Saint-Louis 'for having … incited the people in Banamba, unhappy with our measures for the emancipation of slaves, against our authority' (Nicolas 1943: 19).[58] In 1911, near Kayes another Muslim cleric, Fode Ismaila:

> dealt with the question of slaves and said that the moment to act had not yet arrived, but that a 'marabout', living in the South, would perform a miracle and that it would be necessary to rise up *en masse* and take back the slaves. He announced that at the same time that the reign of Islam would begin, which evidently means that that [the reign] of the French would end. (Marty 1920: 28)

The French quickly imprisoned this man as an agitator. As these examples suggest, the loss of slaves was clearly a shock to slave owners and their associates. The 'millenarian' ideas of certain Muslim religious leaders notwithstanding, they were ultimately unable to prevent many slaves from leaving their owners.

Frequently, such slaves sought 'refuge' in towns under French colonial rule, and the part of Nioro called Nioro-Réfuge or Nioro Liberté (and renamed Malicounda at the request of its inhabitants after independence) was one such place where some of these people settled. Nearly every colonial town and some of the villages near Nioro had such neighbourhoods reserved for servile-status people (see Bouche 1968). Other servile-status persons founded new villages on land allocated to them by the French where they might cultivate or serve as a labour reserve. Around Nioro, there are several such villages of former slaves founded in the first half of the twentieth century.

With the end of slavery, it seems that the distinctions that existed between 'slave' and 'free' for the different ethnic groups in the region became more fluid in at least some areas of social life. While in the period prior to the official French colonial emancipation of slaves in 1905, work in the agricultural fields in this region had been done almost exclusively by servile-status people, this was no longer the case. As some have argued, with the end of slavery, hierarchical principles were weakened not only within the society but also within the family (Pollet and Winter 1971: 371, 394). With the development of the free labour market, people were no longer able to invest capital in slaves (Roberts 1988: 302). Instead, there was an increase in investment in other activities such as trade and livestock (ibid.; Manchuelle 1989). Some of those who were able to diversify were able to keep from direct involvement in agricultural labour, including some of the most prominent people in Nioro associated with the colonial administration. One example is a prominent lineage that was able to accumulate massive livestock holdings. For the majority, however, agricultural labour now became obligatory, sometimes even for high-status people, such as descendants of pre-colonial slave owning elites, who in earlier times would clearly not have engaged in such labour.

It is interesting to note that many colonial administrators claimed (or repeated the claim) that the end of slavery meant a decline in Islam – what might be called the regression thesis – clearly just one variant of prevailing Orientalist ideas of the time. Often the argument was made that the obligation to work in agriculture left little time for religion, not to mention Quranic education (for example Marty 1920: 178).[59] While this is entirely plausible, there is not much evidence that this was the case. In at least one of his books, Marty suggested that in some areas of the Soudan the end of slavery was leading to the spread of Islam since Muslims and non-Muslims actually found themselves in the same situation (ibid.: 24). There is even evidence that the number of students in Islamic education increased in several towns in the Soudan in the first decades after the conquest.[60] This regression thesis most likely comes from the colonial-era scholarly idea that Islam was closely tied to the institution of slavery, an idea promoted most actively by Governor Clozel (Harrison 1988: 99). In this way of thinking, if slavery ceased to exist, then there would certainly be a decline in the religion. But many commentators would later note that the spread of Islam was one of the undeniable changes during French colonial rule in AOF (see Harmon 1988; Launay and Soares 1999).

This still leaves unanswered the question as to what effect, if any, the decline of slavery had on the practice of Islam. As some have suggested, after the official end of slavery, the Sahel experienced considerable economic decline (Roberts 1988: 298). Such decline undoubtedly compelled some people to migrate from the Nioro region with the number of migrants so great at times that colonial administrators expressed concern, and at times alarm, about depopulation of the area.[61] Colonial administrators claimed that agricultural work and labour migration were contributing to decreased interest in the pursuit of Islamic education.[62] Although the educational system that had been in place prior to the colonial conquest no longer existed in the same form, Nioro remained an important centre for Islamic education. According to French colonial statistics, the number of students engaged in Islamic education in Nioro had risen markedly since the colonial conquest. By 1921, there were more students engaged in Islamic education in Nioro than in any other town in the Soudan (Brevié 1923: 215).

In Nioro, the Kabalanke maintained a school that offered advanced education, frequented for the most part by Soninke from the town and its environs. For their part, some Futanke ran schools in neighbouring villages, while several from important lineages identified with the Umarian *jihad* left the region for their studies. While this in itself is not unusual,[63] such travel was necessary because advanced education was not always available from Futanke scholars in the area. Indeed, several Futanke left the Nioro area to go to Mauritania, returning after they had completed their studies,[64] and other groups ran schools of lesser import in the region. Nonetheless, Nioro and the broader region produced and continued to produce religious scholars and leaders. However, it is important to note how such education some-times came to be organised in part along 'ethnic' lines, especially for the Soninke and Futanke near Nioro. Those from each group tended to study with religious leaders from their own ethnic group, a process that may be related to the mutual mistrust that was exacerbated by early colonial policies favouring the Soninke in the region.

Even though the division between free and slave might have been blurred for at least some of those engaged in agricultural labour, the division remained salient in other areas of social life such as marriage. The division was especially important in the realm of religion and religious education. Despite the extent of the social changes associated with the end of slavery, religion remained largely a monopoly of the lineages of religious specialists.[65] That is, hereditary groups of 'free' persons retained control over religious education and leadership positions such as imam and major roles such as muqaddam in the Sufi orders. Almost without exception, most celebrated living or deceased Muslim religious personalities, saintly or otherwise, have come from these same lineages. In fact, there are virtually no examples of servile-status persons or their descendants in the region becoming pro-minent religious specialists and only a few examples of very minor religious specialists of 'caste' origins.[66]

Although it is likely that religious specialists have long had diversified economic activities (cf. Sanneh 1989), it appears that demographic expan-sion compelled certain people, and sometimes even entire lineages of religious specialists, to make a living in other ways, often having to migrate in order to do so.[67] While some lineages became known as minor religious specialists associated in varying degrees with the major religious lineages, many others remained religious specialists in name only. Some from these minor lineages continue to contract marriage alliances with some of the lineages of active religious specialists. Some of them attended colonial schools, that is, French-language schools, and subsequently found employ-ment in the colonial administration locally or elsewhere. Many more worked as merchants, a 'traditional' occupation for many, and/or as tailors and embroiderers, crafts deemed honourable for religious specialists.

Those of servile status who moved to urban settings during the colonial era often found employment opportunities as labourers, butchers and bakers, that is, precisely the kinds of activities that were generally reserved for those of servile status (Ould Cheikh 1993). The descendants of such servile-status persons comprise an important part of the population in Nioro. The servile status of the ancestors of such people has usually not been forgotten. While Muslim political and religious elites were unable to prevent the end of slavery as it had been practised, they were able to exact what might be considered a certain kind of revenge. In nearly all cases, Muslim religious specialists note that slave owners never formally freed their slaves in the region. They claim that, according to the rules of Islamic jurisprudence, such servile-status persons and their descendants remain the property of their owners. Even though such people were no longer considered servile according to French (and later Malian) law, in this interpretation of Islamic jurisprudence, they remained slaves. The ultimate result has been that their marginal status has persisted. Indeed, ambiguity even surrounds the status of their many descendants, influencing their engagement in the local social field and frequently in society at large.

Some of those who left Nioro to work in areas of greater economic activity were able to engage in economic activities from which they might have been excluded in the past because of their servile status. A number of servile-status people from the town and surrounding villages profited in the colonial and postcolonial economy, amassing substantial wealth. Upon return to Nioro, such people had considerable capital to invest, which sometimes helped to mitigate, though not erase, their marginal social status.[68] Such prosperous servile-status persons are a decided minority, and those of servile status who did not make their fortunes elsewhere or migrate to be absorbed into large towns may even constitute the majority in the region. Over the course of several decades, these people whose hereditary status helped to keep them marginal nonetheless began to emulate the Islamic religious practices of those with a monopoly on religious knowledge and education. If former slaves constituted one of the largest groups of Muslims in this region, there were many other Muslims from disparate groups whose status was also ambiguous, at least in relation to members of the lineages of Muslim religious specialists.

After the colonial conquest and the end of slavery, there were huge movements of people for agricultural and wage labour, trading opportunities in new centres of economic activity, conscription in colonial armies, colonial schooling and Islamic education. People of diverse origins from all over were coming together in the new spaces that colonialism had opened up. This new colonial sphere was a much broader and unified sphere of interactions than in the pre-colonial period. Alongside the new political authority of the colonial state was an arena for the relatively autonomous practice of Islam. It was in the space of this new colonial sphere that there was mass Islamisation. Indeed, many non-Muslims from various ethnic and linguistic groups, including urban and agricultural labourers, traders, conscripts, students in colonial schools and their village kin were converting to Islam. As these people converted to Islam, many abandoned their allegedly un-Islamic ritual objects and practices – 'fetishes' and 'fetishism' in the colonial lexicon (see Figure 2.2). Others had never been initiated into the region's various 'secret' societies or renounced their ties to such

2.2 *Boli* or 'power object' (43cm x 55cm x 21.5cm) from Mali, collected in the
1970s, Africa Museum, Berg en Dal   Used with permission

societies. The non-Muslim sources of power and authority, such as the
knowledge of the Bambara or *bamanaya*, to which such objects and
practices were tied eventually lost some of their value. Indeed, such sources
of authority were marginalised and transformed within the broader colonial
sphere and increasingly pushed into the private sphere where individuals
made use of them. Given the widespread Islamisation under colonial rule,
such non-Muslim sources of authority were unlikely to become the basis for
translocal authority in quite the same way that Islam did in the new colonial
sphere. However, some who relied upon such knowledge retained some
measure of authority in certain rural areas and regions.

At the same time, the new colonial sphere also helped to facilitate the
standardisation of Islamic religious practice. In contrast to the pre-colonial
period, ways of being Muslim became much more uniform for all Muslims,
regardless of social differences, hereditary or otherwise. People of diverse
origins – slave, caste, ex-warriors and recent converts – began to emulate the
religious practices of Muslim clerics, such that regular prayer and fasting
during the month of Ramadan became ritual norms for all Muslims
regardless of social distinctions. This helped to make the practice of Islam,

especially in its public ritual forms – more uniform across space and time. However, in addition to regular ritual prayer and fasting during Ramadan, the standardisation of religious practice also usually included affiliation to a Sufi order or at least respect for its leader(s). If prior to colonial rule, affiliation to Sufi orders had been a private affair limited exclusively to scholarly elites, there would be mass affiliation to Sufi orders under colonial rule.

One of the most profound changes during colonial rule was the end of slavery, a veritable shock to some of the slave-owning elites of the region. Nonetheless, throughout the period, some elites – pre-colonial political and/ or religious elites – were able to maintain their positions of dominance, through the diversification of economic activities that frequently entailed migration. While some lineages of religious specialists had to undertake other economic activities to make a living and, in effect, ceased to be religious specialists other than in name only, a number of lineages retained their monopoly on religious knowledge and education, perhaps in no small part because of the colonial *politique musulmane* and the elevation and author-isation of the Muslim establishment. All assertions and predictions – colonial era and otherwise – that the practice of Islam and Islamic education were on the decline were fanciful. As many colonial commentators and even some Muslims would later note, Islamisation seemed to be a direct result of French colonial rule in West Africa. In marked contrast to the era of *jihad*s in the nineteenth century, Islamisation and the standardisation of religious practice were rapid and far-reaching under colonial rule. Such develop-ments were only possible given the complex social transformations occurring under French rule and the expansion of a new colonial sphere of activity in which the practice of Islam could be different than in the past. This was apparent with the new Sufi order, the Hamawiyya, that attracted followers from throughout the broader region. Failing to conform to colonialist expectations, the Hamawiyya, its leader and many of his followers were subjected to prolonged repression and persecution. However, this new colonial sphere of activity continued to develop in ways such that the practice of Islam could be discussed and debated in new ways. But all of these later developments can only be understood within the context of the French colonial policies and the expansion of the colonial economy that helped change Nioro as a socio-political and religious space.

SAINTS AND SUFI ORDERS I:
THE HAMAWIYYA

Over the past few decades, several studies of Muslim societies in sub-Saharan Africa have emphasised the appeal and potential of Islam for resistance, proto-nationalism, or anti-colonialism. Most notably, some have interpreted Islam in Africa as the basis for various kinds of 'counter-society' movements both during and after the colonial period (for example Coulon 1988). Some of the postcolonial interpretations of the rise of the Sufi affiliation around Shaykh Hamallah have, indeed, followed such a model, tending to privilege the colonial encounter and placing considerable emphasis on the purportedly anti-colonial and proto-nationalist features of the Sufi order, its leader and followers (for example Alexandre 1970). Aside from the works of some of Hamallah's followers that we might characterise as hagiographic (for example Ibn Mu'adh 1988) and those that have emphasised Hamallah's status as a Muslim mystic whose concerns were largely spiritual and other-worldly (for example Ba 1980; Dicko 1999), the historian Traoré (1983) has offered the most sustained discussion of Hamallah and the Hamawiyya. Although he presents a rather nuanced view of Hamallah as what he calls a 'man of faith' as well as a resistance figure, his study nonetheless falls within what can be called anti-colonial, if not nation-alist, historiography. The overall cast of Traoré's study is that Hamallah and his followers were anti-colonialists, an orientation that obscures the com-plexity of the movement around Hamallah and contributes little to an understanding of the importance of the Hamawiyya and its transformation in the postcolonial period.

The interpretation offered here is somewhat different, though it too stresses the importance of the colonial context. In my view, Shaykh Hamallah and the Hamawiyya arose at a time when some Muslims in AOF were looking for Muslim leadership, specifically exceptional Muslim leadership, within the new colonial context. It was precisely the new colonial context that allowed the Sufi affiliation that centred around the charismatic Hamallah to spread in unprecedented ways. The colonial economy, the expansion of travel and improved communications helped to create a new space in which the practice of Islam was different to that in the past. Under colonial rule, the standardisation of religious practice that accompanied Islamisation included mass affiliation to Sufi orders and to the Hamawiyya in particular. Such affiliation was to become the norm for many Muslims, regardless of social distinction. Thus, the French colonial presence not only helped to shape what it meant to be Muslim in AOF, but it also helped to provide the conditions for the emergence and spread of the Hamawiyya, which through the charismatic reputation of its leader attracted followers from a variety of social, ethnic and linguistic groups from throughout the French colonies in West Africa.

I also want to explore some of the complexity of the relations between Hamallah, his followers and detractors, the French administration and the Muslim establishment. In this way, I do not unduly privilege the anti-colonialist tendencies of the Hamawiyya nor overstate the purported resistance, passive or otherwise, of Shaykh Hamallah to French non-Muslim rule. When Hamallah and the Hamawiyya seemed to challenge the authority of the existing Sufi orders and their colonial-authorised leader-ship, some Muslims in West Africa opposed him. If some of their reasons for doing so included sheer envy and vested interests in maintaining their own authority and followers, others also objected to Hamallah because of differences and disagreements over doctrine about the licitness of certain religious practices. I will argue that the French, often influenced by Hamallah's opponents, perceived Islam and this increasingly popular Sufi order and its leader as disruptive of order and potentially subversive – anti-colonial, pan-Islamic and fanatical. Although there is no evidence what-soever that Hamallah actually contested colonial rule or sought anything more than the leadership of Muslims and Tijanis living in French West Africa, colonial perceptions of Hamallah and his followers eventually culminated in efforts to eliminate the Hamawiyya: the arrest in 1941 of Hamallah, his subsequent death in detention, and the severe repression of many of his followers in the 1940s. Exploring the reconstitution of the Hamawiyya in the postcolonial period, I show how the history of persecution and repression helped to foster an economy of martyrdom in which a religious community has come to define itself in relation to an absent leader with a saintly reputation.

THE TIJANIYYA BEFORE HAMALLAH

The Sufi affiliation that developed around Shaykh Hamallah began early in the colonial period, shortly after the turn of the century, in Nioro du Sahel. This new affiliation was explicitly a Tijani affiliation and, therefore, linked to the dominant institutional form through which Islam had been practised by some elites in the region since at least the mid-nineteenth century. Although the Qadiriyya through its various branches had also been important here, the Tijaniyya had come to overshadow other affiliations since the *jihad* of Umar Tall.

The early part of colonial rule was a time of considerable social and political economic change in the region. After the establishment of the *paix française* and defeat of armed opponents to French rule, colonial subjects – Muslim and non-Muslim – had to come to terms with the circumstances of French, non-Muslim rule. These included the new system of law and taxation they imposed; changes in production, particularly the end of slavery; forced labour and recruitment; and new restrictions on the movement of persons. At the onset of colonial rule, there was no leadership around which Tijanis, let alone Muslims, were united (Brenner 1984: 43). It was indeed an era in which authority, specifically as it related to Islam, was considerably diffused. Given the existing hierarchical organisational structure that helped to define Islamic practice, many people, most of whom were Muslims, in the region looked to Muslim religious specialists to help them make sense of some of the upheavals of the day (cf. Coulon 1988). Moreover, some Muslims here were actively seeking a new leader in such a time of change. As indicated above in Chapter 1, expectations of exceptional Muslim leadership were commonplace in the pre-colonial period, and this was no less the case after the French conquest.

In the early colonial period, questions of leadership could only have been foremost in the minds of those living in Nioro and the surrounding areas. The lack of leadership was in marked contrast to the mid-nineteenth century when Umar Tall had been a widely recognised, if not uncontested, leader in large parts of the region. The spread of the Tijaniyya in West Africa had been closely tied to the Umar Tall's activities, and many leading scholars and intellectuals from the broader region, including some from North Africa, recognised and praised his overall importance to the Tijaniyya. Although at the time of his death at the height of the *jihad* Umar appears not to have named all the *muqaddams* or deputies he was authorised to appoint, many of the *muqaddams* throughout large parts of West Africa traced their initiation into the Tijaniyya through him.[1] After Umar's death, there was little in the way of unity among his supporters, admirers and descendants.

Immediately prior to the colonial conquest of Nioro, Amadu, who claimed to be the successor to his father Umar and 'commander of the faithful', retained leadership in both political and religious senses. In the region of Nioro, there had been only one or two Tijani *muqaddams* during Amadu's tenure there. In addition to Amadu, there was Sidi Abdallah from Tichit who is reported to have initiated people into the Tijaniyya only in the absence of Amadu.[2] But if there had been disunity after the death of Umar Tall, this was only more so the case during the long periods of internecine struggle and resistance that characterised the rule of Amadu.

In the aftermath of the French conquest and political reorganisation of the region, many people remained in and around Nioro with first-hand experience of the Umarian and immediate successor states. Many, if not all, of these people, defined and continued to define themselves in relation to the *jihad* of Umar Tall, the rule of his sons and the primacy of the Tijaniyya. Although the Tijaniyya remained the dominant institutional form through which Islam was practised, those who considered themselves Tijanis were seriously fragmented, not least because many of the most prominent of their leaders had died in battle, fled or been driven from the area. French colonial policies, particularly those that gave some authority to favoured groups of people in Nioro, only exacerbated this fragmentation.

Shortly after the turn of the twentieth century, there was only one Tijani *muqaddam* in the region of Nioro, according to French colonial sources. This was Muhammad al-Mukhtar (c. 1860–1930), a *sharif* known as both a merchant and religious leader, whose own career in the first decades of the century is absolutely central to the development of the Hamawiyya. First of all, Muhammad al-Mukhtar's presence in the area was one of the consequences of the French political reorganisation of the region.[3] He was the religious advisor and son-in-law of Bodian Coulibaly, the Bambara Massassi leader from Ségou, whom Archinard invited to resettle in the Nioro area shortly after conquest (Méniaud 1931, 2: 363ff.). In 1893, Muhammad al-Mukhtar joined Coulibaly and his retinue, moving to one of the villages from which the French expelled its Futanke inhabitants (de Lartigue 1898b: 81). Not long thereafter, Muhammad al-Mukhtar moved to Nioro proper.

Although Muhammad al-Mukhtar had a most impressive set of credentials that would almost seem to have guaranteed him a pre-eminent position as a Muslim religious specialist in most places in AOF, this was not to be the case in Nioro. In 1885, he seems to have been named a *muqaddam* of the Tijaniyya by a North African visiting West Africa from Fez,[4] site of the tomb of Ahmad al-Tijani and the North African *zawiya* (Ar., Sufi religious centre) with which many Tijanis in sub-Saharan Africa had ties (see Abun-Nasr 1965, and Robinson 2000). Such an appointment and a subsequent visit to Fez in 1907 in conjunction with a trip to the Islamic holy cities undoubtedly helped to facilitate his already extensive connections with Tijanis across AOF and beyond, especially with some of those who would become leading figures of the colonial authorised Muslim establishment. Most notably, he was part of the network of those around Malik Sy (d. 1922), the Tijani leader in Tivaouane (Senegal) who was on very good terms with the French. Muhammad al-Mukhtar had ties in particular with Babakar Sy, Malik Sy's son and designated successor, as well as with Sy's son-in-law, Seydou Nourou Tall, who would later claim Muhammad al-Mukhtar as one of his teachers.[5] As for his relations with the French, Muhammad al-Mukhtar was what might be called a model 'loyal' Muslim. One of his sons died in military service during the First World War while another worked as a colonial interpreter.[6] No less a figure than Blaise Diagne, the first African deputy from Senegal in Paris, intervened on Muhammad al-Mukhtar's behalf with the Governor General of AOF for permission for him to circulate freely throughout the Soudan, ostensibly to collect gifts and offerings of a religious nature.[7]

Despite his credentials – his sharifian descent, his pilgrimage to Mecca and visit to the Tijani *zawiya* in Fez, and ties with prominent individuals – Muhammad al-Mukhtar seems to have had limited influence among the heterogeneous population of Nioro even before Hamallah's rise to prominence.[8] Shortly after his return from his trip to the Hijaz and Fez in 1907, he was almost immediately overshadowed by the young Hamallah, not to mention another Tijani *muqaddam*, Murtada (d. 1922), the son of Umar Tall who had recently returned to live in Nioro.

If, in 1905, Muhammad al-Mukhtar was allegedly the only Tijani *muqaddam* in the area, less than a decade later (and more than twenty years after the conquest) colonial administrators would report that there had been a proliferation of Tijani *muqaddams* appointed by a number of different people in the region.[9] In 1913, a colonial report identified thirteen people who 'claim' to have 'the right to confer the wird', that is, the authority to initiate people into the Sufi order.[10] If some colonial sources claimed that Murtada Tall was the most prominent among them, others would note that his influence was limited almost exclusively to the Futanke associated with his father Umar.[11] More than half the Tijani *muqaddams* listed are Soninke, most of whom lived in villages at considerable distances from Nioro.[12] That there are no Soninke included from the town of Nioro is striking, given that the town was at the time overwhelmingly populated by Soninke and headed by the Kabalanke with their extensive contacts with Soninke groups in the region.[13] At least two of the Soninke *muqaddams* had direct ties to Muhammad al-Amin, who, it was noted earlier, waged *jihad* in the region and whose followers clashed militarily with Amadu and the French. The North African, Sidi Muhammad al-Akhdar (d. 1909), had appointed three of the six *muqaddams* from the town of Nioro and its immediate vicinity, and these were a Futanke, a Fulbe and Hamallah.[14] It is significant that Sidi Muhammad al-Akhdar seems not to have named any *muqaddams* from among the Soninke in the town.

A decade into the twentieth century, the overall situation of the Tijaniyya was such that there were quite a number of *muqaddams* in the Nioro area, but little in the way of unity among those who considered themselves Tijanis. Through *la politique des races* and *la politique musulmane*, the French sought to encourage this lack of unity further since they considered it to be to their ultimate advantage.[15] What might have seemed at the time to have been fragmentation of the Tijaniyya became a polarising situation that only worsened with the advent of mass affiliation to the Sufi order in the following decades.

I now turn to consider Sidi Muhammad al-Akhdar, the North African religious figure to whom the development of the Sufi affiliation around

Hamallah can be traced and with whom any discussion of changes in the organisation of the Tijaniyya in this part of West Africa must begin.

FROM AL-AKHDAR AND HIS 'MISSION' TO THE HAMAWIYYA

Around the turn of the twentieth century, Shaykh Sidi Muhammad al-Akhdar (c. 1856–1909) – hereafter al-Akhdar – a North African with ties to some of the major *zawiyas* of the Tijaniyya in North Africa who claimed to be a *shaykh* of the Sufi order, was travelling widely in AOF and in Mauritania, including areas well beyond direct French control.[16] Al-Akhdar had been the beneficiary of hospitality and support from some noted Muslim religious leaders, including a prominent relative of Muhammad Fadil, the father of Ma' al-'Aynayn, in the region of the Adrar in Mauritania with whom he lived for more than twenty years. He also received support from some of the many Wolof traders who had moved from areas in the west in Senegal to work in colonial towns in Nioro, Kayes and elsewhere.[17] Along his way, al-Akhdar collected gifts to support himself and his family. He explained to a French colonial administrator that he decided to do so only after having seen how successful such notable contemporaries as Amadu Bamba and Sa'ad Buh, among others, had been in doing just this.[18]

Oral sources and written texts sympathetic to the Hamawiyya are unanimous in their view that al-Akhdar was an eminent *shaykh* and *sharif*, indeed, a saint, who had been sent on a mission to West Africa to select a leader of the Tijaniyya. In the book that has the official approval of the present-day leadership of the Hamawiyya in Nioro, Ibn Mu'adh first introduces al-Akhdar as 'the well-known *sharif*, the great pole [Ar., *qutb*, the highest ranking saint]' (1988: 8). Be this as it may, some have pointed out (for example Brenner 1984) that it is very difficult to say with any precision what mission, if any, al-Akhdar had. What does seem clear is that al-Akhdar had something akin to charisma in its Weberian sense, that is, a quality believed to be of divine origin that set him apart from others. In 1906 in an interview while being detained, al-Akhdar claimed to have *iqbal al-khalq* (Ar.), that is, mass support or recognition, a quality that would ensure people were drawn to him.[19] In a second interview, al-Akhdar explained to his colonial interlocutor that two Muslim religious leaders in Mauritania – both of whom happened to be Qadiris from the Tendagha, a group of religious specialists in the Trarza (Mauritania) – had given him a 'divine thing' or 'hadja rabbanyya [Ar., *hajja rabbaniyya*] that consists of something which I cannot say'.[20] What this second 'thing' is, is not at all clear, though it would presumably fall within the realm of secrets (Ar., *asrar*), certain kinds of closely guarded Islamic esoteric knowledge.

Most accounts suggest that al-Akhdar first visited Nioro in 1900.[21] From early on, he seems to have attracted numerous followers, including many women, who gathered around him. Many took or renewed their initiation into the Tijaniyya through him, in a sense confirming his possession of a gift of a charismatic quality.[22] In doing this, such people were recognising al-Akhdar's authority as being above that of others already in the area from whom they may have received earlier initiations into the Sufi order. In 1906, during one of his visits to Nioro that seems to have lasted little more than a week, al-Akhdar met Murtada Tall, who, it was noted above, had only recently moved back to the area. It seems that they disagreed strongly over the number of times a certain prayer associated with the Tijaniyya should be recited. This is the *jawharat al-kamal* (Ar., literally, the pearl of perfection), one of the most important Tijani prayers, that Ahmad al-Tijani claimed the Prophet Muhammad had transmitted directly to him.[23] One index of the importance of this prayer is that one of the rules of the Tijaniyya states that it can only be recited after performing ritual ablutions with water.

In Nioro, Murtada insisted that the *jawharat al-kamal* be recited twelve times, while al-Akhdar insisted on eleven times. Al-Akhdar even went so far as to assert that the Tijani practices of the descendants of Umar Tall were worthless in that they did not recite this special prayer the proper number of times. Moreover, he claimed that West Africans who were initiating people into the Tijaniyya had not been authorised to do so by the real, presumably North African, leaders of the Sufi order.[24] For this reason, their initiation into the Tijaniyya had no value or legitimacy. By al-Akhdar's admission, his disagreement with Murtada was such that his own followers and Murtada's actively avoided each other. While some (for example Marty 1921: 219) claim that the disagreement between al-Akhdar and Murtada was the origin of al-Akhdar's expulsion from Nioro, it is important to recall that al-Akhdar was arrested for allegedly having incited some to resist French authority after the emancipation of their slaves. One colonial administrative report about al-Akhdar suggests that he was merely another one of those wandering religious leaders – *prédicateur errant*, in the language of the report – who could serve as conduits of pan-Islamic and, ultimately, anti-French sentiments and aspirations. Little is known about al-Akhdar's detention, but eventually he was released and allowed to return to Nioro where he later died.

As noted above, al-Akhdar claimed the role of *shaykh* of the Tijaniyya. Over the course of his extensive travels, al-Akhdar named several *muqaddams* of the Tijaniyya in such places as Kaédi in Mauritania and Kayes and Bamako in the Soudan in addition to those from Nioro.[25] It is important to note that many, and perhaps even most, of these *muqaddams* were Soninke and Fulbe/Futanke and not Bidan or Shurfa. Oral and written sources internal to the Hamawiyya claim that al-Akhdar was searching for a leader of the Tijaniyya and that he discovered this leader in the person of Hamallah. A frequently told story in Nioro is that Sidi al-Tahir Butiba,[26] the head of an important Tijani *zawiya* in Tlemcen in Algeria, had instructed al-

Akhdar to go in search of a new leader and that there were five signs to identify the person he was looking for.[27] Four of the five signs are homologies or correspondences between the person and Ahmad al-Tijani, the founder of the Tijaniyya. First, the person was a *sharif*. Second, the person had the same name as Ahmad al-Tijani, that is, Ahmad. Third, the person's father's name was the same as the father of Ahmad al-Tijani, which was Muhammad. Fourth, the person's mother had the same name as Ahmad al-Tijani's mother, 'Aysha, which was also the name of the Prophet Muhammad's allegedly favourite wife.[28] The last sign was knowledge of a secret that consisted of a series of Arabic letters with a special numerological value. Such a secret might refer to the notion of 'God's most exalted name' (Ar., *ism Allah al-a'zam*), the final and secret name, the knowledge of which guarantees effusions of divine grace.

Hamallah, whose real name was Ahmad Hamahu Allah b. Muhammad b. Sayyidina Umar, came from a sharifian lineage from Tichit near Niamina where his father was a merchant and fulfilled all the requirements, the homologies as well as the last one of a mystical nature. While it is not possible to verify the matter of secret or mystical knowledge, it is indeed likely that al-Akhdar either shared his esoteric knowledge with Hamallah or learned from Hamallah that he possessed or shared superior esoteric knowledge as the above story suggests (see Brenner 1984: 50). Some time before he died in 1909, al-Akhdar recognised Hamallah as a *shaykh* and appointed him as his own successor, that is, the leader of those whom he had named *muqaddams* and those he initiated into the Tijaniyya.

It is important to note that the signs al-Akhdar allegedly used to identify Hamallah as leader of the Tijaniyya are reminiscent of the signs used to identify various exceptional Muslims elsewhere in the Muslim world. Most notably, the signs are similar to those used to identify the Mahdi or the divinely guided one, whom some Muslims expect at the end of the world. The signs and characteristics of the Mahdi have been described in various Islamic texts over the centuries.[29] The signs al-Akhdar used are also reminiscent of some that Muslims elsewhere in West Africa have written about and discussed. For example, the scholar and ruler of Sokoto Uthman dan Fodio (1715–1817) wrote several texts about the Mahdi and his attributes that bear a striking resemblance to the signs for identifying Hamallah (see El-Masri et al. 1966). The signs are also similar to those that Amadu Amadu, one of the nineteenth-century rulers of the Dina, used to claim the title of *mujaddid* (Ar.), literally renewer of the religion (see Brown 1969). The veracity of al-Akhdar's use of such identifying signs aside, there were clearly pre-existing motifs for the identification of exceptional Muslims of which Hamallah, from the perspective of his followers, was only the most recent.

After al-Akhdar's death, most, though not all, of the *muqaddams* al-

Akhdar had appointed recognised Hamallah as his successor, renewing their affiliations into the Tijaniyya through him. The Hamawiyya was thus formed by those who took Hamallah as their new leader.[30] A few of the *muqaddams* al-Akhdar appointed never recognised Hamallah's authority, and some were even openly hostile to the idea of Hamallah being the new *shaykh*.[31] Thus, the new group of Tijanis was also formed in the face of an opposition, including such Muslim religious leaders as Muhammad al-Mukhtar, who not only refused to accept Hamallah as a *shaykh* but also became one of his most renowned detractors. From the outset, some of the most ardent opponents of Hamallah were part of, or closely tied to, the Muslim establishment, which in Nioro included Muhammad al-Mukhtar, as well as the Kaba Jakhite family and their associates with their prominent places in the new colonial scheme, and some members of the Tall family, recently returned to Nioro. This is not to suggest, however, that there was in any way a formation of two opposed groups or pro- and anti-colonial factions. Indeed, there is no evidence to suggest that Hamallah's earliest followers were in any way less resigned to the French presence than any others. In some cases, as we will see, some of his followers were certainly not unenthusiastic about the French presence.

I now turn to look at the growth and spread of the Hamawiyya in order to show just how complex the situation was.

THE SPREAD OF THE HAMAWIYYA

I want to contextualise the new Sufi affiliation that developed around Hamallah by exploring the social composition of those associated with this Sufi affiliation in some of its diversity, while also tracing Hamallah's and his followers' relationships to the established Muslim leadership during the colonial period. If there is almost a consensus in much of the colonial literature, not to mention the postcolonial literature, that the movement around Hamallah was emancipatory for social marginals (see, for example, Gouilly 1952; 141; Alexandre 1970), Traoré (1983) has forcefully rejected this position, arguing that the Hamawiyya did not challenge existing social hierarchies in the region, such as the distinction between free-born and slave. Rather, in his view, what made the Hamawiyya unusual was the way in which it successfully attracted a multi-ethnic following. However, it is quite clear that other Sufi orders in the region also had multi-ethnic followings even prior to colonial rule. Most notably, there is the case of the Kunta, who under the leadership of Sidi al-Mukhtar in the late eighteenth and early nineteenth centuries attracted followers to the Qadiriyya from disparate groups of Muslims from across West Africa (see Brenner 1988).

What was new in the case of the Hamawiyya was the colonial context in which people were moving on a much greater scale and with increased rapidity. Under colonial rule, people from all sectors of society were coming together in new spaces that colonialism created. It was in these spaces of the colonial sphere that there was not only mass Islamisation, but also the standardisation of Islamic religious practice. Over time, ways of being Muslim became more uniform for all Muslims, regardless of differences in social status. A set of standardised ritual norms – regular ritual prayer and fasting during Ramadan – that previously had been the preserve of the lineages of Muslim religious specialists became the norm for all Muslims. However, this standardisation of religious practice usually also included affiliation to a Sufi order or, at the very least, great respect for their leaders. Thus, those whose hereditary status was free, 'caste', or slave, along with merchants, colonial civil servants, soldiers, teachers and new converts to Islam, adopted the standardised ritual norms at the same time that they sought affiliation to a Sufi order. In this way, unlike in the pre-colonial period, affiliation to a Sufi order would no longer be limited to scholarly Muslim elites, but rather became a phenomenon of mass affiliation under colonial rule. Many sought out and embraced the new Sufi affiliation around the charismatic Hamallah.

While I agree that some colonial and postcolonial commentators have overstated the emancipatory features of the Hamawiyya, it is quite clear that certain people attracted to Hamallah were indeed rejecting some of the existing social hierarchies. For instance, as some of my informants empha-sised to me, in embracing Hamallah, some young people were rejecting the Sufi affiliations of their elders, and some people of 'caste' and servile status were rejecting their patrons or masters who may have been opposed to Hamallah. Similarly, those non-Muslims who converted to Islam and embraced Hamallah were usually also rejecting the authority of their elders. Those who worked for the colonial administration, including members of the nascent bureaucratic and educational elite, such as teachers, translators and clerks, as well as guardsmen and soldiers, very well may have been attracted to Hamallah for similar reasons. If colonialism provided the condi-tions for the standardisation of religious practice and the mass affiliation and spread of the Hamawiyya, certain social differences continued to be crucial. Indeed, it is quite obvious that Shaykh Hamallah's sharifian descent was a key factor in his rise to prominence as a religious leader. His widely acknowledged status as a *sharif* – however disputed it may have been, particularly by the French – allowed him to be seen as higher in rank than some of the other possible contenders for leadership positions within the Tijaniyya. Moreover, with one known exception, Hamallah only appointed deputies who were members of 'free' lineages, that is, those not of 'caste' or slave origins.

Those who made up the first group to take Hamallah as their leader were Muslim scholars and intellectuals from the immediate area of Nioro and the broader region. Although they were nearly all members of lineages of

Muslim religious specialists, it is significant that very few of Hamallah's earliest followers were particularly exceptional by reputation, nor were any of them from the dominant groups of Muslim religious specialists in or around the town of Nioro, including those whom the French had appointed to administrative positions. Thus, some religious specialists recognised the young Hamallah (b. 1881–3), a *sharif*, who was not yet thirty years old, as a leader or *shaykh*. It is important to note that Hamallah was not part of the Muslim establishment – indeed he was probably too young to be included within their ranks – though in the next few years the French included him among those they saw as important. In 1916, when the French announced the revolt of the Sharif of Mecca against the Turks to selected Muslim religious leaders in AOF, they included the young Hamallah among them.[32]

In the town of Nioro itself, after Hamallah succeeded al-Akhdar many of his early followers came from the various groups of Bidan living in or recently relocated to the town, many of whom had ties to the important trading towns to the north. At the same time, included among these early followers in the town were people from lineages of religious specialists, some (though clearly not all) of whom were not as closely associated with the colonial scheme as the Kaba Jakhite and their associates. Perhaps the earliest of these to take Hamallah as their *shaykh* was the small group of Jakhanke who today point with great pride to their early submission to Hamallah and their enduring attachment to him and the Hamawiyya. From their ranks, Hamallah selected some of his most intimate advisors, including one man who was responsible for explaining the conditions or laws (Ar., *shurut*) of membership in the Tijaniyya to the many people who wanted to join the Sufi order. From among some of the Soninke families in the town and the broader region, Hamallah selected some of his prominent *muqaddams*,[33] who helped to extend his influence into areas around Nioro that are heavily populated by Soninke.

While Hamallah's influence was spreading at the expense of some of those religious leaders closely identified with the French, Hamallah also quickly attracted followers from areas of the Sahel and Sahara that had only recently come under French control. Some of these followers were Muslim clerics whose experience of direct French control of their own land was quite novel, even though many of them had long been involved in trading networks to areas under French control. By the mid-1910s Hamallah could claim as his followers scholars from the most prominent lineages, from the renowned centres of Islamic learning as well as major transit points in the trans-Saharan trade, Oualata and Tichit, the latter of which was also the town of Hamallah's family. Very shortly after Tichit and Oualata (in 1911 and 1912, respectively) came under French administration, Hamallah had *muqaddams* living in those places. Some of these followers were scholars, including some who were initiated into the Qadiriyya, who had very recently looked to Ma' al-Aynayn (d. 1910) for leadership.[34] For example, early in the twentieth century, Buya Ahmad (d. 1960), a young scholar from Tichit, recognised Hamallah as the most elevated Tijani *shaykh* of the day (Ould Cheikh 2000). Buya Ahmad, like many others, had first looked to Ma' al-'Aynayn for leadership but 'destiny' was such that he had been unable to join Ma' al-'Aynayn. In 1912, Buya Ahmad travelled to Nioro to meet Hamallah. After he learned from Hamallah that he had received *al-fath al-akbar* (Ar.), literally, the greatest opening, that is, attainment of the highest stage of spiritual advancement, he submitted to Hamallah as his follower. Hamallah, in turn, named him one of his *muqaddams* (ibid.).

Hamallah soon began to attract many other followers. If, by 1909, he was the *shaykh* around whom some in the local area gathered, by the early 1920s he attracted followers from throughout large parts of AOF. Hamallah and the *muqaddams* he named initiated countless people into the Tijaniyya. Unlike earlier Tijani leaders like Umar Tall, who apparently named only a limited number of *muqaddams*, Hamallah named literally dozens of *muqaddams*, whom he sometimes authorised to appoint other *muqaddams* in turn. When Hamallah and his deputies initiated people into the Tijaniyya or renewed their initiation, they would recite the 'pearl of perfection' prayer eleven times. It is clear that the young Hamallah's influence spread quickly at the expense of some of the existing Muslim establishment, particularly in Nioro. Equally importantly, the new Sufi affiliation was spreading into new areas and at a rate that the conditions of colonial rule made possible. Colonial commentators were apprised of this rapid and broad spread of Hamallah's appeal (see Marty 1920: 221).

This new Sufi affiliation around Hamallah – which might even be called a social movement[35] – was able to spread so far and wide because of the French presence, particularly the *paix française*, the development of the colonial economy and improved communications networks involving accelerated movements of people and objects. In a very important way, the new kinds of communication and travel that colonialism made available and fostered were instrumental in the spread of the reputation of the exceptional leader in Nioro and his Sufi affiliation. African colonial civil service employees, merchants and labour migrants circulated as never before. With the waning of the trans-Saharan trade, merchants worked new trading routes, and labour migrants moved to areas in the south, all areas where the Hamawiyya spread. Many began to travel to Nioro to visit Hamallah, and these even included people from very far away. For example, in 1922, a man from a Mossi lineage in Yatenga (present-day Burkina Faso), whose members had not long been Muslims, travelled to Nioro to meet Hamallah after hearing about him (Kouanda and Sawadogo 1993). Hamallah appointed this man one of his *muqaddams* and, upon return to his home, he spread the Hamawiyya among many recent converts to Islam in that region.[36]

The Hamawiyya was unusual in that it attracted followers from a wide variety of social and ethnic backgrounds throughout the French colonies: first and foremost, religious intellectuals like some of those from prominent lineages from Tichit and Oualata, then some newer religious intellectuals such as the man from Yatenga, and then colonial civil servants, some of whom served in Nioro, recently urbanised social marginals, new converts to Islam, and many ordinary Muslims from different groups – Bidan, Soninke, Futanke, Fulbe, Bambara and so forth.

If the Hamawiyya could be said to have spread at the expense of other Sufi orders, particularly the Qadiriyya, in some cases there was a rapprochement between Hamallah and other Sufi leaders, both Tijanis and Qadiris. At the time, some influential Tijanis pointed out that there was no difference between the way of Hamallah and their own, even though they recited the aforementioned Tijani prayer twelve times and Hamallah did it eleven times. They argued that people should not be opposed to Hamallah.[37] Second, there were regular exchanges between prominent Qadiris in the Soudan (and elsewhere) and Hamallah. For example, members of a high-profile lineage of Qadiris, the Kane Diallo of Dilly, travelled to Nioro to present gifts to Hamallah in order to honour him.[38] Such relations between Hamallah and other leaders of Sufi orders could only have been disquieting to some Tijanis within AOF.

The role of religious intellectuals in the spread of the Hamawiyya in the colonial context cannot be overemphasised. Some of the scholars who took Hamallah as their *shaykh* were part of longstanding trading diasporas in places in the Soudan such as Banamba and Touba. They helped to spread the Hamawiyya to areas quite far from Nioro. For example, Mulay Idris, whose family claimed sharifian ancestry and had settled in Tichit in the nineteenth century, was engaged in extensive trading operations in areas in the Middle Niger. After the slave exodus from Banamba, the important trading centre, early in the twentieth century, Mulay Idris was compelled to move here himself in order to manage his family's trading interests more directly (Marty 1920: 74–5). There, he was known, among other things, for having undertaken missions on behalf of the French colonial administration to areas to the north still not under their control (ibid.). Mulay Idris and some of his nephews, who also lived in Banamba, became prominent *muqaddams* of Hamallah, initiating many people into the new order.[39] By the early 1920s, Banamba, along with the other major trading towns such as Touba, all had *muqaddams* named either directly by Hamallah or by one of his other *muqaddams*. These were some of the important avenues through which Hamallah's reputation was spread far and wide, especially as these traders moved into the new expanding markets of the colonial economy.

By the early 1920s, Hamallah's reputation as a religious leader had spread well beyond the area where he lived. In 1923, one colonial official undertook a mission throughout AOF, Niger and northern Nigeria, and learned that Muslims in these places knew about Hamallah and his reputation as a leader of the Tijaniyya.[40] But Hamallah's reputation extended much further than West Africa. In the mid-1920s, Ibn Mayaba, a Muslim scholar who had fled West Africa at the time of the French colonial conquest, wrote a book in which he denounced Sufi orders and the Tijaniyya in particular for doctrinal reasons.[41] He identified Hamallah as the greatest *shaykh* of the Tijaniyya living under French rule in West Africa, singling him out for condemnation for accepting such non-Muslim rule.

Although the vast majority of Hamallah's followers in West Africa were not scholars or members of lineages known as such, scholars played perhaps the most important role in the spread of the Hamawiyya. In general, non-scholars took their cue from scholars in their selection of Muslim religious leaders as well as of those to whom they accorded respect. Some of the early followers, including some Muslim scholars and intellectuals, began to attribute to Hamallah the titles of *wali* (Ar., saint), *khalifa* and *qutb* or the highest ranking saint. Like Buya Ahmad, many believed that Hamallah had reached the absolute highest level of spiritual advancement. His followers increasingly identified him with the Prophet Muhammad, the Perfect Man (Ar., *al-insan al-kamil*), as both descendant of and successor to the Prophet, and they pointed to the many 'miracles' associated with him.

Hamallah undoubtedly generated much discussion among Muslims, both elite and non-elite. Some of the voluminous poetry in Hamallah's honour written in literary Arabic and in various vernacular languages in the region provide examples of how his reputation was spreading and some of the claims being made about him, including his close identification with the Prophet Muhammad.[42] In one such poem in Arabic, Hamallah is said to have all-encompassing knowledge, including that of 'the secrets', and the poem unambiguously indexes his authority:

> You took control; you sat down on the throne.
> You became *khalifa* with the opening of the closed.

Here, 'control' and 'the opening of the closed' are assertions of Hamallah's ascent to the highest level in the hierarchy of Muslims, in short, his unassailable authority as a Muslim leader.[43] At some point, Muslim scholars in the region also started to circulate and discuss several poems allegedly written in the nineteenth century by a well known scholar from Tichit, Ahmad al-Saghir (d. 1855/6), who had a widespread reputation as a Muslim saint and as a devoted member of the Tijaniyya. In these poems, Ahmad al-Saghir predicted the advent of an important leader of the Tijaniyya who would face enormous difficulties.[44] Scholars claimed that this person was Hamallah. Such poetry in Arabic about Hamallah circulated among scholarly elites, while poetry in vernacular languages, sometimes written by some of the same scholars, was more directly accessible to the many ordinary people who did not know literary Arabic. Many such poems in vernacular languages were committed to memory and recited sometimes collectively among Hamallah's followers. In any case, such poetry clearly helped to spread Hamallah's reputation, often quite far afield. Indeed, copies of some of this poetry in Hamallah's honour, including the poem quoted above, were even circulating in northern Nigeria.

The lofty titles such as *qutb* attributed to Hamallah and the claims of his spiritual advancement could only have dismayed Hamallah's detractors. When religious leaders from the small scholarly elite started to submit to Hamallah and to laud his praises, non-scholarly Muslims frequently followed the scholars with whom they had ties. For those for whom Hamallah was the most spiritually advanced, to pray the 'pearl of perfection' as Hamallah did – eleven times – was clearly the correct way. After Hamallah attracted so many followers, initially scholars and then a flood of non-scholars, some of the established Muslim authorities became concerned.

If, early on, some followers of Hamallah proclaimed him to be a *shaykh* and/or a saint, over time the stakes would get higher. While it is not possible to know to what extent important events in North Africa and the Middle East – from the time of the establishment of the French protectorate in Morocco in 1912 to the events leading up to the abolition of the caliphate by the Turkish Grand National Assembly in 1924 – helped to influence the way Muslims thought and acted in West Africa, it is entirely possible that news of such events had an effect. Indeed, people in the Sahel were often very quickly apprised of such events, with such knowledge coming though a variety of channels. Be that as it may, by the mid-1920s, some of Hamallah's followers had grown more strident in their claims about him. Some of the most serious clashes between Hamallah's followers and his detractors in Nioro came when some Muslims refused to accept his leadership.

I now turn to consider in more detail the opposition to Hamallah that contributed to his first colonial-sanctioned exile from Nioro in 1925 and eventually culminated in the severe repression of the 1940s.

OPPOSITION AND EXILE

If Hamallah eventually attracted notable scholars and members of prominent scholarly lineages from north of Nioro as his followers, he also provoked the ire of others with similar credentials. It has already been noted how Muhammad al-Mukhtar became one of Hamallah's most outspoken critics. Informants in Nioro say that Muhammad al-Mukhtar quit the town for good soon after Hamallah's rise to prominence. Even before that, it is clear that Muhammad al-Mukhtar spent long periods away from Nioro after Hamallah succeeded al-Akhdar, perhaps in part to counter Hamallah's growing popularity and/or to flee from those who maligned him for his opposition to Hamallah.[45] In the period before Hamallah's first exile in 1925, Muhammad al-Mukhtar himself took to insulting Hamallah's followers in public while in neighbouring Kayes.[46]

But there were other Muslim religious specialists who were equally if not more incensed than Muhammad al-Mukhtar over the growing influence of Hamallah. As Hamallah's influence spread, members of some of the other Sufi orders in the broader region became alarmed. In the end, it seems that some were willing to go to great lengths to halt the spread of his influence:

> They never ceased to denounce it [the Hamawiyya] to the public authorities as a dangerous heresy capable of striking a fatal blow to the integrity of Islam, integrity that France, they added, was implicitly committed to defending. (Gouilly 1952: 141)

Most commentators point to another person as one of Hamallah's earliest and most hostile opponents. This was Fah Wuld Shaykh al-Mahdi from the Tinwajiyu, a Bidan group of Muslim religious specialists who also claim descent from the Prophet Muhammad.[47] Fah's father was Shaykh al-Mahdi (d. 1907), who some had thought was the Mahdi during his lifetime (see Chapter 1). Tracing their descent through the renowned North African scholar al-Maghili (d. c. 1504), whom some sources treat as the introducer of the Qadiriyya in Africa south of the Sahara, Fah's family claimed many other illustrious ancestors whose learning, they maintained, eclipsed that of all neighbouring groups in the region.

While some commentators assert that Fah was opposed on principle to Sufi orders (for example Traoré 1983; Hamès 1997a), it seems that most Tinwajiyu who were affiliated with a Sufi order were in fact Qadiris.[48] Moreover, it is doubtful, as some assert (for example Traoré 1983; cf. Ibn Mu'adh 1988), that Fah was opposed to the idea of sainthood (Ar., *wilaya*). It is more likely that Fah, armed as he was with his own very impressive credentials based primarily on descent, was opposed to the idea of Hamallah as a saint rather than to sainthood per se. One of Fah's brothers was the head of a faction of the Tinwajiyu, while another of his brothers himself had the reputation of a saint (Marty 1921: 410, 416). This points to a whole set of privileges, even prerogatives, which Fah and his kin were undoubtedly unwilling to forego. By the mid-1910s, it seems that Fah was unhappy that Hamallah's influence was rising at his and his own family's expense. It appears that some Bidan groups in the Sahel that had historically paid tribute to the Tinwajiyu ceased to do so after taking Hamallah as their *shaykh* (Gouilly 1952: 129–30). Hamallah had even appointed a number of *muqaddams* from within the ranks of the Tinwajiyu.[49] Living near Kayes with a faction of the Ahl Sidi Mahmud composed of many people for whom Hamallah was the leader,[50] Fah spent inordinate amounts of time denouncing Hamallah and his followers. It is reported that Fah even went so far as to brand Hamallah's followers as unbelievers, that is, to perform the act of *takfir*, to condemn them as non-Muslims.[51] The interest of some colonial administrators in using Fah to monitor Hamallah's activities and his growing influence seemed to override the proposal other administrators made for his detention for his activities in 1923. However, in the following year, his activities were apparently so disruptive that he was placed in administrative detention far away from the area in Mauritania.[52]

In any case, Fah's detention did not put an end to the rivalries between various groups in the Sahel, as his opposition to Hamallah must be seen within the larger context of the recently established colonial scheme that came to encompass and transform the pre-existing social and political organisation of the region. If Fah's own lineage and his group, the Tinwajiyu, had been ascendant in the period before French control of the Sahara, things were radically different in the new colonial setting. From the town of Nioro, Hamallah became an axis around which different individuals and groups gravitated. Many of the groups from the Sahel that had interests in promoting trade with the French were drawn to Nioro and then to Hamallah (or vice versa). Not long after the death of al-Akhdar, Hamallah drew followers from nearly all the major Bidan groups in the Sahel near Nioro, the Aghlal, Awlad Nasr, Awlad Mbarak and Mashzuf, that is, from Bidan groups considered *zawaya* (religious specialists) and *hassan* ('warriors'), as well as from groups that were their tributaries.[53] Despite some adherents among the Tinwajiyu in the region, this large group remained for the most part outside Hamallah's sphere of influence. The situation was in a state of flux since many groups in the Sahel and Sahara were still coming to terms with the French colonial presence and the political and economic, not to mention religious, ramifications of this presence.

Of all the disparate groups in the broader region, perhaps the Aghlal, a confederation of religious specialists who historically had not been averse to armed conflict, were among the closest to Hamallah.[54] Al-Akhdar had named a *muqaddam* from this group, Muhammad 'Abd al-Rahman, who took Hamallah as his *shaykh* (Ibn Mu'adh 1988: 233). He, in turn, named several *muqaddams*, including some Aghlal, thereby helping to make members of this group one of the largest blocks of Hamallah's followers among the Bidan. While Hamallah's influence spread quickly among the Aghlal, an important conflict between this group and the Tinwajiyu – Fah Wuld Shaykh al-Mahdi's group – pre-dated Hamallah's rising influence. The conflict between the groups was ongoing and in large measure over economic resources, especially access to grazing lands and wells for live-stock. However, the fact that the Aghlal were largely Hamallah's followers while the Tinwajiyu for the most part were not, clearly exacerbated the conflict. Between 1923 and 1925, there were at least fourteen 'attacks' between members of the two groups.[55] By this time, the French were increasingly concerned with what was referred to as the restless sect (*secte remuante*) around Hamallah.[56] They held Hamallah at least indirectly responsible for the conflicts between the Aghlal and the Tinwajiyu, as well as for other conflicts much further afield in Kiffa (Mauritania) among the Ahl Sidi Mahmud, another group of religious specialists, many of whose members had embraced Hamallah.[57]

In addition to being blamed for these conflicts between groups in the Sahel, Hamallah was around the same time accused of meddling directly in politics, particularly those having to do with the Awlad Nasr, a *hassan* ('warrior') group, which was one of the largest groups of Bidan administered from Nioro.[58] Hamallah had attracted many followers among the Awlad Nasr, most of whose religious leaders had been affiliated at earlier times with one of the various branches of the Qadiriyya. By the late 1910s, Hamallah had named *muqaddams* from the religious specialists among the Awlad Nasr (Marty 1920: 446; Ibn Mu'adh 1988: 233). When the leader of the Awlad Nasr died in 1924, colonial reports indicate that Hamallah wanted one of his supporters, rather than a different French-backed candidate from the group, to be the new leader. From the French perspective, such involvement in politics was unacceptable, since they saw it as a strategy – which it very well may have been – for Hamallah to extend his burgeoning influence among the group and across the broader region.[59]

By the mid-1920s, the claims that some of Hamallah's followers made about him were even more extraordinary. Some became more persistent in calling on others, particularly his opponents, to accept his status as a *shaykh*. What amounted to a struggle over the issue of spiritual ascendancy led to a series of conflicts between some of Hamallah's followers and detractors, who at times came to blows in the town of Nioro in 1924 – that is, around the very same time as the other conflicts in the Sahel mentioned above.[60] All of these events together seem to have induced the French to exile Hamallah from Nioro in 1925 for a period of ten years. Hamallah spent the first part of the exile in Mederdra in Mauritania, not far from where the Ahl Shaykh Sidiyya, pillars of the colonial Muslim establishment, lived. The French expected that this Muslim lineage would either overshadow Hamallah or at least be a positive influence upon him. Hamallah remained in Mederdra until 1930 when there were violent clashes in the town of Kaédi, also in Mauritania, involving some people who were believed to be his followers. The colonial administration decided to move Hamallah to Adzopé in Côte d'Ivoire, an area considered to be non-Muslim and, therefore, well beyond his possible sphere of influence. During this first exile, Hamallah remained in touch with his followers, some of whom visited him while he was in both places.[61]

The seeds of repression that would eventually lead to the economy of martyrdom around Hamallah were sown in this first exile. After Hamallah's arrest and departure from Nioro at the end of 1925, following instructions from his superiors, the local French administrator addressed the local religious leaders.

> [He] insisted on the nature of the measures undertaken, specifying that they constituted neither interference in questions of a religious nature nor public expression of preferential treatment for one rite, but that they had been taken solely with the goal of restoring calm to a troubled region.[62]

But such proclamations were clearly disingenuous. First of all, the reported response of Hamallah's local detractors in Nioro is revealing:

> The Muslims remaining faithful to the tradition of al-Hajj Umar [Tall], to whom I have given advice, greeted this with the greatest impassiveness, which nevertheless fills them with joy.[63]

If not exactly working hand in hand with members of the Muslim establishment, colonial officials shared some of the same sentiments. In fact, they expressed the hope that Hamallah's internment would have deleterious effects on what they called, in very negative terms, 'the new sect':

> One is therefore permitted to hope that, deprived of its leader, the new sect [la nouvelle secte] will rapidly decline, and that the constant agitation in the different conscriptions of the colony following the politico-religious intrigues of Hamallah will disappear in the near future.[64]

In the following year (1926), the administrator in Nioro held a meeting attended by the 'notables' of Nioro in which he explained that:

> We will not constrain any of Hamallah's followers to abandon the form of religion chosen by them, but we do not want a group to use religion [un clan se serve du culte] to disrupt public order.[65]

As these reports suggest, by this time, the colonial administration saw two groups: on the one hand, those 'faithful' to Umar Tall or what was sometimes called the 'Umarian Tijaniyya', tractable Muslim subjects and members of the Muslim establishment; and on the other hand, Hamallah and his disruptive followers and 'sect'.

At some point, the followers of Hamallah in the town made a decision not to pray at the Friday mosque in Nioro because it was under the control of some of Hamallah's most avowed enemies.[66] In this way, they were not able to perform the Friday midday communal prayers, which are shorter in duration than the daily midday prayers and accompanied by a sermon. The decision to abstain from performing the Friday communal prayers was not uncontroversial since Sunni Muslims generally treat Friday communal prayers as obligatory.[67] However, not performing the Friday communal prayers was actually neither unheard of nor even very unusual in this region. For example, one prominent scholar had written a legal opinion against performance of the Friday prayer in the mosque in Oualata because the imamate was under the control of a particular group and was not passed to the most learned in the community in contravention of the rules of Islamic jurisprudence.[68]

However, some in Nioro seem to have worried that they might be forced to pray at the Friday mosque. At some point during Hamallah's first exile, some of his followers apparently raised the issue of building a mosque of their own, that is, a mosque separate from those opposed to Hamallah where they could perform the Friday communal prayers. Colonial administrators apparently would not allow this. When they learned of such discussions about a separate mosque, there was the following response:

> This project does not seem appropriate to me. The administration could always base a possible refusal on a general rule of Islamic law: only large towns can have several mosques when the crowd is too large to meet in a single mosque. In any case, the size of Nioro does not justify two mosques.[69]

It is likely that, in taking the role of the arbiter of Islamic orthodoxy, the French frustrated any attempts by Hamallah's followers to mitigate what must have been a difficult situation for them.[70] It seems that no formal request for permission to build a separate mosque was ever made.[71]

Although things in the town of Nioro itself were simmering, the conflicts between Hamallah's followers and detractors beyond the town did not end with his detention and exile. On the contrary, the Ladem – another Bidan group living near Nioro that was particularly close to Hamallah – attacked the Tinwajiyu, apparently blaming them for Hamallah's arrest.[72] If anything, it is doubtful that Hamallah's absence could have brought 'calm' to the region, even without any kind of religious component to the conflicts.

It is important to note that Hamallah's exile (1925–35) by the French far from his town helped spread his influence, in no small part because of the reputation he developed for having suffered unjustly under French rule. When Hamallah travelled to Bamako to meet with the Governor, large crowds – estimated in the thousands – came to greet him.[73] In Mederdra where he was initially sent, he became acquainted with some important scholars (Hamès 1997a) and may even have appointed some *muqaddams* from there. The length of his detention also helped to spread his reputation.

Even during Hamallah's absence, affiliation to the Hamawiyya continued to spread among various groups in rural areas,[74] as well as among Africans who were deeply imbricated in the administrative operations of the colony. It was especially disquieting to colonial administrators to see how many of Hamallah's followers were employees of the colonial administration, including clerks, interpreters, teachers, guardsmen and soldiers, some of whom had studied in French schools.[75] Many of these people saw Hamallah as a saint and sought him out for his prayers or blessings. Those working for the colonial administration who were unable to make the journey to see Hamallah sometimes wrote him letters, some of which were sent through the colonial postal service and carefully monitored. Over time, colonial administrators worried that African employees of the colonial administration might be more loyal to Hamallah than to the administration. In one intercepted letter, a disgruntled African sergeant from the Soudan wrote to Hamallah and asked him to 'bring God's fury' down on the French (d'Arbaumont 1941: 24).

'RECONCILIATION' AND REPRESSION

Before Hamallah returned to Nioro in 1936 after a ten-year absence, it seems that he had been clearly warned by the French that he could be imprisoned again. On the eve of his return to Nioro, one administrator wrote from the Soudan:

> It will be appropriate upon Sharif Hamallah's release to summon him to Dakar where he will be advised by the head of the Federation [AOF] that he will be rearrested after any demonstration on his part.[76]

It is not possible to know exactly what was said to Hamallah before he returned to Nioro. However, it is safe to assume that he received such a warning. Moreover, it is quite likely this helped to heighten Hamallah's sense of being in a state of insecurity.

After his return to Nioro, Hamallah did not reopen his *zawiya*, which he had closed before leaving on his first exile.[77] Hamallah had also altered the way he performed the ritual daily prayers, and this was eventually to become the focus of considerable discussion and debate among Muslims and the French. That is, he reduced the number of *rak'a* (Ar., literally bows) made in his ritual daily prayers to two rather than the three or four required in the prayers (with the exception of the morning prayer which calls for two *rak'a*s). According to the rules of Islamic jurisprudence in the Maliki school, Muslims are allowed to shorten their prayers when they are travelling, in danger or at war. It seems that Hamallah had started to abridge his prayers during his first exile and continued to do so when he returned to Nioro at the beginning of 1936. In a colonial report, Hamallah is reported to have given the following explanation for his doing so:

> Before I prayed like everyone else, but the Whites exiled me to Côte d'Ivoire where I began to shorten my prayers. They made me come

back to Nioro, but I am not yet free. One day or another, the same Whites could possibly put me to death. I am, therefore, not able to abandon my new way of praying.[78]

It seems, however, that it was several months after Hamallah's return to Nioro before the French became aware that he and at least some of his followers were abridging their prayers.[79] Before the French were aware of this fact, word had begun to spread throughout AOF that Hamallah had changed the way he prayed. Exactly how this happened is not clear. But immediately after Hamallah's return to Nioro, many Africans travelled, sometimes in groups and often over great distances, to visit him there. While some sought and obtained official permission to travel, others visited him without the required travel 'pass'. In any case, it is likely that such visitors learned Hamallah had changed the way that he prayed, and this is how the word spread.[80]

The French looked for a way to convince Hamallah to desist since they thought that abridging his prayers called colonial authority into question and might even be prelude to or substitute for armed struggle. In the words of one colonial administrator, Hamallah was creating 'a real Hamallism of combat [un véritable hamallisme de combat], based on the abridged prayer' because hijra or migration and jihad were not possible under French rule (see Lafeuille 1947). Although it is quite clear that at least some of those who followed Hamallah in abridging the prayers did question French authority, many more followed Hamallah or his muqaddams in accordance with the prevailing practice of following one's shaykh.[81]

The French attempted to investigate those who allegedly followed Hamallah in abridging their prayers. While colonial reports immediately made reference to the textual basis for such practices, most importantly the reference to such ways of praying in the Quran (iv, 102), the administration looked for Muslim subjects, who were willing to say that Hamallah's actions were not licit. Indeed, a few of Hamallah's high-status followers openly criticised the practice of abridged prayers. Most notably, there was the learned Mamadou Doucouré (d. 1946) of Mourdiah, who was not only one of Hamallah's prominent muqaddams, but the author of well-known poetry in Hamallah's honour.[82] Doucouré and some other Muslim scholars argued that it was not justifiable from the perspective of Islamic jurisprudence for Hamallah to abridge his prayers while in Nioro since he was clearly not travelling, at war or in danger.[83] In this way of thinking, it followed that other Muslims would also be wrong to abridge their prayers. In response, some of Hamallah's followers offered legal justifications for Hamallah's actions, most notably in texts, including poetry, that started to circulate in both oral and written forms.[84] Others, including some Muslim scholars in the area, counselled people not to follow Hamallah in abridging prayers, all the while continuing to respect him.[85] At the same time, some reports suggested that

Hamallah said the controversy was between Muslim religious leaders and had nothing whatsoever to do with politics or the French.[86]

In 1937, the French asked Seydou Nourou Tall to travel to Nioro to try to convince Hamallah to give up the practice of abridging his prayers and to effect a 'reconciliation' with the other Tijanis in the town who did not recognise Hamallah's authority.[87] After the death of Murtada Tall, Seydou Nourou Tall, a grandson of Umar Tall, eventually presented himself as the head of the Tall family and a leader of the Tijaniyya.[88] By the 1930s, he was one of the closest Muslim religious leaders to the French. In fact, he was the embodiment of the colonial-authorised Muslim establishment and one of the most prominent leaders of what had come to be called the Umarian Tijaniyya. It was from such a vantage point that Seydou Nourou Tall was one of Hamallah's most outspoken critics. A leader of the Tijaniyya respected by many throughout AOF, Seydou Nourou Tall worked hard in the 1930s to counter Hamallah's growing influence, which seemed to come at the expense of that of his own family. In September of 1937, after receiving assurances from Seydou Nourou Tall that he was not in any danger, Hamallah agreed to abandon the abridged prayers. Although most colonial reports suggest that the 'reconciliation' was a success,[89] Hamallah thought otherwise. In a letter to one of his followers, he noted this was 'all a ruse' that 'the Europeans and the "rejecters"' were plotting.[90]

It is likely that Hamallah was at this time aware of concerted efforts to thwart his influence and even to undermine him and his authority. For example, shortly before the 'reconciliation', the Governor of the Soudan wrote letters to prominent Muslims reminding them how France 'make[s] peace and prosperity reign and respect[s] the true Islam'. In seeking their assistance against Hamallah, the Governor denounced 'the false religion invented through the arrogance of a man who betrays the one true Islam that will always be respected by the French'.[91] Shortly after the 'reconciliation', the local administrator in Nioro was convinced that Hamallah remained hostile, speculating that his reputation had suffered from abandoning the abridged prayers.[92]

Despite the 'reconciliation', the French remained fearful that the movement around Hamallah was potentially anti-colonial and xenophobic, as witnessed in the abridged prayers. It was disturbing to the French and some of Hamallah's African opponents that his influence continued to grow. That Cerno Bokar – a descendant of Umar Tall in Bandiagara and someone closely related to some of the most important pillars of the Muslim establishment and a main figure in the so-called Umarian Tijaniyya – had taken Hamallah as his *shaykh* and had even become one of his *muqaddams* was alarming to them (see Ba 1980, and Brenner 1984). Moreover, Hamallah was amassing considerable wealth that he received as gifts from his followers even during a time of serious economic crisis. In fact, Hamallah was among the first colonial subjects to own an automobile, and he even owned more than one. In the late 1930s, he received a brand new imported Ford Mercury as gift from a group of his followers who lived in the more prosperous neighbouring colony of Côte d'Ivoire.[93] That Hamallah had at his disposal means of transport in considerably better shape than that of the local colonial administration was certainly dismaying to certain French administrators. Hamallah's Muslim followers and detractors could hardly have missed so obvious a fact or 'miracle' (depending on one's perspective), given that he regularly sent his automobiles to neighbouring towns and villages to pick up some of his followers so that they could visit him in Nioro or even join him on picnics in the countryside.

After an incident in 1938 when some members of the Tinwajiyu physically harmed Hamallah's oldest son, this son organised a large group of men from the Aghlal, Ladem and Shurfa, among others, to attack the Tinwajiyu. In August of 1940, most likely taking advantage of the news of the recent French capitulation and perhaps also encouraged by drought conditions in the Sahel (Gouilly 1948: 16), the group led attacks on the Tinwajiyu on the Saharan fringes. Though the French were never able to link Hamallah directly with the attacks, he was held ultimately responsible for the many deaths that occurred during these attacks. In 1941 on a day remembered as Black Thursday, the French forced Hamallah into his second exile for another ten-year period.[94] He was taken by plane – certainly a novelty at the time – from Nioro to Dakar, and then to Algeria before being transferred to France. Early in 1943, Hamallah died in France, although the news of his death was not made public in West Africa until after the Second World War.

In the time leading up to and after the arrest of Hamallah, there was systematic repression of both those suspected of involvement in the armed clashes and of his followers. This began with the trial and subsequent execution of more than two dozen men, including two of his sons, in the neighbouring town of Yelimané for involvement in the violent clashes of 1940.[95] After this time, the French designated 'Hamallism' as one of the principal dangers, and sometimes even 'the principal danger', to the colonial order and took steps to crush it.[96] Many of Hamallah's closest followers, including some prominent *muqaddams*, were among those sent to detention camps in Ansongo, among other places, in the eastern part of the Soudan, an area believed to be outside Hamallah's sphere of influence. Working as forced labourers, a considerable number of these men died in detention.[97] Those followers of Hamallah in Nioro who hailed from places outside the town were forced to return to their home areas in other parts of AOF, including Senegal, Mauritania, Côte d'Ivoire and Niger.[98] All of these measures struck a considerable blow to the Sufi order, even though they did not succeed in eliminating it, as the French seem to have intended.

After Hamallah's exile and the detention of so many of his followers, the French attempted to monitor very closely the activities of all known or suspected followers and associates of Hamallah. While those said to be disrupting public order were summarily arrested, many others not directly punished were threatened with sanctions.[99] In 1942, the colonial administration took its campaign against the Hamawiyya to a new level by undertaking measures that are strikingly similar to events in Europe occurring around the same time. A decision was made to raze the buildings belonging to Hamallah, including the *zawiya* where he had led prayers.[100] In 1944, with 'the main goal of permitting more efficient surveillance of Hamallism', the colonial administration implemented territorial reforms, redrawing the boundary between Mauritania and Soudan so as to keep 'nomadic' Bidan ('Moors') followers of Hamallah isolated from 'sedentary' Africans ('Soudanais').[101]

Throughout this time, followers of Hamallah who remained in Nioro were considerably constrained in their activities and felt they were under constant threat of repression. They were not allowed to gather together for communal prayer and recitation of the special litanies of the Sufi order. Most of them refused, however, to pray at the main Friday mosque in the town, as it was under the control of the local Muslim establishment, some of whose most prominent members had been hostile to Hamallah. Faced with the threat of persecution, many prayed alone in their homes. Some people told me that this was a time when certain people abridged their prayers, but they usually did so discreetly. Those who lived through this time told me they were even afraid to carry their prayer beads or to mention Hamallah's name in public. Hamawis today recall that their enemies would trump up charges against them, as it was easy to get the colonial administration to arrest anyone on suspicion of being a so-called fanatical follower of Hamallah.

The repression was accompanied by an incredible sense of longing on the part of people for their *shaykh*. This was expressed in part through the rumours that abounded about Hamallah's whereabouts, his anticipated return and the imminent departure of the French. One rumour was that Hamallah managed to elude the colonial authorities while the plane in which he was taken was in flight, while others said he was in hiding or visiting 'a sultan'. Privately and occasionally publicly, some cursed the enemies of Hamallah. According to Hamawis in Nioro, many became convinced that his absence from Nioro was part of his divinely inspired mission.[102] Small numbers of Hamallah's Bidan followers living away from Nioro started to tattoo themselves with the identifying symbol Hamallah had used to brand his livestock, and some stopped performing the ritual daily prayers altogether.[103]

During the war, the French colonial administration had orchestrated some prominent Muslims' public renunciation of Hamallah. In 1942, leading Muslim scholars from places such as Oualata, particularly some of those who had not followed Hamallah in abridging their prayers, renounced Hamallah and the Hamawiyya.[104] According to one of Hamallah's *muqaddams*, many abandoned the Hamawiyya in order to be left in peace (Gouilly 1948: 46). However, throughout all of the repression and even after such renunciations, many remained steadfast in their devotion to Hamallah. While some were defiant of the French, saying they would never renounce their *shaykh*, others worked in his name more quietly. For example, certain people continued to serve and to provide for Hamallah's wives and children, since to do so was considered pious activity. Others exhibited their attachment to Hamallah by continuing to name their children after him, his mother, children and wives.

FROM DISARRAY TO ACTIVISM AND RECONSOLIDATION

After the war, the French metropolitan government never conceded that Hamallah and his followers had been mistreated and refused to consider them among the 'victims of Vichy'.[105] Nevertheless, the French Fourth Republic initiated a series of reforms, including the end of forced labour and the use of summary justice (the *indigénat*), eventually allowing for the formation of political parties. These reforms marked the beginning of a period of considerably less repression and persecution for Hamallah's followers. In 1946, the French released the surviving detainees from the labour camps before their sentences ended. Upon return to Nioro, the detainees were explicitly warned that they would be rearrested if public order was disturbed.[106] Although the announcement of Hamallah's death had initially been delayed because of the sense that French 'prestige' had suffered so much since 1940, the formal announcement was made shortly before the detainees' release.[107] Many were incredulous, and some refused to accept the news as true. Others did accept it as true and, as early as 1949, recommended that a mausoleum for Hamallah be built in Nioro.[108]

Because the Hamawiyya no longer had a Sufi centre, some began to gather in small groups at private homes where they prayed together. Most notably, they met at the home of one of the former detainees, a Jakhanke, and at the home of a Bidan scholar.[109] In this era of greater liberality, the French permitted their assembly. With the memory of repression still so fresh, many stayed away, continuing to pray privately, while some returned to pray at the Friday mosque. After all of the repression, the colonial administration noted that Hamawis had become among the most tractable in Nioro. Although the colonial administration hoped the Hamawiyya, deprived of its leader and with no apparent successors, would no longer spread or pose any threat, Hamallah's followers remained under close surveillance.[110] Even into the 1950s, the French assumed that the Hamawiyya was latently anti-colonial and perhaps even in direct contact with the Arab League.[111] Such colonial fears were certainly exacerbated by the localised armed clashes in 1949 in eastern Soudan between the French and Sharif Musa, one of Hamallah's *muqaddams* from near Gao.[112] Considerable administrative attention was also focused on the possible links and ties – collusion, in the language of administrative reports – between followers of Hamallah and the anti-colonial political party Rassemblement Democratique Africain (RDA).

Even though Hamallah never returned to Nioro, his influence and that of his family remained strong. For instance, before elections in Nioro, politicians from the RDA sought blessings or petitionary prayers from one of Hamallah's wives who was living in the town. Her ready willingness to accord these blessings was common knowledge in Nioro.[113] In the absence of a designated successor to Hamallah, many people looked to his surviving children for leadership. But the male children all lived in Mauritania where they were closely monitored. Sharif Ahmad (1915–72) was the oldest living son and assumed the role of head of the family. Many turned to him as the leader of the Hamawiyya. Until the late 1950s, he lived near Oualata and visited Nioro from time to time, but by all accounts, he kept a low profile. In contrast, his siblings were sometimes a source of anxiety for the French because of their frequently open activities on behalf of the Hamawiyya. One of his sisters had been placed under house arrest for her alleged activities on behalf of the Hamawiyya.[114] Likewise, in the 1950s, his younger brothers were said to cause quite a stir, especially among followers of Hamallah, when they travelled around southeastern Mauritania.[115]

In 1957, Sharif Ahmad broke his relative silence and formally requested authorisation from the colonial administration to move to Nioro where he would reclaim his father's land.[116] The authorisation to return was granted. He also requested the return of his father's library that had been seized by the French, and, eventually, part of this library as well as his father's correspondence were returned.[117] On the eve of decolonisation at the end of 1958, Sharif Ahmad supervised the reconstruction of the *zawiya* in the place where it had stood. People came from all over to rebuild the *zawiya*, while others sent cash and money orders to help finance the reconstruction. For many followers of Hamallah, this was the first real break after years of repression since they were finally going to be allowed to pray together at the rebuilt *zawiya*. After this time, some came to Nioro to be close to Hamallah's family and/or to serve at the *zawiya*, sometimes for short periods and, on occasion, to settle permanently in the town.

Sharif Ahmad, however, was not well enough to be actively involved in the running of the *zawiya*. Owing to a long illness, he lived on the outskirts of Nioro and travelled infrequently into the town. After the *zawiya* was rebuilt, Sharif Ahmad authorised his younger brother Muhammadu (a.k.a.

3.1 Muhammadu Ould Shaykh Hamallah at the Hamawi *zawiya*, Nioro
     Photographer: Benjamin F. Soares

Buya) (b. 1937) to serve as head of the *zawiya* and to lead prayers as his
father before him. In addition, following his brother's instructions,
Muhammadu (see Figure 3.1) opened the inner part of the rebuilt *zawiya*,
the place where he would perform prayers. Such an action signalled a return
to a state of affairs prior to the repression since Hamallah had kept this part
of the *zawiya* closed from the time of his first exile in 1925. In his role as the

oldest active son of Hamallah, Muhammadu was to become *de facto* leader of the Hamawiyya in Nioro.

By the time of independence, even though the *zawiya* had been rebuilt in Nioro, the Hamawiyya was in a state of considerable disarray with its recognised leader not well. On the other hand, its *de facto* leader, who was only in his twenties, was enormously popular. Many from the region, drawn by the charisma of Muhammadu, started to renew their ties with the Hamawiyya. In the years before his older brother's death in 1972, Muhammadu also undertook a series of trips, travelling widely to those areas of West Africa where there were many associated with the Hamawiyya. He visited various communities and *muqaddams* in Senegal, Haute Volta (present-day Burkina Faso) and Côte d'Ivoire, among other places. In some places – Haute Volta and the Ségou area of Mali in particular – Muhammadu took wives from various ethnic groups (Bambara and Fulbe), making important alliances. The major consequence of these trips (and marriage alliances) was the partial reconsolidation of the Hamawiyya under the young Muhammadu's authority.

Muhammadu expected Hamallah's followers to be deferential to him, his family and those who had been particularly close to Hamallah. Thus, he seems to have taken measures to assert his authority and the authority of his family over other potential contenders for power within the Hamawiyya. For example, there is the case of Yacouba Sylla (1906–88), one of Hamallah's most well-known followers who hailed from Nioro.[118] After the colonial administration implicated Yacouba Sylla in the clashes in Kaédi in 1930, he was exiled to Côte d'Ivoire where he settled in 1938 after his liberation. In the following year, Yacouba Sylla arranged to send Hamallah the sumptuous gift of the new Ford Mercury from his followers in Côte d'Ivoire. While many of Yacouba's followers recognised him as a saint, he was known until his death to have been deeply committed to Hamallah. His personal stationery proclaimed himself to be the follower of Hamallah, and Hamallah's name was painted on all of his transport vehicles. In the postcolonial period, Yacouba Sylla was a very wealthy and influential person surrounded by many people, who were involved in his extensive commercial and agricultural schemes in Côte d'Ivoire. After an occasion in Côte d'Ivoire when Yacouba failed to treat Muhammadu with the great respect that he felt he deserved as Hamallah's son, there were tensions between Muhammadu and Yacouba's associates, though not a schism.[119] Similarly, the leadership in Nioro has refused to associate with any followers of Hamallah who have made public pronouncements on his death. This has not only served to exclude such persons from the Hamawiyya, as it is recognised in Nioro, but also as a warning to others about the limits of what is deemed acceptable.

Since Sharif Ahmad's death in 1972, Muhammadu has been not only the

3.2 Men between prayers at the Hamawi *zawiya*, Nioro   *Photographer:* Benjamin
     F. Soares

head of Hamallah's family, but also the widely recognised leader of the
Hamawiyya. However, there continues to be some ambiguity about his
actual title. Some consider him a *khalifa* but this is not a title that he claims
for himself. He maintains that he is, above all, a follower or disciple of his
father.[120] In managing the affairs of the Hamawiyya, Muhammadu was
closely advised by his older sister, Zaynab (a.k.a. Nuha) (1920–94), who
lived in neighbouring Aïoun in Mauritania. For more than thirty years,
many followers of Hamallah have recognised Muhammadu as the person
his father chose to lead his followers. In the mid-1970s, a Mauritanian, who
had left the area on *hijra* during the colonial period and had been living in
Medina in Saudi Arabia, sent a series of letters to West Africa. He explained
in his letters that he had seen Shaykh Hamallah in a vision – not in a
dream[121] – who told him to inform people that he, Shaykh Hamallah, had
made his son Muhammadu the *amir* (Ar., leader) of his community.[122] After
the Mauritanian sent the letter to several prominent followers of Hamallah,
including Muhammadu, the contents were made public and circulated. It
was then announced that followers of Hamallah should come to Nioro and
renew their affiliation with Muhammadu. Many travelled to Nioro to do
just this, and today people refer to this as 'the time of the *bay'a*' or act of

3.3 Women at the annual *ziyara* at the Hamawi *zawiya*, Nioro
   Photographer: Benjamin F. Soares

allegiance. This was also an occasion for Muhammadu to make efforts to
expel from the Hamawiyya those whose practices many considered illicit
and possibly even un-Islamic. Thus, those followers of Hamallah known for
their failure to pray the obligatory ritual daily prayers were not allowed to
participate; upon their arrival in Nioro from Mauritania, they were asked to
leave the town. The ultimate effect of this was further consolidation of the
Hamawiyya under Muhammadu's leadership.

Since the time of the exile of its *shaykh*, the Hamawiyya has changed
considerably. While during the colonial period, many of Hamallah's
followers and *muqaddams* came from various Bidan groups in the Sahel, this
is no longer the case today. In Mauritania, the Hamawiyya is only one Sufi
order, among others. Nonetheless, Muhammadu is an important and
influential figure in Mauritania. For instance, in the 1990s he instructed his
followers in the Aïoun region how to cast their votes in elections.

The Hamawiyya is today strongest in western Mali as well as in such
longstanding centres of Hamallah's influence as Banamba and eastern
Mauritania. But Muhammadu's reputation as a religious figure extends
much further. Indeed, he had close ties with Malian president Moussa

3.4 Participants in the annual *ziyara* at the Hamawi *zawiya*, Nioro
      Photographer: Benjamin F. Soares

Traoré whose regime was overthrown in 1991. The Sufi order has also
spread along with migrants, particularly from Mali. In the present, large
concentrations of followers of Hamallah and their *zawiya*s can be found in
Côte d'Ivoire and Central Africa, places where Malian migrants have gone
in great numbers. At the same time, there are frequent contacts and ongoing
relations with other Hamawi communities, most notably in Burkina Faso
and Senegal, established by followers of Hamallah.

     Even though the Hamawiyya faced serious leadership and organisational
difficulties after the exile of its shaykh, Muhammadu worked hard to rebuild
and to reconsolidate the Hamawiyya under his authority. In Nioro, he lives
surrounded by his many followers and is said to lead an even greater number
of people. As one of the principal importers of goods from Mauritania into
Mali through Nioro, he has also become a very prosperous merchant. Each
year, one week after the *mawlud al-nabi*, the celebration of the Prophet
Muhammad's birth, he hosts a *ziyara* (Ar., visit) in Nioro at the *zawiya*.
Known as *ism al-nabi* (Ar., the naming of the Prophet), this is the largest
annual gathering in Nioro by Hamawis and others seeking the blessings of
Hamallah and his descendants (see Figures 3.2–3.4). It is a time when
literally thousands come to Nioro for the celebration and for the affirmation

or initiation, as the case may be, of their ties to Hamallah and his family. By the late twentieth century, all these factors had helped to make Muhammadu a major power broker, whose influence extends to nearly all areas of life in the region, a fact that has not gone unappreciated on both sides of the border separating Mali and Mauritania.

ABSENCE AND MARTYRDOM

As the decades have passed since the exile of Hamallah, the Hamawiyya, despite its postcolonial revitalisation, has faced a serious predicament with far-ranging consequences. This is the issue of Hamallah's death, around which there is almost an enforced silence in the town. While some people admit in private that he is dead, the older generation of Hamallah's followers, along with a smaller group of younger people, insist that he will return. The Arabic texts that discuss Hamallah's exiles from Nioro generally use the term *ghayba*, a concept that occupies a vast semantic field from its conventional sense of absence to a stage of initiation in Sufism, as well as the sense of absence associated with the hidden imam of Shiism.[123] But none of the texts confront the issue of Hamallah's ultimate fate.

It is important to note that over the years there have been initiatives to have Hamallah's alleged remains returned to West Africa from France. In the 1950s, ostensibly in response to some sort of request, the French metropolitan government stated that it would not permit the return of the remains.[124] Such a decision came under the pretext that Hamallah's followers continued to be dangerous.[125] After independence in the 1960s, officials of the Mauritanian government apparently sought permission from the French government to have the remains returned (Traoré 1983: 182–3). Although the French government agreed in principle, it noted that for legal reasons the request for the return of the remains had to come from Hamallah's closest relatives (ibid.). In the end, it seems that no such request was ever made.

In Nioro, some of Hamallah's followers state in the strongest possible terms that their *shaykh* will return. Many people maintain that in the period before 1941, when Hamallah was taken away by the French, he told people that he would go away again at some point but would return. For these people, Hamallah is 'absent', not dead. Coming on the heels of a ten-year 'absence' from Nioro, Hamallah's second exile in 1941 was also supposed to be for a second period of ten years. Thus he was supposed to return. But at least in the Nioro area, French colonial officials stated in unequivocal terms that Hamallah would not return. In mid-1942, while visiting some of the villages around Nioro where Hamallah had many followers, one colonial administrator reported that he informed villagers that 'having repeatedly abused our goodwill toward him, Hamallah has been definitively removed from the Soudan to which he will never return'.[126] One might say that the tenacity with which some cling to the idea that Hamallah will return is a form of resistance to the repression of the colonial era, directed toward those – French and African – who were Hamallah's enemies, as well as toward those who abandoned the Hamawiyya in the wake of the repression.

In contemporary Nioro, those who insist that Hamallah will return tend for the most part to be of the older generation, including some who knew Hamallah, or grew up in his household or around him. But I have also met young people, recently affiliated with the Hamawiyya, who concur with this opinion. At the same time, Hamallah's surviving family has played a crucial role, wittingly or unwittingly, in encouraging the view that he will return. Above all, they have systematically refused to admit or even discuss the possibility of Hamallah's death. Indeed, those known to have spoken openly and publicly about Hamallah's death have been sanctioned or criticised. For instance, after Amadou Hampaté Ba published his book about Cerno Bokar Tall, he faced much criticism from Hamallah's followers for discussing his death.[127] Likewise, the publication of Traoré's (1983) book about Hamallah caused considerable controversy in Nioro. The absent religious leader about whose death one must not speak has become a major reference point in the construction of the community of Hamallah's followers.

For many younger people in Nioro, clearly Hamallah is dead. Many point to the fact that people have gone to visit the site of Hamallah's grave in Montluçon in France, or have read or heard about some of the books in French that have discussed his death.[128] For such people, the belief that Hamallah is not dead is preposterous. But these people have been unable to challenge the older generation openly. This has helped to keep a younger generation, increasingly mobile and educated, from embracing the order. All of this is compounded by the fact that Hamallah has been elevated to the status of an anti-colonial resistance figure in both nationalist historiography and in the postcolonial imagination, and not only in Mali. In fact, informants in Nioro told me the Guinean leader Sékou Touré was so interested in the story of Hamallah and his persecution that he invited some of Hamallah's followers to visit Guinea at his expense. In any case, Muslims in Mali and Mauritania are nearly unanimous in the view that Hamallah had been subjected to injustice during the colonial period.

There is another related issue that has pushed some in the younger generation to question the Hamawiyya: its seeming distrust of other Muslims in Nioro. At the time of my fieldwork, informants told me that there were virtually no followers of Hamallah who have continued to abridge their prayers. However, since Hamallah's exile, his followers have refused to pray in the Friday mosque in Nioro. Indeed, Hamawis in Mali, Mauritania and Senegal often have reputations for not performing their communal prayers in mosques. Instead, they usually pray communally on

Fridays in one of the *zawiyas* of the Hamawiyya. In those places in Mali where Hamawis have control of the imamate, Hamawis do pray in a Friday mosque. As indicated above, most Sunni Muslims in the world see Friday communal prayers as obligatory. But the colonial administration never permitted the construction of a separate Hamawi-controlled mosque in Nioro. The leadership of the Hamawiyya in Nioro has never agreed to build a separate Friday mosque appropriate for Friday communal prayers even after independence when they would have been relatively free to do so. In Nioro, Hamawis pray together on Fridays at the rebuilt *zawiya*, which is not a mosque and, therefore, not appropriate for the shorter communal Friday prayers and sermon.

Some of the various reasons given for the decision not to build a separate Friday mosque are based on jurisprudence and others based more on received and accepted practices. First, many note that, in the absence of the implementation of *shari'a* in the land, communal Friday prayers are not obligatory. Second, the Friday prayers are not obligatory because there has been a lack of confidence in those leading these prayers at the existing Friday mosque. This lack of confidence stems from the alleged machinations of those in control of the imamate against their religious leader. Both of these are reminiscent of the reasoning of Shiite scholars for not performing Friday communal prayers. But another reason is offered that relies on the practices of their religious leader. In this way of thinking, since Hamallah did not pray at the mosque in Nioro and did not construct a separate Friday mosque, it follows that they will not do so.

Younger Muslims, however, see that nearly everywhere else in Mali and beyond, Muslims usually pray together on Fridays in a mosque. When there are differences between Muslims living in one locale, there is usually more than one Friday mosque. More and more influenced by developments in the rest of the country and beyond, some younger people have begun to vote with their feet. In recent years, some youth from prominent families associated with the Hamawiyya have gone to pray at the Friday mosque. As will be discussed in later chapters, such developments are not unrelated to the fact that what it means to be a Muslim has been changing over the past few decades.

Finally, there is a serious organisational problem within the Hamawiyya. Nearly all Hamawis are aware there is a dwindling number of *muqaddams* who can formally initiate people into the order. There are no living *muqaddams* named directly by Hamallah since the last one died in 1992 in Senegal. The remaining *muqaddams* were all named by *muqaddams* whom Hamallah had authorised to appoint other *muqaddams* in turn. Because the few remaining *muqaddams* are not authorised to appoint other *muqaddams*, some see a danger that the Hamawiyya will die out. These organisational problems are somewhat mitigated by the fact that the remaining *muqaddams* are permitted to initiate ordinary followers by telephone and by correspondence. Although Muhammadu claims to be a *muqaddam,* he does not initiate people into the order, explaining that there are others who are able to do so. He leaves open the possibility that he will eventually receive authorisation – ostensibly from his absent father – to appoint *muqaddams.* In the meantime, some devoted followers of Hamallah say wistfully that if the order does die out for the lack of followers, this may have been exactly what Hamallah intended. Others have taken more direct action. For instance, in the 1990s, Ahmada (b. 1951), one of Sharif Ahmad's sons, who lives in Bamako, started to name *muqaddams* who initiated others into the Hamawiyya. Muhammadu is flatly opposed to this. While most in Nioro back Muhammadu in his position, though without openly criticising Ahmada, some worry that this might have the makings of schism.

CONCLUSION

I have tried to give a sense of the resilience of the Hamawiyya and its evolution over time. In the face of years of repression, many remained devoted to their absent *shaykh*; even after independence the order was constrained until Hamallah's young son Muhammadu assumed control of the order. Largely through his efforts over the past thirty years, the Hamawiyya, at least in Mali and Mauritania, has been reconsolidated under his authority. Today, Muhammadu attracts followers, often from outside Nioro, many of whom are drawn by the stories of Hamallah and his saintly intercession. But the Hamawiyya faces some serious challenges, especially in the town of Nioro. If some in the younger generation in Nioro do not embrace the Hamawiyya, this is due in part to the trend away from membership in Sufi orders. At the same time, the young are looking outward from Nioro and see that the Hamawiyya – in refusing to accept openly Hamallah's death and not praying in a Friday mosque – is seemingly out of step with Muslims elsewhere in Mali and beyond. Finally, in spite of Hamallah's son's success in revitalising the Hamawiyya, the dwindling number of *muqaddams* presents a serious challenge.

I have emphasised the importance of French colonialism in providing the conditions for the emergence and spread of the Hamawiyya. What made the Hamawiyya different from some other Sufi orders in West Africa was the fact that Hamallah attracted people from broad sectors of the population and from a variety of different groups in AOF. The Hamawiyya as a Sufi order was also no longer the preserve of a scholarly elite, in the way that other Sufi orders had been in the past. In this way, it was much like other Sufi orders, particularly the Mourides and the Tijaniyya, that also became associated with mass affiliation during the colonial period in neighbouring Senegal. But the Hamawiyya also became a new kind of institution as a direct result of years of systematic colonial repression and policies aimed at containing the Hamawiyya and its members. The French colonial presence helped to shape what it meant to be Muslim in AOF, as is particularly evident in the economy of martyrdom. Long after the colonial period has ended, some members of the Hamawiyya, fashioning themselves deeply devoted to their persecuted and absent *shaykh*, remain wary of other Muslims. Through separate communal prayers, they mark themselves as distinct from other Muslims who might be members of the Tijaniyya or have no Sufi affiliation at all.

In the next chapter, I turn to consider the Tijaniyya, the other important Sufi order, in the town and in the region.

4

SAINTS AND SUFI ORDERS II:
THE TIJANIYYA

As I have argued, the influence of Shaykh Hamallah and the Sufi affiliation around him expanded largely at the expense of the existing Sufi orders and their associated religious leaders during the colonial period. This was especially the case for the Tijaniyya and some of its leaders in the town of Nioro. Although there were people in Nioro who never accepted Hamallah as their *shaykh*, nearly all people report today that such people were a minority, perhaps even in the immediate aftermath of the repression in the 1940s. It is here that I would like to return to one of the points raised in the last chapter, namely how the French colonial presence helped shape what it meant to be Muslim. This is also apparent in the case of Tijanis in Nioro, some of whom had a much closer working relationship with the French than the Hamawis in the period leading up to and after the repression. The history of the Tijaniyya in the town also directly concerns the many Muslim religious specialists and their kin, who had never embraced Hamallah and who were living not only in the numerous villages around Nioro, but also in some of the far reaches of AOF.

In this chapter, I begin with the decline in importance of the Tijaniyya that occurred with the rise in prominence of Hamallah and the Hamawiyya, and I discuss some of the various reactions of the French and the Muslim establishment to this decline. I suggest that, as in the case of the rise of the Hamawiyya, the French colonial presence contributed wittingly and unwittingly to the revitalisation of the Tijaniyya in the town that began quietly, but earnestly, in the 1950s. Through a comparison of the different social trajectories of the major religious lineages associated with the Tijaniyya in the town, I explore the different ways social actors have engaged with the Tijaniyya.

DECLINE

In the previous chapter, I suggested that one of the most important issues facing Muslims in the aftermath of the French conquest and the onset of colonial rule was the question of leadership. In many parts of AOF including Nioro, the Tijaniyya remained important, despite the fact that there was no leadership around which people were united. I have also emphasised how French colonial policies were sometimes explicitly aimed toward maintaining a state of disunity among Muslims, Tijanis or otherwise. Immediately after the French conquest, very few members of the Tall family remained in the Nioro area. Some of those who had been in Nioro and other places in western Mali accompanied Amadu, Umar Tall's oldest son, on *hijra* to the east. After the conquest, the most prominent descendant of Umar Tall to make peace with the French was his youngest son, Aguibou, whom the French appointed as the ruler of the 'kingdom' of Macina with Bandiagara as its seat. Owing to dissatisfaction with his rule, the French eventually demoted him to *chef de province*, a position he held until his death in 1907.[1] Nevertheless, descendants and associates of Umar Tall and his sons, who had not gone on *hijra* or who had done so and returned to the region, gathered around Aguibou, making Bandiagara at least initially the most prominent centre for the Tall family in the new colony.

Shortly after the turn of the twentieth century, Murtada, one of Umar Tall's sons who had been living in Bandiagara and Djenné, returned to live near Nioro. It seems that conflict with his brother Aguibou helped to precipitate his relocation to Nioro.[2] Murtada brought with him an entourage, including some kin, and together they settled in villages near Nioro. As one of the few living sons of Umar Tall, Murtada had considerable prestige, especially among descendants of those who had participated in the *jihad*. Colonial accounts from the first decades of the century suggest that he was among the most influential of the descendants of Umar Tall, indeed considerably more so than his nephew, Seydou Nourou (Marty 1915–16: 357f.; cf. Marty 1920: 229). Reportedly named a Tijani *muqaddam* in 1893 on the eve of the French conquest of Bandiagara (Marty 1920: 228), Murtada personally initiated many people into the Tijaniyya, including considerable numbers of people in the western Soudan.[3] However, some colonial sources emphasised that he had little influence outside those groups of people closely associated with Umar Tall (for example Marty 1915–16: 358–9). Be that as it may, colonial sources repeatedly pointed to Murtada as a pillar of the colonial-authorised Muslim establishment and the so-called Umarian Tijaniyya.

Despite the presence of Murtada in the Nioro area, neither the descendants of Umar Tall, including others who later returned to live in the region, nor the descendants of Umar Tall's followers were unified in any way. Indeed, Umar Tall's descendants were divided into several branches issuing from various sons who, over time, were frequently rivalrous. Moreover, the descendants of Umar Tall's followers were equally, if not more, fragmented, not least because of French colonial policies. There was, however, a sense that the descendants of Umar Tall enjoyed a privileged role within the Tijaniyya that stemmed from Umar Tall's authoritative position in the Tijaniyya, not only in West Africa, but also because of his reputation among Tijanis beyond West Africa, including among them descendants of

Ahmad al-Tijani and his deputies in North Africa. Umar Tall was the widely respected author of several texts about the Tijaniyya, including his most celebrated book on the doctrines of the Sufi order, the *Rimah*. By the late nineteenth century, Tijanis in North Africa considered this text to be among the principal works of the order, and it was widely available, studied and discussed by Tijani scholars.[4] In 1927, when the main text on the life and doctrines of Ahmad al-Tijani, *Jawahir al-Ma'ani*, was published for the first time in Cairo, Umar Tall's book, the *Rimah*, was published in the margins of this book. Republished many times and widely diffused among Tijanis, Umar Tall's book became one of the central authoritative texts on the doctrine of the Sufi order. This has helped to elevate even further the prestige of Umar Tall's descendants.

If, from the French perspective, the presence of Murtada in Nioro would act as a check on the rising influence of Hamallah, things would change considerably after Murtada's death in 1922. After that time, some apparently looked to others in the Tall family for leadership, including Muntaga (d. 1955), the son of Amadu, who lived in Ségou and later became one of the most prominent members of the family in AOF. While Muntaga was also important for initiating people into the Tijaniyya, even to some in the western Soudan, there continued to be considerable diffusion of power within the Tall family. After 1922, no single member of the Tall family in the Nioro area, let alone in the Soudan or Senegal, had been able to exert much authority over the other members of the family or the descendants of those associated with the *jihad*. Without the influence of Murtada in Nioro, it seems that some of his erstwhile followers, especially Fulbe, embraced Hamallah (Nicolas 1943: 33). Some of them became some of Hamallah's most devoted followers and were included among the detainees in the 1940s. After Murtada's death, Hamallah was also able to count some members of prominent Futanke lineages associated with Umar Tall as his followers. These included one of the most learned Futanke scholars in the Nioro area who had gone early in the twentieth century to study with the colonial *qadi* Amadu Mukhtar Sakho (d. 1934) in Boghé in Mauritania, around whom several associated with the Umarian *jihad*, including Seydou Nourou Tall, had gathered.[5] Upon this scholar's return to Nioro, Hamallah named him a *muqaddam* – one of his most prominent in the region.[6] Some descendants of Umar Tall in the area also eventually became followers of Hamallah. Since they were not high-profile members of the Tall family, like Cerno Bokar Tall of Bandiagara, they did not receive the attention of the colonial administration.

While Hamallah attracted many followers in the broader region, there was a core group of people who remained opposed to Hamallah and the Hamawiyya with some of the opposition based at least in part on Tijani principles. Many felt that Hamallah was intruding in areas that were the prerogative of Muslim religious leaders and their time-honoured traditions that came before him. This was particularly the case for some of the descendants of Umar Tall. One interesting example of such a perspective can be found in a letter from a grandson of Umar Tall to the Governor General of AOF. Claiming that Hamallah was anti-French, the author praised the French for their decision to exile him in 1925. As for Hamallah, the author of the letter wrote: 'Since the institutions of al-Hajj Umar [Tall] are sufficient, he does not preach at all for the Muslim religion, but rather against France.'[7] While the author of the letter does not specify the 'institutions' of Umar Tall that he deems sufficient, we can surmise that this related to the Tijaniyya. Indeed, this letter is a particularly good illustration of how some African Muslims specifically linked Islam and the Tijaniyya in particular with Umar Tall, and branded new religious leaders like Hamallah as anti-colonial. The 'institutions' invoked presumably included the chain of initiation into the Tijaniyya that led through Umar Tall, and the related issue of the number of times the 'pearl of perfection' prayer should be recited. Even to this day, most Tall in Nioro indicate that the proper way to recite this prayer is twelve times, as their ancestor Umar Tall explains in his book the *Rimah*. While they note that to recite the prayer eleven times is wrong, they add that they are unable to insist on this point with too much vehemence, as it is clear to all that to recite the prayers twelve times has long been, and remains, a minority view in the town of Nioro.

Another criticism of Hamallah is that he committed a grave error in not respecting one of his teachers or *shaykhs*. This is rather a serious charge given what amounts to the widely accepted rule in pedagogical and Sufi practice that the student follow the teacher or guide – that is, one necessarily respects, honours, even obeys those from whom one has learned. In the *Rimah*, Umar Tall discusses in considerable detail the necessity of following and the perils for not obeying one's *shaykh*. Many claim that before Hamallah encountered al-Akhdar he was a student of Muhammad al-Mukhtar, his future enemy. Although this is likely given Muhammad al-Mukhtar's credentials as a learned man and Tijani *muqaddam* in Nioro, the nature of the relationship between the two men is not entirely clear.[8] In any case, the charge continues that it was a serious mistake to turn against one's own teacher and to disobey him, as Hamallah is alleged to have done. However, followers of Hamallah in Nioro state that even if Hamallah studied with Muhammad al-Mukhtar, the charge is irrelevant since his new teacher, al-Akhdar, was much more spiritually advanced and recognised Hamallah as his own successor. Others point to the fact that Hamallah did not pray the Friday communal prayers as being particularly blameworthy. Not to pray the communal prayers, in this way of thinking, was unequivocally wrong. However, I should note that for some in Nioro who are not Hamawis, this was the only thing that Hamallah ever did – to their knowledge – that was wrong.

Finally and almost paradoxically, some of those who remain opposed to Hamallah try to associate themselves with him, even going so far as to claim that their forebears were at least partly responsible for his coming into the world. In some circles, people state that it was a member of the Tall family who gave the young slave girl Assa Diallo[9] – Hamallah's mother – to Muhammad, Hamallah's father, as a gift in recognition of his status as a descendant of the Prophet Muhammad.[10] It is important to note that this scenario is not implausible. As a trader in the region during the era of Futanke rule, Hamallah's father would most certainly have had dealings with the rulers and/or agents of the Futanke state. In any case, Hamallah's followers roundly dismiss such claims as wishful thinking.

While the Hamawiyya expanded at least until the repression of the 1940s, the Tijaniyya and its leadership in Nioro did not seem able to benefit directly by attracting followers in the wake of the repression. Indeed, French administrators lamented the fact that Hamallah's enemies seemed unable to rally people to their side, blaming this in large part on the personality of Madi Assa Kaba Jakhite (c. 1865–1950), the imam of the Friday mosque in Nioro.[11] More important than the presumed personality flaws of a particular individual is the fact that many people saw some of the Muslim establishment in the town, including the imam and his family, as being if not directly responsible for, then at least complicit in the repressive measures against Hamallah and his followers. In this way of thinking, the reputation of this family – some of whose members served as chiefs (*chefs de canton*), clerks and civil servants – and their associates, had been seriously damaged.

It is likely that this figured in Madi Assa's attempt to be buried after his death near his grandfather, Alfa Umar Kaba Jakhite, the eponymous ancestor of the Kabalanke in Nioro, whose tomb had become, and remains, an important pilgrimage site in the town. To be near this ancestor who has the reputation of a saint might ensure blessings through the saint's intercession, without mentioning the boost in reputation that such a final resting place could provide.[12] Special permission from the French was needed for the burial since Alfa Umar's tomb was located (inconveniently at least for the French) within the old pre-colonial fort in the town that had been converted by the French into a military garrison.[13] The local French administrator granted Madi Assa's request to be buried near Alfa Umar. Madi Assa's descendants report that he received permission to be buried there in exchange for blessings or petitionary prayers on behalf of the French colonial administrator that served ultimately to promote the latter's career to the highest levels within the colonial administration.[14] Upon his death in 1950, Madi Assa was indeed buried near Alfa Umar in a ceremony at which the French colonial administrator eulogised the deceased.[15] Almost immediately, some of Hamallah's followers attempted to have one of their own become the new imam of the Friday mosque.[16] They were ultimately unsuccessful, perhaps only because of the presence of the French. However, some might suggest that it was due to the saintly intervention of Alfa Umar, whose descendants, the Kabalanke, have retained control of the imamate of the mosque since the beginning of colonial rule.

For the immediate postwar period, there seems to be really little to tell about the Tijaniyya in the Nioro area. This is perhaps because Tijanis and the French administration had their working relationship firmly in place. There were some prominent Tijani *muqaddams* in the region who continued to play important roles, quietly initiating others into the Tijaniyya. These included the noted scholar Bakary Alama Jakhite, one of Madi Assa's agnates, as well as a few others in a Futanke village adjacent to Nioro, some of whom had marriage alliances with the Tall family.[17] Without exception, these *muqaddams* traced their initiations into the Tijaniyya in chains of transmission that led to Umar Tall.

At the same time, there is some evidence to suggest an actual decline in membership of the Tijaniyya in the postwar period. Before Hamallah's second exile in 1941, some of those associated with the Kabalanke as clients or as servants had been attracted to Hamallah. While some of these people had openly embraced Hamallah, many more had been sympathetic to him. The discrediting of key figures of the Muslim establishment in Nioro helped to keep many of these people from ever embracing or, as the case may be, re-embracing the Tijaniyya. In some cases, the discrediting of the Sufi order and certain of its leaders may even have helped push some of these people to become formally initiated in the Qadiriyya. Some informants suggested that the French even actively encouraged this spread of the Qadiriyya after 1941. This may have been an extension of the earlier policy whereby the colonial administration relied upon certain prominent members of the Muslim establishment, who were Qadiris, to counter the influence of Hamallah.[18]

REACTION

It is not until the postcolonial period that one can begin to speak of a revival of the Tijaniyya in Nioro. This revival has come largely through the efforts of some of Umar Tall's descendants. Although any discussion of the Tijaniyya in Nioro in the late twentieth century takes Cerno Hady Tall (see Figure 4.1),[19] the present head of the Tall family in Nioro, as its starting point, the most important actor seems initially to have been Seydou Nourou Tall, the Dakar-based grandson of Umar Tall. As I have noted (in Chapter 3), by the 1930s, Seydou Nourou Tall was one of the Muslim religious leaders closest to the colonial administration in AOF. On countless missions sanctioned and financed by the colonial administration, Seydou Nourou Tall literally criss-crossed AOF (and sometimes other French colonies in Africa) to serve as a mediator in disputes and as a messenger from the colonial administration to its subjects, usually, though not

4.1 Cerno Hady Tall   Unknown photographer, widely available hand-coloured
black and white photo

exclusively Muslims. In his many public statements and sermons, quite
often delivered in the vernacular language of his audience, the polyglot and
cosmopolitan *avant la lettre* Seydou Nourou encouraged colonial subjects to
obey colonial authorities and their representatives, pay their taxes, ignore
calls to strike, work in agricultural projects, use new health facilities and
attend colonial schools, among other things. Such 'official' colonial-
authorised duties in mediation and 'propaganda' (as the administration
sometimes called them) were of course highly dependent upon time, place
and the policies of the day.

In addition to his 'official' duties, Seydou Nourou clearly had agendas of
his own of which the colonial administration could only ever be partially
informed. As the model 'loyal' Muslim subject and the embodiment of the
colonial-authorised Muslim establishment in AOF, the colonial administration tended not to pay too much attention to his specifically 'religious'
activities unless of course they might directly serve colonial policies and
objectives. During his peregrinations in the 1930s and 1940s that took him
to the far reaches of the colonies in AOF and neighbouring colonies, Seydou
Nourou frequently intervened directly in the affairs of the Tijaniyya.
Although Seydou Nourou's own rank within the Tijaniyya was not
unambiguous (see Quesnot 1958a), some West African Muslims took
Seydou Nourou to be among the highest ranked in the Tijaniyya. One
prominent Muslim cleric in Niger referred to Seydou Nourou as 'the great

shaykh and well-known exemplar ... my *khalifa*, *shaykh* of *shaykhs*.'[20] Tijani sources published later in Egypt would refer to Seydou Nourou Tall as being among the most important of Muslim religious leaders in all of West Africa.[21] During his travels, Seydou Nourou frequently initiated people into the Tijaniyya, renewed the initiation of many others, and named *muqaddams* in many places throughout AOF, including the Nioro area. While it is not possible to estimate the number of people involved in these activities, they must have been considerable given how extensive his travels were. Like Hamallah, Seydou Nourou also only appointed *muqaddams* who were of hereditary 'free' status and usually those who were from the lineages of Muslim religious specialists.

Some of Seydou Nourou's central concerns seem to have been the status of the Tijaniyya, the position of the Tall family within the Tijaniyya, the Sufi order's long-term prospects in relation to other Sufi orders, and later 'reformist' Muslims. All these concerns were intimately bound up with the fact that the Tall family under Seydou Nourou's tutelage had more or less successfully reverted from a ruling lineage to a clerical lineage during colonial rule. As for Hamallah and the Hamawiyya, it is interesting to note that it seems likely that Seydou Nourou was not initially opposed to Hamallah in the 1920s.[22] By the 1930s, however, Seydou Nourou spent a substantial amount of time convincing Muslim religious leaders to abandon Hamallah and the Hamawiyya and to return to the Tijaniyya under his leadership. For example, during his numerous trips to Soudan in the 1930s, he convinced many Muslims, including some prominent religious leaders, not to recite 'the pearl of perfection' prayer eleven times, but rather twelve times. In accepting to do so, such people usually agreed to renew their initiation into the Tijaniyya through him or through his designated representatives. In this way, they were accepting Seydou Nourou's authority in the Tijaniyya over that of Hamallah. In the period leading up to the 'reconciliation' in 1937 in Nioro between Hamallah and the other Tijanis in Nioro, Seydou Nourou was one of Hamallah's most vocal critics, denouncing Hamallah nearly everywhere he went in the Soudan.[23]

The Hamawiyya was not the only Sufi order that concerned Seydou Nourou. After the repression of the Hamawiyya, Seydou Nourou apparently feared the spread of the Qadiriyya in its place and acted along with his cousin Muntaga in Ségou to discredit an influential family of Qadiris in the Soudan.[24] For Nioro, he could only have been attentive to the situation of the Tijaniyya, where, despite Hamallah's exile and eventual death, his memory and that of the Hamawiyya were strong. If the Tall family had not been united after the death of Murtada in 1922, the lack of unity only intensified over the next few decades. As part of the Muslim establishment, some in the Tall family in Nioro had also been fairly well discredited by their vehement opposition to Hamallah and his followers.

Over the course of his many trips to the Soudan, Seydou Nourou could only have been aware of such difficulties facing the Tijaniyya, especially in Nioro with the weak position of the Tall family and its divisions. Such conditions must have been uppermost in his mind when he decided to send a representative to Nioro. At the same time, any efforts to shepherd the Tijaniyya must also have been taken in relation to what were perceived at the time as potential threats to the already precarious situation of the Tijaniyya. In the 1940s, Mahmud Ba, who hailed from Diowol in Senegal, had opened a 'reformist' Islamic educational institution or *madrasa*[25] in neighbouring Kayes, attracting many students, including some from the immediate Nioro area.[26] Eventually propagating a 'reformist' perspective that was critical of the organised Sufi orders, Mahmud Ba would come into conflict with some members of the Muslim establishment, including Seydou Nourou Tall.

There was also the potential threat of another branch of the Tijaniyya in West Africa. The 1940s witnessed the rapid expansion of the branch of the Tijaniyya associated with another young charismatic leader, Ibrahima Niasse (1900–75), in many places in West Africa, particularly in northern Nigeria.[27] By the early 1950s, Niasse had made several visits to the Soudan and counted quite a number of prominent followers there.[28] While Niasse never seems to have visited Nioro and never gained a foothold there, the expansion of his branch of the Tijaniyya – like the Hamawiyya before it – came at the expense of the branch of the Tijaniyya associated with Umar Tall's descendants.[29] Apprised as he was of developments in AOF, this was certainly a major concern of Seydou Nourou, as it was of other Tijanis, particularly some members of the Sy family, the leaders of the largest branch of the Tijaniyya in Senegal, with whom Seydou Nourou had longstanding ties.[30]

Seydou Nourou, most likely in concert with others, seems to have undertaken a number of actions to counter these threats to the Tijaniyya and the Tall family's stature within it. In the late 1940s, French colonial sources reported an attempt to 're-establish' the Tijani caliphate of Umar Tall, ostensibly the title of *khalifa*, though Seydou Nourou's involvement in such efforts are not clear.[31] This was not uncontroversial and undoubtedly received the criticism of certain Muslim religious leaders.[32] In 1955, Seydou Nourou himself founded an organisation in Dakar that grouped together Tijanis from the Futa region of the Senegal River valley.[33] He named his nephew Muntaga as head of this organisation, which was created largely along ethnic lines, grouping as it did mostly those who considered themselves Futanke or Halpulaaren (as they have come to call themselves in Senegal and Mauritania). In doing so, Seydou Nourou seemed to want to unite Tijanis from Futa under his leadership and, at the same time, link them directly to one of the major *zawiyas* of the Tijaniyya in North Africa.

The membership cards produced for this organisation not only featured Seydou Nourou's own photo, but also that of Ben Amor,[34] a descendant of Ahmad al-Tijani from Algeria, whose trips to AOF and beyond were promoted by the French in the late 1940s and the 1950s.

While it might seem that such an organisation did not involve Nioro, this was not the case, as many people from Nioro, especially the Futanke, were at least indirectly associated through kin and pedagogical ties and networks. From early in the colonial period until the time in question (and long after), there have been important exchanges between Futanke from the Nioro area and the Senegal River Valley, Dakar and much further afield. Some of these exchanges have been migration for the purposes of Islamic education, while perhaps equally, if not more, important has been migration of an economic nature. In fact, the latter has often allowed for the re-establishment and strengthening of ties between Futanke living in some of the different areas of AOF, particularly Mauritania, Senegal and Soudan.

Colonial records indicate that Seydou Nourou visited Nioro in 1955. In an administrative report, it is stated that: 'He gathered the orthodox Muslims [*les musulmans orthodoxes*] at the mosque and gave them a sermon about harmony and obedience to authority.'[35] While the report is silent as to what his activities might have been vis-à-vis the Tijaniyya, this visit occurred either shortly before or after Seydou Nourou travelled to Ségou to visit the grave of his recently deceased cousin Muntaga, who, it was noted, was one of the most prominent descendants of Umar Tall in AOF. Through *la politique musulmane* the French had employed Muntaga – like Seydou Nourou elsewhere in AOF – in their strategy to curb Hamallah's influence.[36] Ties between the two cousins had often been very close, and Seydou Nourou had been largely responsible for the Islamic education of one of Muntaga's sons in Senegal.[37] After Hamallah's second exile, the two cousins had worked closely together to shore up the Tijaniyya.

In any case, as the preceding discussion suggests, there were clearly many factors that can be seen as the seeds for the attempt by Seydou Nourou and others to revitalise the Tijaniyya in Nioro. Toward that end, in the 1950s Seydou Nourou Tall directed his young 'son' Hady Tall to live in Nioro.[38] Hady's father, Amadu Muntaga, was among those who left Nioro to continue his studies with those around Amadu Mukhtar Sakho in Boghé. Born in Boghé, Hady attended French school for a couple of years before continuing with an Islamic education, completing advanced studies in Hore Niwa, near Kayes. There was a celebrated Islamic educational centre in this village where prominent scholars, who were descendants of those associated with the *jihad* of Umar Tall, gave instruction.[39] Many Muslims sent their sons to study in this setting since the teachers there were known to be opposed to the 'reformist' ideas that were beginning to spread in the 1940s and after.

By the early 1950s, Hady's older half-brother Muntaga – named the head of Seydou Nourou's Tijani organisation in 1955 – was living in Dakar with Seydou Nourou and would eventually serve as his successor as head of the Tall family in Dakar.[40] Hady seems to have had a similar mission in Nioro. As Hady himself explained to me, the instructions he received from Seydou Nourou were that he was to act as a leader for the Tijaniyya, but that he would defer in matters to his older brother Muntaga in Dakar. While it is not possible to know the exact reasons for Seydou Nourou's decision to send Hady to Nioro, Seydou Nourou was undoubtedly interested in controlling the evolution of the Tijaniyya. It seems that Hady was a designated representative to that end.[41]

In the 1950s, Hady moved permanently to Nioro. As a descendant of Umar Tall with a reputation for advanced studies and as Seydou Nourou Tall's designated representative, some people, particularly Futanke, confided their young children to him for their education. Although he taught some students, Hady lived a modest and unassuming life for many years in Nioro. Like many other Futanke Muslim religious specialists, Hady spent a fair amount of his time doing embroidery, an income-generating activity considered a noble activity and perhaps not unlike the darning that the Prophet Muhammad is reported to have done himself.

RENEWAL

While Seydou Nourou may have been the person who ordered Hady to move to Nioro, the actual revitalisation of the Tijaniyya in the Nioro area has been largely the work of Hady and his followers. For some of those who remember the modest man who spent countless hours doing embroidery under the shade of a tree, this has come as something of a surprise. For many others, it is nothing short of a 'miracle'. Over the past few decades, Hady has been successful in reconstituting the authority of the Tall family under his leadership over many of the descendants of those involved in the nineteenth-century *jihad* in and around Nioro, many of whom are Futanke. He has done this within the rubric of the Tijaniyya and in the name of Umar Tall. Hady's reputation as a scholar whose learning eclipses most, though perhaps not all, members of the Tall family in the region has certainly facilitated this. Over the course of many years, Hady initiated (or renewed the initiation of) many people into the Tijaniyya.[42] Most of these were Muslim religious leaders – most often descendants of people associated with the *jihad* – who lived in the numerous Fulbe and Futanke villages around Nioro. Many of these villages have few or no Hamawis, while a few are fairly well divided between Tijanis and Hamawis. Once Hady gained the trust of local religious authorities – imams and other religious intellectuals – they submitted to him as disciples to *shaykh*. Repeating this process in many of the villages around Nioro, he and his entourage have crafted a measure of authority over many of these villages. Around this time, he also began to develop a reputation for prodigious powers, especially through the use of the Islamic esoteric sciences.[43]

As the widely recognised leader of some of those associated with the *jihad*, many villagers started to give a portion of their yearly harvests and/or other gifts to Hady. Since the onset of colonial rule, many of the descendants of Umar Tall in the Nioro area have lived on the gifts offered to them by the descendants of those associated with the *jihad*. With the rise in prestige of Hady, many villagers have come to resent other members of the Tall family continuing to expect gifts from them. Over the years, Hady has attracted a huge number of people, including extended family members, followers, servants and retainers, who live near him and for whom he provides. In recent years, those for whom Hady does not provide, including some within the Tall family, have been forced either to try to make a living in other ways or to travel considerably in order to make ends meet. That is, they might have to travel greater distances to visit Muslims from whom they solicit gifts in honour of their descent from Umar Tall.

Many in the Nioro area – almost all of whom come from families that never embraced Hamallah – have taken Hady as the contemporary successor to Umar Tall (cf. Hanson 1989: 245). For such people, his settling in Nioro, the subsequent growth of his influence and personal fortune, and people's taking him as a *shaykh* are all signs of his authority as a leader of those associated with the *jihad*. Many hold that it is under his leadership that there can be a return to the ideals of Umar Tall's original community in Nioro, however vaguely conceived these ideals might be. Indeed, many Futanke have rallied around Hady, asserting their authority as heirs to those who participated in the nineteenth-century *jihad* in the area. They assert this authority against other Muslims in the region, whether they are Hamawis or Tijanis, who are not Futanke.

Hady's reputation has grown such that he is really one of the most prominent Muslim religious leaders in western Mali. In recent years, his influence and authority in and around Nioro have come to rival that of Muhammadu, the head of the Hamawiyya. Arguably, his followers have been central to his rise in status. Some of the many migrants from villages around Nioro and elsewhere in western Mali have gone on to work in places such as Côte d'Ivoire, Central Africa and Europe. Not only have they spread Hady's name and reputation as a learned and pious religious leader, but they have also lavished him with gifts. Equally important for his elevation are the relations which have developed between Hady and the family of President Bongo of Gabon since the marriage of Hady's sister's daughter to a member of the Bongo family (see Diallo 1988). Through their gifts, these and other such well-heeled followers have facilitated the rapid rise in Hady's lifestyle and his displays of wealth.

Since the late 1980s, perhaps the most important communal expression of Tijani identity in Nioro has been the yearly *ziyara* – called the *ziyara* al-Hajj Umar – organised by Hady Tall.[44] After the death of Seydou Nourou Tall in 1980, Muntaga instituted an annual *ziyara* in Dakar that meets around the date of the anniversary of Seydou Nourou's death. The *ziyara* is held at Seydou Nourou's tomb, on a plot of land in central Dakar the Senegalese government gave for a large mosque that is still under construction. In 1987, following Muntaga's lead, Hady initiated a yearly *ziyara* in Nioro that is coordinated with the one in Dakar. It has been held every year in Nioro since then except for one year when there were flash floods in the town.

During the *ziyara*, people, mostly from some of the Futanke villages from around Nioro but also from Kayes, Bamako and beyond, descend upon Nioro for up to a full week. Many travelling long distances come overland, but some also arrive on flights from the capital. Most days are spent reading the Quran and praying, with recitation of the special litany of prayers of the Tijaniyya and preaching in the evenings. It is also a time for Hady to announce the names of new *muqaddams* he has appointed and to give instructions to his followers.

That the *ziyara* is held around the time of Seydou Nourou's death and that Hady defers ultimately to Muntaga in Dakar are facts often lost to many people in Nioro. What most see is that Hady organises, hosts and finances a gathering of thousands in the interest of Islam. Over the last few years, the *ziyara* has come to be not only a Tijani affair but also an assertion of Futanke authority under Tall leadership and specifically that of Hady. While all the communal prayers are (of course) in Arabic, as is some of the programme, nearly all the public speaking during the *ziyara* is in Pulaar (Fulfulde), lending truth to the claim many make that this is strictly an affair of the Futanke or Fulbe. More importantly, the *ziyara* has become a forum for Hady to assert his authority and that of his grandfather. The *ziyara* is held on Hady's private land. As the large banners written in Arabic announce, those attending the *ziyara* are welcome at 'the house of Shaykh Umar al-Futi', that is Umar Tall (see Figure 4.2). The culmination of the week-long *ziyara* is the Friday prayer at the mosque that Umar Tall had built in Nioro (see Figure 2.1). This is followed by a trip by men and boys to the local cemetery for prayers at the grave of Muntaga, Umar Tall's son and Hady's grandfather, who was killed in the conflict with his brother Amadu over rule in the Nioro area after their father's death (Hanson 1989, 1996). This rather public ceremony asserts Hady's authority over any others who might claim to lead, not only within the Tall family but also the Tijaniyya.

Although there are descendants of other sons of Umar Tall living in the region who do not accept the authority of Hady, the *ziyara* and the ceremony at the cemetery downplay, if not negate, whatever claims to authority they might have. Several of the descendants of other sons of Umar Tall in

4.2 Banner, *ziyara* al-Hajj Umar Tall, Nioro   *Photographer:* John Harrelson

the region do not participate in any way in the *ziyara*. But any opposition they might voice is inaudible in the face of the wealth, prestige and influence of Hady. After all, it is Hady, the acknowledged leader of so many, who organises thousands to come together 'in order to pray in the name of God', as the printed *ziyara* programme announcement indicated in 1994. Being lauded as someone able to mobilise people for the sake of Islam has served to spread Hady's reputation even further. Many have seen his ability to bring together so many people as truly extraordinary. This has led some to assert that Hady is not only a Muslim saint like his 'father' Seydou Nourou before him, but that he has also advanced to such an elevated spiritual level that he is indeed the true successor to Umar Tall. Many Futanke in the region point to the fact that they are even more strongly committed as a group to the Tijaniyya under Hady's leadership than they were in the past.

Even though Hady and his followers form the most prominent and well organised group of Tijanis in the region, their authority has not gone unchallenged. However, the problems they face have been mitigated in some cases by their ability to mobilise ties, particularly through Hady's family, to the broader Tijani community.[45] The visit to Nioro by Cerno Mansour Baro of Mbour in Senegal in the late 1980s will serve as an example. Mansour is a very well-known and influential leader of the Tijaniyya associated with Muhammad Sayyid Ba (d. 1980), the founder of a new community, Médina Gounasse in Senegal, that has attracted many Fulbe and Halpulaaren migrants and followers since it was founded in the 1930s. The members of this branch of the Tijaniyya think of themselves as separate from the other main branches in the region.[46] Over the past few decades, from his base in Mbour, Mansour has attracted many followers from among Halpulaaren in the Senegal River valley, Dakar, and from among Halpulaaren migrants in France and elsewhere in Europe. He has been particularly popular among some of those who had previously been close to the established Tijaniyya, especially the Tall family and its associates in the Senegal River valley area. Mansour also has many followers in Mali, particularly in western Mali and Bamako. He regularly visits these followers during his trips to Mali when he usually also goes on pilgrimage to Degembere, the site of Umar Tall's demise in the nineteenth century. Mansour's branch of the Tijaniyya has steadily grown in importance and influence to the extent that it currently rivals other branches of the Sufi order in Senegal and, increasingly, areas of western Mali. This is due in no small part to Mansour's reputation as a learned and pious leader of the Tijaniyya. In fact, many also consider him to be a living Muslim saint.

Before Mansour arrived in Nioro, word of his imminent visit reached the town. Upon arrival, Mansour went almost immediately to a neighbouring village where he has kin who are descendants of those who participated in the *jihad* of Umar Tall. Many noted that the open hostility of some Tijanis in Nioro precipitated his departure from the town. While ostensibly visiting his relatives, Mansour quickly attracted many people's attention. Many, particularly Futanke, had heard about his reputation and sought to see him during his visit to the area. Most of these people were Tijanis, and a number of them renewed their affiliation with the Tijaniyya through him. By renewing their affiliation with the Tijaniyya with Mansour, such people were indicating that they accepted his religious authority over and above that of other religious leaders in the area. Those who sought out Mansour were almost without exception followers of Hady or other Tijanis linked to him. News of people taking Mansour as their *shaykh* reached Nioro almost instantaneously.

In a matter of days, a Moroccan, one of the descendants of Ahmad al-Tijani – the founder of the Tijaniyya – arrived in Nioro from his home in Dakar. This visiting Tijani notable convened a meeting at which he counselled people that Mansour was not authorised to initiate people into the Tijaniyya, and, thus, any initiations he performed were not legitimate or recognised by the Tijaniyya. Most, if not all, of the people whom Mansour had initiated proceeded to renounce their initiations through him. The parallels with Seydou Nourou Tall in his efforts to have people renounce Hamallah and the Hamawiyya during the colonial period are indeed striking. This was the subject of considerable discussion among some people in Nioro even several years after Mansour's visit.

According to some Tijanis in Nioro, Mansour had come under the guise of visiting family, while his real motive had been to attract new followers, thereby disturbing the situation of the Tijaniyya in the area. But it is the larger repercussions that are perhaps even more interesting. Most people were, and still are, only partially informed about the identity of the Moroccan visitor – that he is a long-term resident of Senegal with marriage ties to some of the leading Tijanis there. Indeed, he is one of the descendants of Ahmad al-Tijani whose family left Morocco for Senegal in the 1950s after having been criticised for being too close to the French administration there. Many in Nioro assert or repeat the assertion that Hady is so influential that leaders of the Tijaniyya in North Africa came at his behest to solve problems within the Sufi order, as occasioned by the visit of Mansour. Such claims have only served to boost Hady's reputation further, strengthening some people's attachment to him.

DIFFERENT TRAJECTORIES

If I have focused in this discussion largely on the Futanke, I now want to turn to consider some of the other groups, opposed to Hamallah from the beginning of his career, who seem to have remained committed to the Tijaniyya. I want to argue that people's different social trajectories, particularly educational trajectories – Islamic and otherwise – have helped to shape their ways of being Muslim and their engagement with the Tijaniyya.[47] I focus on some of those groups identified with the Soninke in the area and compare them with the Futanke and the Tall in particular, with whom I begin.

The descendants of Umar Tall in the Nioro area offer an interesting, though not entirely unusual, case of avoidance of French-language Western education. Since returning to the region shortly after the turn of the twentieth century, members of the Tall family have almost without exception refused to send their children to French-language schools.[48] Informants who attended colonial French-language schools in the 1920s reported that even when there were Tall family members in the classroom, they never stayed very long. This is, of course, in marked contrast to the Tall in other towns in Soudan such as Ségou and Bandiagara, where their children attended, or were forced to attend, colonial schools and became civil servants.[49] Moreover, from early in the colonial period, several Tall from these places in the Soudan and beyond also served in the colonial army. If members of the Tall family in Nioro, including Umar's son Murtada, helped the French in the recruitment of soldiers during the colonial period,[50] I learned of no Tall from the Nioro area who had actually served in the colonial or postcolonial army. This is not to suggest that the Tall in Nioro ignored the French colonial presence. On the contrary, as part of the colonial Muslim establishment, various members of the lineage eventually served the French administration in various capacities.

In general, in Nioro, the Tall – like many other lineages of religious specialists – have thought that French-language schools, both colonial and postcolonial, were inherently inferior to Islamic education, even forbidden. This was not least because such schooling seemed to pose a threat to Muslim values, which is understood here as the risk of becoming what people call in the vernacular languages a 'Black European', an African with the values of a European (cf. Fanon 1967; Delafosse 1917).[51] This is somewhat paradoxical given how Seydou Nourou Tall had actively encouraged African colonial subjects to embrace many of the trappings of colonial modernity, not least of which was colonial French-language schooling. As noted above, many of the descendants of Umar Tall in the region have lived for years from the gifts people gave to them in recognition of their descent. Unlike some of the other lineages of religious specialists in the region, they were able to manage without diversifying their activities. In this way, it was perhaps easier for the Tall as a group to avoid French-language education. Hady himself spent a few years in a colonial French-language school in Mauritania – against the will of his family, people like to point out – but he has never sent any of his many children to the state-run French-language schools in the postcolonial period. In an important way, detachment from such colonial and postcolonial educational institutions seems to have helped to keep the Tall and some others focused on 'traditional' Islamic education, as well as to remain committed to the Tijaniyya. This is because Islamic education and the Tijaniyya are so tightly bound together for them.

In contrast, the Kabalanke and many of their associates frequently sent their children to both French-language state schools and 'traditional' schools for Islamic education. In fact, a sizeable number of the male children from such families actually continued their studies in French-language schools to levels considerably more advanced than their studies in Islamic education. In some cases, after completing up to six years of French-language schooling, young boys would then give up such schooling to concentrate on Islamic education. In some families, certain children concentrated exclusively on Islamic education, while others concentrated on French-language schooling. Although early in the colonial period enrolment in the French schools was against the will of some families, as the decades passed such education became increasingly commonplace. Today, among the Kabalanke one finds perhaps some of the highest rates of enrolment of children in French-language state schools.[52] In any case, it seems that sustained exposure to French-language Western education has helped make the Kabalanke and some of their Soninke-speaking associates less enthusiastic about formal membership in the Tijaniyya than their counterparts among the Tall.

Such an argument in no way ignores the fact that the discrediting of some of Hamallah's opponents certainly helped to promote this lack of enthusiasm for formal membership in the Tijaniyya. Furthermore, it does not in any way suggest that they are necessarily opposed to the Tijaniyya or Sufism in general, a subject that will be treated at some length in chapters below. What it does suggest is that the French colonial presence helped to shape what it meant to be a Muslim and that there were different ways of being Muslim. For Kabalanke, as for many others in the town, there was no contradiction between being a Muslim and having an education in French-language state schools. In this way of thinking, such education did not mean that one ceased to be a Muslim, let alone become a 'Black European'. It did, however, change what being a Muslim meant. More specifically, being Muslim was less closely tied to the Tijaniyya, though the knowledge and use of certain practices associated with Sufi orders and their leaders – the esoteric sciences – have remained central to what it means for them to be Muslim. In fact, many of them use the Islamic esoteric sciences for particular desired ends. Thus, students and parents of students in state schools routinely seek out Muslim clerics for amulets, blessings and prayers to help ensure success on exams and in securing employment.

For the Tall and their associates, on the other hand, their avoidance of French-language state education and many of the employment activities associated with such education allowed them to remain more firmly committed to the Tijaniyya. Indeed, for many of them, to be Muslim necessarily means to be Tijani. This entails either formal membership in the Sufi order or, at the very least, great respect for this Sufi order, its leadership and hierarchy, that are so closely identified with their ancestor. If one can speak about a renewal or revitalisation of the Tijaniyya in the Nioro area, it has been largely among the Futanke and led by the Tall family.

PART II

AUTHORITY

5

THE ESOTERIC SCIENCES

In this chapter, I examine more closely the Islamic esoteric sciences in West Africa (Brenner 1985a). The diversity of knowledge and practices that can be grouped under the heading of Islamic esoteric sciences include, among other things, special prayers such as petitionary prayers and blessings (Ar., *du'a*), instruction or guidance in alms-giving (Ar. *sadaqa*), geomancy (Ar., *raml*), mystical retreat (Ar., *khalwa*), decision-making via divine inspiration (Ar., *istikhara*), the confection of written texts or *gris-gris* in the colonial lexicon (to wear or to keep as amulets, to ingest or with which to wash after effacing with water), astrology (Ar., *'ilm al-najum*) and medicine (Ar., *tibb*).[1] Most of these sciences make use of Arabic literacy, including the text of the Quran. And some involve elaborate ideas about and techniques for dealing with spiritual entities, such as *jinn*, known for their interventions in the world. Long central to regionally salient conceptions of Islam, such practices are thought to be perfectly licit and can be justified through reference to the standard Maliki texts of Islamic jurisprudence (Ar., *fiqh*) used here. These esoteric sciences have played and continue to play an enormous role on the social landscape through the practitioners who employ them and their clients who solicit their use. For many in this region, they are a key element in what is thought to constitute Islamic orthodoxy. From the perspective of some people, including so-called 'reformists' (see Chapter 7), most, if not all, of the esoteric sciences considered here are not only un-Islamic, but expressly forbidden according to the precepts of Islam. Be that as it may, the disparate practices I call the Islamic esoteric sciences are among the most important components of authority for at least some, if not most, religious leaders in Nioro, not to mention elsewhere in West Africa. They are also one of the key elements in what I call the prayer economy in this Malian town (see Chapter 6).

It is important to note at the outset that the term 'esoteric sciences' is a convenient way to discuss the various practices enumerated above, as there appears to be no universally accepted local or regional term that covers all of the kinds of knowledge and practices that can be included under this rubric. The term esoteric sciences is, nevertheless, preferable to some of the other options that are based on analytical presuppositions, which are problematical. There is, for instance, the rather clumsy and decidedly modernist

5.1 The Electoral Tribulations of Paco, by Madou

A. Mr. Paco is a candidate for the National Assembly, and he wants to use all means in order to reach his goal.

B. Paco: My dear, I am going away for a few minutes.
Woman: OK

C. Mr. Paco heads towards the house of a *marabout* in the area.
Paco: I must absolutely be elected in my district.

notion of *maraboutage* from the French colonial lexicon that has gained currency, particularly among French-speaking 'modernists' and 'secularists' in West Africa. This notion of *maraboutage* focuses on *marabouts* who presumably engage in 'heterodox' practices, such as 'magic', or other 'animist' practices that they employ to a variety of ends. In this way of thinking, the African masses make up the main clientele for *marabouts*, who are able to exploit them because of their gullibility and ignorance. However, modernising actors in Mali also castigate those educated and well-off Africans, who seek out the services of *marabouts*, for being mired in superstition as well. As the recent cartoon from a Malian newspaper suggests (see Figure 5.1), the enormous sums of money 'modern' politicians seem willing to give to *marabouts* is particularly scandalous.

As I indicated earlier (in Chapter 1), the knowledge and practices discussed here are intimately related to the notion of secret or secrets, locally known as *siru* (Ar., *sirr*) in the region's vernaculars, a term employed for both Islamic and un-Islamic phenomena. In fact, many lay persons use the term *siru* to refer to what I call the Islamic esoteric sciences. In this discussion, I use the notion of esoteric sciences in part because it highlights knowledge and its acquisition through human and/or divine channels in what are usually initiatic processes within a particular social field, here one that is predominantly Muslim. In this way, the term is also analytically more useful than other terms such as 'the occult' with its obvious European and Christian referents (cf. Comaroff and Comaroff 1999). The notion of esoteric sciences also points to a political economy of knowledge (Lambek 1993), that is, the divide between those select persons who know and use these sciences, usually men, and those men and women who make appeals to the knowledgeable ones. Whether we call the latter clients, supplicants or lay persons, they usually remain only partially, if at all, informed about the contents and workings of such sciences. In contrast with other anthropological studies, which tend to treat such esoteric knowledge and practices in West Africa as empty or contentless forms manipulated by actors for gain[2] or tend to spectacularise them as alternative forms of knowledge,[3] I will

---

D. Shortly thereafter...
    Paco: If I am not mistaken, the house of the *marabout* should be here.
E. '*Marabout*': Sir, what is the objective of your visit?
    Paco: The legislative elections are soon, and I want to be elected.
F. *Marabout*: No problem, Sir, but ...
G. *Marabout*: ... You should first make a payment of one million and a black cow for your sacrifice.
H. Paco: Good, I will give you half of what you ask for. I will bring the rest in two days.

Cartoon in *L'Independant*, Bamako, 13 February 1997   Used with permission

focus on the sociology of their knowledge, transmission and use and consider some of their broader social effects. I want to note that I do not discuss the contents of such sciences except in rather general terms. This is largely for ethical reasons since some of my informants explicitly asked that I not reveal the contents of the secrets that they discussed with me.

In a very important sense, all the esoteric sciences to be discussed here are closely tied to questions of power in Muslim West Africa. As I have argued, many see power in all its forms – spiritual, social, political and economic – as related to the possession of secrets, whether secret knowledge or secret object(s). In this conception of power as resource or power as potential, such presumed secrets not only index power, they are the very condition of power. That is, they assure, even guarantee, this power. If it is not possible to assert that such ideas about the close link between power and secrets are universally held, one can say that they are indeed ubiquitous in Mali. In fact, Muslims and non-Muslims regularly articulated such ideas about secrets and power to me during my fieldwork. In this context, one of the certainties in a world characterised by considerable uncertainty is that there are many secrets. Moreover, in this way of thinking, it is an incontrovertible fact that people have differential access to such secrets.

Although my main objective here is to explore the secrets that West African Muslims associate with Islam, its revealed texts and religious figures, I also want to emphasise the importance of the notion of secrets for non-Muslims. From the perspective of many of my informants, non-Muslim rule – in Africa or elsewhere – is tied to the possession of secrets. During my fieldwork, people talked often about the presumed secrets of other non-Muslim Malians. When they did so, they frequently referred to the knowledge of the Bambara or *bamanaya*, which includes various knowledge and practices for the fashioning and use of 'power objects' (*boli* or *basi*), forms of sacrifice, medicines and other medico-religious knowledge. Malian Muslims also pointed to the knowledge and practices of other non-Muslims in Mali, such as that of the Fulbe, though much less so than *bamanaya*.[4] Non-Muslim ritual specialists (*doma* or *soma* in Bambara or *wileebe* in Fulfulde) employ *bamanaya* or other forms of knowledge for a variety of purposes such as divination, protection, healing, accumulation, and so forth. In many cases, such knowledge and practices are thought to be illicit. This is because they are deemed either specifically un-Islamic – that is, in contravention of specific tenets of Islam – or, at the very least, irreconcilable with Islam. Moreover, since such knowledge and practices are within the realm of the activities of non-Muslims – that is, those who have not embraced Islam and are not Christians – they are reprehensible.

Malian Muslims sometimes condemn those who use such knowledge and practices with engaging in activities that fall within the realm of 'sorcery' or *sihr* in Arabic. Since the canonical texts of Islam unequivocally condemn 'sorcery' as unlawful, such practices are particularly blamable. During my fieldwork, Malian Muslims often pointed to various kinds of reprehensible and unlawful 'Bambara' – read non-Muslim – practices that they associate with sorcery. For example, people often spoke about the 'Bambara' techniques of tying knots in pieces of string that some employ for a variety of ends. As some of my informants noted, one even finds unequivocal condemnation of this specific form of 'sorcery' in the Quran. Indeed, in one of the *suras* of the Quran, 'sorceresses who blow incantations over knots' are deemed to be 'evil' (Quran: cxiii, 4).[5] It seems likely that the model for such forbidden practices – that is, the work of non-Muslim ritual specialists and, specifically, those that are un-Islamic in nature – found inspiration in the Quran and other Islamic texts. Although the techniques of tying knots are 'Bambara', as many of my informants noted, this is also a realm of practice that women – 'sorceresses' in the gendered language of the Quran – often use. I will return to the subject of women's knowledge and practices later in this chapter.

Malian Muslims also frequently charge those who employ *bamanaya* with worshipping things other than God. Here, they usually point to the making of 'power objects' and the blood sacrifices made in relation to such 'objects' and/or various beings other than God. They claim that such people are guilty of what is called 'association' or polytheism (Ar., *shirk*), that is, associating other things such as power objects with God. In this way of thinking, such people treat their practices – communicating and interacting with various power objects and/or other beings – as a religion (Ar., *din*). As my informants explained, such un-Islamic practices could never be the true religion, which is Islam. Moreover, Muslim scholars were quick to point out that they know from various *hadith* collections that polytheism – of which such 'Bambara' practices are a perfect example – is the greatest of sins (see Wensinck 1927).

Most in Nioro spoke about such knowledge and objects with considerable derision, invoked, it seems, to distance themselves from those whose practices they deem un-Islamic.[6] Indeed, they regularly call the use of such knowledge and practices as the work of 'unbelievers', 'idolaters' and charlatans. The scorn for such real and imagined people, knowledge and objects does not eliminate the possibility of fear of them. On the contrary, there is constant speculation on the part of Muslims about such secrets and their possibly effective uses, particularly for nefarious ends.

Despite having a repertoire of their own objects and secrets, it has not been uncommon for non-Muslim West Africans to use some of the signs and objects of Islam in the past as well as in the present.[7] For example, some of the practices of non-Muslim Bambara healers and diviners, including divination, blessings and alms-giving, are actually quite similar in form to those of Muslim religious specialists. Indeed, such practices of specifically un-Islamic knowledge or *bamanaya* often seem to have involved the incorporation or appropriation of some of the signs of Islam, such as techniques of writing, the use of amulets, the use of Arabic language in ritual speech, and so forth. However, non-Muslim Bambara ritual specialists explained to me how they would never be able to pray as Muslims and still employ their knowledge and practices. Islam and *bamanaya*, they empha-sised, were necessarily incompatible (cf. Lambek 1993). This is not to exclude the possibility of collaboration between non-Muslim healers and diviners and certain Muslim religious leaders. On the contrary, there is much speculation about their presumed collaboration in efforts to rid places of evil spirits or for purposes of healing.

In the present, Muslims in Nioro (and elsewhere in Mali) sometimes use the medicines and therapies of non-Muslim healers (Bamb., *doma* or *soma*) that they sometimes find to be efficacious.[8] When asked about the use of such medicines, Muslims are quick to note that the use of such 'traditional' medicine is really no different from the use of Western biomedicine that is also made by non-Muslims. As long as illicit ingredients and practices do not taint such medicines, their use is permitted. In a sense, such 'traditional' medicines are only licit for these Muslims because they have been de-sacralised – at least from their perspective. Be that as it may, the knowledge of the preparation and proper use of such 'traditional' medicines is generally only through initiatic chains of transmission analogous to those associated with the Islamic esoteric sciences.

SECRETS, ISLAMIC OR OTHERWISE

If the notion that the possession of secrets was a condition of Muslim and non-Muslim rule prior to the colonial period (see Chapter 1), this was no less the case in the colonial and postcolonial periods. When people in Nioro discuss the colonial period, there is considerable speculation that the French too possessed some secret(s) that allowed for conquest and rule. What this might have been in content, people were unable or unwilling to articulate. But faced with the French and the political power they yielded, West Africans were not defenceless. Many point out that some living under colonial rule were on occasion able to employ their own secrets effectively against the French. A frequently told story in Nioro is that al-Akhdar's detention in 1906 led to the French being cursed which directly resulted in the flooding of Kayes, the capital of colonial Soudan where he was detained. There was, indeed, a major flood in Kayes in August 1906, that is, shortly after al-Akhdar's detention in the town.[9]

Other dramatic examples of the use of such secrets that I heard about during the course of my fieldwork centre around Shaykh Hamallah. Several of Hamallah's followers told me that decolonisation came as the direct, though not immediate, result of the curses that had been placed on the

French after the brutal treatment of their leader and his followers. The expectation, or at least hope, that such curses will continue to be employed or to work is very much alive today. One day I met a man on the street in Nioro who sneered that some time in the future all Europeans[10] (myself included) would be servants of Hamallah's family, ostensibly as retribution for past actions against them. Similarly, people point to misfortune – sudden illness and death, lack of progeny – afflicting some of Hamallah's African Muslim enemies. Although for many people there is considerable ambiguity as to whether such misfortune occurred directly as the result of curses or as the result of some sort of divine recompense, this is perhaps beside the point. On numerous occasions in Nioro, I heard people articulate the view that to be against a saint, let alone to harm a saint, was basically to be against God. Most people acknowledge the power to curse, and the knowledge of such curses and their proper employment are necessarily secret in nature. However, the efficacy of such curses ultimately depends on the will of God.

The interface between Europeans and Muslims, even during the colonial era, across the terrain of the esoteric sciences was not always necessarily adversarial. The story in Chapter 4 of the colonial-era exchange of petition-ary prayers for an administrative favour (burial within the military garrison in the town) between Madi Assa Kaba Jakhite, the imam and one of Nioro's most prominent religious leaders, and the French colonial administrator suggests otherwise. In fact, such a story may provide a precursor to, even a model for, understanding the present. There is the widespread suspicion that North Americans and Europeans have secrets that allow for their great wealth, reputedly efficient medicines and technology. At the same time, many Malians (and other West Africans) assert that they know for a fact that Euro-American political leaders seek out Muslim religious specialists for their knowledge to help them in their quests for power and/or its retention, not to mention their pursuit of other this-worldly goals.[11] Such African Muslim views of Europeans' interest in and use of their 'secrets' have quite a long history. In the nineteenth century, Raffenel, the French traveller who visited parts of present-day Mali, reported that his informants mentioned Europeans consulting Muslim religious leaders (see Raffenel 1856). A century later, the informants of Horace Miner, the American anthropologist who conducted fieldwork in Timbuktu, said very much the same thing (see Miner 1953).

As far as national politics in Mali are concerned, there is much discussion about the secret sources of past presidents' political power. For example, there is much talk about the supposed nature of President Modibo Keita's secret to holding power. Like the defeated rival of Sunjata, the mythical ruler of the Malian empire, Modibo Keita's 'secret' is represented almost invariably as sinister and evil – in short, un-Islamic. People claim that this secret became public knowledge with his loss of power. In fact, the notion of a secret revealed as an index of the loss of power is a recurrent motif in discussions of political power. Given the link between power and secrets and the obvious precariousness of even the most powerful of persons, those who seek power wish to have secrets or, at the very least, knowledgeable ones willing to transmit or employ a secret on their behalf. It is thus not surprising that there is speculation about those seeking power and their interactions with those said to possess secrets, Islamic or otherwise.

The notion that power is contingent upon secret(s) is not merely limited to wielders of political power. Indeed, wealth, good health, success or prosperity, as well as popularity among one's peers or cohort, are often said to be linked to the possession of secrets. It is this broader notion of secrets that permeates more fully the social landscape that I want to illustrate with a few examples. The first concerns what seemed to me was the nearly endless speculation about 'the secret' that a lorry driver in town was said to possess. For years, this man had been the main driver for one of the town's most prosperous merchants, who imported a large volume of basic consumer goods into the town. Driving on roads from Bamako and Kayes that had seriously deteriorated over the past two decades, the driver not only had a reputation for speedy transit, but also for safety. He was consistently success-ful in avoiding the all too commonplace accidents that are the inevitable consequences of poor road conditions. From my perspective, the abundant resources of the merchant and lorry owner permitted the regular purchase of new vehicles, as well as their proper upkeep and maintenance. My friends told me these were, of course, factors, but they were not sufficient to account for the man's outstanding record. Many people asserted that the driver – known incidentally for his regular performance of the ritual daily prayers as a Muslim – had to have some sort of powerful 'secret' and an explicitly Islamic one that allowed for his exemplary record and skilful work.

The next example is from the micro-sociological level where some are said to have a secret that allows them to manipulate others. It is worth noting that people frequently warned me to be wary of such people. One civil servant, descended on his mother's side from one of the most prominent lineages of religious specialists in the broader region, was notorious for his outstanding debts. It was widely discussed how he continued to receive money from a range of people in the town because he 'had a secret' that compelled people to give him money, even against their will. While some – in this setting and elsewhere – might consider this as some sort of extortion, here a 'secret' is the condition of the possibility of obtaining money from others.

Although there is sometimes ambiguity as to whether such secrets are Islamic, the next example is one in which a Muslim wields secrets he explicitly characterises as non-Islamic. Near the end of my stay in Nioro, I learned that a man in his thirties, whom I had known for some time, was believed to possess a wide range of secrets. When I asked him about this, he said it was true. In fact, it was not something that he sought to conceal, even if he wished. He was a member of a lineage known for such knowledge (and about which I had heard countless stories and legends), and he had the distinctive patronym that members of this lineage often have. He explained that his secrets were all non-Islamic secrets obtained from his father and ultimately from their lineage. He eventually told me that he possessed secrets, all of which he expressed as abilities to do things, including the following: the ability to control domestic animals, to prevail over a rival suitor, to enable someone to become a village chief, and even a secret to kill people. By his own admission, his ability to act was fairly well circumscribed in that it was limited to the local area. Indeed, he readily admitted that he could not help those with, say, supralocal political aspirations.

It is interesting to note that although most, if not all, people consider these secrets non-Islamic, though not necessarily un-Islamic, those who possess them do consider themselves Muslims.[12] At the same time, they also see their activities as Muslims constrained in important ways precisely because the secrets are non-Islamic, that is, outside the realm of Islam. The man explained that after employing his secrets he was unable to perform the obligatory ritual daily prayers for extended periods of time.[13] To do so would be harmful to himself, he emphasised, and it would possibly even threaten his ability to use his secrets in the future.[14]

What these secrets consisted of, he explained, were words or incantations that are muttered, the exact content of which he would not reveal to me. This process of muttering incantations usually involves some gentle spitting and is called *tutu* in Fulfulde/Pulaar (his first language), a word that is onomatopoeic since people say it is close to the sound made when spitting. This term *tutu* is used to refer to a certain kind of non-Islamic secrets, which by conventional anthropological definitions would be magic and/or sorcery. He explained that his secrets do not include any 'medicine'[15] derived from plants or other substances. Nor, he noted, did they involve the 'Bambara' technique of tying knots in string. In their use, his secrets are clearly reminiscent – even mimetic – of Islamic *ruqan* (Ar., 'charms' or medicine) that can include the expectorant accompanying the recitation of passages from the Quran or prayers. For some Muslim scholars, such 'charms' clearly fall within the realm of practices Muslims should renounce. For example, the noted North African Muslim scholar al-Maghili (d. 1504), who visited neighbouring areas of West Africa, specifically condemned such practices in some of his writings that have been very influential in this region.[16] However, other scholars whose credentials are no less impeccable have not condemned such practices. In fact, Ibn Abi Zayd al-Qayrawani's *Risala*, one of the standard Maliki legal texts used in the region, points to the

actual licitness of such practices.[17] Herein lies perhaps a partial explanation
of the considerable ambiguity surrounding the practices of my friend and his
lineage and why many consider such practices outside the realm of Islam,
possibly even un-Islamic, and therefore probably best renounced.

Over the course of my fieldwork, I heard a range of people voice vague
apprehensions about this lineage and its abilities. Once this particular man
spoke at length about his secrets, I was able to use such information to ask a
wider range of people about this lineage. What I heard were numerous,
often lengthy, narratives attesting to the powers and abilities of this lineage
from the colonial period to the recent past. Almost invariably such
narratives contained specific examples of misfortune or revenge that served
as warning that one should never offend or cross these people. I learned in
several stories how members of this lineage had employed their secrets
defensively, much like the stories of Hamallah's followers using curses
against his African and French enemies. I heard the following story from a
local civil servant, now retired, who served many years in the town . He told
me that in the 1960s a high-ranking civil servant from elsewhere in Mali was
posted to Nioro, and he had a confrontation with D., a member of this
lineage. At one point, the civil servant struck D., who immediately warned
the former that he would regret his actions. Despite pleas to D. and to
members of his lineage from other civil servants and even an apology, the
civil servant was soon accused of embezzling public funds. He committed
suicide, he explained in a letter, in order to save his honour. After his death,
people learned that in fact no funds had been missing. There was little
doubt for most people, civil servants included, that the charges and,
ultimately, the man's death were the result of the deployment of this
lineage's astonishing secrets.

Although there are certainly parallels in usage between secrets deemed
Islamic and non-Islamic, as this example of postcolonial revenge suggests,
the differences are perhaps equally, if not more, important. Because the
secrets of the lineage of my friend and D. are non-written, they are in a sense
what we might consider the structural opposites of the secrets of the Muslim
religious specialists with whom they sometimes share villages. With their
reputations as noted scholars of the Quran, the Muslim religious specialists
also have their own secrets, but ones that are text-linked, related as they are
to the Quran and, ultimately, to the *umm al-kitab* (Ar.), the original text of
the Quran from which the revelation came. An important part of their
toolkit of secrets, so to speak, stems from the ability of members of their
lineage to memorise the Quran quickly and at an early age. Indeed, there is
a group of lineages with a regional reputation as *hafiz* (Ar., memoriser), that
is, those who have committed the text of the Quran to memory, who share
villages with my friend's lineage. Given that rapid and early memorisation of
the Quran is no small feat, for many people it necessarily follows that the

ability to do so entails a secret. In what might seem to be a tautology (at least from an outsider's vantage point), it follows that once one has memorised the Quran, one also has access to a whole host of secrets.

I suspect that the members of the lineage who possess these allegedly non-Islamic secrets and their Muslim religious specialist neighbours at some time in the past engaged in occupational specialisations that related in some way to differential access to Islamic knowledge. To equate this with merely different levels of Islamisation would be misleading in that it merely adopts the language of 'reformist' Muslims (not to mention Orientalists), who seek to 'purify' the practice of Islam from such non-Islamic accretions. Instead, the existence of these different groups, each with its own secrets – Islamic and otherwise – points to different ways of being Muslim, not only in the past, but also in the present. After all, the lineage with this self-styled non-Islamic knowledge insists that it is Muslim, though the way that it acts Muslim is in some respects different from that of the religious specialists. This is most obvious in the restrictions on the adherence to ritual norms that people claim are obligatory for all Muslims. There are several other lineages from the broader region, also known as Muslims, but also not Muslim religious specialists, who retain their own sources of non-Islamic secrets and power. Although people report that some of these groups had to give up some of their more contemptible secrets – particularly the ability to trans-mogrify – either when they became Muslims or when they joined the *jihad* of Umar Tall, they continue to instill fear among other groups with whom they interact. During the colonial period, administrators sometimes identified specific feared groups and the villages where they lived in the Nioro region, and, decades later, these were some of the same groups and villages my informants and friends also named.[18]

TRANSMISSION

While I have pointed to the structural similarities between non-Islamic and Islamic secrets, I focus in this section more closely on the Islamic, excluding all of those things generally deemed non-Islamic by most people in Nioro, such as *tutu* and other practices, including forms of divination, considered non-Islamic,[19] even though some of those who seek out their use might consider them Islamic.

It is clear that all students, both male and female, who engage in Islamic education at any level are exposed to things that we could call the Islamic esoteric sciences. Since the Quran is seen as a divinely revealed text, it follows that the text necessarily has special properties. Almost every Quranic school student would probably come to appreciate this from the first day of class. One teacher I know explained to me how he wrote a passage from the Quran with the local ink made of a mixture of charcoal and gum Arabic on the palm of the right hand of every new student who came to his school. He instructed the student to ingest the text by licking it off his or her hand. This teacher noted that the particular passage written in ink helped to ensure that the student was able to learn. But even though every person who attends Quranic school would be exposed to such practices, those who actually develop what we might call expertise in the esoteric sciences are perhaps very limited in number. Since girls have usually ended their studies at the point at which they have learned enough of the Quran – usually a few short *suras* – sufficient for them to perform the ritual daily prayers, their ability to develop expertise was much more restricted than boys, who generally studied for much longer periods of time. However, as we will see, not even all male students pursuing advanced Islamic studies will be interested in or able to develop expertise in the esoteric sciences.

Many people point out that esoteric knowledge or secrets must be closely guarded and only transmitted to the appropriate people and at the appropriate times. This is in part because of the prevailing notion that such knowledge is potentially very volatile in nature. While conducting my research, I heard countless narratives about the dangers associated with gaining access to esoteric knowledge with the most recurring motif of a young man or boy who goes crazy while in pursuit or in possession of such knowledge. My friends and informants regularly identified some of these people to me, including some who seem to suffer from permanent affliction. The most prominent of these was a middle-aged man whom I saw nearly every day wandering the streets in the town centre, seemingly oblivious to the many people around him. Although I never heard the man speak, he would sometimes scrawl large symbols in thick black ink on the fronts of buildings, including storefronts, in areas near the market. Everyone I asked told me the symbols, which were vaguely reminiscent of Arabic letters, were nonsensical, at least to them (as they were to me). However, several people told me that these symbols were vestiges of the secret, but dangerous, written knowledge he had tried to use before he had been reduced to a state of madness.

Although the transmission of knowledge of the esoteric sciences is generally from person to person – from father to son, teacher to student, student to student, and, occasionally, from student to teacher – the actual means of transmission can vary considerably. Such knowledge can be shared or given freely, but perhaps it is more frequently exchanged. For instance, a student may work for a couple of years for a teacher, doing manual labour, agricultural work or errands. At the end of a period of time, the teacher may reveal a particular secret of the teacher's choice to the student. In such a case, the secret serves as a reward, to use the language of those who explained such transmission to me.

In some situations, a person might trade his secret for another person's secret, in what people suggest is some sort of equal exchange in which no labour or capital is exchanged. In other cases, a student may learn that a certain teacher possesses a specific secret that effects particular desired results, and the student may be able to receive the secret directly and without delay by exchanging money for it.[20] A friend also told me that certain secrets at the time of my fieldwork fetched as much as the equivalent of $1,000 in local currency,[21] a vast amount of money for most people. During my fieldwork, the oldest living man in the town, who had served as a soldier in Europe during the First World War, told me that for many years he had been curious about secrets, but that his limited Islamic religious education and restricted knowledge of Arabic presented serious obstacles to their acquisition. As a civil servant with a regular income, he was, however, able to hire a Muslim scholar to whom he paid a rather large sum of money in exchange for a very detailed explanation of a form of Islamic divination, geomancy.[22] The man showed me the many notebooks in which he had painstakingly translated the oral instructions into French from Soninke (his own first language) and, ostensibly, from Arabic by the scholar, creating a French-language geomancy manual which, he assured me, he never actually used.

A more important, though certainly less commonplace, mode of transmission is what some consider the divine channel of transmission. It is widely held that some people receive secrets or knowledge directly from God, and this mode of transmission is privileged above all others. These are the 'gifts of God' that people refer to when they speak of the special qualities, abilities and even resources that exceptional Muslim religious leaders possess. Only those believed to be truly extraordinary – Muslim saints – would receive such secrets. It follows that the engagement of members of saintly lineages with the esoteric sciences is quite distinctive as far as transmission is concerned. People seen as recipients of the 'gifts of God' frequently find that others offer esoteric knowledge to them. The motives for such transmission might be very complex – a pious act, an attempt to ingratiate oneself with a supposed saint, or perhaps the hope of exchanging such a secret for others of greater value. In general, a person seeking guidance from a *shaykh* gives – or at least is expected to give – whatever knowledge he might have of the esoteric sciences to his guide higher up in the spiritual hierarchy. In return, the guide *might* give some knowledge to the aspirant, for example, a certain secret litany of prayers for recitation. The guide might also choose to give nothing in return, which would of course be his prerogative given the hierarchical organisation of religious practice.

As suggested in the discussion of al-Akhdar in Chapter 3, once people began to take Hamallah as their leader, they started to share certain intimate knowledge with him. The esoteric knowledge that Hamallah received from the Muslim scholarly elite included text-based knowledge, some of which became part of his library that the French confiscated after his exile.[23] This brings us back to an important issue concerning those religious leaders, whom people think have access to God's favour. People not only see such religious leaders as higher up on the spiritual chain, but also assume that they know more things of a secret nature. For this reason, people frequently want to associate with them. In any case, this pattern in which people give, or are thought to give, secrets to those higher up on the spiritual chain is repeated in a myriad of ways and settings across the social landscape.

Those eager to move up in the spiritual hierarchy or even to secure a firmer position might employ a number of strategies involving the transmission of such knowledge to facilitate their mobility and position. On one occasion, I was with a man with considerable formal Islamic education whose aspirations to the role of Muslim religious leader had been thwarted in no small part by his origins as a member of a hereditary lineage ('caste') of blacksmiths. When we met, he was practising this profession with some financial success, though he continued to be actively involved in the use of the esoteric sciences. During the course of my fieldwork, this blacksmith obtained a copy of a 'secret', an Islamic text in Arabic from a friend, who, in turn, received the text from an aspirant visiting from Guinea. Showing the text to a man in his early twenties who is a member of one of the region's most prominent lineages of religious specialists, the blacksmith seemed to want to use the text as a way to gain access to this person and his resources, material and spiritual, that is, the kind thought to be of divine provenance, though in this case they had also been transmitted hereditarily. Although the young man seemed unimpressed by the text, the blacksmith was successful in getting the young man to commission several pieces of silver jewellery from him. While clearly in the material interest of the blacksmith, the act of working – even for financial gain – for a member of a saintly lineage is at the same time also considered pious behaviour. In fact, there is usually the hope of receiving divine recompense in doing such work (see Chapter 6).

All of this points to the operation of a certain kind of hegemony associated with the Islamic esoteric sciences. Some of my friends with little in the way of formal Islamic education speculated continually about the transmission of such secrets between some of the more prominent religious leaders. Other friends, generally sceptical about the effectiveness, though not the existence, of such secrets, suggested that such speculation helped in no small way to sustain the mystique of the activities of religious leaders. One friend even went so far as to tell me that all of their religious leaders necessarily tricked them. He explained that the religious leaders almost had to bluff since people expected them to be able to accomplish so much via the esoteric sciences, when, in fact, their abilities were much more limited than they were willing or able to admit.

THE USE OF THE SCIENCES

While the Islamic esoteric sciences may be employed in a variety of different ways, many people suggest that they are most often directed toward the attainment of God's favour, which is tied to a range of related ideas such as the gifts of God. Those things such as wealth, good health, power, progeny, good fortune and social prestige that people might want or wish for index God's favour. Many people seek out specialists in the esoteric sciences to ensure such things, but perhaps as often they seek protection from bad or evil things and circumstances, or merely to forestall them. Thus, people seek to employ the esoteric sciences against potential enemies, evil spirits, illness, 'witchcraft' and 'sorcery', among other things.

Although the esoteric sciences are frequently employed for good, I have emphasised how they can also be used for curses or praying against someone. As elsewhere in the Muslim world, there is considerable fear of the power of the Muslim *shaykh*'s curse (Hunwick 1996). It clearly depends on one's perspective as to whether such abilities are good or evil. The curses said to have been directed against the French during colonial rule are examples of what many consider to be socially appropriate uses of curses. But there are other destructive uses which, from some perspectives, are more anti-social – though not necessarily 'sorcery' – and, therefore, condemned as un-Islamic. Examples of destructive uses I heard about included the sciences deployed to defeat or even to kill a rival in a bid for power and/or prestige. In many such cases, there is considerable ambiguity whether the bounds of acceptable behaviour have been overstepped. When socially inappropriate actions are suspected, I have heard some people talk about what they call *batuta*, various kinds of illicit practices they think are indistinguishable from sorcery. Some people told me about and showed me written texts of *batuta*. They explained, however, that they did not use them since they understood them to be un-Islamic.

I want to illustrate some of the uses of the esoteric sciences with the first example taken from the colonial era. In the colonial archives in Nioro[24] and in private collections, I have come across a number of letters that can be considered malevolent uses of the esoteric sciences, at least from the perspective of those to whom the letters were addressed. The French colonial administration ostensibly intercepted the letters, all of which are in Arabic and anonymous. One particular letter posted to Nioro through the colonial mail service seems to have been addressed to Shaykh Hamallah. Written repeatedly on a sheet of paper was the word 'death' (in Arabic), interspersed with the names of prominent religious leaders from the broader region from the first half of the twentieth century. One friend literate in Arabic to whom I showed this particular letter was visibly upset, as the malevolent intentions – the death of the *shaykh*, who was in fact his own *shaykh* – were all too clear to anyone who could read the letter. It seems that this kind of letter, which makes use of the esoteric sciences, is clearly just one of the tools that some may have employed in struggles and rivalries for power and authority.

The next is a much more recent example of uses that, again, some take to be malevolent. Some time after a new Islamic educational institution or *madrasa* opened in Nioro and had been operating, its locally born teacher died.[25] The contemporary Muslim establishment in Nioro had openly opposed this school, organised and run by Muslims with 'reformist' ideas. At some point before his death, the teacher is reported to have found on his property a dead sheep wrapped in a shroud – the white cloth with which a Muslim's corpse is always covered before burial here. It was obvious to all that this was a nefarious gesture on the part of someone or some people. The teacher's sudden death shortly after the discovery of the dead shrouded sheep was widely taken to be the result of actions – of which the dead sheep may have been only one sign – of unidentified Muslims who worked within the realm of secrets of an Islamic nature or possibly even secrets that were un-Islamic.[26]

It is precisely the possibility that one might encounter the kinds of malevolence suggested in these examples that many people seek out those who can deploy the Islamic esoteric sciences on their behalf. People obtain amulets – here often called *hijab*, from the Arabic root meaning to conceal or hide[27] – for protection for themselves, for kin and/or for associates, not to mention animals.[28] One of my friends had such an amulet – a folded piece of white paper – that he kept suspended above the entrance to his retail shop in the market.[29] Although the amulet was not concealed, it was certainly not in plain sight. This amulet contained what he knew to be an Islamic text of some sort that his father, a noted Muslim scholar in the town, had given him when he first opened the shop. Since he had never looked inside, he could not tell me exactly what it contained. He was unenthusiastic, to say the least, about letting me look inside, and I never insisted on doing so. My friend's amulet is fairly typical, if one can say such a thing. Many, if not most, shops in the town contain such amulets, the purpose of which is to protect from misfortune, and, perhaps as equally as often, to attract clients. In many such cases, the contents of the amulet are obscure to the owner. In most cases, people ordinarily have these amulets covered, usually in leather though sometimes in metal, so that they are protected and more likely to last (see Figure 5.2).

Other means of protection work in similar ways. Another friend, a young Bidan from Mauritania who traced his descent from the Prophet Muhammad, also ran a retail shop in the town. Every day at closing, he engaged in what was a protective act drawing from the esoteric sciences. After shutting and locking the doors to his shop, he traced with the index finger of his right hand on each of the doors a shape – what seemed to me an

5.2 Man wearing amulets encased in leather, Nioro   *Photographer:* John Harrelson

Arabic letter and possibly even the same Arabic letter (with a mystical meaning and/or numerical value) that was on a silver ring he wore on his hand. He seemed to bless his shop with his hand in the same kind of way that he might give blessings to people who wish to be touched by him as a descendant of the Prophet. It would be obvious to anyone who watched him that this was a *hijab* and maybe even a blessing, though I doubt his act had much in the way of a performative effect. He seemed to want it to be unseen and was quite annoyed to learn that I watched him. After seeing him do this countless times and after some not too insistent questioning, he told me that he refused to discuss these things of a secret nature with me. This protective act – which he did eventually concede was a *hijab* – was for him protection in an environment of considerable risk (and not just financial risk) as a Mauritanian shopkeeper. In the summer of 1992, retail shops owned (and thought to be owned) by Mauritanians had come under attack as retribution for an attack in a neighbouring village by some thought to be involved in the Tuareg/Arab uprising east of Nioro.[30] After the attacks on shops in 1992, some Mauritanians had abandoned the town for good, and some of those who stayed behind were treated, if not with disdain, then at least with distrust by some residents in the town.[31] Cognisant of the fact that his status as a descendant of the Prophet did not ensure the safety of his shop – though perhaps aware that it did guarantee his own physical safety in the town – the young shopkeeper remained vigilant. He undoubtedly used this particular *hijab* with such ends in mind.

In the period when there were organised demonstrations against the rule of President Moussa Traoré in Mali in 1991, the rumour circulated that one of Traoré's Muslim religious advisors – *marabouts* in the language of the press – had told him that his successor would be from the Tall family, that is, a descendant of Umar Tall.[32] There was the implication that the Muslim religious leader was able, ostensibly via the esoteric sciences, to determine where the threat to his power would come. Within such public discourse, the form in which this knowledge was received – whether in a vision or some sort of divination – is pretty much irrelevant. The content, however, was of utmost importance. It was assumed that the President, taking such words as the truth, would counter such a possible threat. Mountaga Tall, a lawyer from the Ségou branch of the Tall family and also an active figure in the political opposition, left the country clandestinely for fear of arrest.[33]

Although I have considered some of the real and imagined uses of these sciences in somewhat general terms, I want to turn to the issue of content and to ask whether the content and form of the esoteric sciences are relevant. On the one hand, it seems that content is extremely important if one considers the complexity and diversity of the sciences, though perhaps more for the practitioners than for supplicants. Thus, the use of the Islamic esoteric sciences to produce desired results might entail a special litany of prayers, which one recites in an appropriate manner at a designated time, or a particular technique of mystical retreat or other spiritual exercises. A person might consult a practitioner to make a prediction about unforeseen events, as the example about President Traoré seems to suggest. Or, a person may ask someone to use divination to reveal why a particular problem cannot be solved and the possible actions, such as ritual sacrifice, that might help. In yet other cases, texts can be prepared that are erased for drinking or washing that serve a particular purpose such as healing or good fortune. In such cases, a practitioner might have an array of sciences from which to choose, just as the client might also solicit more than one person presumed to have such knowledge. The knowledge and use of such things is very important for the practitioners and those seeking to learn more about them. Form, on the other hand, seems to be more important at least for the supplicants. While ordinary supplicants are generally aware of the various forms, such as prayers, divination, amulets, and so forth, and sometimes have preferences for one or another of these, most of the supplicants have limited knowledge about the content of the forms and the various techniques employed by practitioners. In the end, the status and reputation of the practitioner are of utmost importance. Thus, many are more likely to want to solicit the person with a saintly reputation regardless of the form that person's esoteric practices might actually take.

WOMEN'S KNOWLEDGE

The organisation of religious practice has certainly shaped women's practices in areas related to the Islamic esoteric sciences. Although women are not generally known for their knowledge of the Islamic esoteric sciences, they do regularly seek out practitioners of the Islamic esoteric sciences and other kinds of secret knowledge, including some women are known to possess. Many Malians readily assert that women make up the main clientele for practitioners of the Islamic esoteric sciences. Since girls and women do not proceed very far in Islamic education, it follows that their involvement in the Islamic esoteric sciences, especially as practitioners, is considerably more constrained than that of men. However, some Muslim women do, in fact, have and employ certain kinds of knowledge and practices that they characterise as secret and sometimes as explicitly Islamic. I should note that the gender segregation of the society and the gendered nature of some of this knowledge made it rather difficult for me to learn about women's involvement in knowledge and practices of a secret nature. Thus, what follows is necessarily partial.

Many men in Nioro were quick to note that Muslim women's secrets were not as licit as some of their own secrets, which they claimed were tied directly to Islam and its correct interpretation. They argued that because women have much less knowledge of Islam and its central text, the Quran, than men, their practices were necessarily more questionable, possibly even unlawful. Over the course of my fieldwork, I learned about some women's use of secrets in various realms, particularly in areas related to marriage, though also in other areas such as healing. As most of my informants noted, such practices were clearly different and separate from those of spirit possession whose practitioners, most of whom are women, also make claims to have secret knowledge (see Chapter 7).

Women who faced a particular problem might seek out a range of different people for assistance in resolving the problem, dependent upon the nature of the problem, personal circumstances, social networks, and so forth. While women quite often asked men for assistance via the Islamic esoteric sciences, they sometimes sought out certain kinds of women's secret knowledge and women specialists. In many cases, women claimed their knowledge and practices were grounded in Islam and, therefore, perfectly licit. However, in other cases, there was considerable ambiguity about the licitness of such practices in relation to Islam. For instance, one woman – the daughter of a well-known Muslim cleric – I know used a range of means, such as amulets, prayers and 'medicines', to try to end her marriage. It was common knowledge that she had disliked her husband ever since they had married when they were both teenagers. Over a number of years, she sought out various means, including the esoteric sciences, to end the marriage. Even some of her close male relatives employed various Islamic esoteric practices on her behalf. Frustrated that none of the measures employed seemed to work, she sought something to make her husband impotent so that at least she would not have to have sexual relations with him. Somehow she learned of a toxic substance that she subsequently acquired and mixed into the vessel her husband regularly used to wash himself. When her husband noticed the water in the vessel was unusually dark in colour, he did not use the water. However, he realised her intention to harm him through means that may have been a kind of 'sorcery' and, therefore, possibly un-Islamic. After this incident when the women employed presumably illicit practices, the woman's close relatives worried that she was so desperate to be divorced that she might go mad. Some of them openly supported a divorce, and, indeed, the women and her husband were divorced several months after the incident.

I learned from some other women that if a woman is worried that her husband might divorce her or leave her for another women, there are a variety of 'secret' practices she might use. One particular practice I heard about involved going to an anthill under the cover of night. The woman would remove the string of beads always worn around the waist under her clothing and place it into the opening of the anthill. After making an offering of some grain to the ants, she must leave the beads there for a set period of time. Once this had been accomplished, the woman's husband would not leave her. When I asked why women would do this, one woman, the daughter of a village imam, explained matter-of-factly that they think it is because Suleyman (the Biblical Solomon) could talk to the ants. Although this woman had begun to study the Quran as a child, she, like other girls, stopped her studies after just a few years. However, people here, including girls and young women, often learn about various stories in the Quran from others in the community. In fact, stories about Suleyman are among the most frequently discussed of such stories. In several places in the Quran, there is discussion of Suleyman having extraordinary powers, including control over *jinn* or spirits he was even able to command to do things for him. Many Muslims here say that certain 'secrets' available today, including various techniques for getting spiritual entities to work on one's behalf, have come originally from Suleyman. It was also common knowledge among my informants – learned in Arabic and the Quran or not – that Suleyman could communicate with animals. In fact, many think that the *sura* of the Quran, *al-Naml*, literally 'the Ants' (Quran xxvii), in which there is a passage about Suleyman, 'the Birds' and 'the Ants', means that Suleyman could communicate with all animals. It seems some Muslim women have relied upon some of these stories about Suleyman that circulate orally for 'secret' practices such as the technique of inserting their beads into the anthill. While some women told me they had tried this practice to no avail, others told me they were much more concerned that the practice, its effectiveness notwithstanding, might possibly be illicit since one had to make an offering to ants. As Muslim women, they knew it to be explicitly forbidden to make offerings to anything other than to God.

Other kinds of women's practices are perhaps even more ambiguous as far as what is considered Islamic. I have already mentioned how women sometimes use 'the Bambara' – allegedly un-Islamic – techniques of tying knots in string. When women are having problems, they sometimes ask other women to use their secret knowledge to prepare such strings for them and to explain their proper use. By wearing the string or perhaps by burying it in a specified place, one might be able to resolve a problem such as marital strife, infertility or conflict with one's neighbours or kin. Similarly, women might ask a woman diviner to look 'to see' what their problems are and how they might be resolved. Divination by cowrie shells, one of the pre-colonial forms of currency, was the kind of divination most Muslim women diviners in Nioro used. Not surprisingly, many people here denigrate this form of divination as inferior to other more authentically Islamic forms of divination (see below). Moreover, many think that cowrie shell divination is suspect, not least because of the close association here between cowrie shells and the knowledge of the Bambara. Indeed, most are aware how important cowrie shells are to non-Muslim Bambara ritual specialists. Such ritual specialists regularly wear cowrie shells attached to their clothing, and they also use cowrie shells as ingredients in the confection of un-Islamic 'power objects' and in various forms of blood sacrifice. For these reasons, persons who wear cowrie shells, even as part of jewellery, might be refused access to mosques. In any case, it is striking how many people associate women's 'secret' practices – knots in string, cowrie shell divination and alleged forms of 'sorcery' – with un-Islamic religious practice. The fact that some women's practices seem to borrow from un-Islamic practices would almost seem to guarantee this is the case.

The general ambiguity that surrounds women's practices of a secret nature leads many women to emphasise how their practices are licit. But the ambiguity about the licitness of their practices sometimes even seems to enhance their power. Although many of my friends and informants asserted that Muslim women's practices were less 'powerful' and effective than the Islamic esoteric sciences, some people, including many men I know, expressed concern that some women's practices might be quite effective, possibly even dangerous. Moreover, many people readily acknowledge the effectiveness of some women's knowledge particularly in the realm of 'medicine' and healing (see Chapter 7). Nevertheless, most people, including many women, judge women's 'secret' practices quite unfavourably against men's practices in the esoteric sciences. In this way, women's secret practices just simply do not have the authority and legitimacy in the wider society that men's practices do. Indeed, the example of Hamallah's wife praying on behalf of his followers – that is, standing in for the absent *shaykh* – illustrates how most people value the Islamic esoteric sciences above any specific 'secret', possibly gendered knowledge that women might have.

MINOR RELIGIOUS SPECIALISTS AS PRACTITIONERS

Most people in Nioro would assert that the Islamic esoteric sciences are within the realm of men's knowledge. I now want to consider more closely the educational and career trajectories of some of those men, religious leaders and specialists, who have studied the esoteric sciences. They are all what we might call minor religious leaders, that is, those referred to as *petits marabouts* as opposed to *grands marabouts* in local parlance. The first example is the story of four classificatory brothers – actually sons of three brothers I consider my friends. They studied the Quran and jurisprudence (Ar., *fiqh*) for many years with their 'father', who is among the most learned scholars in Nioro with a reputation extending even to the capital, Bamako. The brothers told me that while they were studying, their teacher (their 'father') never mentioned that he knew much, if anything, about the esoteric sciences. They had always been very curious – like most young people they noted – about these sciences, and they were eager to learn more about them. Over the course of their studies, they had acquired some rudimentary knowledge of things esoteric, the most basic of which, they explained to me, was to appreciate the mysteries of the Quran and how it might be used for divination and problem-solving (see also Mommersteeg 1991).

When one of the brothers travelled to a neighbouring village to continue his studies there, he learned much to his surprise that their 'father' had a reputation for being quite learned in *raml* (Ar., geomancy). Upon his return to Nioro, he informed his 'brothers', and they decided, as a group, to ask their 'father' to teach geomancy to them. He agreed to do so, though perhaps not with the same goals as they had in mind. With him, they studied one of the Egyptian scholar al-Tukhi's Arabic texts about geomancy that was published in Cairo in 1956.[34] Although they told me they had heard about other geomancy texts used in the region, this was the only one they studied. After they completed studying the text and learning the proper practice of geomancy, their father told them that it was not good to practise this science. He warned that if one used geomancy too frequently, one would always be suspicious of other people and even possibly blame them falsely for one's misfortunes.[35] The specific problem with the particular method of geomancy they studied is that it allows one to identify certain characteristics of the person responsible for specific problems, but not to identify that person by name.

None of these 'brothers' earns a living using the esoteric sciences, although all have gone on to learn other esoteric practices of an eclectic nature. For each of them, the sciences play an important, though not a central, role in his life. One earns his living primarily as a teacher of the Quran for very small children, while the second combines his advanced studies of jurisprudence with seasonal agriculture to meet household needs. Another is a merchant whose financial success (not unrelated to his biological father's reputation as a Muslim scholar) allows him to provide for most of the needs of his large extended family. He writes amulets (Ar., *hijab*) for himself and his family, as needed in times of sickness or for protection, and will occasionally make them for others when asked. Because of the reputation of their 'father', people frequently approach each of them to ask for interventions using the esoteric sciences. One of the 'brothers' told me that he tired of people in the village where he lived asking for his intervention for things ranging from help in weaning a child and the treatment of bodily ailments to success in petty trading. Despite repeated declarations of his own limited knowledge of the appropriate secrets, people continually expected him to be able to act successfully on their behalf.

None of the 'brothers' uses geomancy very often and almost never for others they told me. On one occasion, I did come across one of them practising geomancy. As soon as he saw me, he abruptly stopped and would not explain what the consultation had been about. I suspected that he wanted to check whether I, the inquisitive non-Muslim foreigner, had malevolent intentions, given what must have seemed to be endless questions about things 'secret'.

The career of another practitioner of esoteric sciences in Nioro, whom I will call G., contrasts quite sharply with these other men. As a young student, G. was never interested in memorising the Quran or in studying jurisprudence. The son of a Dyula father from the region south of Nioro and a mother of non-free status from a Fulbe group near Nioro, he first went to study with some teachers from his mother's natal village. Although he explained that he decided early on that Quranic studies were not worth his time and effort, it is entirely possible, even likely, that he was frustrated in his efforts to advance in his study of the Quran. Many Muslim religious leaders in Nioro note that people of servile status, almost without exception, never became learned, that is, in areas related to Islam and its central texts, particularly jurisprudence and other exoteric sciences.[36] G.'s own ambiguous status, as the son of a woman of non-free status, may indeed have played a role in his abbreviated Quranic studies. Be that as it may, he pointed out to me that there are many people who have memorised the Quran. In his view, knowledge of Islamic jurisprudence is so widespread that even those who have had the most rudimentary introduction to Quranic studies have managed to pick up knowledge of Islamic jurisprudence in the society.[37]

After learning some things of a secret nature from his father, G. went on to study with several teachers over a number of years. Among these teachers was a Futanke living in Nioro, who had come to the town from Senegal in the 1930s as a young man in order to be next to Shaykh Hamallah, his spiritual guide. After the second exile of Hamallah, this Futanke went on to become extremely well known in the area for his knowledge of the esoteric sciences. Indeed, his reputation extended well beyond Nioro and even as far away as Dakar in neighbouring Senegal. Throughout his studies with this teacher and others, G. was concerned with learning 'names of God', particularly those that are secret and transmitted from teacher to student. He claimed to have learned the 100th and greatest name, that is, the name of God which, according to *hadith* collections, allows those who know it to gain access to paradise. There were many other 'names' that he had been able to learn from various people over the past few years.[38] He also explained to me in some detail about the various divination techniques he employed, which sometimes relied on spiritual entities to predict the future or to explain how to resolve a problem. G. was in his mid-thirties, and he was starting to gain a modest reputation as one who knows secrets. He began to attract a small clientele, including some from far away. In fact, he even had a couple of students who came from Burkina Faso to study with him, hoping, as he explained, to learn secrets. These students work for him, doing chores and errands. As for himself, he says that he too remains a student, constantly trying to learn new things. He even told me that part of his interest in speaking at length with me was that he wanted to know whether I had any secrets that I might be able or willing to share with him.

It is important to note that G. does not make enough money to provide for himself and his two wives and children from his work in the esoteric sciences alone. As his father before him, he combines his work as a practitioner of the esoteric sciences with occasional work on construction projects and road repair in the area. It is not unusual that someone like G. has specialised in the Islamic esoteric sciences or *siru*. In fact, there are many people like him, who have specialised in them in one way or another, and like G., most of these people would not be able to make a living practising the esoteric sciences alone. What is striking in G.'s case is his explicit statement that he had no interest in the study of the Quran and jurisprudence, that is, the exoteric sciences.

I know of others who in the course of their studies have focused on a particular branch of the esoteric sciences. One Soninke man I know studied geomancy with a teacher from whom he learned the intricacies of this science. For a number of years, geomancy has been this man's primary source of income, though most of this income is not earned in Nioro itself. In fact, he spends considerable time in some of the neighbouring towns to the north in Mauritania where he attracts clients. It was pointed out that he was unable to practise geomancy in Nioro, not only because there are so many in the town who are knowledgeable of geomancy, but also because he is fairly young and known throughout the town. Moreover, one friend noted that the fact some people in Nioro know the teacher with whom he studied limits his ability to profit from this skill in the town.

Although the particular trajectories that I have outlined here are perhaps not in any way representative or typical, all of the men discussed here are considered to be part of a group of people who are minor religious specialists in Nioro and its environs. Even though they have not all specialised in the esoteric sciences, the esoteric sciences have been important to them in some way. Each has particular kinds of knowledge, and some of them want and are able to attract enough clients to make a living using such knowledge. But almost always, income gained in the use of the Islamic esoteric sciences is supplemented through other activities, as is the case for nearly every individual discussed above. Similarly, economic and social conditions are such that some must migrate in order to support themselves and their families, whether or not they plan to make a living from the esoteric sciences.

Much of this preceding discussion also applies to the group of people who might be considered an intermediary group between the minor and major religious leaders, and about whom I will say a few words before turning in the next chapter to a consideration of those considered to be *grands marabouts*. As noted in Chapter 4, there are many living in the region who for years have basically earned their livelihood through their descent from Umar Tall, supporting themselves on the gifts given to them by descendants of those associated with the nineteenth-century *jihad*. For many decades, descendants of Umar Tall were able to collect gifts in some of the many villages surrounding Nioro. The gifts were often in exchange for blessings – thought to be especially exceptional blessings given the source – and sometimes for assistance in dispute resolution. A few descendants of Umar Tall have also been widely known for their expertise in the esoteric sciences, and they have made a living primarily through their use. Since the rise to prominence of Cerno Hady Tall, some of the descendants of Umar Tall in the region have had greater difficulties in making a living. Some from the younger generation travel to places where Malian migrants have gone in great numbers – Central Africa in particular – where they often exchange their services in the esoteric sciences for money that frequently returns as remittances to their households in Nioro.

In all such cases, there are limits to the activities of Muslim religious specialists within the realm of the Islamic esoteric sciences that are largely determined by the general configuration of religious practice in the town. In short, practitioners of the esoteric sciences are seriously constrained in what they might hope to achieve, particularly because of the way that the most celebrated religious leaders have come to dominate the affairs of the town through what I call the prayer economy.

CONCLUSION

As I have tried to suggest, the Islamic esoteric sciences play a central role on many levels of the social landscape in Nioro. In fact, I would even go so far as to say that they are among its central defining characteristics. Not only are they important in some way in most people's daily lives, but they also bring renown to the town's most celebrated religious leaders and, by extension, their followers. In the next chapter, I turn to consider the development of the prayer economy in which the celebrated religious leaders of Nioro are the major actors. I then turn to consider some of the people in contemporary Nioro and beyond who are vehemently opposed to the use of the esoteric sciences. These are the 'reformists' who have become known for their strong opposition to the esoteric sciences, as well as to much that is associated with the way Islam has long been practised in the region.

6

THE PRAYER ECONOMY

In some of the previous chapters, I explored power and authority as they have related to Islam before the onset of colonial rule and during the colonial period. In this chapter, I focus more explicitly on the shifts in power and authority from the colonial to postcolonial periods, and the contemporary organisation of religious practice in the town of Nioro. If the most obvious of shifts came in the wake of independence with the departure of the French, I consider perhaps the most dramatic of such shifts in religious practice in the postcolonial era. This is the development of what I call, following Murray Last (1988), the prayer economy in this religious centre. The prayer economy is, in effect, an economy of religious practice in which people give gifts to certain religious leaders on a large scale in exchange for prayers and blessings. I argue that certain processes of commodification – the exchange of blessings and prayers for commodities, the proliferation of personal and impersonal Islamic religious commodities – have proliferated and intensified around such religious leaders in the postcolonial period. Such processes of commodification have helped to transform the relations between religious leaders and followers. In fact, they have facilitated the personalisation of religious authority in certain Muslim religious leaders with reputations as saints, to whom many ordinary and elite persons have turned for succour. That is, religious authority has come to be centred on a few individuals rather than institutions like the Sufi orders with which they have historically been associated. Two religious leaders in particular have become major actors, on a regional and sometimes international scale, attracting numerous followers. While the vast majority of their followers are ordinary Muslims, some of the elite followers include prosperous merchants, high-ranking government officials, politicians, even African heads of state and their kin, including some from much further afield. The religious leaders attract these elites, offering spiritual and political guidance, blessings and petitionary prayers, which are rendered in exchange for large gifts, further reinforcing their power and authority. I show how these religious leaders have become more privatised religious figures – effectively free-floating sanctifiers – in a religious economy that has come to be more like a market. I consider some of the broader implications of such an economy of religious practice and, in Chapter 7, I explore the Islamic 'reformist' currents that sometimes call this economy of religious practice into question.

CONTEMPORARY SAINTS

As I have argued, hierarchy and charisma have been enduring features of the social landscape in Nioro. Indeed, hierarchy and charisma have been among the central defining characteristics of the organisation of religious practice in this region. If this was the case prior to the onset of colonial rule, it has been no less the case in the colonial and postcolonial periods. Over time, hierarchy and charisma have come to have a very close association with the Sufi orders that have been the primary institutional forms for Islamic religious practice in this region since at least the mid-nineteenth century. With the rise in prominence of the Tijaniyya and the subsequent development of the Hamawiyya under French colonial rule, these Sufi orders became even more pervasive in this region. Indeed, they were taken for granted as central to Islamic religious practice.

As I have already indicated, there are particular Muslim religious specialists in Nioro who clearly overshadow others. These religious specialists belong to the three major lineages of Muslim religious specialists in the town that descend from the three religious figures: Umar Tall, Alfa Umar Kaba Jakhite, and Shaykh Hamallah. That is, the lineages descend from the key pre-colonial and colonial-era Muslim religious figures with reputations for piety, association with miracles, and propagating Islam in the region. In the case of Umar Tall and Alfa Umar, they also have reputations for scholarship and learning, and in the case of Hamallah, he has the special reputation of having endured persecution under French colonial rule. Perhaps most importantly, all three figures have widespread reputations as saints. In a process akin to Weber's notion of the routinisation of charisma, the three lineages have become what some have called saintly lineages.[1] Even though contemporary representatives of all three lineages are not taken to be saints, they nonetheless do exert a hold over the economy of religious practice in the town. As I will suggest, these lineages and their putative heads effectively restrict the activities of others within this economy.

At the time of my fieldwork, two of the most celebrated religious leaders resident in the town were considered to be saints by many, though not by any means all, of their respective followers. The first, Muhammadu, is the only living son of Shaykh Hamallah. Since Muhammadu is the widely recognised leader of the Hamawiyya, he is at the pinnacle of this particular Sufi hierarchical structure and its institutional form. Many people call him 'the *sharif*' in the region's vernaculars, almost as if *sharif* is the title of an officeholder. In a sense, *sharif* is a title in that many people take Muhammadu to be the head of Hamallah's family that claims sharifian descent, as well as the legitimate leader of his father's community. Moreover, Muhammadu's followers extol him for managing the affairs of the Hamawiyya and the *zawiya*. They praise him for what they call his prodigious powers and his knowledge and use of the esoteric sciences. He has many followers and associates drawn from the broader region who are not in any way limited to a particular ethnic or linguistic group. Muhammadu also has enormous personal wealth, which he receives as gifts from his followers and also acquires through his extensive commercial activities. This wealth is most visible in the large imposing home he has built, the latest imported automobiles he owns, and the horses and herds of livestock he has acquired. Some of Muhammadu's followers state quite explicitly that he is neither a saint, nor does he pretend to be. But many of his followers do proclaim him to be a saint and point to his modesty in not declaring himself as such.[2] Some people even go so far as to say that all of Hamallah's children were saints. Although one of the sons of Muhammadu's older brother has challenged his authority (see Chapter 3), Muhammadu remains the undisputed head of the Hamawiyya at least in Nioro and much of the surrounding areas.

The second and considerably older of the two religious leaders is Cerno Hady Tall, a direct descendent of Umar Tall. Clearly among the most prominent of Umar Tall's descendants in contemporary western Mali and a celebrated leader of the Tijaniyya, Hady is perhaps the most renowned descendant of Umar Tall over the past fifty years from this part of West Africa. Many praise him for his activities on behalf of Islam and as the most prominent leader of the Tijaniyya in the region. People praise Hady for his involvement in religious activities, most notably for the *zawiya* he runs and the annual *ziyara* he organises that attracts thousands of participants. They also speak often about his prodigious powers and renown for the use of the esoteric sciences. Hady too has enormous personal wealth which, in his case, can be seen in the large, modern-style homes he has built in the town and the fleet of cars he and his family use. Unlike Muhammadu, Hady and the other descendants of Umar Tall in the region are generally not involved in commercial activities.[3] Rather, Hady and his immediate family live from the gifts he receives from his many followers from the broader region. In contrast to Muhammadu's rather ethnically and linguistically diverse followers, Hady's followers come mostly from the descendants of those associated with the Umarian *jihad* and state. In many cases, these followers are either Futanke or members of other groups who speak Pulaar/Fulfulde. Many of Hady's followers also claim that he is a saint. Some see Hady not only as a saint, but also as the successor to Umar Tall. That is, they consider him the leader of the descendants of those associated with the nineteenth-century *jihad* in the region. Like Muhammadu, his authority has not gone uncontested.

These *grands marabouts* – to use the language of the French colonial lexicon – attract many followers. Like their saintly ancestors, they too have reputations for learning, piety and prodigious powers. They live surrounded by their numerous followers, associates, including minor religious leaders, clients and dependants. They both operate large *zawiya*s where people gather for prayers, blessings, instruction and guidance. Each year thousands participate in the annual visits or *ziyara*s that they organise. Given that each religious leader has so many people around them, many take such wealth in people to be a sign from God that he is favoured, even an indication that *vox populi vox Dei*. Indeed, many take the two religious leaders to be closer to God than ordinary Muslims, that is, higher in the spiritual hierarchy with more privileged access to God's favour. For this reason, many people tie their own destiny to these two religious leaders. One friend, who is a devoted follower of Hady, told me that his association with Hady was the reason for his considerable success in business activities. Another friend, who is a close follower of Muhammadu, told me that his ability to make a good living – better than most in the town – by selling the tassels that one attaches to prayer beads was unquestionably, *hurma* Shaykh Hamallah, literally the sanctity or holiness of Shaykh Hamallah. Others told me that their reasonably good standards of living and health could only be explained by the closeness of one of the religious leaders to God and, in turn, their own closeness to that religious leader.

While neither of the two religious leaders openly proclaims himself as a saint, ordinary Malian Muslims readily point to various signs that index them as saints. Many people associate them with the exemplary life of the Prophet Muhammad. Pointing to their piety, devotion to God and commitment to their respective Sufi order, many people think they embody a certain kind of morality. Both of the religious leaders also have reputations for association with miracles (Ar., *karamat*), most notably, the ability to predict unforeseen events. Likewise, it is widely reported that their supplicatory prayers will be, or at least are more likely to be, answered by God. Many readily discuss the 'power' of these religious leaders in terms of force in both its spiritual and material senses (cf. Chapter 1). On several occasions and in reference to the two religious leaders, people said to me, 'he is very powerful'. I understood this to be a way to underscore to the seemingly or potentially incredulous visiting Westerner the leaders' exceptional qualities. As elsewhere in the Muslim world, people here are often predisposed to identify particular events or happenings around the *shaykh* as miraculous (see Gilsenan 1982).

Given the reputation for miracles, many seek out the two religious leaders for their intercession with God. The two religious leaders have more than just local reputations. In fact, their reputations are regional and even international in scope. I have met followers and aspirants in Nioro visiting from neighbouring countries, including Mauritania, Senegal, Burkina Faso, Côte d'Ivoire and Guinea. But the two religious leaders also have close ties with people in those places where Malian migrants have gone in great numbers, particularly Central Africa and France.

People can learn about the two religious leaders through eyewitness accounts and oral narratives about the miracles associated with them, but perhaps as often through radio, television, and popular culture, more generally. Malians can view coverage of the annual visits with saints on national television in programmes that usually feature images of the large crowds in attendance, or they can listen to coverage of the annual events on national radio. They can also listen to audio-cassette recordings of *griots* and other such 'traditionalists' who laud the virtues of one of the saints or hear songs in praise of them and their ancestors on the radio.[4] The two saints have what is effectively celebrity status in Mali. We might even call them among the superstars of contemporary Muslim religious leaders in Mali.

As I have indicated in Chapter 1, it is the truly exceptional person whom Malians think are saints. However, there can be considerable complexity, ambiguity and debate surrounding the question of saints and sainthood. As we have seen in the case of Shaykh Hamallah, many recognised him as the *qutb* or supreme saint of the day, and many continue to take him as such today. However, it is obvious that Hamallah's status as a saint and his authority as a religious leader did not go uncontested. Such issues as they relate to saints and sainthood are not a relic of the past. They are being debated, sometimes quite intensely, in Nioro.

On more than one occasion, I witnessed heated discussions about the status of a particular religious leader, and I know that some of these were instigated by my questions. Once, a man in his eighties, whom I knew to have been close to the Côte d'Ivoire-based Yacouba Sylla, proclaimed him to be a saint. Another man around fifty years old immediately pointed out that this was patently false. For him, Yacouba was a person much inferior to a saint. Obviously angered by this, the first man responded that all the wealth and followers that Yacouba had amassed were signs of his sainthood. The second man's swift rebuttal was that everything came from God, even madness, with the implication here that madness applied in Yacouba's case.[5] The discussion ended rather abruptly with the younger man walking away, thereby avoiding escalation into a more heated exchange, which would have been inappropriate given the considerable difference in age between the two men.

When the subject is the presumed sainthood of living Muslim religious leaders, the discussions are often even more discreet. This is particularly the case when some of those present have conflicting affiliations and alliances. For instance, I have listened as people have discussed the possible signs of the sainthood of Hady and Muhammadu. In such discussions, the participants invariably talk about the alleged respective miracles, numerous followers and great wealth of these two figures. Interestingly, people also frequently pointed to the physical appearance of the two religious leaders and, most specifically, how their appearance seems to undergo sudden and unpredictable change. On several occasions, I listened as people discounted the alleged signs of sainthood and miracles of one of the religious leaders. While many seemed cautious not to criticise a supposed saint openly, some intimated that one or the other leader failed to exhibit the exemplary comportment expected of saints.

That the career of major religious figure, not to mention sainthood, is not open to just anyone in Nioro, even other religious leaders, cannot be emphasised enough. Others who might actually develop reputations as minor religious personalities in Nioro must necessarily submit to the authority of one of the two main religious leaders or be associated with the town's third most prominent lineage of religious specialists, the Kabalanke. In order to elaborate on this very important point, I want to consider a little more closely the Kabalanke in Nioro. It is interesting to compare this lineage with the situation of the two religious leaders with their reputations as saints and their respective lineages. One of the most striking things about this lineage is that it no longer seems to produce 'saints'. This is clearly reminiscent of the situation of other lineages of Muslim religious specialists whose power and authority have waxed and waned in other settings. Perhaps the most widely known (and arguably more extreme) example of this phenomenon in West Africa is that of the Ahl Shaykh Sidiyya, the lineage of religious specialists in Mauritania that was among the closest to the French administration during the colonial period.[6] In the words of the sociologist Abdel Wedoud Ould Cheikh, their '*baraka* est epuisée', and they are no longer able to reproduce themselves as a saintly lineage.[7]

Although the ability of the Kabalanke to produce saints seems limited, if not completely exhausted, matters are much more complex than the simple drying-up of their charisma. In fact, the Kabalanke do retain a measure of authority in the town of Nioro, in no small part because of the saintly reputation of their ancestor, Alfa Umar, and the not unrelated fact that they have succeeded in retaining control of the imamate of the town's sole Friday mosque. Perhaps of equal importance is the fact that members of the lineage operate a large, well-respected Islamic educational institution that offers advanced studies, particularly in jurisprudence, to students who come from the broader region. Through this educational institution, the pedagogical ties between teachers and students that it fosters, and the frequent marriage alliances accompanying such ties, they have been able to renew and, in some cases, to reinforce their relations with different groups from across the region, many of whom are Soninke.[8]

At the same time, it is significant that none among the Kabalanke can boast the kind of wealth in people associated with the other two saintly lineages. However, the ability of the Kabalanke to diversify their economic activities has certainly helped them as a group to maintain a measure of authority in the town.[9] As has been suggested before (in Chapter 4), many of the Kabalanke were able – often more successfully than some other lineages – to benefit from opportunities afforded to them not only in the colonial period, but also in the postcolonial period. Their sustained involvement with French-language state education has certainly been an important factor here. Thus, the history of the Kabalanke, as a group, contrasts rather sharply with the other two saintly lineages. Its history is much closer to many of the other lineages of religious specialists in the town and region whose members have often had to make a living in entirely different ways than through the use of their expert Islamic religious knowledge. The difference is that the Kabalanke do have relatively more charismatic authority than some of the other more minor lineages of religious specialists.

It is significant, though perhaps not surprising, that some Kabalanke are most vehement in denying the existence of saints in contemporary Nioro. One friend from this lineage told me that it was a clear and indisputable fact that the time of saints was long past. My friend stated that they know there were saints in the past in Nioro – indeed the grave of their illustrious ancestor Alfa Umar stands as proof. But today, he continued, there were no saints to be found in the town or anywhere else in the world for that matter. Over the course of my fieldwork, many from this lineage and those associated with it voiced such sentiments to me in one way or another. While such people were not willing to deny the existence of sainthood per se, from their perspective the present world and its conditions were such – disenchanted, in the language of Weber (cf. Bourdieu 1979) – that in no uncertain terms were living saints within the realm of the possible.

Although this discourse seems to echo some 'reformist' ideas about saints (see Chapter 7), I learned from many discussions that such sentiments were not quite so unequivocal. I noticed that this questioning of contemporary sainthood was almost invariably accompanied by an assertion of the noble qualities of the man they called their 'spiritual leader', Sadikou, the imam of the town's sole Friday mosque and a member of their lineage, who died in 2003. I heard repeatedly how 'the imam', as he was often called, led a very modest life in contradistinction to the town's two major religious leaders, who are known for their lavish lifestyles. Moreover, the imam was actually involved in the major rituals of the life cycle – naming ceremonies for newborns, weddings and funerals – at which he officiated. Such activities took up a considerable amount of his time given that he performed these rituals for the broader community that recognised his authority as imam. They included many Muslim 'strangers' to the town, particularly the many

Muslim civil servants and their families posted to the town from elsewhere in the country. Because of their very elevated status, the other two religious leaders would never engage in these kinds of activities directly. Many of the people who denied the existence of saints also frequently noted that those really close to God have no need for this world (Ar., *dunya*) and the material possessions associated with it. In this way of thinking, those looking to the next world (Ar., *akhira*) eschew the things of this world.[10] In such discourse, there is clearly the suggestion that the imam is closer in his comportment to that of a true saint, even if no one asserted his status as such.

I suspect that some of this discourse, not to mention the imam's comportment, relates to – is even in a way a response to – some of the criticism, even disdain, that the Kabalanke have encountered over the years. The imam was the son of the imam Madi Assa (d. 1950), one of Hamallah's most ardent opponents in Nioro at the time of his second exile in 1941. To this day, some followers of Hamallah see Madi Assa as the personification of the opposition to Hamallah and genealogical closeness to such a figure as a liability. Moreover, since the French conquest, the 'office' of imam has been transmitted to the most learned among the Kabalanke. During times of succession and even fairly recently, candidates from other families have been put forth. Only one of these, however, has ever been successful, and this was very early in the colonial period. Most Kabalanke maintain that such outside candidates could never be successful. After the imam died, his eldest son, Madi Assa, succeeded him as imam. Many in Nioro state that Alfa Umar Kaba Jakhite led the first prayers – that is, acted as imam – in Nioro when Umar Tall arrived there in the mid-nineteenth century. In this way of thinking, Umar Tall entrusted the imamate of the mosque in Nioro to them. The *de facto* institutionalisation of Kabalanke control of the imamate has met some criticism. Over the years, some have noted that the transmission of the imamate of a Friday mosque within a particular family amounts to questionable, possibly, unlawful practice. In this way of thinking, the imamate should pass to the most learned in the community, and there is no reason to assume that this person would issue from a specific family.

The contemporary organisation of religious practice in the town is the outcome of the conditions of decades of colonial rule and the exigencies of the postcolonial situation in which some groups have been able to maintain and, in some cases, to reinforce their power and authority. It is presently such that, on the one hand, there are two lineages in town from which major religious leaders have emerged and from which saints may be proclaimed at least by some of their followers. On the other hand, there is another lineage that denies the possibility of sainthood in the present, all the while pointing to the exemplary comportment of one of their own. The three lineages have what, at times, seem to be competing and, at other times, complementary claims to authority.

Moreover, the organisation of religious practice in the town constrains social actors. There are very real limits to the activities of religious specialists – not only junior members of the saintly lineages, but also those from other minor religious lineages – which are not merely a function of demographics. One can see such constraints in the controversy surrounding Yacouba Sylla's status as a religious leader. However, I want to emphasise that some people in Nioro continually stressed to me that any religious specialist in the town had to be allied with one of the town's major religious leaders – or, as one friend put it, at least seem to be allied with one of them. One cannot seek openly or even covertly (or so it seems) to challenge their authority in any way. In other words, the 'rules' of religious practice are such that people have to be outwardly deferential to one of the three religious leaders. This point cannot be overemphasised. It is not something just taken for granted; rather, I heard it explicitly articulated on many occasions.

Minor religious figures, who might have expectations of, or aspirations for, a more lofty position, have been unable to rise above a certain rank within the town. Becoming too influential or well known without remaining ultimately deferential to one of the major religious leaders in the town carries risks. If one did establish a reputation, one could – many insist that one would inevitably – provoke the ire of the leading religious leaders and their followers. By seeming to be independent of the authority of the major religious leaders in the town, one seems to contest the order of things. In fact, there is constant speculation about the downfall of previous minor figures, who seemed to act as though they did not respect the authority of the major leaders. Many think that the death of the *madrasa* teacher discussed in the previous chapter was just one example of such an upstart's demise.

The following example will serve as further illustration. It concerns a young man born in the 1960s into a lineage of religious specialists whose father was one of the most renowned practitioners of the Islamic esoteric sciences in the region. After his father's death, the young man amassed a following in spite of his own inability to secure the diploma or licence (Ar., *ijaza*) that would certify his completion of advanced Islamic educational studies. While resident in the town, the young man, like his father, became revered for what people consider unusual powers. Nonetheless, while in Nioro, he remained – like his father before him – a follower of one of the town's major religious leaders. The existing organisational structure and religious leadership effectively prevented him and others like him from rising too high in prominence. At the time of my fieldwork, the man had taken up residence in Bamako where his activities were not subject to the same kinds of constraints as they were in Nioro.[11] The same could be said about Yacouba Sylla who apparently never returned to Nioro after leaving in the 1930s. Living so far from Nioro in Côte d'Ivoire, his reputation could grow and spread relatively unhindered.

Such restrictions on the activities of would-be Muslim religious specialists point to the existence of a certain kind of hegemony in the town. This is as much a product of the colonial freezing of influence of religious leaders in the town, as it is of the reconfiguration of relations that have occurred since independence with the rise in prominence of the two major religious leaders. Unlike some other larger towns in Mali, the options for those who would like to be religious specialists and even for ordinary followers are fairly limited. One can either be allied with the Kabalanke, the family of Hamallah or the Tall family. To be allied with the latter two is by extension to be Hamawi or Tijani. Another option, to be discussed in the next chapter, is to be 'reformist', which almost always entails leaving the town if one is or aspires to be a religious leader, scholar, teacher or preacher. Another option, to be discussed in Chapter 8, is that of remaining neutral or at least seeming to be, something that an expanded public sphere allows.

SAINTS AND FOLLOWERS

He who has no *shaykh* has the devil as his guide.
(Attributed to Bayazid al-Bistami, 3rd century A.H.)[12]

I am convinced that it is very difficult for many social scientists to deal even-handedly with the subject of the relationship between Muslim religious leaders and followers in this kind of setting. The idea that a person could, or even should, submit to another for whatever purposes (religious or otherwise) challenges deeply embedded, Western, commonsense notions of autonomous individuals, not to mention platitudes about the venality of clerics and the virtues of secularism – ideas not unknown to some of the actors I encountered during my fieldwork. Moreover, deeply entrenched, Western, rationalised understandings of religion as a sphere separate from the world of commodities and commerce often leads to moralising discourses about social actors whose very religious practices are suffused with the commodity form and money.[13]

In what follows, I will try to sketch out the contours of such relations between religious leaders and their followers and some of their meanings and interpretations in contemporary Nioro. The actual establishment of a relationship with a Muslim religious leader, even a one-time visit (Ar., *ziyara*), may have many layers of meaning. An individual actor – a man or a woman, young or old – may have complex motives and interests in culti-vating a relationship with a religious leader. Attempts to explain such relationships as rationally maximising behaviour or as some sort of cost-benefit analysis on the part of Muslims, while perhaps applicable in some cases, are, it seems to me, at best tendentious (cf. O'Brien 1971, 1975). In fact, because people are expected to have a religious leader or guide, a relationship with a religious leader is often considered a pious act or at least an attempt to adhere to conventions of proper behaviour for a Muslim (cf.

Gellner 1969). That some people might remain in relative poverty or even impoverish themselves in the cultivation of their relationship with a religious leader seems to suggest that more is at work than simply the maximisation of material interests or some crude form of false consciousness.

In Nioro, many people are members of lineages that have had historical ties to one or more of the religious leader's lineages. Many of these people take their relationships with one of the religious leaders in the town for granted, even if such relationships are not enacted mechanically. Around each of the three major lineages, there are individuals, lineages, sometimes even whole communities or neighbourhoods, whose ancestors were followers or sometimes clients of these lineages. Many of these people continue to be followers in some way. Indeed, one finds many said to have been born followers of a certain religious leader, and they often consider themselves at least nominal members of one of the two Sufi orders, the Tijaniyya or the Hamawiyya.

In practice, one finds considerable variation in the nature of interactions with religious leaders and in style of religiosity, dependent upon a number of factors, including – but not limited to – age, gender, education, social status and individual temperament. While the relationship to a religious leader might be premised on nominal membership and attachment to a Sufi order and/or its titular head, others might actually become formally initiated into one of the two Sufi orders in the town. Certain individuals might initiate new ties with one of the religious leaders. Some might move to Nioro to be close to the religious leader and, in some cases, might even cut ties with family to cultivate those ties. Others who initiate a relationship with one of the religious leaders might give a child – a boy or girl – to be raised in the religious leader's household, perhaps to work in domestic service and eventually marry into the saint's entourage. Over time, individuals, groups of people and, on occasion, entire communities may initiate, renew, strengthen, downplay or actually sever ties with a religious leader for a whole host of reasons.[14]

Despite the existence of inherited and nominal ties, followers – individuals and groups of people – might have reasons of a very pragmatic or instrumental nature for interacting with a particular religious leader. The major religious leaders assume, or are called upon by their followers to assume, a number of important roles, most notably as mediators in dispute resolution. During my fieldwork, I learned of numerous occasions when people asked the religious leaders to intervene in various kinds of often acrimonious disputes, including conflicts over land used for agriculture and livestock grazing. In a few cases, the religious leader himself served as mediator, while more often the religious leader selected a representative from among his followers to act as a mediator on his behalf. The religious leaders also have reputations for giving alms to the poor and to members of their large entourages. In some cases, someone might make appeals for food or money directly to the religious leader or, as is more often the case, to a member of the religious leader's entourage.

In addition, individuals might cultivate a relationship with a particular religious leader with the intention, or at least hope, of having other personal concerns or interests addressed by the religious leader, whom they assume has considerable power. On the one hand, with primarily spiritual goals in mind, some might seek instruction from a religious leader or one of his associates or kin that leads to advancement within the Sufi order. Such a person might receive guidance on techniques of concentration or various forms of spiritual exercises, additional litanies of prayers or 'names' for recitation, that might facilitate advancement to higher states or stages, here called *maqamat* (Ar.). On the other hand, reasons of a more this-worldly nature for individuals to interact with a religious leader might include the pursuit of wealth, power, social prestige, progeny or good health, or simply to avoid misfortune. It is worth emphasising that such goals, whether 'spiritual' or 'material', are not necessarily mutually exclusive.

The ties between a religious leader and ordinary Muslims, or lack thereof, receive perhaps their most tangible, public expression in the place where a person performs communal prayers, the weekly communal prayers on Fridays, as well as the communal prayers held on the occasion of the main Islamic holidays. For example, if a person performs the communal prayers at the *zawiya* of the Hamawiyya on Fridays, that person's ties to the Hamawiyya and its leader are clear. This is the case even if the person is not formally initiated into the Hamawiyya and, thus, would not gather for and participate in the weekly communal recitations of the special litany of prayers of the Sufi order. There is, however, somewhat more ambiguity if one performs communal prayers at the town's sole Friday mosque. If a person performs some of the daily prayers at the small mosque within the compound of Cerno Hady Tall or meets there for the communal recitations of the special litany of prayers, then that person's ties are patently clear.

Another important index of ties to a particular leader is participation in one of the annual 'visits' the saints in the town organise. There are representatives of each saintly lineage living in the capital, not to mention in other towns and cities in Mali and in neighbouring countries. These representatives coordinate the trips of individuals and delegations – both men and women – to Nioro for the annual visits, which have become highly organised affairs involving thousands of people. During the visits, people gather for performance of the ritual daily prayers. They listen to poetry in honour of the Prophet Muhammad, the respective saint and his ancestor(s). In the afternoons and evenings, people also listen to other, usually more junior, religious leaders who give sermons – often in the vernaculars – about Islam and the way to conduct oneself as a proper Muslim. Those who are members of the Sufi order to which the saint belongs also meet to recite collectively the special litany of prayers of the Sufi order. Visitors also eat meals with groups of other visitors and, usually, at least once, all together.

GIFTS AND COMMODITIES

One of the most salient features of the relationships between Muslim religious leaders and others is the giving of gifts. Muslims in West Africa have long brought gifts to religious leaders, usually seeking blessings from them or their intercession with God. It is important to see such gifts and gift-giving in relation to regionally salient conceptions of Islam and what is thought to be the proper comportment of Muslims. In Islam, Muslims are not only encouraged, but also commanded, to give to others. One of the so-called five pillars of Islam is *zakat*, or the alms expected from all Muslims. Such alms are obligatory, and many, if not all, Malian Muslims would state this is the case. Prior to colonial rule, certain Muslim religious leaders and rulers in this part of West Africa collected and distributed what they considered *zakat*. Under colonial rule, the French suppressed the collection of *zakat* and imposed a system of taxation not based on Islamic juris-prudence that has survived into the postcolonial period. Today, what many Muslims in Mali, including saints, give annually to the poor and needy, and what they also give to the poor at the end of Ramadan, the yearly month of fasting from dawn to dusk, they call *zakat*, as do many people elsewhere in the Muslim world.

There is another notion of alms, *sadaqa*, that is rather different from *zakat*, but equally, if not more, important in Muslim West Africa. In general, what one gives willingly and informally to others in one's daily life or what one gives, sometimes even sacrifices, following the recommenda-tions of a Muslim religious leader is considered *sadaqa*.[15] It is this second notion of alms or charity that is undoubtedly more widespread in this part of West Africa. According to the Quran and other Islamic texts, such as *hadith*s, such alms are usually for the poor (see Quran: ix, 60). Therefore, the gifts that Muslim religious leaders receive are not considered alms. This clearly relates to the idea that descendants of the Prophet Muhammad never keep alms for themselves. One finds this in local discourse and practice, as well as in statements attributed to the Prophet Muhammad (see El Bokhari 1964: 138). In principle, those lineages claiming descent from the Prophet Muhammad and, by extension, all religious leaders of elevated status in this part of West Africa, never accept gifts designated as *sadaqa* for their own consumption. That is, at least in theory. In practice, some people do give alms to elevated religious leaders for distribution to the poor on their behalf.

The word gift most accurately captures the local and regional idiom for describing the transfers of objects from followers to Muslim religious leaders. The gifts that the most esteemed Muslim religious leaders in Mali ordinarily receive are called *hadaya* in the region's vernaculars.[16] This word, *hadaya*, comes from the Arabic (*hadîya*; pl., *hadaya*) meaning 'gift' or 'present'. If in some places in the Arabic-speaking world, such as nineteenth-century Egypt, the word simply meant 'gift', the term is used exclusively in this part of West Africa for gifts given to descendants of the Prophet Muhammad, descendants of Umar Tall, as well as others of similar stature. Although some gifts offered to the Sultan in Morocco have been so designated (Dannerlein 2001), the longer history of the practices of gift-giving in West Africa and their possible relationship to practices in North Africa are not at all clear.

It is striking that *hadîya* – gift-giving to religious leaders – does not figure as a category discussed in the standard Islamic legal texts used in this region.[17] According to one of these legal texts, things transferred 'in view of a reward in another world' are not to be considered gifts, but rather alms (Ruxton 1916: 263). Be that as it may, one can say in this context that by giving gifts to others and quite often preferably to religious leaders of elevated status, people are following longstanding and widely accepted practice considered to be religious commands. But it is also clear that people are doing more than simply following Islamic legal texts, mechanically enacting rules for alms or gift-giving. By giving gifts to religious leaders, people are often seeking to assure their place in the next world. However, they frequently wish to obtain merit and God's blessings in the world in which they are living as well.

As many of my informants noted, in giving gifts they wished to obtain *baraji*, which translates from the region's vernaculars as merit or divine recompense. Although there was no consensus among my informants about the origins of this word *baraji*,[18] some Muslim scholars explained that the term corresponds to the notion of merit (Ar., *thawâb*) one finds in Islamic religious texts, while other scholars suggested other terms with similar meanings (for example, Ar., *'ajr*).[19] There was, however, agreement among my informants that *baraji* clearly has a sense of merit, which, they explained, is the reward from God for one's actions. One receives such a reward in this world – wealth, good health, progeny, and so forth – or in the hereafter, that is, either access to heaven and eternal life or hell. There is a prevailing notion that one receives such merit for alms – obligatory alms (*zakat*), voluntary alms (*sadaqa*), gifts and generosity more generally. Those who gave to others, including gifts to religious leaders, explicitly stated that in doing so they hoped to receive such merit. Because the religious leaders in question are thought to be close to God, one honours God through gift-giving to them, thereby possibly obtaining merit and, ultimately, God's favour. Uncertainty is, however, inevitable. One never knows whether or how exactly one will benefit from such merit in this world or the next. In any case, I want to emphasise that it is this notion of *baraji* that is perhaps as equally important here as *baraka*, which many anthropologists have high-lighted, even overemphasised.

In exchange for gifts, Muslim religious leaders, give blessings or petition-ary prayers – in the local vernaculars *duwaw*, another loan word from Arabic – exactly as the Prophet Muhammad is reported to have done when he received gifts. That is, in conformity with the *sunna* as recounted in the collections of *hadith* (see Wensinck 1927: 88). Many claim that all that the religious leaders of Nioro have – wealth, numerous followers, as well as the intangible knowledge and power associated with 'secrets' – is a gift from God.[20] They, the ordinary followers, in turn pay homage to the religious leaders in part through gift-giving to them because, by being blessed and favoured, they are foremost in the hierarchy of authority before God. What one finds then is not unlike a situation that the fourteenth-century writer Ibn Khaldun described in which persons with a reputation for piety are frequently the recipients of gifts because 'the great mass believes that when they give them presents [gifts], they serve God' (1958, 2: 327).

In Nioro, there is near unanimity in the view that people can, even should, give *hadaya* to descendants of the Prophet Muhammad, which would include Hamallah's descendants. There is some debate as to whether other religious leaders who are not *sharifs* can also accepts gifts that people deem *hadaya*, not whether they can receive gifts. In any case, most of the descendants of Umar Tall who collect gifts from followers and most of those giving such gifts refer to them as *hadaya*. In contrast, the Kabalanke also receive their share of gifts, but I never heard anyone say that such gifts could by any criteria be considered *hadaya*.[21] This would seem to be in keeping with their diminished, almost secondary role in the postcolonial period and possibly even earlier.

Because people think that it is basically good, morally correct and even potentially meritorious to give gifts to religious leaders, a strong sense of obligation permeates the practice of such gift-giving. Indeed, many feel compelled to give gifts to a religious leader. In Nioro, one finds not only a wide variety of persons, both local and non-local, who visit and give gifts to the prominent religious leaders, but also a considerable range in the value of their gifts. If one usually gives according to one's means (but compare below), people note that a gift should correspond to the stature of both the person giving and the recipient.[22] As one of the religious leaders explained, he accepts all gifts, regardless of size or value, that people offer to him. Such gifts can range from the very modest – a few measures of grain or a single coin – to the munificent – large sums of cash and commodities such as new cars. Thus, those things considered gifts (*hadaya*) might include some of the most important material tokens of value in the wider society. In this context, no clear break exists between gifts and commodities (Appadurai 1986; cf. Gregory 1982), since many commodities and 'luxury' goods are given as gifts.

If people feel compelled to give gifts to religious leaders, this is particularly the case during the annual visits in the town. Indeed, for many, the highpoint of participation in one of the annual visits is the time during which they are able to deliver gifts to the religious leader. In rather formally structured rituals, the religious leaders, or possibly one of their sons, receive visitors – both men and women. I have watched ordinary followers lining up by the hundreds, waiting as individuals or in groups to hand over their gifts – livestock, agricultural products, consumer goods, envelopes filled with cash – to a member of the religious leader's entourage as the religious leader stood close by. If one is lucky, one might be able to shake the religious leader's hand or be touched by him at this time. For example, Muhammadu might place his hand on one's shoulder or head, or touch one's prayer beads. These are all ways of blessing or transmitting charisma, to use the language of Weber. Such contact, however fleeting, is greatly anticipated and eagerly sought. I have seen people trembling with anticipation as they waited to hand over their gifts and possibly be touched by the religious leader. Given the number of people involved in the annual visits, these ritualised exchanges would be the closest direct contact that most ordinary people visiting the town would have with a religious leader.

In fact, most ordinary people are kept socially and spatially apart from the two religious leaders, and access to them is consistently and emphatically regulated. The religious leader's retainers, who are often privileged members of their entourages, act as intermediaries with almost all of those seeking access to them. I encountered many people – followers, those with some sort of problem, or simply the curious – who explained how they had made the journey to Nioro at times other than during the annual visits, but had been unable to see the religious leader.

Access to the religious leaders is even restricted for many of those who live in the town, including those who might be able to gain access by mobilising kin or client ties with one of the religious leaders. At the weekly Friday communal prayers, social and spatial distance between the religious leaders and their respective followers is sharply marked. For example, Hady always travels the short distance from his home to the Friday mosque by automobile. He generally arrives after almost everyone else has taken a place in the mosque and he does not mingle with people. Back at his compound, Hady often addresses the many people who gather at his *zawiya* from a position inside his personal quarters from which he is barely visible.

On Fridays, at his *zawiya*, Muhammadu prays inside a building, unseen by most others who pray together in the more public space of the *zawiya*. Before and after prayer, he usually moves in and out of the more public space. As he does so, women seated together in an area behind the men, as in a mosque, watch him, and some of the women ululate when he is in their view in order to signal their devotion to him. Usually, Muhammadu and his retainers allow men and boys to approach him between prayers. Women and girls are not permitted in the central space of the *zawiya* during prayer times and thus watch from afar. He often stands for a few minutes inside the portal of the building housing his private space for prayer. Gathering on the veranda before him, men and boys, including many of lower status – the unemployed, the infirm and the destitute – but also some of his well-heeled devoted followers approach to touch his outstretched hand, which they sometimes also kiss, out of respect and/or in order to be blessed (cf. Messick 1993; Gilsenan 1982). Others lower their heads so that he might touch them. Throughout, several retainers engage in crowd control. They prevent people from lingering too long or getting too close to Muhammadu.

While it is clear that the regulation of access to such religious leaders is important in no small part because of the sheer number of followers involved, their limited visibility helps to enhance their sanctity and power (Graeber 1996). A visitor or even someone living in Nioro might catch a glimpse of one of the religious leaders during communal prayers, possibly hear a message delivered on his behalf over a loudspeaker, or even kiss his hand after communal prayers. But a private audience with one of the two religious leaders – no matter how much desired – is nearly unattainable for most ordinary people who, thus, are usually unable to communicate their own this- or other-worldly concerns directly to the religious leader. We might say, in neo-Durkheimian fashion, that such people, residents or visitors to the towns, with often quite different backgrounds, forge a collective religious identity, expressing this identity as followers of one of the saints. While the experience of those involved is not akin to the 'communitas' described by Victor Turner (1973) in which individuals are essentially equals, people are engaging in what might be characterised as 'ritual communication' (van der Veer 1994). That is, people express an overall group identity as they communicate to themselves and to others as pious Muslims submitting to a leader whom they believe to be close to God. In doing so, such people receive blessings and/or potential merit in exchange for their gifts. To put this even more starkly in the language of the outside analyst, they have access to the religious leader's symbolic capital, which they receive in the form of blessings and/or merit. Additionally, individuals or groups may also benefit materially through the networks of redistribution or the intervention of the religious leader as mediator, though these might ultimately be of less importance than the group identity expressed or the symbolic capital acquired.

Although for centuries, certain Muslim saints in West Africa have been associated with commodities, such as the gold, salt, and slaves they accumulated and exchanged during the trans-Saharan trade and, more recently, with major cash crops, such as groundnuts in neighbouring Senegal, recent processes of commodification have complicated matters.[23] In recent years, visits to the religious leaders have increasingly come to resemble a market-place, in that contact with them has come to be mediated on an unprece-dented scale by both commodities and money. In what are clearly new ways of indirect access to the religious leaders, people are able to purchase desirable Islamic religious commodities (cf. Starrett 1995; Tambiah 1984). Depending on one's means, one can purchase the religious leader's photo, which might easily cost more than the average daily wage. Or, since the late 1980s, one can also usually purchase a video recording of the proceedings of the annual visit that features close-ups of the religious leader, members of his inner circle and sometimes even the anthropologist. Needless to say, such videos – produced where public electricity has been unavailable – are many times more expensive than a religious leader's photo. In some cases, the religious leaders have authorised certain individuals to make what amount to official video recordings of the annual visits and sometimes to take their portraits. Guaranteed such privileges, some of these people – entrepreneurs so to speak – have profited handsomely from the sale and distribution of these religious commodities. Given how eager people are to add such a photo to their collections, many recognise the potential profit to be had from the reproduction and sale of the saints' photos. At the annual visits, I have watched as crowds have quickly gathered around those announcing the sale of official and unofficial photos.

These religious commodities – photos and videos – can be widely diffused. Indeed, they circulate with the visitors who pass them on through trade and exchange with others at home and among migrant communities elsewhere in Africa and beyond who might not be able to travel to the provincial towns for the annual visits. I have found such religious commodities – photos of the religious leaders prominently displayed in living rooms, and videos of the annual visits – in the homes of Malian migrants living in France. More than one Malian in France told me he recognised me from viewing the official videotaped recordings of those annual visits I attended (and during which I was invariably videotaped). Because of my association with and relatively easy access to the religious leaders, Malians repeatedly asked me to give them or even to sell them photos of the religious leaders.

Such religious commodities have certainly helped to spread the reputa-tions of such religious leaders and their 'fame' (Munn 1986), but also their presumed arc of power. For many, these religious commodities unambi-guously index the religious leader's influence and, indeed, his sanctity. These religious commodities have undoubtedly helped to make the two religious leaders of Nioro superstars, not least because most are aware that it is not just anyone whose image can be commercially viable. Many seem truly awed by the video and photographic images of the enormous crowds gathered under the leadership of the respective saints during the annual visits. Some have told me that they have made plans to attend or have actually attended the annual visits after the lasting impression such images have made on them. This has not, however, meant the unproblematic spread of the religious leaders' influence along with the flow of such religious commodities. On the contrary, certain Muslims, who have been opposed to such representational art, have been critical of the use of the religious leaders' images, though they are perhaps in the minority. Such people – we might call them 'reformist' Muslims – see such images as evidence that the religious leader or, at the very least, some of his followers are guilty of idolatry or 'association' (Ar., *shirk*), that is, treating things other than God as a deity – in short, un-Islamic behaviour. This is just one feature of a larger Muslim 'reformist' discourse that contests the legitimacy of all supposed living Muslim saints, their alleged powers of intercession and, by extension, gift-giving to them (see Chapter 7).

Such criticisms are very serious indeed and may partly explain why some religious leaders have taken steps to restrict the commercialisation of their images or what they see as excessive profiteering in the sale of such images. Clearly, the religious leaders do not savour the idea of just anyone profiting financially from the sale of their images. On more than one occasion, I have seen the religious leaders stop someone from taking his photo or video-taping him. Once I watched as one of the religious leaders instructed a member of his entourage to prevent a young man from videotaping him and the activities at the annual visit. I later learned that the young man was the son of a migrant without any particular attachment or relationship to the religious leader who was merely seeking to exploit the commercial possibilities of videotaping the religious leader. While the two religious leaders have sometimes reacted angrily to the unauthorised commercialisation of their images or excessive profiteering, they have not been able to control the proliferation and circulation of these commodities, even if they wished to.

THE PRAYER ECONOMY

Murray Last has used the notion of prayer economy to describe the rather complex but pervasive practices in Kano in northern Nigeria in which considerable sums of money are given to Muslim 'scholars' for prayers, blessings and Islamic medicine (1988: 196f.). People make such transactions, he argues, in order to ensure political and financial success and/or to build a base for such success. As he points out, the oil boom of the 1970s made unprecedented levels of capital available for such transactions with profound effects on the Kano economy.[24] Contemporary Nioro of course contrasts rather sharply with Kano. Differently situated within the world economy, Mali has not experienced such levels of economic growth and today remains a very poor country. But despite the obvious differences in national income and resources, the giving of gifts to religious leaders on a large scale makes it entirely appropriate to speak about a prayer economy in

Nioro. Indeed, it would be virtually impossible to understand contemporary Nioro without an examination of this local and, in many senses, trans-regional economy, which links the town to the wider political economy.

As I have already suggested, some of the considerable wealth one finds in Nioro does come from some of its inhabitants. Indeed, a sizeable amount of the wealth of the two religious leaders in Nioro is traceable to ordinary non-elite followers living in and around the town. Nioro is also the birthplace and home of many prosperous merchants and traders, some of whom have built considerable fortunes in the postcolonial period. A number of these enterprising individuals and families are based in Nioro, but some are based in other Malian towns and cities, neighbouring countries, and as far away as Central Africa and Europe. Some of the most financially successful among them have longstanding ties with the town's religious leaders.

In addition to ordinary local Muslims and the more well-to-do merchants, the two religious leaders attract other prominent followers, including some who are affluent by any standards. People from across francophone West Africa visit and make gifts to the two religious leaders in Nioro. Such visitors include high-ranking civil servants, influential political appointees and other Muslim religious leaders. In fact, the relations between Nioro's religious leaders and African heads of state are almost legendary.[25] As I have noted, Muhammadu was very close to Mali's president Moussa Traoré before the latter was removed from power in 1991. Muhammadu also had very close ties to Ould Saleck in neighbouring Mauritania, while Cerno Hady has been close to the Bongo family of Gabon. Such high-status followers – heads of state, merchants, government ministers, and their kin – give large and expensive gifts, while many others of similar means and status who are unable or unwilling to go openly to Nioro send gifts on their behalf. Association with such high-status people undoubtedly enhances the reputations of the religious leaders, though too close association with figures of power, especially political power, might carry potential dangers. Clearly, it would not be accurate to state that the role of Islam is that of a counter-society movement or a refuge for the weak in this postcolonial setting, as some have argued was the case in some places under colonial rule in West Africa (cf. Coulon 1988; Brenner 1993a).

For some members of the elite – successful merchants, government officials, civil servants, politicians, even heads of state, and their kin – visits to either of the religious leaders are, as one might imagine, rather different from the visits of ordinary Muslims. The vast economic and political capital of such people facilitate their interactions and ties with the religious leaders. Since travel to Nioro is expensive and more difficult than to many other areas of Mali because of poor road conditions, it takes considerable expenditure – not to mention effort – to reach the town. It is clearly the economic resources and greater 'leisure' time available to many successful merchants, civil servants and politicians that gives them greater mobility to initiate or renew and maintain ties with the celebrated religious leaders in Nioro. When there has been a regular commercial airline service between Bamako and Nioro and between Mauritanian towns and Nioro, many, if not the majority, of the passengers on the flights have been followers and/or kin of the two religious leaders.

In general, many – perhaps most – of the elites interested in the religious leaders do not participate in the annual large-scale visits. If some of them simply want to avoid the crowds, others prefer their interactions with a religious leader to be discreet, possibly even secret. After all, many such people want to visit a religious leader for help with this-worldly matters – wealth, commercial success, political power – and they may hope to keep these private. Moreover, they would want to ensure that they have the undivided attention of the religious leader – something very difficult, if not impossible, during the large-scale visits with thousands of participants.

It might not be an exaggeration to say that the world of commodities saturates the interactions between the two religious leaders and the elite. For some members of this elite, their visits have come to be like holiday tours: they arrive in private or hired cars, and by commercial or chartered flights from the capital. Sometimes they send their private cars overland to meet them at the airport in Nioro. In certain cases, they lodge in luxury accommodations that have been specially constructed since the late 1980s for visitors not accustomed to provincial living. A few have even built their own private, modern-style homes for their regular visits to Nioro.

Unlike the overwhelming majority of visitors to the towns, these visitors are usually guaranteed relatively direct access to the religious leaders. Their visits invariably include a private audience with the religious leader during which they are able to communicate their concerns to him. It seems that they gain this less restricted access because of the lavish nature of their gifts. Although the religious leaders and their entourages readily deny the truthfulness of such a statement and note that the religious leaders dispense blessings to one and all, those who are the bearers of gifts of great value – new cars, wristwatches and large sums of cash – never have difficulties in seeing the religious leaders and meeting with them personally. Thus, those with access to or even at times control of some of the society's central tokens of value – cash and commodities – also have greater access to the religious leaders and, ultimately, their symbolic capital. There seems to be a process whereby commercial and bureaucratic elites are joined or fused with religious leaders.[26]

In exchange for their often sumptuous gifts, the religious leaders give blessings to members of the elite, as they do for the ordinary followers. But the religious leaders also perform much more personalised services for them. They usually employ special prayers so that the elites might obtain what they desire. The religious leaders might also use some of the other Islamic esoteric sciences, including forms of mystical retreat (Ar., *khalwa*) and Islamic 'divination' (Ar., *istikhara*) for these high-status visitors. It is possible that the religious leader or a member of his entourage will write special, presumably personalised texts in Arabic, the language of the sacred texts in Islam, for them to wear or to keep as amulets, or they may write texts for them to ingest or wash with after effacing with water. These blessings, prayers and amulets are also religious commodities, and they also seem to possess some of the charisma of the religious leader (cf. Tambiah 1984).

These religious commodities – blessings, prayers and amulets – are different in a number of ways that make them potentially more powerful than the other commodities like photos and videocassettes.[27] They are not only presumably more personalised, but they are always concealed, rather than being publicly displayed. Moreover, the actual contents of such religious commodities will almost always remain mysterious to the recipient, thereby enhancing their power. Finally, most people assume that such powerful religious commodities would almost always be given in exchange for gifts of great value. Thus, the personalised religious commodities are much more highly valued and coveted than those available and affordable to most ordinary people. In exchange for their gifts, elite followers have relatively unfettered access to the religious leaders and their blessings, and access to more personalised and, therefore, more powerful religious commodities.

Since gifts are expected to be commensurate with the prestige and status of both the religious leader and the giver, as well as with the nature of a giver's request (cf. Eickelman 1976: 178), an extravagant gift often indexes a major intervention via the esoteric sciences. The following example will help to illustrate how large gifts might be extended in return for such an intervention. One person told me that when one of the religious leaders was helping him with his personal problems, the latter not once mentioned what was required in exchange for his services rendered via the esoteric sciences. He said that he simply had an idea of what an appropriate gift would be. When the follower's problem had been resolved, he transferred an appro- priately large sum of cash to the religious leader. This is clearly in keeping with what the religious leaders told me. For instance, Muhammadu explained to me that his father never once specified that someone give him something, anything in particular. For his father – and he stresses that he tries as much as possible to follow his father's ways – a gift must always be 'freely' given. Be that as it may, there is evidence to suggest that gift-giving by certain high- status followers and supplicants is part of the quest for what Bourdieu (1984) calls social 'distinction'. For example, it is sometimes common knowledge which wealthy individual has given one of the religious leaders his latest imported vehicles or other publicly visible gifts. Such public knowledge seems to contribute to a climate in which some people might engage in competitive gift-giving, not unlike what Appadurai (1986) has called 'tournaments of value'. Thus, as some of my informants pointed out, certain individuals try to outdo others in the lavishness of the often public gifts they make to the religious leaders.

At least some of the elites, who do not necessarily have any long-range spiritual – even ideological – commitments to the religious leaders, effectively pay them fees for services.[28] In fact, certain elite followers are known to solicit more than one religious leader. That is, after visiting one of the religious leaders for help with a particular problem, a person might visit another one for the same, still unresolved problem. It is significant that such practice is explicitly forbidden in locally understood Islamic religious doctrine, whereby one must not frequent Muslim religious leaders, including saints, indiscriminately.[29] Such practice contrasts quite sharply with that of ordinary Muslims whose relationships with either religious leader is usually premised on at least nominal membership in his Sufi order. This also signals a significant shift in the organisation of religious practice, a situation where ties between religious leaders and some elite followers are no longer mediated primarily through membership in a particular Sufi order, but rather through access to political and economic forms of capital and other central tokens of value in the society. In their relations with some members of the elite, the religious leaders are more privatised than their saintly predecessors. In other words, the nature of the relationship between some followers and certain religious leaders approaches a fee-for-service religion. In such cases, the Muslim saints have become what we might even call free-floating sanctifiers in a religious economy that is more like a market. In this way, the postcolonial saints are unlike earlier pre-colonial and colonial-era saints, such as Umar Tall and Shaykh Hamallah. Although the actual signs of sainthood – miracles, numerous followers, great wealth – do not seem to have changed that much over the past few centuries, the relations between the more privatised saints and some of their followers have been dramatically transformed.

If the idea of saints as free-floating sanctifiers might seem to be the language of the outside analyst, I want to note that I have indeed heard some Malians express such views about saints. They criticise the activities of certain Muslim religious leaders, though generally without naming names, denouncing them as petty traders or merchants who sell their prayers and amulets, sometimes to the highest bidder. While there is general agreement that religious leaders do not have set fees for their services, many point to inflation – rising fees for particular services – as well as inflationary pressures in this service economy. That is, even without set fees, more is often expected in return for their services.

If some Malians suggested to me that the privileged relations between elites and the two religious leaders would eventually undermine the religious leaders' authority (cf. Soares 1996b), it is striking that such criticisms generally do not target the individual religious leaders or the notion of saints or sainthood. This might relate of course to the quite widespread fear of saints and their power to curse. In fact, many people direct their criticisms toward those who act as intermediaries with the saints, frequently accusing them not only of hindering access to the religious leaders, but also of graft and corruption. This is not unlike the person around a charismatic ruler, described by Weber, 'who can take over responsibility for the acts of government, especially for failures and unpopular measures' (Weber 1978: 1,147). Needless to say, the fact that the religious leaders themselves generally remain above criticism is dismaying to certain modernising actors in Mali, particularly members of the small, urban secular elite (cf. Chapter 8). For some members of this elite, such religious leaders embody all that they find reprehensible about the 'traditional'. For instance, I know Malian civil servants who condemn in moralising – though always rather hushed – tones what they see as the profligacy of the religious leaders.

Be that as it may, one can say that for many people in postcolonial Mali, religious authority has been personalised in these two religious leaders with reputations as saints. Although this notion of personalisation draws upon the writings of Weber, it departs significantly from them. According to Weber, when charisma becomes routinised, it is necessarily less 'revolutionary' and less important. In this way of thinking, if charisma becomes hereditary and attached to a particular lineage, it also becomes 'depersonalized' (Weber 1978: 1,135ff.). However, what I want to argue is that charisma in this setting has not undergone a process of 'suffocation' in the face of material interests (ibid.: 1,120). Rather, charisma is a potentiality that manifests itself in the personalised authority of certain religious leaders, who come from certain lineages with hereditary charisma. Indeed, such figures have been able to re-personalise charisma. The commodity form has been a key element in this process of personalisation.

Religious authority has come to be centred on a few individuals rather than any institutions like the Sufi organisations with which they have historically been associated (cf. ibid: 1,135f.). Indeed, if anything, the institutional basis of the Sufi orders has been shrinking in postcolonial Mali, a situation that, by almost all reports, does not seem to be the case in neighbouring Senegal.[30] Even in those regions in Mali where the Sufi orders have been important historically, it is increasingly rare for people to be initiated formally into any Sufi order. However, the decline in the organisational importance of the Sufi orders does not mean that notions of hierarchy and charisma, embodied most importantly in the notion of the Muslim saint, are any less important. Nor does it suggest that people have been embracing more 'reformist' ideas about Islam – though this is happening in some cases – or even that some are finding 'secularism' more appealing (cf. Chapters 7 and 8). On the contrary, with the decline in the organisational importance of the Sufi orders, certain religious leaders have become known for their individual saintly qualities, association with miracles, in short, their charisma.

It is interesting to note how many Malians from all sectors of society express disdain for certain kinds of ordinary religious specialists, particularly those minor 'traditional' Muslim religious figures who make a living as diviners or sellers of amulets – *maraboutaillons* or *petits marabouts* in the colonial lexicon. They also regularly disparage those *marabouts d'affaires*, who are directly analogous to *hommes d'affaires* or businessmen, who offer their services for money (see Conclusion). In fact, many denounce all such minor Muslim religious specialists as impostors and charlatans. These very same people often consider a particular Muslim religious leader an authentic saint. This is the case even though many admit that one might never know for sure if someone is truly a saint. In any case, the two religious leaders in Nioro attract followers and clients from all sectors of society, from the very poorest to the most influential, not all of whom, one should note, are necessarily Muslims (see Diallo 1988). Similarly, I know self-professed 'reformist' Muslims who have travelled themselves to visit the saints, seeking blessings from them or their intercession with God.

Although visits with Muslim religious leaders have been occurring for centuries in West Africa, such activities have expanded and accelerated, especially in the postcolonial period. As I have noted, the French colonial state took particular note of gifts given to Muslim religious leaders and often tried to restrict considerable accumulation on their part, not to mention ordinary people's visits to them. Unlike the colonial state, the postcolonial Malian state has not restricted the interactions between religious leaders and their followers, nor the exchange, accumulation and redistribution of resources around them. In fact, the postcolonial state has often facilitated such interactions and accumulation, thereby helping to boost the reputations of certain religious leaders who sometimes attract followers from across the region. It is widely discussed in Mali how the postcolonial state and its agents exempted the two religious leaders from paying import duties on those things considered *hadaya*. If Moussa Traoré, Mali's second president, lavished gifts upon religious leaders, including the two in question, it is worth emphasising that extravagant gifts from officials from the highest levels of the government to the very same religious leaders have continued in the era of multi-party elections in Mali.

Modern means of communication and transportation have been important to the activities around the religious leaders. On a much greater scale, people – elite and non-elite – are able to travel relatively easily over greater distances to the towns for the annual visits and at other times of the year, and to give gifts to the religious leaders. I have been present on several occasions when new imported cars have been delivered to the religious leaders, who not only have better and newer vehicles than the local post-colonial administration, but generally a wider selection of cars, including the latest models. In the 1990s, the religious leaders received Toyota Landcruisers and pick-up trucks – preferred vehicles for navigating roads that have seriously deteriorated since the colonial era when they were built and maintained through the use of forced labour.

Central to understanding the prayer economy is a prevailing notion that there can be only one spiritual head of a particular lineage of religious specialists and saintly lineages in particular. Thus, certain individuals – either the oldest or most charismatic – become a major, if not the sole, locus of gift-giving for a particular saintly lineage. In recent times of economic and political uncertainty – structural adjustment, currency devaluation, political upheaval – many ordinary Muslims have turned to the religious leaders of Nioro who are thought to be close to God. Many of those looking to them are urban-dwellers or migrants associated with urban economic activities, market trading and commerce. Many such people are struggling to attain wealth and economic success or simply to maintain and to reproduce what they have already acquired in a precarious economic environment. Given such uncertainties and the seeming precariousness of all wealth, those who have experienced new-found financial success will often start immediately to give gifts to the saints or to seek out their services.

In many cases, people appeal to one of the religious leaders when their chances of economic success seem dim. Those facing bankruptcy will sometimes even try to secure loans in order to extend to saints expensive gifts they otherwise cannot afford. One struggling petty merchant I know pleaded with his friends and relatives to loan him the money he needed to purchase a gift of significant value for one of the religious leaders. It is surprising (at least to me) though apparently not unusual for a saint's retainer – whose own economic situation might also be precarious – to inform someone, even publicly, that an intended gift to a saint is woefully inadequate. Others facing ruin in risky trading schemes travel to Nioro in a desperate bid to reverse their fortunes. I have met still yet others involved in the traffic in precious gemstones who do the same. Such ordinary people revere the same religious leaders as the elites, drawn by a reputation they may well have learned about through word of mouth or the mass media and popular culture. With such attention on the saints' miracles and with gift-giving focused so closely upon them, people have effectively pushed other members of the saintly lineages out of the religious economy, permanently or at least until a period of succession in the event that the saintly character of a particular lineage has not been exhausted.

It is significant that the two religious leaders usually remain in Nioro or close by (in the case of Muhammadu, at a neighbouring hamlet near where he keeps his livestock). With very few exceptions, they do not visit other people in the town. They travel rarely to the large towns in Mali, and when they do visit, say, the capital, Bamako, they never stay very long. They might do so when in transit or possibly to seek medical attention. Hady's visits to Bamako have usually been on his way to catch a flight to perform the *hajj* or to visit followers in Europe, while Muhammadu's only recent trips to Bamako were for medical care in one of the private clinics there. Their avoidance of cities and other towns in Mali might relate to the fact that these are places where decadence and impiety are known to reign – that is, the exact opposite of what saints are thought to embody. More important, perhaps, is the fact that the religious economy in such large urban centres is invariably more complex and diverse. In short, competition is much more intensive there. All of this is without mentioning their potential critics – urban-based secularists and 'reformist' Muslims who contest the legitimacy of these celebrated religious leaders.

In Nioro, it is quite clear that the two religious leaders, in some ways more privatised saintly figures, influence nearly all areas of social life in the town. However, people also readily acknowledge and even openly discuss the potential instability of authority, particularly as it relates to questions of succession. At the beginning of the twenty-first century, no one anticipates another new absent religious leader associated with the town. On the contrary, people acknowledge and anticipate that once the two powerful saints are no longer alive, there will inevitably be succession disputes and struggles. Given the number of their followers, enormous wealth, reputation for miracles, and their many male descendants, not to mention others who might pretend to be their successors, people talk about future succession struggles on a scale that would have been unimaginable before the saints had such personalised authority.

CONCLUSION

An expanded network of persons – elite and non-elite – is in patronage relations with the religious leaders and their lineages, transferring commodities and money to them. In the past two decades, the scale of the annual visits has increased, and there have been huge infusions of capital, construction of expensive homes and the acquisition of luxury items by the religious leaders. The great wealth of the religious leaders has allowed them to maintain enormous households in which the women – wives and daughters – usually live in seclusion and in great comfort. Although it should be clear by now that the religious leaders are not necessarily expected to lead austere lives, they do, however, provide alms – never enough some critics note – for the many poor individuals who gather around them. They also reward their faithful followers with gifts and largesse. Through accumulation, the religious leaders have been able to exhibit the signs of wealth, very large families and support of followers – the 'gifts of God' that index their sanctity – and seeming immunity from the incredible political and economic uncertainty most people face – in short, their 'power'. The religious leaders seem to have been immune to the 1991 overthrow of seemingly omnipotent President Traoré with whom they both had ties. Moreover, as many Malians point out, they seem not to have suffered financially (and may even have profited) when the currency was devalued by half at the beginning of 1994.

The elite followers have been key actors, facilitating, as they have, the displays of wealth that have helped to boost the reputations of the religious leaders, reinforcing and extending their religious power and authority. But non-elite followers have been no less important here, because of their number, the volume of their gifts and the religious commodities they help to diffuse. If the two religious leaders in postcolonial Mali have the reputation of being more pious than ordinary people – moral exemplars and, in this way, somewhat like Weberian puritans – they are *not* ascetic, even if they do live far from major urban and economic centres. In Mali, commodification has been perhaps one of the most important factors in the personalisation of religious authority in certain presumed Muslim saints, ensuring that they embody much that is elusive – sainthood, wealth, fame – though no less desirable, to many, if not most, ordinary people.

'REFORM'

In preceding chapters, I outlined the evolution of the Hamawiyya and the Tijaniyya, and emphasised the strength and resilience of these two Sufi orders and the power and authority of their present leaders, particularly in the prayer economy. Although the two Sufi orders and their respective leaders dominate the field of religious practice in Nioro, other Islamic discourses are hardly inconsequential in Nioro and its hinterland. In fact, Islamic 'reformist' ideas, including anti-Sufi currents, have long been important in this region of West Africa. In general, reformists in West Africa have been opposed in principle to the way that Islam has historically been practised there; they usually seek to bring religious practice more in line with what are deemed more 'correct' practices, modelled on the presumed centre of the Islamic world, the Arab Middle East. They have, for example, criticised the veneration of Muslim religious leaders, the Sufi orders and the use of esoteric practices. If reformism, its emergence, and spread have been documented for colonial and postcolonial Mali, the broader influence of reformism has not.[1] Although reformism does not exist in the form of separate institutions such as mosques or schools in the town of Nioro proper, it has, nevertheless, been on the rise in the area from at least the 1940s, if not earlier. In this chapter, I trace the presence and influence of reformism and certain reformist ideas in the region of Nioro and some of the local responses to them. In doing so, one of my objectives is to understand some of the ways in which the Sufi tradition might be transformed.

During the colonial period, French colonial administrators used the terms 'Wahhabi', 'Wahhabism' and 'Wahhabiyya' rather loosely to refer to reformist Muslims in West Africa. Although such language continues to be used there today in both French and in the region's vernaculars, it is in fact somewhat misleading. Wahhabiyya is generally the term used to designate the community Muhammad ibn 'Abd al-Wahhab (d. 1787) formed in Arabia. The House of Sa'ud adopted and propagated his teachings, which emphasised the oneness of God (Ar., *tawhid*) and the need to extirpate un-Islamic practices. Those the French labelled Wahhabis in West Africa were never simply the advocates of such 'Wahhabi' doctrines. Indeed, they were always a more heterogeneous group of individuals. However, Salafi doctrine has been a very important influence on such reformists, and modern

Salafiyya ideas about Muslims facing Western colonial rule and domination and the perceived need for the reform of Muslim society have been key here.[2] Thus, the teachings of such modern reformist writers as the Egyptian Muhammad Abduh (d. 1905), the Syrian Rashid Rida (d. 1935) and the Algerian Abd al-Hamid ibn Badis (d. 1940) have been particularly influential among some 'reformists' in Mali.

Although it is clear that the colonial administration borrowed the terminology about 'Wahhabis' and 'the Wahhabiyya' from French Orientalist scholarship, it is not clear when they first started to use such terminology in West Africa. However, by the early 1950s, the administration was regularly using this terminology to designate various alleged reformists in West Africa. The African Muslim opponents of such reformists in AOF adopted the very same colonial terminology in the region's vernaculars. In this discussion, I have decided to use the terms, 'reformist' and 'reformism'. While this language departs from most local and scholarly conventions, it is perhaps more sensitive to the reformists themselves. In Nioro, the overwhelming majority, who are not reformists, do in fact use the terms Wahhabis and the Wahhabiyya to refer to reformists. However, these so-called Wahhabis invariably reject these terms. In fact, those I have met usually prefer to call themselves *Ahl al-Sunna* (Ar., the people of the Sunna) or, simply, Sunnis, that is, those who follow the *sunna*, the authoritative practice of the Prophet Muhammad. I use the terms reformists and reformism in order to avoid any confusion (not to mention controversy) since Tijanis and Hamawis also say that they follow the Sunna and are, therefore, Sunnis. I also employ such language since it reflects the discourse of some of my 'reformist' informants who emphasised to me that they saw themselves in a position analogous to that of Protestants who object to or protest about the way others practise the religion.

If the history of the Sufi orders in Nioro is inextricably linked to colonial and postcolonial history, this is no less the case for reformism. As I have noted, the colonial repression and persecution of those affiliated with the Hamawiyya reached their peak in the 1940s. After the war, and particularly in the 1950s, the colonial administration increasingly focused its attention on those Muslims perceived to be the latest threat to the colonial order – so-called Wahhabis, including those with educational ties and affinities with the Arab Middle East.[3] This is not in any way to suggest that Hamawis and the Hamawiyya were no longer the objects of colonial administrative surveillance (see Chapter 3).

It is important to recognise, however, that reformist ideas were present in this part of Africa long before any colonial administrative actions were taken against reformists (Triaud 1986). By 1929, the Mauritanian scholar Ibn Mayaba's criticisms of the Tijaniyya on doctrinal and other grounds were circulating in written form in AOF. The colonial authorities were not only aware of his writings, but they had also sometimes even seized them.[4] In the two decades prior to independence, the colonial sphere with modern communications, increased travel for trade, labour migration, the *hajj* and the spread of education (both religious and secular) facilitated the dissemination of such reformist ideas, including anti-Sufi ideas. As in earlier episodes in the long history of *la politique musulmane* in French West Africa, colonial experiences with Muslim reformists and nationalist currents elsewhere, especially in North Africa, informed administrative actions against the advocates of such ideas in West Africa.[5]

Although the colonial fear of Islam, pan-Islamism and pan-Arabism remained fairly constant during the colonial period, the 1950s – the decade in which reformism spread in West Africa – was a time when the whole colonial enterprise seemed increasingly precarious.[6] The nationalism sweeping the Arab world and the independence of British colonies, most notably India and Pakistan in 1947, and, then the independence of Indonesia in 1949, all with large Muslim populations, were especially alarming to the French.[7] In North Africa, the imminent independence of Libya from Italy in the early 1950s seemed to pose a direct threat to the French colonial project in the Maghreb, not to mention sub-Saharan Africa, more generally.[8] In 1954, the war in Algeria began, and the French suffered defeat in Indochina. In 1956, there was the Suez crisis.

In addition to such events occurring beyond West Africa, there were indications that the *Islam noir* of the colonial imagination was coming unstuck at least in some quarters of AOF. In 1952, in a long report on the state of Islam in AOF, the former governor Beyriès identified the presence of 'Wahhabi' ideas in various places in AOF, as well as the popularity of the ideas of the 'modernist' Muhammad Abduh.[9] Some of the presumed main carriers of such ideas were a number of West Africans who returned to the region in the 1940s after studying at the Islamic university of al-Azhar in Cairo or at other institutions in the Hijaz. Upon return, some of them specifically sought to reform the way Islam was practised in West Africa.

These people, whom the French and their West African Muslim critics labelled Wahhabis, were usually critical of the existing hierarchy associated with Islamic religious practice and the Muslim establishment in particular with its working relationship with the French. They thought this hierarchy and establishment prevented people from being proper Muslims. Such ideas were explicitly stated, for example in the Senegalese reformist Cheikh Touré's 1957 book, *Afin que tu deviennes un croyant*, written in both Arabic and French and published in Dakar. Reformists wrote and spoke forcefully about the need to combat *bid'a* (Ar., innovation), which means unlawful innovation in Islam. Not only did they argue that the idea of intercession with God through religious leaders, including saints, was fraudulent, but they even went so far as to condemn the Sufi orders as *bid'a* and Muslim saints as dangerous (see Touré 1957: *passim*). In a direct challenge to the use of the Islamic esoteric sciences widespread in West Africa, they argued that amulets – and by extension all such things – are identified with a state of unbelief (Ar., *kufr*)[10] and 'association' or idolatry (Ar., *shirk*), that is treating things other than God as a deity (ibid.).[11] That is, they used the same argument that many Muslims here have used against the use of un-Islamic knowledge or *bamanaya* to criticise the Sufi orders. Interestingly, reformists also quite readily adopted both the language of the French colonial lexicon, such as *gris-gris* for amulets, and the 'modernist' perspective in order to denounce such practices as 'charlatanism', 'trickery' and 'lies'.[12]

It is important to recognise that there was a decidedly anti-colonial slant to some, though clearly not all, reformist critiques at this time.[13] For example, in the introduction to his book, Cheikh Touré boldly identified 'the trio' of the 'Capitalist, Marabout, Colonialist', who 'exploited, misled, and oppressed' people in West Africa (1957: 1), a theme upon which his book did not elaborate any further. He did, however, decry 'the collabora-tion' with colonial authorities 'carried on even in our mosques, meetings, and religious holidays' (ibid.: 9–10; see also Diané 1956, and Chailley 1962). In 1954, after the outbreak of war in Algeria, some reformists demanded that West African Muslims not be sent to serve in North Africa. Toward their goal of bringing the practice of Islam in line with their views, some reformists sought to give students an Islamic religious education that emphasised literacy in Arabic. This was to enable students to have direct and more immediate access to Islamic religious texts so as to help them to break away from local religious practices they found suspect. The French saw the advanced and widespread education in Arabic that reformists advocated as a potential and dangerous threat to their own authority.

Needless to say, from the perspective of other Muslims living in West Africa, the charges of innovation, idolatry and unbelief reformists made against them were highly inflammatory. Not only did they openly challenge the way Islam had long been practised in the region, but also they suggested that many, if not most, people in West Africa were not Muslims, even though they might consider themselves as such. To equate them with non-Muslims was deeply offensive to them. Consequently, many West African Muslims, regardless of perspective or opinion on the French colonial presence, were immediately opposed to these people and the schools they opened in various places in AOF.

By the early 1950s, colonial administrators were aware that some Muslim religious leaders, without direct contact with the Middle East or North Africa, had themselves broken with the Sufi orders and had begun to embrace what seemed to be more reformist ideas about Islam. One of the most prominent of these Muslims was Demba Wagué (d. 1978) from Barouéli, a renowned centre of Islamic learning near Ségou. Although

Hamallah had named Wagué one of his *muqaddams*, he eventually renounced this title.[14] In the early 1950s, colonial reports did not identify Wagué as a 'Wahhabi', but noted that he belonged to no Sufi order and 'appears in his remarks rather reserved towards Sufis and saints'.[15] If, at the height of the repression of Hamallah's followers, the French might have lauded the renunciation of Hamallah or any distancing from him, they later came to appreciate this turning-away from established Muslim leaders and the Sufi orders, including the Hamawiyya, as a possible threat to the *Islam noir* with which they thought they were familiar.

It is significant that one of Wagué's teachers was Mamadou Doucouré, the imam of Mourdiah (another centre for Islamic education), who had also broken with Hamallah in the late 1930s, over the issue of Hamallah abridging his prayers (see Chapter 3). According to colonial sources, despite his break with Hamallah, Doucouré remained part of what the French called the 'traditional Islamic culture' they wanted to resist any Islamic currents that sought inspiration from outside West Africa.[16] One of Doucouré's sons, Abdoul Wahhab, had studied at the Zaytuna, the renowned North African Islamic educational institution in Tunis, and, upon his return, became one of the leaders of the so-called counter-reform 'movement' along with Amadou Hampâté Ba.[17] Beginning in the early 1950s (Cardaire 1954: 155), this counter-reform movement was directed against reformists, who already had a noticeable presence in the form of schools in some of the larger towns in Soudan and Côte d'Ivoire. If the counter-reform movement was not completely controlled by the colonial administration, it was, as one administrator put it, 'under the benevolent watch of the administration'.[18] With what must have been the approval of the colonial administration, the movement also tried to cultivate relations with some of the most prominent Muslim religious leaders from AOF, including those with saintly reputations, in order to curb the influence of the reformists.

As some have pointed out, the reformists specifically chose Bamako, the political and economic capital of the Soudan, as the site for the propagation of their ideas in part because of the city's distance from potential Muslim critics (Kaba 1974: 85ff.). Thus, they seem to have avoided established centres of religious activity in the Soudan such as Nioro. Where there was a reformist presence in the form of schools, the counter-reform movement tried to establish rival educational institutions, which generally failed to attract as many students as the reformists' schools. During the late 1950s, there were serious confrontations between reformists and their opponents in Bamako and elsewhere in southern Mali and Côte d'Ivoire (see Kaba 1974). The counter-reform movement was, however, ultimately unable to prevent reformists from establishing a strong and visible presence in Soudan and postcolonial Mali.

REFORMISTS IN NIORO

What is perhaps most notable about the town of Nioro proper is the very negligible direct influence reformists seem to have had. This is not to suggest that people in Nioro were unaware of reformism. In fact, that would have been practically impossible. It has been noted how in the 1940s, Mahmud Ba (1905–78) opened a 'reformist' *madrasa* in Kayes, the largest town and colonial urban centre closest to Nioro.[19] Ba was among those who had studied in the Hijaz before returning to West Africa where he opened new schools. At some point in the 1940s, Ba even seems to have recruited some students for his school in Kayes from the immediate Nioro area. Informants in Nioro (both those sympathetic and those hostile to his teachings) report that he visited Nioro and some of the surrounding villages, attracting people by claiming he would renew their initiation into the Tijaniyya, using this as a pretext to draw people so that he could spread his ideas against the Sufi orders. Eventually, he would come into conflict with prominent members of the Muslim establishment in Kayes and elsewhere in AOF, as he increasingly spoke out more forcefully against the Sufi orders.

In the mid-1950s, colonial administrative reports identified a few indivi-duals in villages near Nioro as 'Wahhabis',[20] but the presence of reformists in Nioro itself seems to have been virtually non-existent.[21] Although some from the Nioro area have been involved in the spread of reformist ideas elsewhere (see below), reformists seem to have made few inroads in the town itself. At the present time, perhaps unlike any other large town in Mali, Nioro has no reformist institutions such as mosques or schools, not least because the number of those who would characterise themselves as reform-ists in Nioro is very small indeed. In 1994, reformists in Nioro claimed that there were no more than twelve such people in the town, and, in 1998, they told me the number had not changed. Such a restricted presence seems to confirm Jean-Loup Amselle's claim that reformists can more easily establish a presence in those places where there are no Muslim scholars to oppose them (1985: 355 n.1).

Although I mentioned at the outset some of the prevailing reformist criticisms of other Muslims, I want to consider reformist ideas as expressed by reformists themselves in Nioro. To do so, I draw from conversations with various reformists in the town. The man whom most take to have been the first reformist to live in Nioro enumerated to me the differences that he sees between himself and other Muslims in Nioro. These differences are all things that he and most other reformists find illegitimate. In the order in which he listed them, they are: (1) predicting the future, which may be by way of geomancy or other such methods, (2) the veneration of religious leaders, (3) use of *gris-gris* or amulets, and (4) *sadaqa* (Ar., 'sacrifice') or prestations that accompany the recitation of the Quran upon people's deaths.[22] The first three of these call the authority of nearly all religious leaders in the town directly in question. The town's major and minor religious leaders accept and use the esoteric sciences in one way or another, though not necessarily for predicting the future, and they do venerate those higher up in the presumed hierarchy. The fourth on his list calls into question one of the most important life-cycle rituals – the recitation of the Quran after a person's death and the prestations that accompany this recitation – that is widespread among Muslims in many parts of West Africa. It is noteworthy, however, that Sufism as devotional practice is not singled out for condemnation.

While some have noted that Muslim reformists in other places have attacked established legal formalism (Launay 1992: 86), this has been less the case in Nioro where none of the reformists in the town has anything in the way of scholarly credentials that could begin to rival the established Muslim leadership and those associated with them. As in some of the discourses mentioned above, I heard reformists in Nioro talk about the need to combat *bid'a* and *shirk* and to bring local Islamic practice into line with what they consider to be the universalistic imperatives of the principle of the oneness of God (Ar., *tawhid*) from which many Malian Muslims, in their view, necessarily diverge.

As elsewhere, most reformists in Nioro pray with their arms crossed – the reason their opponents, French and African, called them *les bras croisés* – unlike most Muslims in the immediate region who pray with their arms hanging by their sides.[23] What this means is that a person prays with 'the right arm over the left arm' held 'on the chest or between the chest and the navel', as a popular book written by Kabiné Diané in the 1950s explains (Diané 1973).[24] Praying with one's arms crossed is definitely a doctrinal issue over which people have strongly disagreed. As Diané points out in his book, Muslims should follow the example set by the Prophet Muhammad. Since the Prophet Muhammad crossed his arms when he prayed, and this is attested to by eminent scholars, then Muslims should follow him in doing so (ibid.). Reformists in Nioro told me that praying with crossed arms was absolutely central to their sense of being Muslim, and they could not pray otherwise.

While the manner of praying is a doctrinal issue, at least for those able and permitted to engage in discussions of doctrine, it is clear that how one prays has also come to have enormous symbolic import, although in some cases, this seems to have lessened over time. Not too long ago, some Muslims in Nioro (and elsewhere) denounced those who prayed with their arms crossed as non-Muslims (Ar., *kafir*). Even to this day, the sight of someone praying with crossed arms is profoundly unsettling to many people in Nioro. This is because the manner of prayer conjures up for many people all that they find offensive about reformists. However, increased travel and exposure to images of Muslims praying elsewhere in the world, particularly on television, have certainly helped to make such postures of prayer seem more commonplace, if not entirely acceptable, to many Malian Muslims.

I now turn to consider the social trajectories of some of Nioro's reformists before giving the portrait of a typical reformist, if there were ever such a thing. The first reformist to live in Nioro was born in the town in the early 1920s. He studied for six years at the Quranic school run by Madi Assa Kaba Jakhite, the imam of Nioro, before getting involved in commerce in Mali and then later in Central Africa. Over the course of about ten years, while working in the precious gemstone trade in the area of Lumumbashi in Zaire (now the Democratic Republic of Congo), he came into contact with many other Malians, including some prominent reformists, whose ideas helped to influence him. In the 1960s, he eventually decided to become a reformist. In 1972, when he returned with his Zairean wife and savings to re-establish permanent residence in Nioro, he was, by nearly all accounts, the first reformist from the town to live there. When he went to the mosque and prayed with his arms crossed, people moved away from him. Some even went so far as to say he was a *kafir*, that is, not a Muslim, after seeing him pray this way. Because of this hostility, he decided to pray at his own house instead of at the mosque and did so even at the time of my fieldwork, when there were other reformists who prayed regularly at the mosque. Not issuing from a very prominent or populous lineage, this man remained fairly marginal, and most people ignored his presence.

A man from one of the most prominent lineages of Muslim religious specialists, who was born in 1929, told me that his experiences as a reformist are not unusual. In contrast to the first man, his religious studies in Nioro were more advanced than the average student. Over a period of thirteen years, he read through the Quran more than once and studied some of the basic texts of jurisprudence used in the region.[25] Like the first man, he worked in the trade of precious gemstones in Central Africa – in Congo and Zaire, among other places – in his case, for twenty years during which time he made several trips to Europe. During this period, he too was exposed to ideas critical of the way Islam is practised in West Africa. The most sustained influence was that of an older man, who was also part of the West African trading diaspora in Central Africa and whose family, another lineage of Muslim religious specialists, also came from Nioro. This older man acted as his mentor and influenced him with reformist ideas. At the same time, other West African Muslims who periodically visited and preached reformist ideas were an important influence on him. He told me the most prominent of these included Mahmud Ba, the founder of the *madrasa* in Kayes.

In 1975 or 1976 – he said he could not remember exactly when – this second man decided to become a reformist. About five years later, he returned to Nioro because his female relatives asked him to do so as there were no other surviving adult males in their immediate family. By this time in his life, he had gone on the *hajj* twice – a clear indication of having a substantial amount of money, at least at that time. Although the *hajj* had certainly become more commonplace than in the not-so-distant past, it was still rather prestigious to have accomplished it. Unlike the first reformist, this man does pray at the Friday mosque and does so with his arms crossed. It is important to note that his being a reformist has caused tensions and strains in his relations with the rest of his extended family of religious specialists. Some in his family told me that his becoming a reformist was not at all unexpected. One of his cousins even attributed it to his longstanding tendency to be a zealot in much that he did.

One of the most recent examples of someone from the town to become a reformist is a wealthy man who is not only a successful merchant, but also one of the largest owners of rental properties in the town. In comparison with the other two, his religious education was much more limited. Unlike many adult men in the town, he has had limited experience of working away from Nioro. He does, however, come from a lineage of religious specialists with enduring ties with the family of Hamallah and the Hamawiyya. Upon return from a recent trip to Saudi Arabia for the *hajj*, he immediately began to pray at the Friday mosque and also adopted the manner of praying with crossed arms. Praying at the mosque constituted a sharp and much-discussed break with the Hamawiyya given that nearly all his extended family in the town prays on Fridays at the *zawiya* and not at the Friday mosque. His many critics pointed out that, as one of the wealthiest people in town, he had simply decided to become part of the larger network of well-to-do reformists in Bamako and elsewhere. His extended family also worries that he will be able to use his abundant resources to attract others, especially young men, to reformism by offering them financial support.

In general, the reformists in Nioro are all men, who have travelled extensively, usually as migrant labourers and traders, frequently to Central Africa and sometimes to Europe. Although most are relatively well-off, they are not, with the one notable exception, among the most prosperous merchants in the town (cf. Amselle 1985). At the time of my fieldwork, all were adult men at least fifty years old, and nearly all were Soninke. From these stories and others, I would like to describe the typical profile and trajectory of reformists in Nioro. After several years away from Nioro, such people, who, in most cases, have had some religious education, have been changed as Muslims, undergoing what might be called 'conversion'. After returning to the town, they have been earnest in their concern to change the way that Islam is practised locally. None of them leads an ostentatious lifestyle, though in all cases they have a certain amount of money or level of income. This, it seems, allows them to resist the social pressures that they undoubtedly encounter from the wider community not to forsake the way Islam has long been practised in the town.

Given the relative size of the town of Nioro and the considerable number of people involved in migration, the small number of reformists is striking. I suspect that the social pressures not to become a reformist are so strong that others, who might share some of their views, are reluctant to identify themselves as such. In fact, there is a group of men who do not consider themselves reformists nor do they pray with their arms crossed, but nevertheless they have gathered around one of the most prominent reformists in town. Although they have not had anything like an advanced religious education, they all have engaged in advanced secular education. After working for years in the Malian civil service, they are all now retired and draw their pensions. They consider themselves devoted Muslims and seem to agree with many of the reformist ideas critical of the way that Islam is practised in the town. But they told me they were not willing to embrace reformism. Not only would they not unequivocally accept reformist ideas, they were unwilling or unable to be Muslim in the reformist style, that is, to pray with arms crossed or to abandon the *sadaqa* associated with important rituals of the life-cycle. Ironically enough, the relationship that these men have with the reformist is not unlike that which ordinary Muslims have with religious leaders. Some of the younger kin of these men even like to joke about this, calling them (behind their backs) 'the Wahhabi's children' since he seems to give them instruction as a father might give instruction to his children or, indeed, as a religious guide might give instructions to a follower.

In sociological discussions of reformism in West Africa, some have pointed out that reformism 'absolutely takes exception to pre-colonial hereditary caste and class distinctions' and that 'all Muslims are equal, whether they are chiefs, griots or slaves' (Amselle 1985: 349). If one considers the social bases of reformism in Nioro, it is clear that this is quite simply not the case. Reformists living in Nioro are all from free-born lineages, that is, their status is neither servile nor 'caste'. This is also the case for their associates, who do not embrace reformism, with the exception of one man from a family of blacksmiths ('caste') – though neither he nor his father ever practised this profession. Even though some reformists might decry the hereditary distinctions of 'caste' and servile status, such distinctions are in full force for these men, as they are for many others in Nioro. In fact, the reformists in question told me they would never marry or even give consent to one of their children to marry a person of servile or 'caste' status.[26] Be this as it may, such questioning of hereditary social distinctions does indeed seem to occur in some of the surrounding areas of Nioro and also in other large urban centres in Mali, particularly in Bamako.

Although pre-colonial hereditary distinctions are still relevant to reformists in Nioro, such reformists do seem to advocate an ideology in which all people, regardless of hereditary distinctions, are expected to work (cf.

Amselle 1985). With their extensive experience as long-term migrants and/ or their substantial accumulation of resources, the reformists in the town are more individualistic, not only in the conduct of their economic affairs, but also in their style of religiosity, as they question the existing organisation of religious practice.[27] On many occasions, reformists and their supporters in Nioro explained to me how objectionable they found the relationships between ordinary followers and religious leaders that are associated with the Sufi orders. In their view, what they see as the complete submission of people to elevated religious leaders is unacceptable in that it essentially allows the latter to live off the labour and resources of the former.

How these self-styled Sunnis have attempted to go about changing the way Islam is practised in the town has been very much constrained by the fact that the Sufi orders and their leaders dominate the town and the broader region. The individual temperaments of the different reformists have also been an important factor. On the whole, reformists in Nioro have had to be cautiously critical of the Sufi orders, the town's leading religious leaders and their practices. While some reformists in Nioro referred in private to those who do not share their ideas as *Ahl al-bid'a* (Ar., innovators), they did not use such inflammatory language in public pronouncements. The restricted number of reformists would almost seem to guarantee that stridency would not only be imprudent but futile.

As most people, reformist and otherwise, are quick to point out, many people from Nioro have been exposed to reformist ideas while living elsewhere in Mali and beyond. The high rates of migration, seasonal and more permanent, make this almost inevitable. In many cases, such people frequently adopt some of the outward signs of reformism, particularly praying with crossed arms, when they are away from the town. Upon return to Nioro, their families and the broader community expect them to abandon – and they usually do abandon – such practices and follow the accepted practices of their forebears.

One man in his sixties, who was formally initiated in the Tijaniyya decades ago, expressed views that I think are fairly representative of those opposed to reformists. He told me that in Nioro they have almost come to expect their relatives to embrace reformist trappings, such as praying with crossed arms, while away from Nioro but to conform to local conventions when they return. He himself undoubtedly had regular and frequent contact with reformists, in some of the different places he worked over many years as a migrant labourer and merchant, particularly in Bouaké, Côte d'Ivoire, long an important centre of reformist activities. In this man's view, the serious problem is those few people who do not abandon reformist practices upon return to Nioro, and thereby refuse to follow locally accepted and time-honoured practices such as respecting their religious leaders and their authority, praying with arms uncrossed, and engaging in the important *sadaqa* rituals associated with the life-cycle.[28] Such people, he noted, are not numerous, though they are, nonetheless, pernicious.

As for the many people from Nioro who have established more permanent residence in other places, particularly Bamako, many of them have indeed openly embraced reformist ideas. There are many people in Nioro from families with long ties to the Hamawiyya and Tijaniyya who are committed reformists in Bamako and elsewhere. Some of these people are scholars, which suggests that scholars with reformist inclinations would necessarily have to leave Nioro. While, for many in the town, the existence of reformists from Nioro is cause for considerable dismay, it has become so commonplace that it is no longer quite so jarring as it must have been in the past. In casual conversation, I have heard Hamawis and Tijanis in Nioro inquire in jest about their respective 'Wahhabi' relatives in Bamako. One man from a lineage of religious specialists with long ties to the Hamawiyya pointed out to me that such relatives of his own had at least not forsaken Islam and become atheists. From the perspective of those in Nioro sympathetic to reformism, the fact that there are so many people from the town and broader region living elsewhere who are reformists points to the wave of the future. Several people assured me that this would be the normal, even rational, route of social evolution. One man told me that on future visits to Nioro, I too would be able to notice the evolution in this direction. When I asked about this upon return in 1998, another reformist told me the religious leaders of Nioro just had too many devoted followers for this to have happened.

Despite their restricted numbers, some reformists have, over the years, made efforts to have a more visible presence in the town, particularly through the construction of new schools. In the end, all such efforts seem to have been thwarted. The man identified above as the town's first reformist was the first to initiate such efforts.[29] On several occasions, this man has tried to organise a private school in the town that would give fee-paying students a religious education and promote literacy in Arabic. Eventually, he tried to organise a *madrasa* that would give instruction in a broader range of subjects than in the kind of religious education available in the town.[30] In the late 1970s, he acquired a piece of land close to the centre of town and organised a small school,[31] which at first seems to have been primarily for the education of his own children, whom he did not want studying in the state-run French-language schools. He was able to hire a local teacher to give instruction. Almost immediately, prominent citizens in the town with ties to the major religious leaders demanded that the school be closed, claiming that serious problems would arise if it were not. Faced with what he (and many others) saw to be a thinly veiled threat of violence, the sponsor of the school felt compelled to close it and did so. Since some reformists had been able to establish a *madrasa* in a neighbouring village by this time, the man sent his children there for their education. It is significant that if the school's first teacher, who came from Nioro, had been sympathetic to reformism, this changed rather quickly. After the closure of the school, the teacher apparently became a close and devoted follower of one of the town's major religious leaders. As many suggested to me, this illustrates both enormous pressure not to associate with reformists and their activities, and the very 'power' of the major religious leaders.

A few years later, the town's first reformist was able to secure official permission from the local government administration to open a *madrasa* in Nioro. He stressed to me that this had only been possible through the support he received from the highest administrator in the town, the *commandant du cercle*, who was from eastern Mali and sympathetic to reformism. At the same time, the then mayor of the town – today known for his good rapport with some of the town's reformists – helped him to secure a piece of land for the *madrasa*. The religious establishment in Nioro – Tijani and Hamawi alike – was still hostile to this new educational institution, which attracted a fair number of students. Although there were no specific objections to the actual curriculum of the *madrasa* or its pedagogical style, some claimed that the school and its teachers infringed on local prerogatives and could serve as a conduit for unwelcome reformist ideas, not to mention the fact that it might siphon off students from other established schools. The teachers, local and non-local, faced relentless opposition, and interested parties worked hard to force the closure of the school. Nevertheless, the school was open for several years and, at its peak, attracted several hundred students. This was not surprising to people in Nioro, as there are many in the town who want to send their children to a *madrasa* rather than to the state-run schools. Sadikou, the imam of the Friday mosque in Nioro, told me that for many years people have asked his family to open a *madrasa* in Nioro, but they have declined to do so, preferring instead to continue giving instruction in the way they have for years.

According to the school's backer as well as some of his opponents, efforts to recruit and to retain teachers from Nioro in the prevailing climate proved to be difficult, if not impossible. Through his connections with reformists in Bamako, the backer of the school was able to recruit two teachers, who came to live in Nioro. Discouraged by the hostility they encountered and convinced that the town was under the sway of the town's prominent religious leaders, they left after about a year. In addition to these non-local teachers, there were a few local teachers, the most prominent of whom came from a family with long ties to the Hamawiyya. As discussed in Chapter 5, many attributed the death of this teacher to the machinations – via the esoteric sciences – of those opposed to the school and its backers. After the teacher's death, enrolment at the school fell sharply, and the school ceased operations. Many see the ultimate failure of the school as the success of the town's religious establishment in preventing the spread of reformist ideas and institutions that have the potential to challenge their authority. At the same time, some of those in Nioro, who wished to send their children to this type of school and had the means to do so, sent their children either to Bamako or Ségou or to one of the neighbouring villages where *madrasas* have opened in recent years.

REFORMIST INTERVENTIONS

While the failure of reformists to establish schools in Nioro is striking, this is perhaps not surprising given what we have learned about Islam in the town. At the same time, it is also important to consider some of the other areas in which reformists have devoted their efforts to changing the way Islam is practised in the town. Here I will examine some of the complexity, ambiguity and limitations to some of their interventions in areas that directly concern women. I will also consider the case of a 'radical' reformist whose inter-ventions provide an example of the outright failure to propagate reformist ideas as well as an illustration of some of the enduring obstacles some reformists face.

The first issue concerns women and their dress. In Mali, women who are reformists or are married to reformists, generally wear long black veils in public, that is, when they are outside their own homes. Usually worn over ordinary clothes, such veils cover the head, leaving the face uncovered, though there may be a flap of diaphanous fabric that can be pulled down over the face. In towns with a large reformist presence, such as Bamako, it is not uncommon to see women wearing such veils, though the numbers of such women are fairly restricted. In Nioro, where there are very few reformists, women wearing such veils are very noticeable, standing out to all, not only to the visiting anthropologist. Near the beginning of my fieldwork in Nioro, I think that I saw a woman wearing such a veil in public only once or twice in town, and then never again. When I asked reformists in Nioro about the veils, they explained that they asked their wives to wear them because it was proper to do so according to the precepts of Islam. On one occasion while visiting the home of one reformist, I asked about the use of the veil. The man immediately called his wife, whom I noticed was wearing what we can call normal, everyday attire, a long dress made of printed cotton fabric, most likely of Chinese provenance. When she came to where we were seated, he asked her to show me her veil. She went into the house, and, to my surprise, she returned with a veil in her hands. While standing in front of us, she proceeded to put it on over her clothes. Once it was on, the man remarked that this was how the veil is normally worn when going outside the home. After this demonstration, she removed the veil and left us alone. At the time, I seemed to be the only one embarrassed by the demonstration, and the man and I continued our conversation.

It is significant that those people opposed in principle to reformists and their ideas insisted that even though one sometimes sees women in Nioro wearing a veil in public, for instance, while visiting the market, the fact remains that the wives of reformists in Nioro do not always wear the veil when they are expected to do so. I have no way of knowing for sure about the accuracy of such statements, and, besides, I thought this to be an inappropriate field of sustained inquiry, especially after learning about some of the controversy surrounding the veil. But if the wives of reformists in the town are not always wearing their veils, I suspect that this may not be unrelated to negative reactions to both veils and reformists.

Some men and women objected to the veils on the grounds that they were impractical and burdensome. In this way of thinking, wearing such a veil in the hot local climate amounted to wearing twice as many clothes. Some noted that such veils were unnecessary since local standards of women's dress were appropriately modest. Others had more visceral reactions to the veil. In a discussion about the wearing of veils, one friend, who fashions himself a very observant Muslim, asked rhetorically why Muslim women have to wear a 'sack' while in public. For this person and many others, these veils are not only unsightly – devoid of the ornamentation and style that are so important to the aesthetic senses of most women and men – but downright repulsive. Just as in the case of praying with crossed arms, the veil is a highly charged symbol.

If getting women to wear the veil in such an unfriendly environment posed difficulties, the effort to stamp out other practices that reformists consider *bid'a*, even within their own households, is no less problematical. Some reformists told me that sometimes it was just not possible, as much as they might try, 'to force' women to act in accordance with their ideas. One man readily admitted that despite his repeated objections to the use of amulets, he was well aware that women in his family might continue to procure and to use them. Moreover, he noted that even if women said they have forsaken such things, it is a distinct possibility that they might use them covertly. This is without even mentioning some of the other kinds of knowledge and practice, which remains largely outside men's competence, that some women might use (see Chapter 5).

In some instances, however, reformists have been effective in preventing some women from engaging in practices that they find objectionable. In the course of my fieldwork, I learned that one of the reformists from a prominent lineage of religious specialists had forced his mother to stop using what people call 'traditional' medical practices. For years, this woman had treated children for physical ailments using knowledge of a secret nature that had been passed on among women in her family for generations. Although the secret and gendered nature of this knowledge posed some difficulties for my inquiry, I learned that her 'medicine' involved the use of secret prayers or incantations that she recited over sick children.

When the woman's son returned to Nioro as a reformist, he forbade her to use such knowledge because it was not only objectionable, but also *bid'a* or unlawful innovation and, therefore, un-Islamic. In his view, one could not be a Muslim and do such things. It is interesting to note that his objections had nothing whatsoever to do with the alleged efficacy of the medicine. He himself uses Western biomedicine – the kind for sale in the local pharmacies at prices often well beyond the reach of many people – which is, in his view, perfectly licit. By most accounts, once the man told his mother to stop using her medicine, she stopped treating children. But this did not happen without offending many in their extended kin group and even the broader community. Most people did not think that her 'traditional' medicine was in any way forbidden according to the precepts of Islam. On the contrary, many respected her for her medical knowledge and the treatments she had provided to many children over the years. If anything, this particular episode helped to convince certain people – both men and women – how misguided some reformists might be in their attempts to change things about which they had little knowledge, and, because of their new rigid ideas, they could only be misinformed.

At the end of 1994, one of my friends told me that a well known reformist, originally from a small village near Nioro but living for many years in another francophone West African country, had returned to the town for a visit. Shortly after his return, he had been arrested in the market after proclaiming that he was a messenger (Ar., *rasul*) of God, or so my friend insisted he had heard. I was not prepared to accept this account at face value, given my friend's very strong anti-reformist opinions. I immediately thought at the time – and it is probably true – that asserting that the man professed to be a 'messenger of God' was a way to anathematise someone whose views my friend and many others could under no circumstances accept. Indeed, most Muslims hold that messengers of God are prophets and that the Prophet Muhammad was the last and final prophet. In this way, there can be no more messengers.

After asking a number of people, I learned the man had been arrested because he had stood in the market and publicly insulted the town's major religious leaders by name. But people were reluctant to give many more details. From his comportment, many people thought that the man might be crazy. Indeed, people do not ordinarily stand in public and hurl insults. One man, who apparently heard the visiting reformist, told me that most of what the man had said was so offensive he was unable to repeat it. After the man's release from custody, I could find no one who would agree to help me locate him. I later learned that once he had been released, he had gone to his natal village where he has kin.

When I asked one of the town's most prominent reformists about the man who had been arrested, he acknowledged that he knew him and that he was a fellow reformist. He explained that while he did not think the man's ideas – specifically that the town's religious leaders were astray – were wrong, the man's approach to changing people was seriously misguided, if only because the relatives and followers of the people he was insulting are all around. He too remarked that the man might be crazy given the way he acted on this occasion.

Others, including one of the man's closest friends – who incidentally does not fashion himself a reformist – told me that this man has a long history of reprehensible behaviour. He explained that once he and the man had been working together in the precious gemstone trade in Côte d'Ivoire when they had some difficulties with one of their debtors. They went to see Amadou Hampâté Ba (d. 1991), at the time a prominent Malian (the former ambassador) living in Abidjan in Côte d'Ivoire, in order to ask for his help. After they met Ba, the man asked him whether he was a Tijani. When Ba responded in the affirmative, the man immediately replied that Ba was, therefore, not a Muslim and, moreover, that he wanted no assistance from him. The man's friend told me that even though he had known the man for decades he was stunned and profoundly embarrassed by such impertinence, the flagrant flouting of widely accepted conventions of respecting one's elders. He added that there were others present, and they too were visibly shocked by the man's words.

Others told me that the man had become, at least from the perspective of many local people, the region's most notoriously rude reformist. Over the past few years, cassette recordings of some of his fiery pronouncements against Muslim religious leaders and the Sufi orders in Mali have made their way back to Nioro. In one of these cassettes, the man derides Nioro's major religious leaders, saying that they are like orchestra leaders because they organise groups of people to sit around singing – here a reference to the communal recitation of litanies of prayers by Tijanis and Hamawis. While some in Nioro were able to see some humour in the man's analogy, they nonetheless took great offence at his mockery of people's commitment to Islam and what they see as the exemplary standards of piety in Nioro.

In discussions, some people offered some sociological readings of the man's actions – readings, incidentally, that the man's friend did not discount. They told me that this man was from a 'caste' lineage, as I had suspected from his patronym. They pointed out that it was quite typical for those from such lineages, much like many others from some of the villages around Nioro, to spend great lengths of time as labour migrants or traders in places like Côte d'Ivoire. Like most other migrants, they are often exposed to reformist ideas, and, in some cases, they accumulate considerable capital. The problem, one person remarked, is that those from 'caste' lineages have almost always had little in the way of religious education. For many people, it is the highest affront that such people return to Nioro and try to tell others, including members of hereditary lineages of religious specialists, to change the way they practise Islam. In this way of thinking, such people were ignorant of Islam when they left and can only remain as such, regardless of any education they might have acquired elsewhere.

In these cases, such people do seem to want to contest some of the pre-colonial hereditary social categories such as 'caste' or slave. As I have emphasised, the major lineages of religious specialists have been able to maintain almost a monopoly on Islamic religious knowledge, leadership positions, such as imam and *muqaddam* in the Sufi orders, as well as over Islamic education. Moreover, they generally do not seem to encourage other groups – 'caste' or servile-status persons – to engage in advanced studies. In the present, those from servile and 'caste' groups, who have engaged in advanced religious studies, continue to be exceptions. Those from established lineages of religious specialists often mistrust and/or resent the few individuals from such groups who do have an advanced education. For example, I know a very learned man from a 'caste' lineage who is occasionally invited to serve as imam in a local mosque when the regular imam is absent or otherwise unable to lead the prayers. The young man often falls ill, many point out, as the direct result of the machinations – via the esoteric sciences – by members of lineages of religious specialists, who categorically refuse to pray behind a person of presumably lower status, his scholarly credentials notwithstanding.

As the preceding discussion suggests, it is somewhat tempting to attribute the 'radical' reformist's approach to frustrated ambition[32] because the organisation of religious practice is such that this carrier of reformist ideas, as a member of a 'caste' lineage, can have little in the way of local religious authority. The irony is that his strident message only seems to make this even more so the case. There are rumours that some of the most prominent Muslim religious leaders in Mali, Mauritania or Senegal were actually of 'caste' and sometimes even of 'servile' status. Although many readily admit that such rumours might be attempts to cast doubt on the authority of certain influential figures and, by extension, their descendants and followers, it is striking that none of the accused or their descendants – unlike the radical reformist – ever seems to have adopted the comportment of a member of such a caste.

AROUND NIORO

In marked contrast to the situation in Nioro, reformists have been more successful in establishing themselves in certain neighbouring villages. In fact, there are around half a dozen villages near Nioro with a large reformist presence, nearly all of which have a majority of Soninke inhabitants. In recent years, reformists have gone on to build separate mosques and schools in several other villages in the immediate area. By all accounts, in every case, this has been accompanied by considerable controversy. In general, a group initially makes a claim that a separate mosque is needed because of doctrinal differences with other Muslims. Almost invariably, they call into question the roles religious leaders and, especially, Sufi leaders play in religion. On the whole, it has been migrants living elsewhere in Mali or abroad with ties to reformist institutions who have provided the funds for the construction of these mosques and schools.

A particularly rancorous dispute occurred in a medium-sized village where the inhabitants are mostly descendants of migrants from the Senegal River valley who came to participate in the *jihad* in the nineteenth century. The village has a Friday mosque and a large Hamawi *zawiya* and is home to several families known for Islamic scholarship and longstanding ties to the two major religious leaders in Nioro. The reformists in the village received important support – moral and material – from some sectors of the village, including some who lived elsewhere as migrant labourers and traders, who had over the years grown disaffected from the local Muslim establishment. In the words of some of these people, they no longer had the need for the elevated religious leaders one finds in Nioro.

A group of reformists in the village decided to construct a new mosque and eventually appointed as imam a young man barely thirty years old, who had been a devoted follower of one of Nioro's two major religious leaders just a short time before. The young imam told me that, after considerable study, discussion with others and reflection, he was convinced of the veracity of reformist ideas. The construction of the mosque and the selection of the imam were taken as a direct affront to the village religious establishment – Hamawi and Tijani – as well as to Hamawis and Tijanis in the broader region with whom they have close ties. The young imam's father, an educated religious leader in his own right, immediately denounced his son and banned him from his home. Efforts by an alliance of Tijanis and Hamawis to prevent the opening of the mosque by appealing to the government failed.

In this same village, the imam also opened a new Quranic school – not a *madrasa* – which attracted students from the village and surrounding areas, causing further tensions. When I visited the school, I saw more than 100 boys and girls in attendance. The religious authorities of the village and Nioro – Tijanis and Hamawis – asserted that those supporting the creation of the new mosque and school were simply well-to-do migrant labourers, who were clearly not learned. The reformists countered that though they were not primarily scholars, they had chosen the most learned among them as imam. Indeed, the young imam has engaged in very advanced studies within the local and regional Islamic educational system in Mali and in Mauritania, though not within the *madrasa* system. In this way, the young imam is quite different from the reformists in Nioro, none of whom have

such educational credentials. The reformists remained convinced that they
know the truth while the others – Tijanis and Hamawis alike – have gone
astray with the veneration of their leaders, the Sufi orders and esoteric
practices. However convinced of the truth they might be, the reformists do
not dare to say that the others in the village are not Muslims. But in their
actions – symbolic separation in prayer and in education and sometimes
even the refusal to give daughters in marriage to non-reformists – they do
seem to suggest as much.

It is interesting to contrast this situation with that in one of the largest
neighbouring Bambara-speaking villages where most people are descendants
of former slaves and, despite a long tradition of migration, no one is particularly prosperous. Very few villagers have actually sought formal initiation
into any Sufi order, and no prominent religious leader in the region seems in
the least bit interested in attracting them as followers. The imam of the
mosque in the village told me that the not insignificant number of reformists
there have prayed together with other Muslims – affiliated to a Sufi order or
not – without any controversy whatsoever for many years. This seems to be
due in part to the relative lack of prestige of such people, who continue to be
marginal in the broader society because of their hereditary slave status.

STANDARDISATION AND PURIFICATION

As I have suggested, reformists offer some very serious criticisms of some of
the religious practices of their co-religionists. Moreover, there have
sometimes been heated debates about religious practice, for example about
whether to cross one's arms across the chest during prayer. However, I have
not intended to give the impression that reformists and those who support
the Sufi tradition are never united in their views about Islam. What is
remarkable is the actual convergence between such 'reformists' and those
they criticise over the past few decades. In fact, both groups generally agree
that all Muslims should practise the standardised Islam that has become
more widespread since the colonial period began. That is, both groups
actively encourage the standardised ritual norms of regular prayer, fasting
during the month of Ramadan, and the *hajj* whenever possible. Moreover,
the two groups are quite frequently in agreement about the kinds of
'traditional' religious practices and the 'customs' of Muslims and non-
Muslims in Mali that they find objectionable. Some of these practices fall
within the realm of the activities of non-Muslim ritual specialists who
employ non-Islamic knowledge such as *bamanaya* and use various 'power'
objects they find objectionable. Others are the practices of Muslims, including some women's practices. Indeed, many who consider themselves
Muslims engage in certain practices that many, if not most, Muslim religious
leaders and some laypersons in the country characterise, in some cases, as
questionable and probably illicit and, in other cases, as unequivocally un-

Islamic. Although these practices range from various forms of traffic with spirits, certain kinds of medico-religious knowledge and sacrifice, 'spirit possession' is one of the most frequently discussed (and familiar to outside observers) of these practices. Indeed, for a variety of reasons that I will discuss, both reformists and supporters of the Sufi tradition have made spirit possession a favoured target of their criticism.

Although there have been no studies of the history of spirit possession in this region, we know that it has long been practised here. European travellers to the region in the eighteenth and nineteenth centuries, including Mungo Park and Raffenel, described the existence of various practices that analysts would today label as spirit possession and mediumship.[33] Colonial ethnological and historical materials collected in the region of Nioro in the early and mid-twentieth century suggest that one particular form of spirit possession has been important here since at least the nineteenth century.[34] In this form of spirit possession, a medium, who might be either a man or a woman, had a relationship with a particular spirit that allowed the medium to enter into trance, to predict the future and to resolve problems. In one village close to Nioro, a spirit medium would lead people to the spirit's abode in a hill adjacent to the village where people's requests would be presented to the spirit. In general, people would make an oath that an offering would be made to the spirit in the event that a particular request was granted. Many thought that the failure to fulfil such an oath was to invite inevitable misfortune.

Some of these colonial ethnological sources and later oral sources suggest that certain Muslim leaders in the region tolerated and sometimes even patronised this particular form of spirit possession. According to some of these sources, Muntaga, the son of Umar Tall, had very close ties with one prominent woman medium who lived in a village not far from Nioro.[35] He relied upon this spirit medium for her ability to predict the future, particularly the outcome of future conflicts with his enemies. It is reported that when Muntaga fell ill, he not only turned to this medium for treatment, but even spent the night in the spirit's abode. Some Futanke Muslims living under Muntaga's rule allegedly complained to Amadu, Muntaga's older brother in Ségou, that Muntaga had ceased to be a Muslim through his actions. Such a serious charge of what was effectively un-Islamic behaviour may have been one of the factors in the conflict between the two brothers prior to the French conquest. However, these same sources indicate that once Amadu removed Muntaga from power, he did not impede the activities of the very same spirit medium.

I should note that many of my informants in Nioro strenuously denied that there have ever been any ties between Muslim leaders and those who organise spirit possession in the region. Although such past ties are certainly plausible, these claims might have been attempts to legitimise or at least to justify the practice of spirit possession, which has long come under attack. Today, spirit possession is regularly practised in various places in both urban and rural settings throughout Mali. In Nioro and in some of the neighbouring regions, those involved in spirit possession are organised into groups called *jiné-ton*, literally, the society of spirits in Bambara or *jiné don*, literally, the dance of the spirits.[36] *Jiné-tigis*, literally 'owners of the spirits', are spirit mediums who organise and run these spirit societies. These mediums are the hosts of various spirits, and they also possess 'secret' know-ledge for communicating with these and other spirits. The spirit societies usually meet quite regularly in order to summon spirits through drumming and dancing for purposes of divination, healing and so forth. In Nioro and the surrounding areas, those involved in spirit possession are overwhelm-ingly women, and all the mediums are without exception women. Although as a group they are socially, ethnically and linguistically diverse, the majority of the active and regular participants are socially marginal women (cf. Stoller 1989). Many of the women are descendants of former slaves, that is, they are of hereditary servile status. They are among the poorest in the town, often petty traders, trying to eke out a marginal existence for themselves and their families. If the vast majority of these women are poor and marginal, the spirit mediums tend to be of 'free' status and sometimes quite well-off.

It is striking how remarkably similar the spirit societies are in structure and organisation to Sufi orders.[37] Most notably, the spirit societies have a structure that is equally hierarchical. As the leaders and organisers of the activities of the societies, the mediums are analogous to the Sufi *shaykh*.[38] The mediums' associates and followers are in relations of subordination to the mediums who are thought to be closer than ordinary people to the spirits. Moreover, some participants who are close to the leaders might receive instructions and 'secrets' that allow them to rise higher in the hierarchy. Certain spirit mediums in the region have considerable wealth and engage in conspicuous consumption, that is, much like the town's major religious leaders, though on a lesser scale. Within the pantheon of spirits, certain spirits are actually Muslim saints, including Ahmad al-Tijani, the founder of the Tijaniyya. It is noteworthy, however, that there are no recent saints in the pantheon from the immediate region.

In contemporary Nioro, people approach the spirit societies for many of the same reasons that they might solicit the practitioners of the esoteric sciences. That is, for good health, wealth, to avert misfortune, or simply to help make sense of the world (cf. Boddy 1989; Lewis et al. 1991; Masquelier 2001). However, in contrast to the esoteric sciences, the predominant reason given for seeking out the spirit societies and/or the mediums is for the specifically therapeutic services for which the spirit societies are renowned. This is exactly what leading spirit mediums in the Nioro area told me. In fact, the most celebrated spirit medium in Nioro explained to me that her reputation was based on her successful treatment of people for a wide range of ailments. Her followers and even some of her critics pointed to her exceptional ability to treat ailments for which Western biomedicine and the Islamic esoteric sciences seemed to offer no cure.

Unlike the Sufi orders and their leaders, the spirit societies and their individual mediums often have regular interactions with and ties to non-Muslim ritual specialists with their knowledge of medicines. The spirit society in Nioro regularly has such a non-Muslim ritual expert on hand for consultations and for the preparation of various medicines made from a range of organic and inorganic substances. In the event of a more intractable problem, the medium might even summon one of the more renowned non-Muslim healers from the region or a particular healer with expertise in a specific area. In some cases, such ties to healers and access to their medicines have helped to enhance the reputation of individual mediums and particular societies of spirits for their therapeutic effectiveness.

Many Malian Muslims – both reformists and those committed to the Sufi tradition – state quite emphatically that spirit possession in all its forms is completely incompatible with Islam. In other words, one cannot be a Muslim and engage in spirit possession. Thus, for many of the people, spirit possession is unequivocally evil. In this way, their objections to spirit possession are quite similar to the objections many Muslims have to *bamanaya*. It is, however, instructive to consider the specific criticisms people make of spirit possession. In Nioro, on numerous occasions I heard both reformists and Sufis condemn those involved in spirit possession for 'association' or polytheism (Ar., *shirk*). In this way of thinking, spirit possession is un-Islamic. Once I heard a man state with disgust how his neighbours were in no uncertain terms *mushrikun*, which translates somewhat loosely from the Arabic as idolaters. It was the day after his neighbours had hosted a meeting of a spirit society in their home in Nioro during which there had been much drumming and dancing to summon the spirits. The man's charge against his neighbours was that they were worshipping things other than God. That this particular meeting had been held in order to heal a young child in the household was for this man quite simply beside the point.

Many people also state explicitly that the problem with spirit possession is that people treat it as a religion. Since Islam is the only true religion, those who engage in spirit possession are effectively unbelievers (Ar., *kafir*). In addition, people often object to the blood sacrifices those involved in spirit possession allegedly make during their ceremonies. They charge that the participants sacrifice animals for spirits, rather than for God. Again, in this way of thinking, this constitutes un-Islamic behaviour. All of these objections lead many to go so far as to say that even though those who engage in spirit possession might call themselves Muslims and possibly even pray and fast during Ramadan like Muslims, they are not really Muslims. It follows that many keep their social distance from those involved in spirit possession, and some might even sever ties with relatives whose activities they despise. I know one renowned spirit medium whose Muslim cleric husband divorced her in order to distance himself from her activities. Similarly, some of her relatives do not acknowledge that they are even related to her.

As all of this suggests, there is considerable opprobrium around spirit possession. Indeed, this opprobrium is such that it contributes to considerable social pressures for people not to become involved in it. However, even some of those who do not dispute that spirit possession is incompatible with Islam might, in some instances, be willing to engage with it. This is often during personal crises such as serious illness when they will sometimes engage with spirit possession clandestinely. I know of a number of people who have been unable to find any effective treatment for debilitating illnesses they themselves or their relatives had, and as a last resort, they have contacted spirit societies and their mediums for their therapeutic services. In some cases, the medium organises meetings of the spirit society to facilitate the treatment of the person who would attend and participate in the ceremonies. During the meeting of the society, the medium might invoke the spirits in order to learn the name and the nature of the possessing spirit(s), as well as the actions – medicines, sacrifices, offerings – required for healing to take place. One seriously ill man I know had first sought treatment at the local hospital and from various specialists in the esoteric sciences in the region before approaching a medium in Nioro. After the medium said she could help him, he agreed to attend the possession ceremony. In other cases, some people work through intermediaries in order to obtain various kinds of medicines and even treatment from a spirit medium. That is, they do not deal directly with the medium, and they never participate in spirit possession ceremonies during which the spirits are summoned. In this way, they are able to avoid making public their use of such therapies.

Since the most prominent spirit mediums are widely known, their involvement in spirit possession is public knowledge. Despite the social pressures not to participate or even to observe spirit possession, many ordinary women are still loath to give up their involvement in spirit possession. However, many try to conceal their interactions with the spirit societies from others, including relatives, neighbours, friends and acquaintances. I know quite a few women who have secretly taken their daughters to spirit possession ceremonies in the hope of finding a cure to a problem.

If spirit possession is just one of a wide range of practices that many people in Mali find questionable, even un-Islamic, from explicitly and usually self-consciously *Muslim* perspectives, it has been the subject of much criticism in Mali, particularly over the past few decades. This is perhaps because spirit possession is much more visible and public than the more diffused practices of, say, *bamanaya*, that many Malian Muslims also find objectionable. Spirit possession is organised into identifiable groups – spirit societies – that host semi-public ceremonies. During these ceremonies, crowds often gather and make quite a bit of noise, sometimes in close proximity to those who object to their practices. That these are largely women's activities usually held in the evening in semi-public venues has also made them a target of criticism for possibly fostering immoral behaviour.

The opposition to spirit possession in Mali has sometimes taken very public forms. In the 1980s and the early 1990s, a celebrated Muslim religious leader with a reputation as a saint, who is not incidentally from Nioro, undertook a series of campaigns throughout the Malian countryside to spread Islam among non-Muslims and to eradicate spirit possession among those who consider themselves Muslims (Soares 1999). Many people I know in Nioro saw this man's ability to get women to renounce spirit possession as just one index of his sainthood. Although he never undertook his campaigns in Nioro, many told me they wished that he would have done so.

In Nioro, those involved in spirit possession have faced considerable opposition and constraints on their activities though it has often been less direct than the organised campaigns against spirit possession. Since the spirit societies are in general associated with the socially marginal, they have been unable to counter the rather pointed criticism they receive from many Muslims – reformists and Sufis – in the area. In contrast to the major religious leaders in Nioro, the spirit societies have no prominent public figures who defend their activities. Those involved in spirit possession have, however, been able to secure a measure of protection to continue their practices from the Malian state and its agents with regular assertions of the secular nature of the state. While the man mentioned above complained bitterly about his neighbours' allegedly un-Islamic activities, he was unable to prevent them from hosting a meeting of the spirit society in their home. Indeed, the participants had secured the costly permit from the local administrative authorities that allowed them to host the meeting. If some people in Nioro practise spirit possession openly, many others do so with discretion. Constantly aware of the criticisms addressed to them, most of those involved in spirit possession have tended to keep a fairly low profile. Indeed, the practices have been increasingly relegated to private or at least semi-public venues, that is, out of view of their critics. Although the spirit societies and the services of mediums have remained popular for some of the reasons cited above, they may be transformed in the face of the relentless criticism they endure.

As I have tried to suggest, reformists and Sufis share some of the same values, which includes a commitment to the standardised ritual norms, as well as disdain for the spirit possession that both groups state is un-Islamic. This shared animosity has certainly helped to constrain the activities of those involved in spirit possession in Nioro and in the broader region. But it is important to recall that reformists also specifically accuse the Sufis of transgressing in almost the same way as those who participate in spirit possession – something the latter find deeply offensive and have not easily forgotten.

DEBATE

For many years, discourses associated with reformism, not to mention secularism, have been a feature of the social landscape in Mali. As has been suggested, reformist discourses come mainly from outside Nioro, while reformists in town are cautiously critical of other Muslims. Such discourses, often rather vocal at times, call directly into question the kinds of roles that religious leaders like those in Nioro assume, questioning their elevated status and frequently criticising some of their and their followers' practices. By exploring some of the debates that such reformist discourses have helped to launch in Nioro, I want to show how, in many cases, people directly contest such reformist criticisms and accusations of un-Islamic practices. At the very same time, such reformist discourses seem to have influenced some of the religious practices of Sufis, or at least the discourse on religious practices.

I mentioned at the outset that reformists make the claim that the Sufi orders are *bid'a*, or unlawful innovation. In this way of thinking, all that was not done by the Prophet Muhammad is *bid'a*, and since the Sufi orders did not exist at the time of the Prophet then they are unlawful. It follows that all of the trappings of the Sufi orders, including the special litanies of the Sufi orders, the prayers members recite daily, are considered *bid'a* as well.[39] It almost goes without saying that those committed to the Sufi orders find such ideas a serious affront. Faced with such charges, they counter that their practices are indeed licit, having been received and authorised in a chain of transmission that leads directly to the Prophet Muhammad. In the case of the Tijaniyya, they note that Ahmad al-Tijani, the founder of their order, received his litany of prayers directly from the Prophet Muhammad. Those opposed to the Sufi orders, they proclaim, are guilty of ignorance as well as the failure to accord past religious leaders, like Ahmad al-Tijani, not to mention the Prophet Muhammad and his descendants, their due respect.

On a few occasions, some people suggested to me in private that such 'Wahhabis' could not possibly be Muslims, given their brazen contempt for past celebrated religious leaders, such as Ahmad al-Tijani. Even if one could allow that they were Muslims, their behaviour is unquestionably odious. Many people evoked, as evidence of such behaviour, the destruction of tombs in Arabia by Wahhabis after they came to power. While their intentions may have been to stamp out what they thought were un-Islamic practices, such as the adoration of tombs, their actions were blameable. 'Wahhabis' in Mali, some people suggested, cannot be any different.

In some cases, I have also heard some people assert that reformists are often too quick to denounce things as *bid'a*. Once I heard a person point out that it is obvious to all that there are many things today that certainly did not exist at the time of the Prophet Muhammad. These include running water, aeroplanes, and automobiles. How, he asked, can such reformists make use of these things? According to their own criteria for what constitutes innovation, he continued, should they not forego using them? Undoubtedly, they will not, he noted.

Another man told me that what might be a valid concern with unlawful innovation can be taken to extremes by the overzealous and ignorant. He said that he once witnessed a reformist tell a religious leader that the clock he owned was *bid'a*, because it had an image of the Ka'ba, the central sanctuary in Mecca, on it. The owner of the clock found the charge annoying and immediately retorted that reformists freely accepted money with 'idols' – he used the Bambara/Fulfulde word *boli* – on it. The man proceeded to show me on a bill of CFA francs some of the images – carved objects and such – in question. The man noted that the religious leader's point was valid, as such 'idols' are unambiguously un-Islamic. He added, however, that clearly reformists were not going to stop accepting such currency for their transactions. A second man, who was present during the telling of this story, was visibly upset by this realisation that there were such 'idols' on the currency they use. He said this just showed how little they, as Muslims, controlled their own affairs. In any case, such examples give an idea of how some people deal with reformist criticisms, which, in these cases, seems to be by trivialising them.

As noted, reformists also criticise Sufi orders and their leaders for the use of esoteric practices. It has been suggested that religious leaders often gain considerable prestige, not to mention income, from the use of such esoteric knowledge and practices. Some people told me that while reformists might openly condemn the esoteric sciences – the use of amulets, secret litanies of prayers, and so forth – they are convinced that reformists are hypocrites in these matters. In their view, reformists clearly have secrets of their own. For example, the cousin of one of the most prominent reformists in Nioro told me that he has no doubt his cousin has a secret special litany of prayers that, when recited, brings him certain desired outcomes. What this litany might be in content he cannot know – it is secret! – but its existence is not in doubt. Moreover, people around celebrated religious leaders in Nioro and elsewhere frequently mention the clandestine visits of reformists to religious leaders – or the use of relatively anonymous intermediaries – in order to engage the religious leaders to act via the esoteric sciences on their behalf. Many people expressed such ideas that undoubtedly stem, at least in part, from the pervasiveness of the notion of secrets and the widespread and almost taken-for-granted nature of the esoteric sciences in everyday life.

If reformists claim that saints are dangerous, their actions, many of their critics point out, betray them. Although reformists often state that they are opposed in principle to the giving of gifts to elevated religious leaders, things are rather ambiguous in practice. Indeed, some reformists from Nioro, living elsewhere in Mali, are known for their large and overt gifts to some of Mali's religious leaders in Nioro and elsewhere. For example, in recent years, one of Bamako's wealthiest merchants, who is a reformist, made regular, extravagant gifts to Hamallah's descendants in a semi-public venue. Needless to say, some take pleasure in citing such people by name in order to flaunt what they take to be the shallowness of reformists' convictions as well as their obvious mendacity.

Over the years, reformists in Mali have been particularly intent on spreading the idea that it is *shirk* or idolatry to invoke the name of any prophet or saint in any prayer whatsoever.[40] Although Muslims are not supposed to address anyone other than God in their obligatory ritual daily prayers, it is quite usual for Muslims in this region to invoke the name of a saint in petitionary prayers (*du'a*), those personal prayers being quite distinct from the former. Some people told me that this is what either they or others did in relation to a particular saint, whom they mentioned by name. On a few occasions, I visited graves where prayers were directed in this way (or so I suspect since the prayers were inaudible). I also noticed that when certain people – usually those with a religious education – discussed this subject with me, they were very cautious about what they said. Some people close to important religious leaders told me that if they visited the grave of a saint, they might pray, addressing a particular demand to God. They stressed that they would not address anything directly to the saint. When I asked others, who were not reformists, about this, they pointed out that this was clearly disingenuous. One person asked what the point would be in visiting the grave of a saint if the saint was not addressed in some way.[41] He averred that reformists seem to have been so effective in circulating their ideas that they have been able to get people to doubt some of their practices – here petitioning a saint to intercede with God – that very well might have been unreflected upon and unquestioned not long before. As this seems to suggest, reformist discourses have been able to influence in subtle ways the discourse – and perhaps even the practices – of those who ordinarily characterise themselves as opponents of such discourses.

In this chapter, I have tried to explore some of the local responses to the presence of reformism and the influence of their discourses. Reformists have encountered serious obstacles in efforts to establish a more visible presence, especially in the town of Nioro. This is not least the case because of the authority of the two religious leaders in the town and the fact that the overwhelming majority is not favourably inclined toward reformism. Reformist discourses have nonetheless had an important influence in Nioro.

Continually aware of reformist critiques and their pervasiveness in areas away from Nioro, those opposed to reformism in the region have been increasingly forced to defend themselves and the way that they practise Islam. Moreover, reformist discourses have become such a feature of the landscape that their effects can be seen, for example, on the discourse on some taken-for-granted religious practices.

THE PUBLIC SPHERE AND THE POSTCOLONY

In the previous chapter, I discussed the presence and influence of reformists and their discourses in Nioro and its hinterland, and their relationship to the understanding of Islam centred around the Sufi orders, their leaders and practices. In this chapter, I want to extend the discussion of the changes in Nioro as a social and religious landscape. Over the past few decades, there have been a number of inter-related factors helping to shape what it means to be Muslim, changing the way Islam is practised at least for some people in the town. These factors include the proliferation of Western-style education, the promulgation of notions of secularism or *laïcité* by the state and its agents, the more g eneral spread of ideas critical of Sufi orders, leaders and their practices, and the availability of information and ideas about Islam and other areas of knowledge from beyond the local area. Most of these relate directly or indirectly to the conditions of living in a *laïc* or secular postcolonial state. They also relate to the expansion of the public sphere in which Islam has been very important. The objectives of this chapter are to consider the impact of such changes on Nioro as a social and religious space. First, I discuss the nature of the postcolonial state, the complexity of relations with Muslim religious leaders, and changes in religiosity in Nioro. Second, I trace the development and contours of the public sphere in colonial and postcolonial Mali. As I will argue, the public sphere helps to encourage particular conceptions of what it means to be Muslim that are sometimes at odds with some of the local and regional conceptions discussed earlier. Such a discussion of the postcolonial state, Islam and the public sphere allows us to see some of the limits of the understanding and discourse of civil society that became so fashionable in the 1990s. Moreover, in contrast to the pervasive analytical frames of Islamic fundamentalism and political Islam, it provides greater insight into the different ways of being Muslim in postcolonial Mali and arguably much further afield.

THE POSTCOLONIAL STATE

As discussed in Chapter 2, in 1905 French law formally separated religion and state, which meant that the state should not intervene in religious matters. Religion was to be private and confessional – in short, belief or faith

– with freedom of religion guaranteed only as long as those of a particular religious faith did not go beyond the private religious or confessional domain and engage in politics, that is, to enter the public arena. Given this conception of the secular or *laïc* state with its explicit limits to religious toleration, paradoxically enough, colonial officials in French West Africa promoted a Muslim establishment organised around tractable colonial Muslim subjects, who did not seem to manifest any objections to French rule. As I have argued, it followed that they intervened not infrequently against certain religious figures and groups, claiming that the latter were interfering in politics and were, therefore, a threat to the colonial public order.

Perhaps one of the most egregious examples of religious intolerance in West Africa under French colonial rule was the repression and persecution of those affiliated with the Hamawiyya. French perceptions of the Hamawiyya as potentially subversive – pan-Islamic, anti-colonial, irrational – though arguably wrong, led to demonisation and, eventually, to efforts to eliminate it. Though the French were ultimately unsuccessful in stifling the Hamawiyya, it was, as a Sufi order, profoundly transformed. Similarly, in the postwar period, the colonial administration redirected its energies toward neutralising so-called Wahhabis or reformists, whom they considered to be the latest group of Muslims, which might pose a challenge to French colonial rule and the colonial-authorised Muslim establishment. However, by the 1950s with the implementation of various reforms, the colonial administration could no longer justify the kinds of repressive measures that had been used against the Hamawis. In the case of reformists, colonial authorities were also unable to stamp them or their ideas out.

The postcolonial Malian state has inherited the idea that the state is to be *laïc* or secular and, like its colonial predecessor, the Malian state has ostensibly been committed to the principle of *laïcité*. In recent Malian law, this means that the state 'adopts an attitude of total neutrality with regard to religious problems' (Diaby 1992: 121). However, secularism in postcolonial practice has arguably been even more problematical than in the colonial era. Since independence, the Malian state, through its leaders and agents has frequently asserted its secular nature. In spite of such assertions, every postcolonial Malian regime, much like the colonial administration, has sought to associate itself in one way or another with Islam. Regardless of motivations and intentions, the association with Islam has provoked the criticism of Mali's small, but influential, group of largely urban-based secularists, who insist that the state uphold the principle of *laïcité*.

The – at least, theoretical – separation of religion and politics grants the secular state – colonial and postcolonial – sources of power and authority with which most Muslim religious specialists in Mali would have difficulties competing. The expansion of the state, not to mention the Western-style education for training the state's agents, has helped to contribute over time to changes in the roles of Muslim religious specialists in Mali. Indeed, Muslim religious specialists, who in the pre-colonial period might have been involved in various ways in the affairs of a particular political unit – as rulers, councillors or advisors – had their roles sharply curtailed during the colonial period. As we have seen, the French colonial administration attempted to limit the 'political' activities of most Muslim religious specialists and sought to freeze them into spheres of influence where their activities were largely restricted to the religious and educational spheres, such as prayer and Quranic education or the running of a particular Sufi order. There were always important exceptions, such as Seydou Nourou Tall, the quintessential member of the 'loyal' Muslim establishment, whose interventions in politics, religion and public policy were integral to the colonial administration's policies toward Islam and Muslims. Similarly, in the 1950s, the colonial administration encouraged the activities of Muslims involved in 'counter-reform' activities.

It is arguably the case that Muslim religious specialists have been even further marginalised in postcolonial Mali (Brenner 1993a: 77f.). Like the colonial state, the postcolonial Malian state has also sought to restrict the activities of some Muslim religious specialists. For instance, the postcolonial socialist regime of Modibo Keita disbanded the UCM, the Union Culturelle Musulmane (the Muslim Cultural Union), an association of reformist Muslims. After the overthrow of the Keita regime in 1968, the new regime allowed the UCM to reorganise, but disbanded it a second time shortly thereafter.[1] Over the past few decades, the discourse of 'development', with its own coterie of technical and administrative experts who view 'development' as the panacea for many of the country's problems, has certainly helped to marginalise even further Muslim religious specialists with their expert religious knowledge (ibid.). For this reason, it seems almost inconceivable for the postcolonial Malian state to include Muslim religious specialists *qua* religious experts in the making of public policy decisions.

Many contemporary Muslim religious specialists in Mali continue to play important roles in education, broadly conceived. Not only do they transmit knowledge of the Quran and other religious texts, but they also impart knowledge of the basic principles of Islam and give instruction and guidance on how to be a Muslim. The other roles that Muslim religious specialists play relate to the major life-cycle rituals associated with Islam – naming ceremonies, weddings and funerals – during which they lead prayers and give blessings, as well as the redistribution of alms. Muslim religious leaders, who are members of Sufi orders as a matter of course, organise certain religious activities such as the annual visits during which people gather at different places in the country.

One of the most important areas in which the Malian state impinges on what some take to be the prerogatives of Muslim religious leaders is the realm of law. Like the colonial state, the postcolonial Malian state uses modern European-derived codes of law and does not rely upon Islamic jurisprudence. To some Muslim religious leaders and ordinary Muslims in Nioro, this is perplexing. Some told me that they quite easily understood why the French had not implemented law based on the principles of Islamic jurisprudence. The French were, after all, not Muslims. In their way of thinking, the postcolonial Malian state is an entirely different case. Not only is Mali overwhelmingly Muslim, but almost all the country's leaders are also Muslims. Despite these criticisms of the postcolonial state, it is striking that most Malian Muslim religious leaders and other ordinary Muslims are not usually calling for the implementation of *shari'a* unlike elsewhere in the Islamic world or even in other places in West Africa such as Nigeria. Muslim religious specialists in contemporary Mali might, and regularly do, apply Islamic legal principles in the conduct of their own lives and affairs (and that of their families and associates), particularly in those areas such as marriage, divorce and inheritance, directly related to the family. Although many also apply such principles in other areas such as commerce, the broader applica-tion of Islamic jurisprudence to other areas and to society at large is simply not possible given the secular nature of the state. Some Muslim religious specialists told me how they often gave advice to people on how to behave in accordance with the precepts of Islam. Such advice, however, they usually only give when it is solicited. In sermons and in written works, other Muslim religious leaders and sometimes laypersons, generally from outside Nioro, do exhort people in often very moralistic language about how to conduct themselves as proper Muslims.[2] But, in all such cases, there is no doubt that such advice or exhortation has little in the way of binding force within the secular postcolonial state.

Despite such constraints, some Muslim religious leaders in Mali clearly do play roles that go well beyond some of the restricted ones discussed above. This is not, however, merely in those rural areas where the presence of the state, its agents or even international organisations is less pronounced. As I have argued, religious authority in Nioro has been in part personalised in the town's most prominent religious leaders, who dominate the prayer economy. Given the political economic changes of the past few decades, this prayer economy encompasses an expanded network of persons from all sectors of society who are in relations of exchange with the town's major religious leaders and their families. It is precisely in this prayer economy – involving, among other things, the transfer of gifts on a large scale – that one can see the extent to which certain Muslim religious leaders are imbricated in nearly all areas of social life.

It is important to note, however, that the religious leaders in Nioro are, by no means, the only Malian religious leaders with such personalised authority. There are, indeed, others of equal and comparable stature and influence living elsewhere in the country. There are some, who like Nioro's religious leaders, have national reputations and, in some cases, reputations that extend into neighbouring countries such as Mauritania, Senegal, Burkina Faso, Côte d'Ivoire and Guinea.[3] Other Muslim religious leaders have reputations in these and other places where Malian migrants have gone in great numbers. Despite the very real marginalisation of many Muslim religious specialists mentioned above, some religious leaders – and not only those in Nioro – have enormous influence and the ability to act not only locally but also supralocally.

At the outset, I noted that Western-style education has been a very important factor that has influenced how some people think about and practise Islam. It is not surprising that many of those, who have been educated in the state-run French-language schools, are more committed to the idea of secularism than those who have not been so educated. One might even say that secularism is an ideology that many – though clearly not all – with a secular education advocate. This seems to apply whether an individual identifies as Muslim, Christian, or neither.

Most civil servants from Nioro and elsewhere in Mali – most of whom are Muslim – have had to travel for their education and/or training and have therefore come in contact with others from disparate places and from different backgrounds. Many such people often come to imagine themselves with a connection to the state – a connection that also reflects their material interests as a class of civil servants – that might continue over the course of a career trajectory that can take an individual and family to postings in different places in the country (cf. Anderson 1991; Bowen 1993). When such people work as civil servants, that is, as agents of the state, they frequently expect to see the ideology of secularism in practice. The commonly held view among many such people is that religious leaders should be concerned with those kinds of specifically religious activities mentioned above, including prayer, religious education and the major rituals of the life-cycle. Similarly, in performance of official duties, civil servants should not ordinarily be involved in religious matters.

In Nioro, the distinctive organisation of religious practice and the prayer economy in particular are such that there have sometimes been tensions between agents of the state promoting secularist principles and other people in the town. In what is essentially a replay of the mistrust of Muslims under colonial rule, some suspect certain agents of the state might be more loyal to a particular religious leader than to the state. In at least one much discussed case, one of the highest-ranking officials in Nioro was removed from his job because he was said to have become such a devoted follower of one of the town's religious leaders that he neglected his official duties. Despite having been posted elsewhere in the country, he continues to visit the religious leader in Nioro where I have met him.

It is also the case that many – but again certainly not all – people with a secular education are quite sympathetic to some of the criticisms that are made of Sufi orders and their leaders. Such people have their own sources of power and authority linked to the state – however limited these may be – and tend to disparage what they regard as the blind submission to and veneration of certain religious leaders. Such 'modernist' views are not, however, in any way unambiguous evidence of the process of 'rationalisation' in religion that Weber has described (Weber 1978). On the contrary, some of these same people, who espouse such ideas, seek out and employ – clandestinely in many cases – the Islamic esoteric sciences, not to mention purportedly un-Islamic practices, for particular desired ends.

Many people with a secular education are also frequently quite critical of those Muslim religious leaders whose actions do not respect what they see as secularism's neat separation of religion and politics. During the course of my fieldwork, I heard repeated criticisms of certain religious leaders who were said to act within the realm of politics, that is, beyond that which was considered the religious realm – the exclusive area in which it was stated that they should act. On several occasions, people identified religious leaders who, in their view were acting 'like politicians' – behaviour that was, in this way of thinking, unquestionably inappropriate. Almost invariably, people drew a contrast between such 'renegades' and those Muslim religious leaders who were more seemingly compliant with the conventional behaviour that secularist principles dictate.

At other times, I heard angry, though private, denunciations of those Muslim religious leaders whose actions had obvious political and economic motives. Muhammadu, the head of the Hamawiyya, was often singled out for criticism, in part, it seems, because of his role in lucrative regional commerce. He is one of the most important importers of goods into the region from Aïoun, the town in Mauritania linked by paved road to the capital and port, Nouakchott. Some civil servants charged with the regulation and levying of duties on imports often saw their authority trounced when they dealt with this religious leader and the vast quantities of his imports.[4] This was perhaps unavoidable given the possibly not unintentional ambiguity of the boundary between his commerce in the form of imported goods and those ostensibly duty-free gifts (*hadaya*) people from across the border in Mauritania have made to him.

Although Muhammadu has stated that he will not be directly involved in politics – some of his public pronouncements say that this is not the role of his family[5] – he has made several conspicuous interventions in electoral politics in both Mali and Mauritania. During electoral campaigns in the 1990s in Mali, Muhammadu sometimes openly supported particular candidates for political office. As for Mauritanian politics, he has occasionally given his followers explicit instructions on how to cast their votes in some elections. While Hady Tall has also made public statements about his unwillingness to support any political candidate or party, several of his sons' active interest and involvement in electoral politics is common knowledge. In fact, they maintain close ties with their cousin from elsewhere in Mali who is a high-profile politician and leader of a prominent political party. As one can imagine, those committed to the idea of secularism have decried such involvement in politics, stating that religious leaders and, by extension, their sons (and probable successors) should deal with religion and religion only.

But matters are certainly more complicated than such criticisms of religious leaders would suggest. When Muslim religious leaders act in other areas – for instance when they serve as mediators in dispute resolution, an extra-legal channel at least from the perspective of the state – such activities are of course political in nature. From the perspective of those who may have had a dispute resolved through such mediation, not to mention those agents of the state for whom such mediation might serve to alleviate administrative burdens, the charge of acting beyond the realm of the religious is simply beside the point. As this suggests, the relationships between the state and its agents, on the one hand, and Muslim religious specialists, on the other, have sometimes been rather contradictory.

RELIGIOSITY

While the preceding discussion tried to give a general sense of the nature of the impact of the postcolonial state with its ideology of secularism, I now want to examine some of the complexities of the changes in the style of religiosity among people in Nioro over the past few decades. As I will suggest, some of these changes seem to reflect generational differences, while others show the influence of those discourses critical of Sufi orders and their leaders.

In contrast to those from older generations, many younger people in Nioro have less of a direct link with the town's Sufi orders and leaders. Although many such people would consider themselves Tijanis or Hamawis simply by having been born into families who were identified as such, they never formally join either of the Sufi orders. Indeed, it is fairly unusual for anyone from the generation of men in their forties and fifties in the town to seek formal initiation into the Tijaniyya or the Hamawiyya. When I asked why this might be the case, many people told me the conditions or rules for doing so were just too onerous. They noted that joining the Sufi order was a life-long commitment. Failure to perform the special litany of prayers of the Sufi order was to invite divine retribution; one even risked dying an apostate. Muslim religious leaders in Nioro do not of course dispute in any way the hardships associated with being a Tijani or Hamawi. On the contrary, they often stress such hardships, but without failing to extol the benefits. During visits between religious leaders and followers, it is quite common for religious leaders to emphasise the very strict demands of Tijani or Hamawi practice as well as the incomparable rewards, such as access to paradise, if one does adhere strictly to such practice, particularly the performance of the special prayers of the Sufi order.

The reluctance to embrace formally the Tijaniyya and/or the Hamawiyya has become fairly widespread in Nioro. If previously most adult men sought at least nominal membership in one of the town's two Sufi orders, this is no longer the case. This effectively signals an overall decline in the numbers of people, at least in the town of Nioro, seeking formal initiation into any Sufi order. Some of those closely associated with the two Sufi orders comment on this development and seem quite concerned about it. As I suggested in Chapter 6, this does not in any way imply that such people are necessarily swayed by secularist ideas. Nor has this meant the decline in importance of certain charismatic religious leaders or any necessary opposition to some of their esoteric practices. Rather, it suggests that what it means to be a Muslim in this context has been changing. Many younger people in the town admire those able and willing to be formally initiated in a Sufi order. Indeed, they often see such initiation as a mark of exceptional piety. However, many others find the discourse extolling the rewards accruing to those with formal initiation almost irrelevant to them. These people seem to think formal affiliation with a Sufi order has become almost superfluous but, unlike the reformists, they do not condemn the Sufi orders outright.

This waning of formal affiliation to the Sufi orders is neither unambiguous, nor a simple matter of Muslims abandoning more 'magical' or 'traditional' practices, as some social theorists might assert. It is, in fact, very complicated. Some people – rather staunch opponents of reformists – told me that while they have no objections to formal initiation into a Sufi order, they think it is simply unnecessary. One person pointed out that the benefits from affiliation to a Sufi order were hardly obvious, and may even, in some cases, prove to be detrimental. He noted that many people had suffered tremendously for their affiliation with the Hamawiyya during the colonial repression – witness the many people from Nioro who had been persecuted. He asked, rhetorically, what, if anything, those who had suffered had gained from such devotion to and affiliation with their *shaykh* and Sufi order. As far as he was concerned, there had been little in the way of tangible reward for them or their families. He said that quite a few people think that perhaps they had been wrong to have risked so much for the sake of a Sufi order and a particular religious leader. Needless to say, the rejoinders of those who support the Sufi orders point to some of their intangible rewards in this world and in the next.

In contrast to such discourse, which seems to be a 'rational' weighing of the benefits of affiliation with a Sufi order, the following perspective on religious practice reveals how complicated the changes have been. Several people, who incidentally are also unyielding in their opposition to reformists, explained to me that they had no need for a special litany of prayers from one of the Sufi orders in the town. This is not because they objected to special litanies of prayers per se, but rather that they had what they called the *wird* or litany of prayers of the Prophet Muhammad himself. What they meant by this was that they perform the supererogatory prayers the Prophet Muhammad is himself reported to have performed, according to various collections of *hadith* (see Wensinck 1927). In this way of thinking, such prayers, de-linked as they are from a particular Sufi order, nonetheless seem to have the same objective, that is, being a pious Muslim. Moreover, such people think these prayers are just as efficacious as those of the Sufi orders and, quite possibly, even superior since they ostensibly emulate the example of the Prophet Muhammad. From this perspective, the special prayers associated with initiation into a Sufi order are basically irrelevant but not un-Islamic, as reformists would have it. In such cases, the influence of discourses, such as those of reformists, that stress the imperative of following the example of the Prophet Muhammad is obvious.

As this last example suggests, the persistent and longstanding reformist discourses critical of Sufi orders, coming for the most part, but not exclusively, from outside Nioro, have undoubtedly had an influence on the interest in formal membership in the Sufi orders. Such discourses question not only the authority of certain religious leaders, but also frequently some of their and their followers' practices, including the gift-giving associated with the prayer economy. These discourses are what might be called an external critique that many people in Nioro, the major religious leaders included, have tried to counter in part through their opposition to the establishment of reformist institutions in Nioro and its environs.

Over the past few years, ideas such as the criticism of religious leaders have gained currency among some residents in Nioro such that they are no longer exclusively limited – if they ever were – to reformists and secularists. From conversations with people from broad sectors of the society represented in the town, I learned that such ideas are more widespread than in earlier periods. The spread of such ideas cannot, however, be attributed solely to reformists, whose presence in Nioro is very restricted. Arguably, one of the broader effects of Western education in conjunction with secular ideology has been the more general spread of ideas critical of Muslim religious leaders of elevated status. As in the case of secularists discussed above, this does not mean that such people have adopted reformist ideas wholesale. In fact, many of the people in the town who harbour views critical of Sufi leaders and/or seem reluctant to join a Sufi order, nevertheless also seek out the use of the Islamic esoteric sciences. In some cases, this is even from some of the same religious leaders from whom they might, at earlier times, have actually sought initiation into a Sufi order.

I discussed in Chapter 6 how some people have been quite critical of the privileged relations between elites and the prominent religious leaders in Nioro. However, sainthood and the authority of saintly religious leaders are almost never called into question. In discussing the relations between such religious leaders and followers, some people expressed the view that their own interests and those of the broader community have sometimes been slighted. Such views are part of what might be called some of the internal critiques of the present organisation of religious practice in Nioro. In some cases, such critiques have been rather pointed. In recent years, a number of ordinary followers of the religious leaders in Nioro have questioned the preferential access some elites seem to have to the religious leaders. I have heard some people complain that they too have serious problems – individual and communal – which need addressing, but that they, unlike the more affluent, are unable to obtain direct access to the religious leaders, their prayers and blessings. Individuals and groups have, in some specific instances, curtailed, and, in a few cases I know about, even suspended their transfers of gifts to religious leaders. In doing so, they sometimes stated quite explicitly that they think their interests have been ignored in favour of those who happen to give gifts of much greater value.[6] While I initially thought such criticisms might disrupt the prayer economy and even threaten its reproduction, the suspension of gift-giving has been only temporary in all the cases I learned about. In some cases, individuals and groups have simply shifted their gift-giving from one of the religious leaders in Nioro to the other, effectively signalling a public transfer of affiliation.

In one much discussed case, once the religious leader became aware the inhabitants of a particular village had actually stopped giving gifts, the religious leader actively attempted to prevent a permanent rift from developing. Members of the religious leader's entourage almost immediately travelled to the village and communicated the religious leader's appreciation to villagers for past collective gifts they made to him. Shortly thereafter, the villagers decided as a group to resume their gift-giving. Some of the people from the village subsequently told me they expected their interests to be slighted again in the future. They explained that they recognised this as one of the realities of the relationship with their 'powerful' religious leader. They also told me the religious leader himself was not at fault; rather, those around him were ultimately responsible. In the end, the religious leader's authority remained intact.

Some people in Nioro have made what is perhaps an even more trenchant critique, at least from the perspective of the outside observer. I have heard several people assert that the celebrated religious leaders of Nioro, their piety notwithstanding, cannot possibly be saints because true saints have no need for the lavish homes, cars and ostentation that so mark their presence. In conversations about the town's religious leaders, one person asked me whether saints could possibly have so much wealth and continue to live so close to people living in conditions of poverty without seeming to care. Of course, the specific discourse of the Tijaniyya on the licitness of material wealth that is gained through licit means is relevant here. Moreover, those around the major religious leaders often point to their largesse and how some of their wealth is used as alms for the poor and to support their large entourages. In the end, however, such critiques do not preclude those who articulate them from making gifts to one or the other of the religious leaders for a variety of ends.

As I have pointed out, over the years the two major religious leaders in Nioro have been associated with high-ranking officials in postcolonial regimes in Mali and elsewhere. Both religious leaders have had close ties with regimes that have been overthrown or have faltered, or with political figures whose fortunes have waned. While some people in the town suggested privately that the religious leaders would necessarily be blamed for such misfortune or at least the inability to forestall it, this has not been the case. In fact, the efficacy of the symbolic capital of the religious leaders seems not to have suffered in the least. It is, indeed, striking that in spite of such critiques of the organisation of religious practice and even doubts about particular individual religious leaders, most people in Nioro generally continue to defer to the town's religious leaders. This includes those who do not seek formal initiation into a Sufi order, as well as those who might possibly be less enthusiastic about an affiliation they already have. Although I have noted (in Chapter 6) that many seem reluctant to criticise possible saints, it is quite difficult to generalise about such deference. While some clearly defer out of sheer respect for religious leaders and their status, some people discussed such deference in terms of *realpolitik*. In this way of thinking, people have no choice but to act deferential when faced with the considerable power of the religious leaders who, after all, have the potential to curse or at least to invite divine retribution.

These various critiques of Sufi orders, their leaders and associated practices are in no way universally shared. Even though the Sufi orders seem to be less directly appealing to many within the town of Nioro, there are many for whom affiliation with a particular Sufi order and/or direct ties with a religious leader are still central to what it means to be Muslim. It is significant that for some of these people, including some with a religious education, the boundary between the Tijaniyya and the Hamawiyya has been, to a certain extent, blurred. There is a sense among some people that what they share in common in their commitment to the Sufi orders and their leaders is greater than what separates them from both reformists and secularists. I suspect that such a rapprochement might be, in part, a reaction to the pervasiveness of the reformist discourses coming from outside Nioro, as well as to the increased influence of reformists in the area. In addition, it may be related to the fact that so much time (more than sixty years) has passed since the exile of Hamallah and some, though not all, are unwilling to uphold old animosities. Many committed to the idea of Sufi orders see Tijani and Hamawi religious leaders as equally legitimate, though most have personal and partisan preferences that they sometimes articulate and act upon. One of my friends, who is a very devoted member of one of the Sufi orders, occasionally makes visits to the head of the other Sufi order in Nioro. He goes on behalf of a friend, a migrant from the area living far from Nioro, who makes regular gifts of cash to the religious leader. In recent years, some people have even gone so far as to participate in the communal rituals and annual visits of both communities, Tijani and Hamawi – something almost inconceivable just a few decades ago.

During my fieldwork, there was discussion of a potentially even broader rapprochement between Tijanis and Hamawis during multi-party elections. In fact, those who identify as Tijanis and Hamawis have sometimes forged alliances against certain candidates for elected office who are either secularists or reformists or are supported by secularists or reformists. While in some places Tijanis and Hamawis have successfully organised voters to defeat certain candidates, they have failed in others. If some noted the alliance between Hamawis and Tijanis was a makeshift one, it is perhaps more accurately characterised as a détente, the outcome of the predicament of living in a postcolonial state, when some see that what unites them as supporters of the Sufi orders and their leaders is more important than what divides them from their critics, both reformists and secularists.

Despite the declining interest in formal affiliation with the Sufi orders in Nioro, other ordinary people from all sectors of society, often from outside the town, have been formally joining the two Sufi orders. These include civil servants, military personnel and merchants, who have lived or worked in the town at some point or who travel there to seek formal initiation. Many others from the surrounding villages and further afield who work as agriculturalists, petty traders or herders have also been joining the two Sufi orders. There are also, of course, the many elite followers for whom the celebrated religious leaders are more privatised religious leaders.

While some analysts have pointed to a decline in influence of the Sufi orders and saints with the spread of education, urbanisation and the rise of a middle class, I have tried to provide a more nuanced view of the evolution of Sufi organisation and practice in Nioro. While it might be tempting to assert that, after regaining the authority that they had earlier in this century, the Sufi orders are declining along with the expansion of the forces of 'modernisation', this would not be an entirely accurate assessment of the rather complex situation. Clearly, some people, many of whom are urban dwellers, are less enthusiastic about formally embracing the Sufi orders. Although such people are usually not reformists, some of them have either adopted reformist ideas or have been profoundly influenced by them. At the same time, many others seem to have moved in the opposite direction, establishing and/or renewing ties to the Sufi orders and their leaders, if anything further strengthening their position. The various criticisms made of the organisation of religious practice do not seem to threaten the cele-brated religious leaders with their personalised authority, and Nioro's living Muslim saints remain enormously influential. But if the authority of such religious leaders might be certain, many people in Nioro acknowledge that the authority of their successors is certainly not.

THE PUBLIC SPHERE

In earlier chapters, I argued that the French colonial presence helped to foster a new sphere of activity in which people from all sectors of society were coming together. In this new colonial sphere, the practice of Islam was different to that in the period prior to colonial rule. In addition to the many conversions to Islam, people from all sectors of society were also adopting a standardised set of ritual norms that included regular prayer, and fasting during Ramadan, as well as affiliation to a Sufi order. If the colonial sphere fostered such standardisation of religious practice for virtually all Muslims, the standardisation of religious practice has also continued in the postcolonial period and must be understood in relation to the expansion of the public sphere in Mali. Indeed, a consideration of the genesis, history and nature of this sphere is absolutely crucial to understanding religious practice in contemporary Nioro and in Mali more generally.

Arguably, a public sphere has been developing over the past several decades in Mali. This public sphere differs quite considerably from the idealised bourgeois public sphere that Habermas (1989; cf. Calhoun 1992) has described, in which there is a space for so-called rational critical debate. In such a bourgeois public sphere, religion clearly has no place at all. Following John Bowen who has written about Aceh in Indonesia, I would argue that in Mali there is a 'public sphere of discourse that combines religious, social, and political messages' (Bowen 1993: 325). In Mali, a country where Muslims constitute a clear and overwhelming majority, we can talk about a public sphere of debate and deliberation in which the religious messages have come to be centred predominantly around Islam.[7] One could even go so far as to say that Islam has come to saturate the sphere of public discourse in postcolonial Mali.[8] The public sphere in postcolonial Mali is a loose and somewhat intangible sphere where many Malians have come to imagine themselves as Muslims (cf. Anderson 1991).

Although some elements of the public sphere in Mali can be traced back to the colonial period when certain kinds of new spaces were opened for debate, such a sphere actually has roots in generally overlooked antecedents in non-secular discursive forms in this part of West Africa.[9] Prior to colonial rule, debates between Muslim religious figures sometimes centred on such questions as the legitimacy of rule by particular Muslims and non-Muslims, including the French, the licitness of trade with non-Muslims, the licitness of practices such as spirit possession (see Chapter 7), and so forth. We have evidence of such debates in the form of various treatises in Arabic and oral histories and narratives from the precolonial and colonial periods.[10] Under colonial rule, once Muslim religious leaders came to accept French rule or at least were resigned to the colonial presence, 'Muslim' debate and deliberation about political and economic issues such as the legitimacy of non-Muslim rule were, on the whole, attenuated.

However, as I have suggested, colonialism did indeed provide openings for certain kinds of debate and deliberation between African Muslim subjects. Some of these debates between Muslims living under colonial rule were specifically about the leadership of the Muslim community, such as whether to accept Hamallah or another as a religious leader. Other debates were about orthodoxy, such as whether to abridge one's prayers or to cross one's arms during prayer or the licitness of the esoteric sciences and Sufi orders. In the 1950s, the decade leading up to independence, Muslim debate about such 'political' issues as non-Muslim rule would again became important. As we have seen, certain Muslim reformists entered the public arena in new ways and sometimes began to question the legitimacy of colonial rule.

In spite of the restrictions on the nature of 'Muslim' debate and deliberation during colonial rule, the spread of colonial newspapers, publications, pamphlets, political parties, associations and organisations within the new colonial sphere helped to contribute to the development of a public sphere. In contrast to the Habermasian notion of the idealised secular public sphere, there were significant restraints and constrictions on debate in this sphere in colonial Soudan. Moreover, religious messages were sometimes very important in this sphere. This is particularly the case if one considers, for example, new forms of associational life in colonial urban areas. Beginning in the 1920s and the 1930s, individuals and groups founded Muslim associations in various urban centres in AOF.[11] While the most prominent of these were 'reformist' Muslim associations, there were several associations that ostensibly admitted all Muslims as members. In practice, these associations, which grew considerably in number in the postwar period, attracted as members those men who were African colonial civil servants, former soldiers and others involved in the colonial urban centres of economic activity. If some of the early associations had as a main goal the promotion of the *hajj*, increasingly an objective of an expanding and aspirant African Muslim bourgeoisie, others centred their attention on the building of mosques or the promotion of Islamic education.

Several of the Muslim associations organised public meetings where invited speakers, including prominent African Muslim intellectuals, sometimes gave lectures about such topics as Muslim unity and morality.[12] According to colonial accounts, thousands of people sometimes attended the public meetings of such associations in Bamako. Working with one of these Muslim associations, Fraternité Musulmane (Muslim Fraternity), Mahmud Ba gave public addresses in which he condemned young Muslims for their greater interest in drink and the pursuit of pleasure than in the practice of Islam.[13] In 1954, on a visit to Bamako from Senegal, Ibrahima Niasse addressed a large audience at the Club Africain. He instructed his listeners to practise Islam according to the precepts of the Quran without failing to perform the *hajj* if they had the means to do so. Moreover, Niasse encouraged them to contribute funds towards the construction of a new Friday mosque in central Bamako.[14] Most of these Muslim associations were decidedly non-political or at least generally avoided political issues (at least from the perspective of the French). That is, they did not seem to contest French authority directly.[15] Be that as it may, such Muslim associations were helping to animate discussions about Islam and how to be Muslim in the colonial context.

During the late colonial period, newspapers also contributed in important ways to the dissemination of certain kinds of messages about religion and Islam in particular in the public sphere. Although no newspapers were published in the Soudan until after the Second World War, *Paris-Dakar*, the French-owned daily published in Dakar, was distributed in the Soudan before the war (Bourgault 1995). In 1950, the Bamako-based weekly *Le Soudan Français* was launched and immediately became an important medium in which Islam was a topic of discussion. In the 1950s, the circulation of *Le Soudan Français* was around 2,000 and regularly featured articles about Islam ostensibly addressed to a new reading public educated in French. Such coverage of matters Islamic is all the more interesting when one considers that there were considerably fewer articles about Christianity published in the newspaper. On the one hand, the newspaper seemed to promote what Dale Eickelman has called a 'generic Islam' that is centred around the assumed universals of Islam (Eickelman 1989a). On the other, the colonial newspaper advocated a notion of 'modern' African (or French) Muslims whose modernity was closely tied to France and not to closer association with the Arab world.

Such a generic Islam of assumed universals can be seen in numerous articles about the main Islamic holidays, rituals and even certain Muslim personalities in AOF, which had a prominent place in this weekly newspaper. For example, at the beginning of the month of Ramadan, the yearly month of fasting from sunrise to sundown, front-page articles in the newspaper highlighted the obligatory fasting 'all true Muslims should respect'. At the end of the month, there was regular coverage of the communal prayers at the Friday mosque in Bamako and the ensuing holiday marking the end of the fast. Quite often a photo of the imam of the main Friday mosque in Bamako accompanied these front-page articles.[16] For the Feast of the Sacrifice, various African correspondents sometimes wrote articles about the celebration of the holiday in different places in the colony.[17] Every year, there was also coverage of the *hajj* and sometimes even rather extensive coverage by some of those from the Soudan performing the *hajj*. In addition to death announcements of prominent members of the colonial-authorised Muslim establishment, some African Muslims – members of the colonial-authorised Muslim establishment – contributed articles about such topics as 'Muslim marriage', singing and music from the perspective of Islam, and the *hajj*.[18] In this way, all of the articles about Islam in *Le Soudan Français* seem to present a very generic Islam – an Islam of communal prayers, Ramadan, holidays and the *hajj*.

In this vision of Islam, most of the salient differences or even debates between Muslims in the colony are passed over in silence, and what made the practice of Islam possibly different in West Africa from anywhere else in the world seems to be ignored. Thus, readers are not able to read about differences between Hamawis, Tijanis, reformist or others, though they would undoubtedly know about the differences between such Muslims and their often heated debates about religious authority, leadership, doctrine and practice. While this might seem to be a departure from the colonial policy of promoting an African Islam, it is clear that this Islam of assumed universals was a vision of Islam palatable to the French. Moreover, it was a vision that conformed to larger geopolitics in play at the time. It was after all the 1950s, the heyday of Arab nationalism at the same time that the position of the US as a world power was being consolidated. There were, of course, no reformists, with their affinities beyond West Africa, published in the newspaper – indeed, it is inconceivable they would have been allowed to publish articles. Excluded from this press, some reformists were in fact starting to publish some of their own pamphlets and books at this time (see Chapter 7). Muslims in Soudan sometimes ordered publications such as Cheikh Touré's reformist review, *Reveil Islamique*, from Dakar and sold them in Bamako.[19] In contrast, *Le Soudan Français* became a privileged site and forum for particular kinds of 'loyal' Muslim subjects who were deemed newsworthy. In the inaugural issue of the newspaper, there was a front-page story about the visit of Shaykh Fanta Madi from Guinea to Bamako.[20] During the life of the newspaper, features about the colonial-authorised Muslim establishment were a regular occurrence. Thus, the imam of the main mosque in Bamako was invariably featured in photos sporting his colonial medals, and Seydou Nourou Tall's visits from Dakar to various places in the Soudan received coverage.

In addition to occasional articles where the anti-reformist opinions of certain Muslim religious leaders were expressed,[21] the most prominent 'counter-reform' activists – Amadou Hampaté Ba and Abdoul Wahhab Doucouré – regularly published articles about Islam (and other topics) in the newspaper. For example, the prolific Doucouré, who was an employee of the colonial administration in Bamako and one of main leaders of the counter-reform movement, advanced some very telling arguments in a series of articles in *Le Soudan Français*. In an article about 'modern times' published in 1952, Doucouré argued that Black Africans (*Africains noirs*) have basically nothing to learn from Muslims elsewhere in the world and specifically not from Arabs. With French assistance, he argued, Black Africans can draw upon specific African Muslim spirituality and wisdom in order to remain 'French Muslims' in their quest for the modernity and 'progress' that is only attainable through Western science.[22] This African Muslim spirituality is thought to be embodied in the teachings of Cerno Bokar, the *shaykh* of Amadou Hampaté Ba, the latter actively promoted in the 1950s (and long after), culminating in a book co-authored with Marcel Cardaire, the colonial administrator responsible for *la politique musulmane* in Soudan (see Ba and Cardaire 1957). However, other African Muslim authors also highlighted the wisdom of other African Muslims, as for example, in the story of a wise *marabout*, who offers perfect advice, published in the late 1950s.[23]

In subsequent articles in the newspaper, Doucouré continued to promote Islam and close association with France. For example, in one article, which is a seemingly innocuous discussion of the *hajj*, he raises criticisms of the Saudis for demanding too much money from pilgrims while they are on Saudi territory. He concludes this article by noting that 'the life of Saudi Arabia is entirely a condition of the royalties American oil companies pay to the royal treasury'.[24] Thus, pointing not only to Saudi exploitation of pilgrims, Doucouré also questions the very legitimacy of the Saudi regime with its ties to the US, which had become an important reference point in African nationalist discourse, especially in the postwar period. However, Doucouré was not alone in advancing the agenda of keeping African Muslims separate from Arab Muslims. In a long interview, a colonial chief who had performed the *hajj* enumerated in great detail the very high cost of the *hajj* in Saudi Arabia and the difficult physical conditions there. After making the *hajj* seem a thoroughly unpleasant experience for those wishing to accomplish such an important religious duty, the chief stated that African Muslims have absolutely no 'interest' in remaining in Saudi Arabia.[25]

Although radio was also developed rather late in the colonial period in the Soudan, it has also helped to spread religious messages in the public sphere. In June 1957, the new colonial radio station *Radio Soudan* began daily broadcasting of various news, culture and educational programmes, mostly in French, but also in a few different vernacular languages for news. Such programming was spread out over a limited number of hours in the day over the week.[26] It is striking how the radio station almost immediately created a space in its weekly schedule for specific Muslim religious programming. Most notably, on Fridays, there was a weekly programme – *émissions musulmanes* – broadcast in the afternoon around the time of the midday Friday communal prayers;[27] it too promoted a generic Islam of assumed universals. The promotion of 'Muslim' programming on the colonial radio is even more remarkable given the almost total lack of 'Christian' programming. In fact, the only seemingly 'Christian' programming was the so-called 'spiritual music' broadcast on Sunday mornings. In any case, the promotion of Muslim radio programming was a continuation of the colonial policy of making space for a certain kind of Islam in various public forums.

It is also important to note the ways in which political parties also helped to spread religious messages in the new public sphere during colonial rule. While generally secular in orientation, political parties and nationalist movements nevertheless actively and openly identified with some of the signs of Islam. As several commentators have noted, almost all the leaders of the parties in Soudan were Muslims. Moreover, they usually sought openly to identify themselves as such. If some observers have drawn attention to the fact that many politicians wore distinctive 'Muslim' dress and hairstyles, which indexed their differences from the French,[28] some politicians actively sought to associate themselves with various lineages of Muslim religious specialists or other charismatic individual Muslims. The politicians from the anti-colonialist party, who asked Hamallah's wife for petitionary prayers, provide just one such example of this association with Muslim religious figures.

The public sphere that was developing under colonial rule has continued to expand even further in the postcolonial period. Today some of the many religious messages in the public sphere come through religious education, sermons, print and audio-visual media and the country's Islamic associations, all of which have been influenced by transnational and global interconnections.[29] After tracing the contours of the public sphere in postcolonial Mali, I want to show how this public sphere allows for the practice of Islam to be discussed and debated in new, though not entirely unprecedented, ways in a religious centre like Nioro. I will also demonstrate some of the ways in which the public sphere has helped to foster a more supralocal sense of Muslim identity among many Malians.

In the past few decades, there has been an expansion of new private Muslim educational institutions (*madrasas*) in Mali that relates in part to increased educational and financial ties with the presumed centre of the Islamic world, the Arab Middle East, which the availability of petrodollars began to facilitate in the 1970s.[30] In these schools, students receive not only an Islamic religious education but also instruction in Arabic in a much broader range of subjects than in a 'traditional' Islamic education. Because many Muslims prefer to send their children to these private schools rather than to French-language state schools, there has been an enormous influx of students into the schools. Since independence in 1960, there has also been a rapid and sustained increase in mosque construction in Mali, often financed externally or through the remittances of Malian migrants.[31] These newer Islamic educational institutions, along with the pre-existing older educational institutions, and the proliferation of mosques have all helped to shape Mali as a social landscape that is predominantly Muslim.

Islamic organisations and associations have also had an important influence on the public sphere in postcolonial Mali. They include the Sufi orders long present in the region, the more recent foreign-funded Islamic cultural centres and institutes in the capital,[32] and formal associations such as AMUPI, L'Association Malienne pour l'unité et le progrès de l'Islam (the Malian Association for the Unity and Progress of Islam). In 1980 the Malian government founded AMUPI, which at the time was the only officially authorised Islamic association in the country. It seems that this national association was created in order to try to contain some of the conflicts between reformists and those affiliated with Sufi orders with their different understandings of Islam. Undoubtedly, one of AMUPI's goals was to promote the idea of harmonious Muslim subjects compliant with what was at the time an authoritarian regime. Perhaps equally importantly, AMUPI also had responsibility for coordinating financial aid from abroad, particularly the petrodollars from various countries for the construction of mosques, *madrasas*, and Islamic cultural centres and institutes, primarily in the capital.

In 1991, after a coup d'état led by military officers, leaders of a transitional government convened a national conference to draft a new constitution for the Malian Third Republic. During the conference, several individuals, including some representing a small group calling itself 'Hezbolla' – from the Arabic, 'party of God', thereby making known affinities with groups elsewhere in the Islamic world – argued rather forcefully for allowing the formation of Islamic political parties in Mali. Since defenders of the principle of secularism were in the majority, the new constitution drafted and approved by a referendum reaffirmed the commitment to secularism and explicitly forbade the formation of political parties based on or around religion. However, given the state's greater commitment to freedom of association and expression since 1991, there has been a proliferation of new Islamic associations. This has meant that the government-initiated Islamic association AMUPI suddenly lost its monopoly. No longer the only officially recognised Islamic association in the country, AMUPI now had to compete for members. If Hezbolla was initially one of the most visible and vocal of the new Islamic associations, it seems to have ceased to operate shortly after 1991. There are now literally dozens of Islamic associations that have been officially registered with the Malian government since 1991.[33] Most of the associations are based in Bamako since Mali, on the French model, is a very centralised state. However, these associations vary not only in size, but also in their stated objectives. In addition to several Muslim youth, women's, and reformist associations, there are associations that group together Muslim preachers. Several of the new Islamic associations advocate 'development', 'socialism', 'democracy' or even 'individual rights', goals and objectives, which they sometimes signal in their names. Many of the associations are actively attempting to gain access to funds from overseas for projects such as mosque and school construction and educational activities. Since 1991, individuals and members of some of the different associations have attempted to create umbrella organisations that unite or coordinate the activities of some of the disparate Islamic associations.

While some of the founders and leaders of these new associations have engaged in French-language secular schooling, in many cases they are graduates of the private *madrasas* and have sometimes pursued further advanced Islamic education abroad. Indeed, some of them are new intellectuals from the highly educated Muslim elite that has expanded considerably in the past few decades. While some of the new Islamic associations are small and focused around a particular charismatic leader such as a preacher or Muslim intellectual, others have much wider appeal. One of the most prominent of the new associations has been AISLAM, Association Islamique pour le salut (Islamic Salvation Association), an association founded at least in part in opposition to AMUPI. If AISLAM has a reputation for being a reformist association, others are known more for charitable work or the promotion of 'development' and are effectively Islamic NGOs. At the time of my long fieldwork in Mali, I did not meet any members of these associations in Nioro, with the exception of AMUPI. While the existence of so many Islamic associations is arguably evidence of the expansion of civil society in Mali, many Malians committed to the principle of *laïcité* find their very existence alarming.

In the wake of greater freedom of expression, there has also been a rapid increase in the number of privately owned newspapers published in Mali. While these numerous newspapers – more than seventeen at the time of my fieldwork – are nearly all strongly secular in orientation and actively promote a secularising modernist discourse, a few had a specifically Muslim religious perspective. In 1991, one such newspaper, *Témoignage afro-musulman*, exalted Mali's 'Afro-Muslim Heritage' (*héritage négro-musulman*) and likened those Malians who had opposed the Traoré regime to Muslim 'martyrs'.[34] A few years later, the founder of this newspaper wrote an opinion piece in a secular newspaper where he emphatically embraced the appellation 'Islamist' and argued that Islamists were actually committed to peace in Mali.[35] In August 1993, another religiously oriented newspaper, *Le*

Politicien musulman (The Muslim Politician), asked rhetorically when Mali would become an Islamic Republic.[36] But such religiously oriented newspapers with 'Islamic' – even 'Islamist' – perspectives and agendas have not thrived in the way the secular press has, and they have without exception been published irregularly. In most cases, they have actually ceased publication altogether. On the whole, Malian newspapers – all of which have somewhat restricted circulation in that they are generally available only in the capital and in a few of the larger towns – are addressed to the small secular elite. In this way, they almost completely ignore the concerns of many, if not most, ordinary and elite Malian Muslims.

While it is not surprising those Malians critical of secularism or possibly interested in promoting Islam are largely excluded from secular newspapers, it is rather striking that the commitment to secularism in the other newspapers is so strong that one finds an almost complete avoidance of the discussion of religion as it is practised in Mali. For example, in nearly all the secular newspapers, there are regular death notices for prominent Malians, particularly those with some connection to the presumed readership of these newspapers, that is, the secular elite. Unlike the colonial newspapers, the deaths of Muslim religious leaders, including the most prominent in Mali, are never acknowledged in print.[37] This is perhaps an indication of the extent of anti-clericalism in the French republican tradition detectable in the press. More importantly, it indexes the wide gap between such newspapers and most ordinary Malian Muslims.

When the topic of religion is broached in the secular press, it is usually discussed in a few different ways. First, journalists usually focus attention on questions of conflict, whether religious disputes between Muslims in Mali or between Muslims and Christians in the country.[38] At the time of my fieldwork in the 1990s, there was considerable coverage of the civil war between Islamists and government forces in Algeria, a country with which Mali shares a long Saharan border. A subset here are the many sensationalist stories about the alleged dangers of rising Islamism, *intégrisme* or 'fundamentalism' in Mali and the threats to the secular nature of the state. Such threats are usually thought to come in the form of the new Islamic associations with their presumed international and sometimes even 'terrorist' connections. For example, one hyperbolic and condescending front-page piece entitled 'Islamism' warned that 'the bearded ones are amongst us'.[39] Second, there are regular anti-clerical exposés, which usually focus on the alleged improper behaviour of various Muslim clerics in Bamako, including embezzlement of funds, sexual impropriety and their 'fraudulent' and superstitious practices (see Figure 5.1).[40] Third, there are occasional articles, often by non-journalists, who present general information about Islam, again a generic Islam. For example, in various articles, laypersons – often retired civil servants – enumerate the so-called five pillars of Islam or discuss uncontroversial rules for Muslim worship, such as how to perform one's ablutions properly.[41] In this way, like the articles in the colonial newspaper, they studiously avoid discussion of what might make the practice of Islam in Mali different from elsewhere in the Islamic world. In other words, they do not consider the religious discourses and practices of the overwhelming majority of Malian Muslims. Thus, when the secular press in Mali is not focusing on conflict or the venality of Muslim clerics, it tends to give space to, if not actively promote, what Peter van der Veer has called 'the reformist religion of the bourgeoisie' (1994: xiii).

Along with the proliferation of newspapers has been the even more important expansion of the availability of print media related to Islam. During French colonial rule, vernacular languages were generally not developed as a means of written communication, a situation quite unlike in Anglophone Africa. Therefore, Islamic religious literature in postcolonial Mali tends to be either in Arabic or in French and not in vernacular languages. For several decades, bookshops in Bamako have been selling a range of often inexpensive Islam-related books and pamphlets in French and Arabic, including some written by Malian authors.[42] Many of the books for sale are imported from publishers in various places in the Arab world such as Casablanca, Cairo and Beirut. Since the 1980s, the range of subjects that such books and pamphlets cover has broadened considerably. Some of the books for sale include the following: rules for proper Muslim worship, guides for supererogatory prayers, Islamic jurisprudence, details of the life of the Prophet Muhammad, stories of Muslim saints and other pious Muslims from history, and the Islamic esoteric sciences.[43] If many of these published texts present rationalised understandings of religion, some of the most popular Islamic religious texts in French available in Mali deal with the Islamic esoteric sciences (see Figure 8.1). Although some of these are inexpensive, others are among the most expensive texts available in French. Most notably, Cheikh Ahmad Tall, a Senegal-based descendant of Umar Tall with no direct ties to the Tall in Nioro, has published a series of books about 'secrets' in Islam in French translation (for example Tall 1995). In addition, those Malians who are literate in Arabic now have access to a wide array of published texts on many different subjects, including a broad range of esoteric sciences, something that would have been difficult for their forebears.

Although perhaps the greatest market for some of these published texts is among those associated with the new Islamic educational institutions, a new general reading public of men and women – however restricted in number or difficult to quantify it might be – with varying degrees of education seems to be using these texts about Islam. If some people read such texts on their own, I know others who have discussions and debates about certain texts with their peers and elders. One woman I know, a schoolteacher in Nioro, had regular discussions about such texts about Islam in French with her

8.1 Book cover, *Les noms les plus exaltés d'Allah* (*The Most Exalted Names of God*),
     with no listed author, publisher or copyright

cousin, the imam of a mosque. She said she relied upon her cousin's knowledge of Islam and Arabic to check the validity of the content of the texts. In any case, the access to knowledge about Islam that such published materials in French and Arabic has allowed constitutes an important transformation in the sociology of Islamic knowledge that has not been in any way limited to urban areas.

However, the print media are not the only important media here. Indeed, the electronic media have been particularly important in recent years. Regularly scheduled Islamic-themed programming on state-operated media, particularly the radio, has played a crucial role in the postcolonial period. Such Islam-related programming on the radio apparently increased shortly after the 1968 coup against Mali's first postcolonial socialist regime and, in 1983, began on television (see Sanankoua 1991). Many people listen to such radio programming, some of which is broadcast in the region's vernaculars, making it more accessible to those who do not understand the usual standard languages – French and Arabic – of Islamic-themed radio programming. In addition to the special and extensive radio programming on Islamic holidays and during the month of Ramadan, there is usually coverage of the annual visits to saints in Nioro and elsewhere in the country. One popular long-running radio programme is *Les Règles de l'Islam (The Rules of Islam)*, one of whose presenters, Ismaïl Dramé, is a director of a large *madrasa* in Bamako and a prominent member of the Hamawiyya. If he invariably discusses a 'generic Islam' of universals in his radio programme, he has a widespread and public reputation for his knowledge and use of the esoteric sciences. In addition to such programmes on Malian national radio, many Malians also listen to Islamic-themed programming about Islam from various countries on short-wave radio that provides a wide variety of information about religion, international affairs and so forth.

Within what we might call the more 'informal' sector, there are the tape-recorded sermons of Malian Muslim preachers that circulate widely in the country and among Malian migrants elsewhere in Africa and beyond.[44] Some of the most popular preachers come from some of the country's leading lineages of Muslim religious specialists and have national and sometimes regional reputations. The direct predecessors of such religious leaders would seem to be some of the colonial-era preachers, such as Seydou Nourou Tall, whose peregrinations were authorised by the colonial state. Copies of the most popular preachers' sermons on cassette can be purchased in almost any market where one can also find cassettes of popular music for sale. Since the spread of private radio stations in the 1990s, recorded sermons have also been regularly aired on various stations in Bamako and elsewhere in the country. These recorded sermons cover topics ranging from the five pillars of Islam and questions of doctrine to questions of morality, marriage, divorce, and so forth, and in many cases, the themes of the sermons are uncontroversial. These sermons on cassette and on the radio are also helping to transform the sociology of Islamic knowledge, and their importance should not be underestimated. Although such recorded sermons seem to be most popular among those with little formal Islamic religious education, including many Malians who are illiterate in French and Arabic, their appeal is not limited to these people. If listening to sermons on cassette or on the radio is popular among certain young people, some women also told me they enjoy listening to recorded sermons since they are usually not permitted to attend public sermons. In fact, many ordinary Muslims listen to recorded sermons while they are working or relaxing.

One preacher, whose recorded sermons are enormously popular, is Chérif Ousmane Madani Haïdara (b. 1955) (see Figure 8.2). He is also the head of an association called *Ançar Dine*, which he translates as 'those who help the religion [Islam]',[45] one of the more successful of the many new Muslim associations in Mali. In some of his sermons, Haïdara has argued for the translation of the Quran and *hadith* into Bambara so that the tenets of Islam are accessible to the overwhelming majority of Malians who are not literate in Arabic. Most Malian Muslims religious leaders – whether or not affiliated with a Sufi order – are categorically opposed to such efforts to translate the sacred scriptures, which they see as fraught with insurmountable problems. Beginning in 1993, Haïdara has also preached in his sermons that Malian Muslims – many of whom know very little Arabic – are able to perform the ritual daily prayers in Bambara or whatever vernacular language they happen to speak.[46] This too has provoked considerable controversy, with the overwhelmingly majority of Malian Muslim religious leaders insisting that such prayers would not be valid. Indeed, I have heard many people in Nioro denounce Haïdara for making such arguments in his sermons which circulate on cassette and, more recently, on video.

Recorded sermons give Muslims – both those who listen to them and those who hear about their contents from others – access to knowledge about Islam and instruction on how to be a Muslim in the contemporary world. In some cases, they allow listeners to confirm what they might already know about Islam and religious practice. In other cases, listeners augment the knowledge they have with supralocal sources of information, which might at times contradict what they have learned or heard from local sources. It is a notable and much discussed fact that there are no preachers who come from Nioro with anything like a national reputation.[47] This is, in part a question of language, since preachers with a national reputation usually give their sermons in Bambara, increasingly the country's lingua franca. However, Bambara is not the first language for any of the lineages of Muslim religious specialists in Nioro. As many of my informants told me, no Muslim religious leader in Nioro or even any aspiring preacher would ever deign to record sermons in that language. The lack of preachers from Nioro with a national

8.2 Poster, Chérif Ousmane Madani Haïdara, Muslim preacher and media star

reputation may partly explain why many Muslim religious specialists in Nioro resent such recorded sermons. Indeed, some of my friends and informants told me they even saw these sermons as a potential threat to their own authority in matters related to Islam and its correct interpretation. In any case, the overall effect of the proliferation of recorded sermons like those of Haïdara has been the opening-up of debate about Islam and how to be Muslim that sometimes seems to impinge on the prerogatives of existing Muslim religious leaders in a place like Nioro.

The increased availability and use of video recorders have also been significant in Mali. While most videos available for purchase and rental in Mali are from East and South Asia, there are many popular videos dealing with Islamic themes.[48] In this area, perhaps the most influential actor has been Ahmed Deedat, the Indian-born South Africa-based preacher, who has campaigned as a Muslim against Christian missionaries and Christian ideas. Videos featuring Deedat, the best known of which is a 'debate' between Deedat and the American televangelist Jimmy Swaggart, are enormously popular in Mali and available even in some of the smallest towns where there is at least one video recorder and a generator.[49] The cassette is so popular in Mali that I have heard European Protestant missionaries complain about its ubiquity, not to mention the way they think Deedat distorts Christianity and the Bible.

In this study, I have repeatedly stressed how movements of people, objects and ideas have been key to some of the major developments discussed here. Migration and other movements of people have been no less important in the making of the public sphere in Mali. When migrants are outside Mali, they frequently re-imagine themselves both as Malians and as Muslims. Some of the more prosperous Malian migrants have become key actors in the development and the expansion of the public sphere. Such migrants have helped to shape this sphere through their largesse in the construction of mosques and the educational institutions discussed above and, more recently, in providing funding for a private radio station, Radio Islamique, to air Islamic religious programming in the capital.

Any discussion of the public sphere and Islam in postcolonial Mali must also consider the changing role of the state. Since independence, every Malian government – democratically elected or not – has attempted to associate itself with Islam and its public expression. This is, of course, a continuation of colonial policies, with the difference that every Malian head of state has sought to identify himself publicly as a Muslim. If the government announces the beginning of the month of Ramadan, it has never forced any Malians to undertake the monthly fast. As in the neighbouring country of Senegal (see Villalón 1995), it has, however, become routine for local government officials to pay what some refer to as a courtesy visit to Muslim religious leaders on the occasion of Islamic holidays, including the holiday that marks the end of Ramadan. I have been present in Nioro when large delegations of the town's senior civil servants have sought to gain audiences with the town's prominent religious leaders on the major Islamic holidays, and they have sometimes given them gifts. As groups and individuals, such people also visit many of the minor, though well respected, local Muslim religious specialists.

Beyond such practices, which might be considered mundane, the Malian state's association with Islam was very pronounced in the 1980s under the regime of President Moussa Traoré who sought to identify himself and his regime rather closely with Islam in a number of ways. On the international stage, during Traoré's regime, Mali became a member of the Organization of Islamic Conference (OIC) based in Saudi Arabia, thereby making Mali eligible for certain kinds of foreign assistance and cultural activities through the OIC. Even more tangible to ordinary Malians was compulsory public worship in the main Friday mosque for those high-ranking government officials who were Muslims (Brenner 1993a). In addition, there have been close and often open relationships between the head of state and other officials and some of the country's leading Muslim religious leaders, including heads of Sufi orders. In fact, it has been rather commonplace for government officials to solicit Muslim religious leaders publicly and semi-publicly for blessings or petitionary prayers and to give them lavish gifts in return. But this association with Islam has not been limited to the Traoré regime. Even in the 1960s, the socialist government of Modibo Keita made efforts to associate itself with Islam and Muslim religious leaders. In the face of criticism for allegedly being socialists and possibly even being against Islam, members of the ruling party of the socialist regime had frequent recourse to Muslim religious leaders for, among other things, petitionary prayers.[50] Even officials in the recent democratically elected governments of Mali, despite very strong stated commitments to secularism, have made efforts to assert Islamic credentials or at least to downplay suspicions that those in power are anti-religious. Indeed, representatives of the government and sometimes high-ranking officials from various political parties attend the large annual gatherings at Sufi centres in different parts of the country, including those in Nioro. Some politicians, including a recent Prime Minister, are known for their sumptuous and often public gifts to certain religious leaders in Mali.

It has been much to the dismay of secularists in Mali that the postcolonial state has actively promoted its identification with Islam. If during the late colonial period, some Muslim reformists explicitly criticised the colonial administration for its involvement in the public expression of Islam, Malian secularists have been among the most vehement critics of the state's identification with Islam in the postcolonial period. In fact, they were particularly incensed in the 1980s when the Malian government took administrative measures to ensure that all bars and nightclubs were closed during the month of Ramadan.[51] After 1991, when the transitional government reversed this policy, Malian secularists defended it in the face of much criticism, sometimes using the secular press to advance their views.

The conferring of a decidedly Islamic cast to the state has had some broader consequences that have helped to shape Mali as a predominantly Muslim space. Most notably, there seems to have been the almost tacit encouragement of the spread of Islam in Mali. As I indicated in Chapter 7, in recent decades, some Malian Muslim religious leaders have undertaken campaigns to convert rural non-Muslims and to enjoin others to give up practices, including spirit possession, that they and most others deem un-Islamic. In some cases, the Malian state and its representatives – most of whom are Muslims – have encouraged, or at least have lent legitimacy to, these conversion campaigns by regularly providing them with administrative authorisation and almost always greeting the campaigns' leaders enthusiastically. Although the actual outcomes of such campaigns are uncertain, direct or indirect association with them has promoted the state's identification with Islam even further. It also contributes to the further marginalisation of other allegedly un-Islamic sources of authority, which in the face of criticism have been increasingly relegated to less public spaces.

Over time, religious education, sermons, print and audio-visual media, the country's Islamic associations and the state have helped to animate some of the religious messages in the public sphere. In Mali, many of the specifically religious messages in the public sphere centre largely around Islam. It is through this public sphere that information and ideas about Islam (as well as other areas of knowledge), including that from beyond the immediate area, have become more readily available to the public.

BEING MUSLIM IN THE POSTCOLONY

While the public sphere is perhaps more vibrant in the towns and cities in Mali, it also extends into some of the far reaches of the country where, for many people, to be Malian means to be Muslim. Indeed, the public sphere has helped to foster a supralocal sense of shared Muslim identity in Mali, an imagined community of Muslims often linked to the Malian state whose members are to varying degrees attentive to the broader Islamic world that lies beyond the state boundaries.[52] It is quite clear that there are necessarily exclusions in such a public sphere where the religious messages are centred predominantly around Islam. Most obviously, those excluded from such a sphere include Malian Christians and non-Muslims, not to mention secularists. Moreover, those Malians, who might actually consider themselves Muslims, whose various 'religious' practices such as spirit possession other Malians deem un-Islamic are another important group of those excluded from such a public sphere. Although many such people are all too aware of their exclusion, it is less clear whether these beleaguered individuals or groups of people constitute any sort of counterpublics (Warner 2002).

In some ways, the notion of a supralocal sense of shared Muslim identity in Mali seems to contradict some of the major themes of this study. As we have seen, Muslims are often divided in important ways from other Muslims, and there are different ways of being Muslim in Mali. In Nioro, there are differences between Tijanis and Hamawis, between both of these two groups on the one hand, and reformists on the other. There are also noticeable differences between those moving away from a conception of Islam centred around the Sufi orders and their leaders – most of whom are not reformists – and those who remain committed to such conceptions. In addition, there are salient differences between those who advocate secularist principles and those who do not. In spite of such differences, the public sphere helps to foster a sense of a Muslim community tied in important ways to the idea of Mali as a state. In fact, many Muslims in Nioro imagine themselves as part of a broader Muslim community, particularly a community of Muslims within the Malian state. Perhaps this is because for many Malians the state has had a tangible influence on their lives. Although some Malians see themselves as participating directly and unambiguously in the global Islamic community – the *umma* – many other Malian Muslims recognise too many differences between themselves and others on that scale that cannot be elided in the imagining of such a global community.[53] Whatever differences people in Nioro know exist between themselves and other Muslims in the town and beyond, many do have a sense of shared Muslim identity. The imagined community of Muslims in Mali helps to shape the way ordinary Muslims practise Islam.

In fact, there have been a number of interrelated effects of the expanded public sphere and the shared Muslim identity that it has fostered. Most notably, the public sphere of debate and deliberation helps to promote unity between Muslims in Mali. In other words, it compels many to aspire to, or, at least to yearn for, more unity as a community of Muslims. It also encourages some, though certainly not all, Malian Muslims to want to transcend differences that might separate them from other Muslims in the country and beyond. In practice, this means that it encourages some people to opt out of certain religious practices that many Muslims have come to see as particularistic. Such effects are a continuation of the standardisation of religious practice that got underway during the colonial period. However, increased transnational and global interconnections in the postcolonial period have certainly had an important influence.

The aspiration for unity among Muslims in Mali can be seen, for example, in the celebration of the major Islamic holidays, which follow the Islamic lunar calendar, and are determined by sightings of the moon. In Mali, the state-operated media (radio and television) generally broadcast an announcement of reported sightings of the moon in the country along with the provenance of such sightings. These are vetted by the state-organised Commission Nationale d'Observation de la Lune. Such an announcement, as far as the state is concerned, is an indication that the celebration of the holiday will begin. Given the vast size of the country and differing regional weather conditions, the moon will sometimes not be sighted in all places at the same time. Since some people do not have confidence in the radio or television announcements and might be reluctant to follow their lead, it is not uncommon for different groups of people within the same community to begin celebrating Islamic holidays on successive days.[54] This happened a few times during my fieldwork in Nioro, including once when the head of the Hamawiyya said that he was not prepared to celebrate the holiday because he did not know about the trustworthiness of those reported on the radio to have sighted the moon (television was not available in Nioro until the late 1990s). Most, if not all, Hamawis followed his lead and waited until the following day. Others in the town followed the radio announcement. On such occasions, I noticed that many people from broad sectors of the society were bothered that all Muslims in the town were not celebrating the holiday at the same time. On other occasions, when the entire community of Muslims in Nioro did celebrate Islamic holidays simultaneously, people were quite pleased. Indeed, when this did happen, there was much discussion of this fact. Some people, especially reformists, were even more pleased when they happened to celebrate holidays on the same day as Muslims in Mecca, something they would have learned about from the radio. These examples help to illustrate the desire many have for more shared Islamic religious practice, which the expanded public sphere seems to have heightened.

At the same time, the public sphere also creates pressures for Islamic practices to be more uniform.[55] As I argued for earlier periods, many people of marginal social status, including those of hereditary servile status and recent converts, have emulated the conventions of religious practice, as well as standards of piety of Muslim religious specialists. Over time, this has helped in some ways to improve their otherwise marginal status (cf. Soares 2000). Such processes seem to have been deepened and intensified in the postcolonial period. In fact, the public sphere encourages some people to come to expect that certain particularistic religious practices be put aside in order to come into line with what some take to be more broadly accepted conventions of proper Islamic practice.[56] As I have noted in Chapter 3, some of the difficulties facing the Hamawiyya have to do with relations between Hamawis and other Muslims in the town and beyond. I pointed out how some young people from Hamawi families have gone to pray regularly at the Friday mosque in the town, effectively leaving the *zawiya*, though without necessarily ceasing to identify as Hamawis. What they encounter is the pressure for practices to be more uniform, or at least that is how I want to gloss what I heard people express. Many Muslims pointed out that in most places in the country and elsewhere, Muslims pray together on Fridays in a mosque, and it is obligatory to do so. Reasons (juridical or otherwise) for not praying at the Friday mosque notwithstanding, many people – Hamawi or not – are uncomfortable with the fact that Hamawis fail to perform the Friday communal prayers in a mosque. Thus, when some Hamawis from Nioro are away from the town in places where there are few Hamawis, they sometimes do begin to pray the Friday communal prayers in a mosque.

This departure of younger people from the *zawiya* in Nioro also seems to relate to the silence surrounding Hamallah's death. There is an unspoken rift between those Hamawis who insist that Hamallah is going to return, and those who accept that he must be dead. In certain cases, some of the people from the younger generation, not to mention the secularised national elite, have adopted what can be characterised as the colonialist and modernist view that those people who anticipate Hamallah's return are necessarily irrational. Here, too, we can see the pressures of the public sphere at work.

In addition, some who do pray at the *zawiya* criticise the way that it is managed, claiming that affairs there are often too much at the whim of the leadership. For instance, communal prayers held there on Fridays do not ordinarily begin until Muhammadu arrives to lead prayer. Not infrequently, he arrives late, and people have to delay their prayers. More than a few people find this to be a problem. In this way of thinking, to pray late is blamable.[57] Some people have cited this as the reason they have decided to perform their communal prayers at the Friday mosque – again leaving the *zawiya*. It is precisely this matter of conformity to more uniform Islamic practices that has figured in the conflict between Muhammadu and his nephew Ahmada over the future of the Hamawiyya (see Chapter 3). In fact, Ahmada broke with longstanding Hamawi practice and started to perform the Friday prayers in a mosque that he has built in a neighbourhood in Bamako.

Although it might seem that Tijanis in Nioro do not encounter the same pressures from the public sphere as Hamawis, I want to emphasise that this is most emphatically not the case. To illustrate the broader influence of the expanded public sphere, I want to consider some ordinary Muslims in Nioro. Clearly some non-elite Muslims, including many with a secular education, have what we might call a more 'modernist' approach to Islam. Like so-called religious modernists elsewhere, some Muslims think that they should be able to understand the meaning of religious texts and scripture. At the time of my fieldwork, one thoughtful civil servant in his thirties told me that he considered himself a Muslim and intended to continue conducting himself as such by following the accepted precepts such as regular prayer and fasting during Ramadan. However, he sensed a certain inadequacy in his sense of being Muslim. He said he was unhappy that he did not understand the meaning of the obligatory ritual daily prayers or even the meaning of the individual words he repeated every day in these prayers. Since the prayers are in Arabic, a language he does not understand, the literal meaning of his daily prayers is lost to him. This is the case for many Muslims in the world who, despite being unable to understand Arabic, are able at some point in their lives, usually at an early age, to memorise enough of the language to recite their prayers.

Many other ordinary Muslims, including some with little formal Islamic education, are concerned with the contents of their prayers, as well as with other questions about Islam. Because they are literate in French and/or in Arabic, they have been able to procure books and pamphlets that provide explanations and instructions about various subjects related to Islam. I know both men and women who have relied upon such texts to increase their own knowledge about the religion, and they are quite satisfied that they have been able to do so. Similarly, I know people who rely upon sermons on cassette for such information about Islam and how to be a Muslim.

It would be hasty to attribute the inquisitiveness of such ordinary, often non-elite, Muslims to 'rationalization' in the religion (Weber 1978), though clearly they might now be in a position where they might pay less heed to local Muslim religious specialists. At the same time, it would be equally unwise to suggest that this represents either a withering-away of earlier, more 'magical' practices as the secularisation thesis might have it, or even a process of desacralisation that Durkheim described (1961). The example of the self-styled curious civil servant (see Chapter 5) who managed to write his own French translation of an Arabic-language geomancy text, suggests otherwise, as does the popularity of texts about the Islamic esoteric sciences. In fact, the most popular and inexpensive French-language Islamic religious texts – books and pamphlets – in Nioro and elsewhere in contemporary Mali (and neighbouring Senegal) deal with the esoteric sciences. At the time of my fieldwork in Mali, perhaps the most popular of such texts was a short book in French, by an anonymous author, that lists the so-called ninety-nine names of God, transliterated from the Arabic, along with the ensuing benefits – good fortune, progeny, and so forth – to those who recite a particular name of God (see Figure 8.1). This published text, *Les noms les plus exaltés d'Allah (Soub-hana-wa-ta-Allah)* (The most exalted names of God), has no publisher or publication date listed. The text contains a short statement attacking as idolatry the pursuit of secret names of God (cf. Chapters 5 and 7), and this would seem to be the reason for the anonymity. In any case, I cannot remember in how many places and with how many different people I saw such texts. Since the books are usually written in the most basic French, they are accessible to anyone with just a few years of schooling.

At the same time, the angst of the civil servant should not be attributed to some sort of crisis of 'modern' consciousness (cf. Ewing 1997). Many other Malian Muslims I know expressed no such anguish about their inability to understand the literal meaning of their prayers. In fact, a fair number found the issue of understanding the content of one's prayers altogether unimportant. As far as they were concerned, they were committed Muslims and regularly performed their ritual daily prayers. They usually fasted during the month of Ramadan and sometimes hoped they might be able to accomplish the *hajj* one day. Or, perhaps they would be able to save enough money to send their parents on the *hajj*. All of this was sufficient for them. Needless to say, many Muslim religious specialists I know do not agree with such complacency. In conversations, some noted that the lack of concern about the details of one's practice of Islam was in itself dangerous. In their way of thinking, such people, ignorant as they were of the original and time-honoured religious texts and their correct interpretation, might not know when their own seemingly proper and licit acts – say, for example, in the way they conducted their obligatory ritual daily prayers – were invalid. But the existence of this broader public sphere allows many people without much formal Islamic education, such as civil servants, and those of marginal social status, such as those of caste or servile status and recent converts to Islam, to ignore such concerns or at least to bypass them. After all, those who require such knowledge can find it readily available in some of the popular published texts, possibly discussed in sermons on cassette, or from ordinary Muslims who are not members of lineages of religious specialists.

As this suggests, there is a not entirely new, though clearly different, way of being Muslim that has become much more widespread in the postcolony. For the sake of convenience, I have called this incipient tradition of Islam the postcolonial tradition. People in Nioro are well aware of the significant differences between Muslims in the town and beyond. They are equally aware of the enormous influence of the major Muslim religious leaders in the town with their widespread reputations and personalised authority. Some prefer, however, to remain neutral, or at least appear to be neutral, in relation to these leaders and the Sufi orders they head. One can be a Muslim without allying oneself with any of the major actors in the town, an option that an expanded public sphere in the postcolonial secular state has allowed.

CONCLUSION: THE MARKET, THE PUBLIC AND ISLAM

I began this study with Shaykh Hamallah, the absent religious leader, who retains a strong hold on the social imagination, especially of those living in the town of Nioro, but also elsewhere in Mali and beyond. Shaykh Hamallah also seems to exert a hold on the imagination of scholars, both African and Western, as the number of works that invoke him seems to suggest. It is this history of Shaykh Hamallah and the earlier nineteenth-century history of al-Hajj Umar Tall in the town and the broader region that has helped to guarantee a special place for Nioro in the social imagination. A relatively small and economically marginal town, Nioro has remained an important Islamic religious centre for well over a century. To be an inhabitant of Nioro or its neighbouring villages today almost automatically means that one is Muslim. However, the association between this place and Islam is so strong that many regard the town as actually blessed and its inhabitants as more pious Muslims. Some of the descendants of Hamallah and Umar Tall have been central to the reshaping of Nioro's reputation as an Islamic religious centre, and they too have a prominent place in the contemporary social imagination.

One of the central premises of this study has been that what it means to be a Muslim has changed considerably from the nineteenth century through the colonial period and closer to the present. In trying to understand some of the shifts and transformations in ways of being Muslim, I have found it analytically useful to talk about different traditions of Islam. Although I have identified three traditions – the Sufi, the reformist and the postcolonial – that have appeared chronologically in this region, these traditions currently co-exist. In this final chapter, I would like to return to the question of the changing ideas about and practices of Islam and some of the ongoing tensions around Islam and authority in this setting. In this way, I want to reflect on Nioro as a profoundly transformed Islamic religious centre in postcolonial Mali.

A major thread running through this study has been the figure of the exceptional Muslim religious leader or Muslim saint. The juxtaposition of the absent colonial-era *shaykh* with the town's two presumed living Muslim saints to whom a coterie of businessmen, civil servants and politicians regularly turn for blessings, prayers and amulets is rather instructive. The

Muslim saint living under French colonial rule, whether the persecuted and absent Shaykh Hamallah or colonial-authorised Muslim Seydou Nourou Tall, was not entirely unlike his pre-colonial saintly predecessors. Most notably, the actual signs of sainthood – the reputation for 'miracles', numerous followers and material resources – remained remarkably similar after the onset of colonial, non-Muslim rule. Likewise, descent and knowledge, particularly the secret knowledge of the Islamic esoteric sciences, continued to be among the key bases of religious authority for colonial-era saints. In spite of such continuities, the colonial context was markedly different in a number of very important ways. Under colonial rule, there were of course new tensions between Muslim leaders (saintly or otherwise) authorised by the French, and those with other bases of authority. At the same time, there was the unprecedented standardisation of religious practice and mass Islamisation that accompanied the reorganisation of the political economy under colonial rule. It was the expansion of a new colonial sphere of activities, increasing the movement of persons and ideas, that facilitated a relative shift toward a more uniform way of being Muslim with a standardised set of ritual norms and, at least for some time, affiliation to the Sufi orders around various figures with saintly reputations. This same colonial sphere also allowed for the greater mobility of reformist Muslims and the spread of their activities within and between different colonies in French West Africa and beyond.

If some scholars of Africa have wanted to downplay the importance of the colonial period, treating it merely as an interlude, it must be clear that this is not a perspective I find useful for understanding Islam in Nioro and Mali more generally. In addition, I have emphasised the importance of understanding further changes in how Islam has been practised in this region in the postcolonial period. As I have suggested, the prayer economy with its more privatised Muslim saints was only possible within the context of a postcolonial state in which the rulers were overwhelmingly Muslim, and in which the state, and many of its agents, actively promoted identification with Islam and prominent Muslim religious leaders like those in Nioro. In recent decades, religious authority has been increasingly personalised in these figures, whom many think of as saints with privileged access to God's favour. Although the religious authority of these postcolonial religious leaders is based in large part on descent from the key historical figures of Hamallah and Umar Tall, their reputations are closely tied to their knowledge and use of secrets and the Islamic esoteric sciences. In this way, they are similar to the pre-colonial and colonial-era Muslim saints. By the late twentieth century, the two leaders had become major actors on a regional and, sometimes international, scale with followers giving them gifts in exchange for prayers, blessings and esoteric interventions. Processes of commodification, especially the exchange of blessings and prayers for gifts, have served to reinforce even further the power and authority of these religious leaders. The two leaders of the town's Sufi orders have become pivots around which an economy of religious practice turns. It is striking how qualitatively different the postcolonial Muslim saints are from the colonial-era saints, not to mention their pre-colonial predecessors. As relations have come to be organised more along the lines of the logic of the market, the nature of the relationship between the saints and some people has changed rather dramatically. In the analytical language I have used, the saints have become free-floating sanctifiers in a broader religious economy that is itself much more like a market. In some instances, the postcolonial prayer economy approaches a fee-for-service religion.

As this suggests, the Sufi tradition of Islam with its particular emphasis on Muslim saints and their authority has been shifting and changing. Important challenges to the authority of Muslim saints and the Sufi tradition have come from the increased influence of Muslim reformists and the pervasiveness of their discourses. Moreover, processes of the standardisation of religious practice, which were so significant during the colonial period, have even accelerated in the postcolonial period. As I have argued, processes of standardisation in the postcolonial period are tied to the expansion of the public sphere, and this has had implications for the practice of Islam in Mali. The postcolonial public sphere is a sphere of debate and deliberation, which includes religious messages that are centred predominantly about Islam. In Mali, informal and formal religious educa-tion, including various types of Islamic educational institutions, new Islamic associations, sermons and print and electronic media – all of which have been heavily influenced by transnational and global interconnections – have helped to animate religious messages in the public sphere. The public sphere has helped to foster a supralocal sense of shared Muslim identity in Mali, an imagined community of Muslims. If one of the consequences of the expanded public sphere has been that it has sometimes allowed for the practice of Islam to be debated in new ways, it has also exerted pressure for the practice of Islam to be more uniform or at least to conform to more broadly accepted conventions of proper Islamic practice. These include regular ritual daily prayer, fasting during Ramadan, and the increased importance of the *hajj*. Moreover, certain Muslims have been giving up what they have come to think of as particularistic religious practices, especially some associated with the Sufi orders, for instance, the longstanding practice of Hamallah's followers not to perform communal Friday prayers in a mosque.

In Mali, one can see a more generally shared, though hardly uniform, way of being Muslim and a commitment to Islam as a religion that has developed over the past few decades, a way which encourages Muslims to identify with a more supralocal Islamic community within Mali as a state and also beyond. In Nioro, the public sphere has afforded some Muslims the possibility of not having to ally with any of the major religious leaders in the town. This enables them to sidestep, so to speak, the prayer economy without openly contesting it. If such a tradition of Islam is a distinctly postcolonial way of being Muslim, it is also, arguably, the one that best characterises how many, perhaps even most, Muslims in Mali practise Islam today. In fact, most Muslims I have encountered during the course of my research in Mali are neither formally affiliated with any of the Sufi orders present in West Africa nor are they reformists. Moreover, many Malian Muslims categorically reject these and other such labels. This is not, however, to deny the importance of Sufi orders, Sufism or even reformism in Mali. On the contrary, it is crucial to recognise how the postcolonial way of being Muslim partakes of the traditions of Islam that appeared chronologically earlier. From the Sufi tradition in particular, we can see the very prevalent recourse to the esoteric sciences and what might be called spiritual clientage, that is, personal relations with individual religious leaders that often involve gift-giving for material and immaterial benefits without formal initiation into a Sufi order.

In postcolonial Mali, there is a certain kind of consensus about what most Malian Muslims consider proper Islamic religious conduct, particularly in its public manifestations. Among many Malian Muslims, one can trace identifiable processes of the standardisation of religious practice and the giving-up of certain kinds of particularistic practices, especially some of those that are public. In short, one can identify the broader appeal of a more 'generic Islam' of assumed universals, which indexes a publicly acknowledged or at least tacitly accepted consensus. But at one level, such a notion of consensus among Muslims is clearly tendentious. After all, any such consensus excludes all of those whose actions in private or in semi-public venues do not partake of it. Various others – Muslim and non-Muslim – have regularly faced exclusions from a public sphere in which Islam has increasingly dominated the messages about religion. Those excluded include Malian Christians, non-Muslims and ardent secularists, as well as those Muslims whose 'religious' practices include spirit possession or certain forms of healing that many deem un-Islamic. Different groups of Muslims regularly intimate that others, who consider themselves Muslims, are not really Muslims at all. Indeed, the extent to which the public sphere has systematically excluded such people and has sometimes even provided space for various kinds of intolerance is certainly striking (cf. Asad 1993). One of the major contradictions of the public sphere follows from these attendant exclusions. For the recent changes associated with expansion of the public sphere cannot be considered the unproblematic flourishing of civil society with its much vaunted potential for civic pluralism (cf. Eickelman and Piscatori 1996; Hefner 2000).

At the same time, there also seems to be a tension – perhaps an outright contradiction – between, on the one hand, a public sphere in which Muslims orientated toward a more generic Islam are presumed to be potential equals as Muslims and, on the other, the prayer economy, premised as it is on hierarchy, charisma and its own obvious exclusions. It would seem to follow that the changes associated with the expanded public sphere in postcolonial Mali pose a significant challenge to the esteemed Muslim religious leaders with their personalised religious authority and, indeed, to the operation of the prayer economy. Many of the transactions between individuals and saints within the prayer economy are private and sometimes even secret. Those who solicit the saints usually do so for personal reasons, to help them obtain their own individual goals. It would thus seem that the prayer economy is inimical to an expanded public sphere, which is premised at least in theory on the very opposite of that which is private and individual or personalised. However, the relationship between contemporary Muslim saints and the public sphere is much more complicated than this suggests. Indeed, the separation between private and public within the prayer economy has never been so clear-cut; the two often even intersect. Although the public sphere has helped to make a much broader range of information about Islam available to the public, it has also helped to spread information about the esoteric sciences, secrets and saints. There is, for example, much contemporary discussion about how published texts of the Islamic esoteric sciences have become much easier to buy, especially in bookshops in Bamako. This contrasts with earlier periods when such access to esoteric knowledge was largely dependent upon personal relations between student and teacher. But there is widespread suspicion that these texts can never reveal all their secrets to just anyone who reads them. As many people emphasise, one might be able to gain access to some secrets and esoteric practices from these available printed texts, but they will always remain necessarily partial and incomplete. In addition to such general information about the esoteric sciences, the public sphere has also facilitated the spread of rather specific information about individual Muslim saints. In fact, it has been via such public culture as oral narratives, rumour, televised coverage of the annual visits with saints, recorded praise poems and Islamic religious commodities that the saints' fame and their arc of power have been able to spread even further. Indeed, all of these have served as means of publicity that have helped to enlarge the reputations of the postcolonial saints. It has been within an expanded public sphere that so many ordinary Malian Muslims have come to see certain Muslim religious leaders as embodying the sainthood, wealth and fame many of them find so alluring.

Despite the fact that many of the actual transactions of the prayer economy do take place in private, it is significant that the prayer economy is simultaneously public in orientation, as in the following example. In the early evenings, many men in Nioro go to the livestock market on the outskirts of the town in order to appraise animals as they are returning from daytime grazing in the countryside. For a time during my fieldwork, a prosperous young merchant I know went to the market nearly every day because he wished to buy some mature, pure white bulls that had no observable imperfections. After several visits to the market in the early evening, the news circulated that he was in the market for such bulls. It was obvious to everyone that the animals would be for some sort of ritual sacrifice, and sellers and brokers eventually brought them to the market. After purchasing a set number of white bulls, one of the merchant's employees led the animals from the livestock market through the streets to the man's large compound in the town centre. Soon thereafter, the merchant himself proceeded to sacrifice the bulls, and to distribute most of the meat to his relatives, neighbours and the poor. He also invited a group of his friends with whom he had grown up to eat some of the meat with him at his home. Most of the actions leading up to the sacrifice, from the market visits, the purchase and delivery of the animals to the actual slaughter, took place largely in public. At each stage, there was much public, as well as private, discussion of the man in question and his actions. I heard some of those who depend on the merchant's largesse speak rather matter-of-factly about the sacrifice of the bulls, and they praised him for his generosity on this occasion and others. Alongside such praise came considerable speculation and various rumours about the man's possible motives. Although such a sacrifice could most certainly have followed the instructions of those involved in spirit possession or other non-Muslim religious specialists, it is unlikely, though not inconceivable, this was the case. No one doubted the merchant was following the instructions of one of the town's religious leaders and, presumably, one of the Muslim saints, who would have employed secret knowledge or the esoteric sciences on his behalf. And no one doubted he would have paid a large sum of money or extended gifts of great value in exchange for detailed instructions about the type of animal, colour, requisite number, the most auspicious time and other necessary conditions for the sacrifice to be effective. Several of my friends noted that the merchant's actions coincided almost exactly with the delivery of a new lorry that he had purchased and had had shipped to the town. The arrival of such a new vehicle was itself a very public act, indeed, a rather conspicuous display of wealth. But the new lorry also indexed the man's aspirations to become a member of the town's small commercial elite. I myself wondered whether his recent publicly discussed marriage troubles and the fact that he had only one child and no male heirs were not also factors that figured in the ritual transactions. Although it was public knowledge that the man had long-standing and close ties to one of the town's saints, rumours circulated that in this case of the sacrifice of bulls he may have been following the instructions of the town's other saint. That is, many suspected the merchant had solicited the services of the religious leader who was not his own. Some suggested this was perhaps because of the magnitude of his problem or request, which his regular saint, so to speak, might not have been able to resolve.

The merchant undoubtedly received a personalised intervention via the esoteric sciences and probably also some sort of personalised religious commodities, such as special prayers, blessings or amulets that would remain private. Be this as it may, it does not necessarily follow that his motives were merely individual or personal. In fact, it is quite clear that the interests of many of those in the merchant's larger kin and social networks were closely intertwined with some of his own. Various individuals and groups within his networks stood to gain from his achieving whatever it was that he wanted, whether wealth, male heirs, good fortune in commerce, social prestige or some combination of these. It was common knowledge that his lack of a male heir was one of the reasons he had recently married a second wife, and this had led to conflict between him and his first wife and in-laws. Around the same time, many in the town had begun to talk about the merchant becoming a member of the economic elite. Some less pros-perous merchants I know either resented or envied his success, and more established merchants dismissed him as a *parvenu*. I know that his kin and dependants took it for granted that rituals like the sacrifice of bulls (surely not the only but perhaps the most conspicuous of the ritual actions he had undertaken) might possibly alleviate existing or mounting social conflict and contribute to the social reproduction upon which they too were depen-dent. However, everyone was readily aware that the personalised religious services of the saints are not available and affordable to just anyone. For many people, the merchant's privileged access to the privatised saints and their services confirmed his own social power and authority and perhaps also the security of those who saw their own destiny linked to his. In this case, one can see some of the paradoxical ways in which the prayer economy is both public and private. Indeed, one of the central features of the prayer economy seems to be the way in which it links up the individual and private with the public. One can see this link between public and private in the rumours, speculation, suspicions and discussions about the ties between various saints and members of the elite that circulate widely in public and private. I cannot recall how often I have heard ordinary Malians discuss the fantastic wealth of the country's most prominent merchants or the power of politicians having come as a direct result of their association with the saints.

The privatised Muslim saints are not the only new Muslim religious figures that have appeared in postcolonial Mali. There are two other kinds of Muslim religious figures – both of whom are, in effect, religious entre-preneurs – who have become much more prominent in recent years. The first of these is the *marabout d'affaires*. In contemporary Mali and especially in urban areas, one finds Muslim religious specialists referred to as *marabouts d'affaires*, who are directly analogous to *hommes d'affaires* or businessmen. If many Malians, members of Sufi orders, reformist Muslims and secularists regularly invoke *marabout d'affaires* as a term of abuse, there is considerable ambiguity surrounding these figures and their activities. These men are basically religious entrepreneurs who often say they can help guarantee wealth, success or prosperity. As in a business relationship, clients usually pay such *marabouts* directly for services that ordinarily involve the use of the esoteric sciences. Unlike the privatised saints who are descendants of some of the most prominent Muslim religious figures, many of these *marabouts d'affaires* are descendants of the numerous minor pre-colonial lineages of Muslim religious specialists. In marked contrast to the saints, the *marabouts d'affaires* seem to engage almost exclusively in this kind of freelance or contract work. These *marabouts* usually do not have pretensions to be Muslim religious leaders nor do they usually make any claims to religious authority. In some cases, they are followers of one of the saints and members of the Sufi orders. It is significant, however, that their clients are generally unaware of any such links between these *marabouts* and individual saints or even the Sufi order to which they might belong. Many of these religious entrepreneurs live in Bamako – the Malian urban centre of fee-for-service religion – and travel regularly to places outside Mali where many Malians live. In fact, I myself have run into some of these *marabouts d'affaires* at the airport in a neighbouring country. Since these *marabouts d'affaires* are more accessible and their services often considerably less expensive than those of the privatised saints, they have been able to attract many clients and accumulate substantial wealth. This is especially the case for those *marabouts d'affaires* who have developed reputations for getting their clients quick results. It is therefore not surprising that *marabout d'affaires* is a career to which many young Muslim religious specialists, particularly those with a more 'traditional' Islamic education, aspire. I know quite a few people who look forward to and strive toward such a potentially lucrative career. On several occasions, one of my friends joked he would eventually like to have an office – in Bamako of course – where he would have a price list for the different services he would be able to provide via the esoteric sciences.

Many Malians periodically consult a *marabout d'affaires* or other minor religious specialists – Muslim or otherwise – as the need might arise. The popularity or success of certain *marabouts d'affaires* notwithstanding, many openly mock and criticise them. Although some decry the high prices the saints command or expect for their services, many see a big difference between saints and other Muslim religious figures and *marabouts d'affaires* in particular. Many condemn the latter for operating in a way that is virtually indistinguishable from businessmen. From an outside perspective, it might appear that the saint and the *marabout d'affaires* are virtually interchangeable, equivalent kinds of free-floating sanctifiers in a religious economy that obeys the logic of the market. But as Weber suggested long ago, the relationship of religious practices and the market is very complex indeed. Here too, it would be tendentious to claim that religion has been reduced entirely to the logic of the market. In fact, one of the most salient differences between the two types of sanctifiers is that *marabouts d'affaires* have no base of supporters or followers. As many note, even though the saints might provide personalised services to members of the elite, there are also thousands of ordinary Muslims who are their followers. While *marabouts d'affaires* must travel to their clients or attract them in the city, the saints – with their competitive advantage in charisma – stay in one place where people visit them during the annual visits or at other times in the year. Such people seek them out for their privileged access to God's favour and possibly to obtain merit. Along with the blessings they dispense, the saints redistribute some of what they receive, and they often act as mediators and stand as exemplars for ordinary Muslims. In the end, religious entrepreneurs like the *marabouts d'affaires* simply do not have the allure of the living Muslim saints like those in Nioro. Indeed, many presume that one should address one's greatest concerns, needs and desires to more reputable Muslim religious specialists than those who are no different from businessmen. This seems to be even more the case when one is a member of the economic or political elite. It is here one can see how elite and non-elite Muslims stand firm in their attachment to particular Muslim religious leaders, whom many think of as authentic saints.

This leads me to the second kind of religious entrepreneur in postcolonial Mali. These are Muslims whose presence as specifically Muslim public figures within the broader public sphere has become more important, especially over the last decade. These new public figures include the writers of books, pamphlets and newspaper articles about Islam, preachers whose sermons are aired on the radio and television, and circulate on audio and videocassette, those involved in Muslim educational institutions, and the activists and leaders of the many Islamic associations that have been founded since the early 1990s. With one very notable exception (see below), none of these Muslim public figures has anything like the charisma of the Muslim saints who live in Nioro or elsewhere in the country. Even in those cases when they are highly respected public figures, they generally do not command the authority or respect of the Muslim saints.

The one new Muslim public figure in Mali who does command considerable attention and respect is Chérif Ousmane Madani Haïdara. He is a Bamako-based preacher and the head of *Ançar Dine*, the most successful of the new Islamic organisations, which has thousands of members (see Chapter

8). Although Haïdara is a rather unusual religious entrepreneur in Mali, his own career trajectory helps to illustrate the continuing importance of hereditary charisma and its transformations in postcolonial Mali. Like many other Muslim public figures, Haïdara comes from a lineage of Muslim religious specialists with long and close ties to the Sufi orders. Haïdara's own father was a member of the Tijaniyya, and the person who initiated him into the Sufi order traced his own initiation to Hamallah. Although Haïdara is himself not a member of any Sufi order nor does he identify himself as a Sufi, he is not against Sufi orders per se. He does, however, fashion himself in opposition to 'Wahhabis', those reformists he criticises in his sermons as hypocrites or for insulting the name of Hamallah whom some denounce as a proponent of Sufi orders. It is noteworthy that Haïdara does not ordinarily engage in the use of the esoteric sciences on behalf of others, and he is quick to condemn the country's many *marabouts d'affaires* as frauds.

Unlike the living Muslim saints who never give public sermons and rarely make public pronouncements, Haïdara has become famous for his sermons that deal with such issues as morality, honesty and doctrinal issues about prayer. Ever since being arrested and banned from preaching on several occasions in the late 1980s for allegedly insulting remarks, Haïdara has managed to garner considerable public attention. Haïdara is perhaps Mali's most controversial and flamboyant Muslim media personality, indeed, a Muslim media star. He appeals to a mass public, including many who are illiterate, in Mali and among Malian migrants elsewhere in Africa and in Europe largely through his sermons (in Bamana/Bambara) on audio-cassette, video and radio. Haïdara has received considerable media attention for provocative public statements he has made about the immorality and dishonesty of politicians, merchants and other clerics, as well as for his interventions in debates about morality and the correct practice of Islam. In some ways, his is a project focused on the shaping of moral subjects in the public sphere, a very public Islam that also includes a social agenda advocating fund-raising for education and the poor. In this way, he is not unlike such colonial-era Muslim preachers as Seydou Nourou Tall. The discussions and controversies about whether Muslims can perform ritual daily prayers in whatever vernacular language they speak and other subjects raised in some of his sermons and other public pronouncements have undoubtedly helped to spread his reputation, even notoriety.

Despite the obvious differences between Haïdara and a Muslim saint, he is in some very important ways rather like one. Even if he is not a self-proclaimed Sufi and certainly not a *marabout d'affaires*, he readily dispenses his prayers and blessings to the many people and numerous followers who specifically seek him out for these. In return, he receives many gifts and offerings from people who wish to obtain merit and/or blessings. The volume of the gifts Haïdara receives helps to support a comfortable lifestyle

– witness the almost *de rigueur* Mercedes and multi-storey villa where he and his family live in Bamako. Interestingly, Haïdara is also the only Malian preacher whose photo has become commercially viable and is regularly sold alongside the photos of the country's past and present Muslim saints. Some of his followers sport buttons with his photo, display his photo in their homes or places of business, or wear printed fabric with his image, that is, exactly like some followers of saints in Mali. Although the media have been central to the making of Haïdara's career, his ability to receive a forum, when, for example, he enters public debate about Islam, relates in no small part to his status as a member of a lineage claiming descent from the Prophet Muhammad. In fact, his patronym, Haïdara, indicates sharifian descent here as it does in large parts of Muslim West Africa. As in the case of Hamallah's son, Muhammadu, many people refer to Haïdara simply as Chérif or Haïdara, as if these were titles of an officeholder, presumably the highest-ranking descendant of the Prophet. In many of his sermons, Haïdara makes explicit reference to his very limited formal education, and, in this way, he seems to draw parallels between himself and the Prophet Muhammad who was known as 'the unlettered prophet'. However important Haïdara's personal charisma, which includes his skills as a talented orator and his media savvy, authoritative hereditary charisma seems to have been an essential condition of possibility for the making of his career.

Not only does Haïdara the preacher bear striking resemblance to a Sufi *shaykh*, but the structure and organisation of *Ançar Dine* are rather like those of a Sufi order. Most notably, formal membership of *Ançar Dine* is in the form of the *bay'a*, an act of allegiance. If *Ançar Dine*'s brochures suggest this allegiance is to Islam, in practice many see this also as allegiance to Haïdara and his association. In an obvious parallel with the Sufi orders, Haïdara also refers to himself as 'the guide'. Moreover, many of his followers pledge to work on his behalf and that of his organisation. Some of these individuals might work on construction work on one of his properties, while others might labour in his agricultural fields near Bamako or in the much larger fields in the agricultural scheme of the Office de Niger in central Mali. In this way, Haïdara and his followers draw on the widespread practice of members of Sufi orders working physically for their *shaykh*. The most important and largest annual gathering of Haïdara's followers is the *mawlud*, the anniversary of the birth of the Prophet Muhammad, that is, the same day that many members of Sufi orders in Mali (and elsewhere in the world) gather together. If this gathering is sometimes in the neighbourhood of Bamako where Haïdara lives, in 2003 he actually held the gathering in a large stadium in central Bamako. Just as in the case of Muslim saints, access to Haïdara has become increasingly difficult, as the number of his followers has risen.

Many of the people who have gathered around Haïdara treat him as though they would a Muslim saint. I have watched as people have approached him to kiss his hand or be touched by him, that is, in exactly the same way many Malian Muslims approach descendants of the Prophet Muhammad or other saintly figures. And many Malians explicitly talk about Haïdara as though he might possibly be a saint. This is not least the case because of his many followers, the accumulated wealth and even some of the miracles that are reported around him. I think that it is also worth emphasising that Haïdara does not seem to wish to discourage such views. The fact that he has been able to bring together thousands of followers in a stadium in Bamako has not been lost to the broader public, whether they admire him or not. This would include the many Muslim public figures, including Muslim reformists and those within the Sufi tradition, who might disagree with some of his positions or resent his popularity. This is equally the case for those secularists who sometimes condemn any expression of Islam in public, especially when it does not conform to their rationalised and privatised understandings of religion. Many secularists openly worry that Haïdara might possibly become the most popular Muslim public figure in contemporary Mali. As I have heard Malians say, not one living politician in the country could so easily fill a stadium with his supporters. It is obvious that Haïdara is a new kind of Muslim public figure. However, his rather unique career as a Muslim media star depends heavily upon both the Sufi tradition with its understandings of authority, and an expanded public sphere. Whether Haïdara is actually a new kind of saintly figure – indeed, a new kind of sanctifier – who might be able to supplant or displace the existing Muslim saints is another matter altogether. It goes without saying that any such predictions on my part would be foolhardy.

Hereditary sanctity remains extremely important in how Islam is practised in postcolonial Mali, and many people continue to have expectations of exceptional Muslim leadership. Much to the dismay of modernising and secularising Muslims, the desire for intermediaries, especially living saints with their presumed access to God's favour and the true secret knowledge – not that knowledge found in published books for sale in the market or available from *marabouts d'affaires* and clearly unavailable from most Muslim public figures with the possible exception of Haïdara – has been no less diminished in the postcolony. Even though Haïdara might bear some of the signs of sainthood and has numerous follows who treat him as a saint, I have heard many Malians claim that one cannot possibly find living Muslim saints in Bamako. Over the course of fieldwork in Mali, I repeatedly heard Malians say that real, authentic living Muslim saints, if they exist at all, live far from such urban centres. To find Muslim saints, one needs to look to provincial towns like Nioro or other renowned Islamic religious centres elsewhere in the country. It is from such a vantage point that we must understand Nioro as a religious centre that has been transformed from the time of the colonial period. Although there are different traditions of Islam that currently co-exist, what has remained dominant has been an understanding of Islam built on hierarchy and charisma centred around the Sufi orders and their saintly leaders. But from the nineteenth century through the colonial period to the present, what it means to be a saint has changed considerably. At the beginning of the twenty-first century, the privatised Muslim saints of Nioro are clearly different from their pre-colonial predecessors, the absent *shaykh* of the colonial period, *marabouts d'affaires* and contemporary Muslim public figures. As I have argued, such transformations in an Islamic religious centre like Nioro can only be understood at the intersection of the local, regional, national and transnational.

Although there is little evidence to suggest that hierarchy and charisma are becoming any less consequential in Nioro or further afield in Mali, the ultimate future of Nioro as a religious centre is far from obvious. The town is not typical of Mali's other urban areas or, indeed, of wider Malian society. If some might criticise one or other saint for being too close to a past regime or for inflated fees, there is usually the idea that a more authentic saint is surely to be found or might eventually appear. But for those who doubt the authenticity of individual saints, many readily point out that saints like those in Nioro have been able to outlast secular political regimes and economic decline and crises. The authority of the leaders of the Sufi orders in Nioro seems quite certain at this point in time. Indeed, for most people, the saintly character of the present leaders and their lineages is not in doubt. But there are uncertainties about what lies ahead. In Nioro, people talk openly (though not usually publicly) about the potential precariousness of the authority of the saints' successors and the almost inevitable segmentation their lineages will face once the two present leaders are gone. It is impossible for me to make predictions about outcomes here.

What emerges from this historical and ethnographic study of understandings of Islam and authority in a West African religious centre is the tension that exists between local settings, larger social formations and the broader world in the articulation and transformation of such understandings and religious practices over time. I have pointed to the pull between the local, regional, national and the transnational in the changing understandings of Islam and authority and the practice of Islam, a perspective as it relates to religion that is relevant not only for the study of Islam. Such a perspective clearly transcends Nioro and is directly applicable to the study of all world religions.

NOTES

INTRODUCTION

1. The Sufi order has been called 'Hamallism' and sometimes the Hamalliya in the colonial and scholarly literatures. I use here the term Hamawiyya as it is the name used by the contemporary leadership of the Sufi order. Although those affiliated with this Sufi order are often called 'Hamalliste' in French, I will refer to them as Hamawis, as many of them prefer to be called. I will refer to those affiliated with the Tijaniyya as Tijanis.
2. Traoré 1983: 161–7 discusses these events in some detail. Cf. Rocaboy 1947a, 1947b, 1993. On this period in AOF more generally, see Akpo-Vaché 1996.
3. See Centre des Archives d'Outre-Mer, Archives Nationales, Aix-en-Provence, France (hereafter CAOM) Aff Pol 2258/3, 'Décès Hamallah'. This file contains various documents from the 1940s about Hamallah's internment in Vals-les-Bains and Montluçon. In some of the Vichy-era documents, Vals-les-Bains, where Hamallah was initially held in France, is referred to as a *camp de concentration* and in others as an *établissement d'internement administratif.*
4. See Archives Nationales du Mali, Koulouba (hereafter ANM), 4E 21 (FR), Circulaire (Secret), Gov. Gen. AOF to Gov. Colonies, 18 December 1944.
5. This information comes from French archival sources. See CAOM, Aff Pol 2258/3, letter, General de Corps d'Armée Secrétaire d'Etat à la Défense to M. Le Contre-Amiral, Secrétaire d'Etat à la Marine & aux Colonies Etat Major des Colonies, Vichy, 7 April 1944.
6. CAOM, Aff Pol 2258/3, Amadou Doucouré, Conseiller de la République du Soudan français, 'Pèlerinage à Montluçon sur la tombe du Cheick Hamallah', Montluçon, 21 February 1948.
7. See ANM, 4E 1256(ii), note, Capitaine Cardaire, n.d., but presumably 1952 or 1953.
8. Whether this was the perspective of Weber or his interpreters, particularly Talcott Parsons, is a subject of debate. See, for example, Meyer 1999.
9. This has been the case at various conferences and lectures where I have presented some of my material.
10. Cf. Chapter 8 below.
11. See, for example, the contributions to 'the fundamentalism project' in Marty and Appleby 1991.
12. For reviews of the literature on the anthropology of Islam, see Asad 1986; Eickelman 1982, 1987; Abu-Lughod 1989; Launay 1992, 1998; Bowen 1993; Starrett 1997; and Soares 2000.
13. See Gellner 1968, an article that was eventually expanded to be the introduction to his *Muslim Society* (1981). Some of these issues were also discussed in Gellner 1963; cf. Gellner 1981.
14. There is a considerable body of literature in anthropology, sociology, and

Middle Eastern, Asian and Islamic studies that assesses the contribution of both authors. My discussion is particularly indebted to Asad 1986. See also Zubaida 1995 and Salvatore 1997.

15. For studies of 'popular' and local Islam, see, for example, Lewis 1986.

16. See el-Zein 1977 and Eickelman 1976. While this is a perspective that many (such as Eickelman 1987) have renounced, it lingers, for example, in discussions of so-called African Islam or *Islam noir* in French scholarship. See Soares 2000.

17. It would be perhaps more accurate to refer to the Sufi orders as 'paths' or simply orders. In this context, people make a distinction between the orders and Sufis. One can be a member of an order without necessarily being a Sufi. The term Sufi is generally applied to those who devote most of their time to prayer and mystical practices. Because much of the scholarly literature uses the term Sufi orders, I will do so as well.

18. On sorcery and witchcraft, see, for example, Austen 1993; Geschiere 1997; and Rowlands and Warnier 1988. On the occult, see Comaroff and Comaroff 1999 and Mbembe 1992. The few notable exceptions to discuss Islam in relation to these topics include Shaw 2002 and the work of political scientists such as O'Brien 1975, and Villalón 1995.

CHAPTER 1

1. This discussion of Islam and religious practice is indebted to Launay 1992; see also Launay and Soares 1999.

2. These Muslim lineages included those who called themselves Soninke/Marka (particularly those who trace a connection to the empire of Wagadu/Ghana), Dyula, Jakhanke, Fulbe/Futanke, Bidan/Arab/Shurfa, and so forth.

3. Members of these Muslim lineages also tended to have reputations for not consuming the alcoholic beverages produced in the region and for not having more than the maximum of four wives permitted according to the rules of Islamic jurisprudence.

4. For example, certain groups of Bidan ceased to engage in warfare and became religious specialists and traders or *zawaya* and sought the protection of armed 'warrior' or *hassan* groups. On Bidan social organisation and history, see Ould Cheikh 1985.

5. Cf. Levtzion 1973, 2000; Hiskett 1984.

6. On these commercial networks, see Launay 1982 and Roberts 1987. On the clerical networks, see Wilks 1968, Sanneh 1989, Saad 1983, and Launay 1992.

7. See Ba and Daget 1962; Brown 1969; and Sanankoua 1990.

8. On Umar Tall, see Robinson 1985 and Ly-Tall 1991.

9. Although it is debatable whether this was a 'state', here I am following scholars such as Robinson 1985, Roberts 1987, and Hanson 1996.

10. See Sanneh 1989 and Hunter 1977.

11. On Umar Tall's successors, see Hanson and Robinson 1991, and Hanson 1996. Muhammad al-Amin is often referred to as Mamadu Lamine. On his career, see Bathily 1970, Fisher 1970, Gomez 1994, Hrbek 1979, Oloruntimehin 1971, and Sanneh 1989.

12. I follow Eickelman's (1976) discussion of the reputation of *marabouts*.

13. According to Cornell 1998, it was in the fifteenth century that the notion that *sharifs* had the authority to rule spread in Morocco. Of course the sixteenth-century Moroccan conquest of parts of West Africa might also have been a factor in the increased importance attached to sharifian descent in West Africa.

14. On the mid- to late nineteenth century, see Hanson 1996.

15. This is in contrast to some of the stereotypes of Muslim religious leaders as rural-

dwelling and non-literate found in colonial and postcolonial scholarship. Cf. Gellner 1969; Geertz 1968; Munson 1993.

16. For some of the extant literature from the region, see Hunwick 2003a.
17. These are some of the terms in Arabic used to describe certain historical figures that have equivalents in the region's vernaculars.
18. Cf. Geertz 1968; Gilsenan 1973; Eickelman 1976; Cruise O'Brien and Coulon 1988; and Hammoudi 1997, to name only some of the most influential studies. I would not, however, go so far as Bourdieu who writes about 'the *almost empty notion of baraka*' [emphasis in original] (Bourdieu 1977: 228, n. 89).
19. For an extended discussion of the names of God, see Gimaret 1988; cf. Doutté 1984: 199.
20. See Wensinck 1927.
21. Bazin 1985, 1986 and MacNaughton 1988 use the term 'power objects' for such objects as *boli* or *basi*. See also Monteil 1924. For an example of such a contemporary object, see Figure 2.2.
22. This tradition reported by Delafosse comes from an Arabic manuscript from the Kaba Jakhite family of Nioro. 'Wale' in Soninke is the insignia of power (see Delafosse 1913: 302 n.1). See also Dieterlen and Sylla 1992.
23. On the kingdom of Jara, see Diawara 1990 and Boyer 1953.
24. The full title is *Kitab al-rimah hizb rahim 'ala nuhur hizb al-rajim* (The Lances of the Party of the Merciful One upon the Throats of the Party of the Accursed One).
25. See Abun-Nasr 1965: 110ff.; Hunwick 1992; cf. Robinson 1985: 33–4.
26. See Delafosse 1913, and Tyam 1935.
27. On al-Maghili, see Hunwick 1985. Some French colonial sources, for example Marty 1921, point to al-Maghili as the person to introduce the Qadiriyya south of the Sahara. Such claims probably initially came from the Kunta. See Norris 1986.
28. See Robinson 1985: 96–8; Willis 1989: 83–5; cf. Abun-Nasr 1965: 110ff.
29. Cf. Willis 1989: 85–6; cf. Hunwick 1994.
30. See Marty 1915–16: *passim*.
31. *Wali* is from the Arabic root meaning to be near. See 'Wali' in SEI. The term is used in all the major languages spoken in the region of my research, including Bambara/ Bamana, Hassaniyya, Jakhanke, Pulaar/Fulfulde, and Soninke.
32. See Radtke and O'Kane 1996, and Cornell 1998.
33. Much of the scholarly literature refers to these people as saints, for example Gellner 1969; Cruise O'Brien and Coulon 1988.
34. On the notion of the perfect man, see Nicholson 1921, ch. 2. See also Werbner (1998, 2003) for a consideration of this notion among Sufis in Pakistan and Britain.
35. This is not in any way to deny the relevance of the model of the unlettered Prophet Muhammad (Ar., *al-nabi al-'ummi*) here. See the discussion of Shaykh Hamallah in Chapter 3, and of Chérif Haïdara in the Conclusion.
36. For the Tijani discourse on religious leaders and material wealth, the most relevant text for this context is perhaps Umar Tall's book, the *Rimah*.
37. Abun-Nasr 1965: 139. According to Robinson 1985, some criticised Umar Tall for having Mahdist pretensions.
38. On Umar Tall's death, see Robinson 1985, and Hanson and Robinson 1991.
39. See Marty 1927: *passim*, and Hunwick 2003b.
40. On the Tinwajiyu, see Marty 1921: 401–22.
41. This information comes from the Arabic chronicles from Oualata and Nema translated by Marty 1927: 551; cf. Marty 1921: 416.

42. For some of those in Oualata, see Marty 1921: 339. For Tichit, see Ould Cheikh 2000.

CHAPTER 2

1. Some of the migrants arrived as late as the 1880s. On the migrations to the region, see Hanson 1996. On the earlier Massassi state, see Boyer 1953 and Monteil 1924.
2. For the most detailed discussion of this period, see Hanson 1989, 1996, and Hanson and Robinson 1991.
3. On the 'resistance' to the Umarian states, see Hanson 1989, 1996, Robinson 1985, and Roberts 1987.
4. The best account of conquest is by Kanya-Forstner 1969.
5. On this subject, see Hanson and Robinson 1991. For the details of the last days of Amadu and his followers on *hijra*, see CAOM, 75 APOM 5/6, Renseignements sur la mort de Cheikhou Amadou.
6. For a general discussion of French representations of the Fulbe over time, see Robinson 1985, and Williams 1988.
7. On the return to Futa Toro, see Kane 1987.
8. At least one French colonial administrator called this 'passive resistance'. See Bertin 1955.
9. Lanrezac 1905 discusses the economic potential of Nioro.
10. ANM, 1E 212 (FA), Nioro, correspondence, 1902. See also Désiré-Vuillemin 1962.
11. On Ma' al-'Aynayn, see Martin 1976, Marty 1915–16, and Désiré-Vuillemin 1962. On his relatives in the Hodh, see Marty 1921.
12. For the colonial reorganisation of the region and its rationale, see Méniaud 1931, 2: 56–67. For French stereotypes of the Soninke, see, for example, Rançon 1894 and de Lartigue 1898a; cf. Manchuelle 1987, 1997.
13. On the Kaba Jakhite, see Rançon 1894: 175–7.
14. On Alfa Umar Kaba Jakhite, see Adam 1903–4 and Dramé 1988, as well as a Wesleyan missionary's account of an encounter with him in Bundu in 1838 in Fox 1851: 462.
15. On Kisma, see ANM, 1E 212 (FA), letter, Admin. Nioro to Gov. HSN, 21 December 1906; cf. Marty 1920. Although made chiefs of the Soninke, the Kabalanke do not claim to be Soninke themselves. Those in Nioro do speak the Soninke language and have long had marriage ties with Soninke groups in the region.
16. Each of the three families settled in areas of the town that became neighbourhoods bearing their names: Kabala (literally, the place of Kaba), Maguiragacounda, and Syllacounda.
17. In an Arabic chronicle from Nioro, there is mention of 'the people of Diàgha' who called Umar Tall to liberate them from the infidels. See Delafosse 1913: 358.
18. In 1897 the population of Nioro was about 4,500 people with more than 70 per cent of these people described as Soninke. See Archives Nationales du Sénégal (hereafter ANS), 1G 156, Notice Géographique sur la Région du Sahel, 1897.
19. Although the French intended cantons to represent traditional political units (*chefferies*) in at least some parts of its colonies, in Nioro the situation is somewhat more complicated. A number of the 'ethnies' grouped into cantons were actually followers and/or descendants of followers of Umar Tall who had migrated to the region and had displaced or driven out previous inhabitants. There were also some cantons based on some pre-*jihad* political units, such as the Canton des Diawaras. At least one Bambara canton was created by inviting

some Bambara from Ségou to move to Nioro after the conquest. See Blanc 1924 and Monteil 1924.

20. Méniaud 1931, 2 suggested that this would continue until they were more disciplined.

21. They have retained control until the present except for a brief interlude when a member of the Maguiraga family – with whom the Kabalanke have marriage alliances – was imam. Cf. Marty 1920: 264.

22. Although *qadis* (judges) were not officially named after 1903, those named as such prior to this date were allowed to perform these duties until they died. ANM, 1E 212 (FA), letter Admin. Nioro to Gov. HSN, 21 December 1906. On the subject of colonial law in AOF, see Sarr and Roberts 1991 and Shereikis 2001, 2003.

23. With the coming of the end of military rule, colonial administrators debated about the kinds of African intermediaries they would use in the Nioro area. Initially, they intended to use *les bambaras fétichistes*, that is, non-Muslim Bambara, whom they perceived to be more pliable and loyal and, therefore, more effective as intermediaries. It was proposed that Bambara be employed to subvert Islam and the influence of the Futanke and other important Muslims in the region. See ANM, 1E 60 (FA), Rapport politique, Nioro, April 1891, May 1891, and July 1891.

24. For a discussion of these issues for neighbouring Senegal, see Coulon 1981.

25. Valuable contributions to the study of *la politique musulmane* in West Africa have been made by O'Brien 1967, Harrison 1988, Launay 1996, 1997a, Robinson 1988, 2000, Robinson and Triaud 1997, and Triaud 1974, 1992. Given that such renderings of *la politique musulmane* as 'Muslim policy' are inadequate, I have decided not to translate the phrase.

26. Other French scholar-administrators went so far as to claim that France never had a *politique musulmane*. Cf. Gouilly 1952: 248; O'Brien 1967; and Robinson 1988.

27. I translate *laïcité* as secularism, even though the latter term is inadequate, as the following discussion suggests. See Bauberot 1998.

28. This draws on the discussion of the rights of subjects under French colonial rule in West Africa in Moreau 1938. See also Conklin 1997.

29. Some of these were published as 'Le Salut au drapeau: témoignages de loyalisme des musulmans français' and 'Les musulmans français et la guerre: adresses et témoignages de fidelité des chefs musulmans et des personnages religieux' in issues of *Revue du Monde Musulman* in 1914 and 1915–16. Those from Nioro were published in the latter.

30. The height of anxiety and the amount of administrative effort in this direction at least by scholar-administrators is reflected in such colonial-era scholarly publications as the special issue of *Revue du Monde Musulman*, 'Le Bolchevisme et l'Islam' in 1920 and André 1922, vol. 2.

31. William Ponty quoted in Marty 1915–16: 16. See also Conklin 1997.

32. Early in the twentieth century, some referred to *Islam africain* (for example Arnaud 1912) while later the term *Islam noir* was used more frequently. For an example of the perdurable concept of *Islam noir*, see Monteil 1980.

33. On the Italian-Sanusi war in present-day Libya, see Evans-Pritchard 1949.

34. Harrison (1988: 42f., 55) notes that the Governor General of AOF requested such files as early as 1906 but they were not systematically collected until after 1911.

35. See, for example, the early studies of the different Sufi orders and their leaders, by Depont and Coppolani 1897, and Le Chatelier 1899.

36. Paul Marty's books consist of compilations of local reports that were often copied verbatim. See, for example, Marty 1915–16, 1920, 1921. These books have in turn been used as the basis for many studies right up to the present.

37. These cases are too numerous to mention but can be found throughout the political reports of the first decades of colonial rule in the Archives Nationales du Mali.

38. This was often a long process, as the example of the implementation of restrictions on the collection of *zakat* (Ar., alms tax) by one family of religious specialists indicates. See ANM, 4E 25 (FR), Marabouts, personnages religieux, Nara, 1912–35.

39. See Harrison 1988, Sanankoua and Brenner 1991, Sall 1998, and especially Brenner 2001.

40. ANM, 4E 19–8 (FR), Nioro, Rap. sur la pol. musul., Commandant Blanc, 31 December 1922.

41. Both Behrman 1970 and Coulon 1981 use the expression 'exchange of services'.

42. Cf. Robinson 1997, 2000 on the cooperation between colonial authorities and Muslims in northern Senegal and southern Mauritania with Launay 1996, 1997a.

43. See Marty 1915–16.

44. See, for example, CAOM, Aff Pol 2260/5, Synthèse des rens. concernant les Communautés Musulmanes de l'Union Française, 2d sem. 1948.

45. The career of Seydou Nourou Tall as it relates to Nioro will be discussed in Chapters 3 and 4.

46. CAOM, Aff Pol 159, Rapport sur la situation politique, HSN, 4th trim., 1917, Région du Sahel.

47. Ibid.

48. Ibid.

49. The notion of freezing is Eickelman's language (1976).

50. On the development of the early colonial economy in this region, see Roberts 1987; Manchuelle 1987; and Suret-Canale 1971.

51. On forced labour in AOF, see Fall 1993.

52. Manchuelle 1987, 1997 unnecessarily downplays such 'push' factors in migration.

53. On the gum trade, see ANM 1D 107 (FA), Soudan, Etude commerciale, Le marché de Nioro, Lt Guillaume, 1 July 1902.

54. The effects of interactions with the French were undoubtedly complex and may even have had a directly negative influence on the economic situation of some religious specialists. See Soares 2003.

55. This discussion draws on Klein 1987, 1998, Lovejoy 1983, Meillassoux 1991, Roberts 1987, 1988, and Roberts and Klein 1980.

56. Cf. Klein 1987: 52, 1998, and CAOM, 75 APOM 8/11, Letter Lt-Gov. HSN to Gov. Gen. Dakar, Bamako, 2 July 1918. While such estimates are not reliable, I should note that I noticed during my stay that the subject of the prevalence of slave descent among Nioro's inhabitants was frequently a topic of discussion.

57. On the important slave exodus from Banamba, see Roberts and Klein 1980.

58. See also CAOM, Soudan I/11, Affaires Politiques, Rapport sur la situation pol. du HSN, 2nd trim., 1906. The career of Shaykh al-Akhdar is discussed in Chapter 3.

59. Some more recent commentators have taken up such ideas rather uncritically. See, for example, Roberts 1987: 200.

60. For statistics on students for 1897 to 1921, see Brevié 1923: 215.

61. See ANM, 1E 212, Aff. Pol., Nioro (1902–11); cf. Manchuelle 1987.

62. ANM, 4E 62, Rap. annuel sur la question musulmane, 1913.

63. See Eickelman and Piscatori 1990.
64. Some of these kinds of educational and/or scholarly migrants are discussed in chapters below.
65. I know of only one example of a non-religious specialist from the region successfully undertaking the career of religious specialist, although there are undoubtedly others. It is interesting to note the great distances this man travelled. The man was from a Soninke ('free') 'warrior' lineage from the Diafounou area (Mali) who studied in Kaédi (Mauritania) and then carried out his career as a religious specialist in a village of Bambara migrants near the peanut basin in western Senegal.
66. The latter are all attached as clients to one of the lineages of religious specialists with whom they studied. On these monopolies among the Futanke, see Wane 1969; cf. Willis 1978.
67. Brenner 1984 and Niezen 1987 also make this point.
68. In marriage, they were almost without exception unable to marry women from 'free' lineages. Thereby constrained, some men have married women of 'caste' origins. The children that issue from such unions are not considered servile status. Those who might have a claim over ego have no claims to these children.

CHAPTER 3

1. See Marty 1915–16: *passim.*
2. ANM, 4E 19 (FA), letter Admin. Nioro to Gov. HSN, 12 June 1913. On Sidi Abdallah, see Robinson 1985: 363–4, and Marty 1920: 69, 205.
3. ANM, 4E 62 (FA), Rapport sur les associations catholiques ou indigènes et sur les confréries musulmanes, 16 August 1905. See also Marty 1920: 217–18.
4. ANS, 15G 103, Personnages Relig., Nioro, HSN, 1909.
5. ANM, 4E 32 (FR), Questions religieuses, 1925. Garcia (1994) reports that her informants said that Tall claimed Muhammad al-Mukhtar as one of his teachers.
6. ANS, 17G 298 (126), Demande d'autorisation de circuler au Soudan français pour le Chériff Ahmadou Mouktar Aydara [signed in Arabic, Sharif Muhammad al-Mukhtar], 1925.
7. ANS, 17G 298 (126), letter, Deputy of Senegal, Blaise Diagne, to Gov. Gen. AOF, 30 June 1925.
8. ANM, 4E 62 (FA), Rapport sur les associations catholiques ou indigènes et sur les confréries musulmanes, 16 August 1905.
9. ANM, 4E 19 (FA), letter, Admin. Nioro to Gov. HSN, 12 June 1913.
10. Ibid.
11. Ibid.; cf. Marty 1915–16: 357–8, Marty 1920: 228–9.
12. These Soninke were named *muqaddams* by a number of different people from Saint-Louis and Bakel in Senegal as well as from Nioro. See Marty 1920: 239–48.
13. Madi Assa Kaba Jakhite, who became imam of the Friday mosque in Nioro, is listed elsewhere as a *muqaddam* as early as 1909. See ANS, 15G 103, Affaires musulmanes, Fiche de renseignements, June 1909; and Marty 1920: 214. His omission from the 1913 report cited above is puzzling. He is, however, listed as a *muqaddam* in the declarations of loyalty to the French published in 'Le Salut au drapeau: témoignages de loyalisme des musulmans français' 1915–16.
14. ANM, 4E 19 (FA), letter, Admin. Nioro to Gov. HSN, 12 June 1913.
15. This is expressed in the same 1913 report cited above.
16. CAOM, 75 APOM 9/13, Robert Arnaud, Mission de 1906, Kayes, HSN, Rapport sur le marabout Moh.d [*sic*] Moktar ben Abdallah.
17. Ibid. The name of al-Akhdar's patron in the Adrar was Muhammad Fadil b. Muhammad Abaydi. Like others at this time, Muhammad Fadil seems to have

had multiple affiliations to Sufi orders. See ANM, 2D 64 (FR), Rapport de Mission en Mauritanie, December 1933–March 1934, Beyriès. Cf. Marty 1915–16: 145–6. Muhammad Fadil is briefly discussed by Poulet 1904: 144, 147, and Bonte 1982. The date of his death is given as 1321 A.H./1903 in al-Mahjubi 2001: 370.

18. CAOM, 75 APOM 9/13. See also ANS, 19G 3–1, Marabouts, fiches de renseignements, Nioro, 1923; and Nicolas 1943.

19. CAOM, 75 APOM 9/13, Robert Arnaud, Mission de 1906, Kayes, HSN, Rapport sur le marabout Moh.d Moktar ben Abdallah. Handwritten interview notes, undated but presumably May 1906. The handwritten note describes this as 'the gift of attraction [*le don de sympathie*]; when seeing him, humans are drawn to him and welcome him ...'

20. Ibid., handwritten interview notes, 19 May 1906.

21. In 1906, he said that he had been initiating people in the area for four or five years. See CAOM, 75 APOM 9/13, Robert Arnaud, Mission de 1906, Kayes, HSN, Rapport sur le marabout Moh.d Moktar ben Abdallah.

22. For Al-Akhdar's first associates in the region, see Ba 1980, Ba 1989, and Doucouré 1976. The information about women followers comes from an informant whose father's brother was a *muqaddam* al-Akhdar named in Nioro.

23. For this prayer in Arabic and its translation into English, see Abun-Nasr 1965: 187, 52.

24. CAOM, 75 APOM 9/13, Robert Arnaud, Mission de 1906, HSN, Rapport sur le marabout Moh.d Moktar ben Abdallah, letter to Gov. Gen. a/s du marabout Mohammed ben Abdallah, Kayes, 24 May 1906.

25. Some of the *muqaddams* are listed by Traoré 1983, while a more extensive listing can be found in Ibn Mu'adh 1988. Cf. Marty 1920: *passim*.

26. The accounts by Hamawi scholars, including Ibn Mu'adh 1988 and Doucouré 1976, stress the link to Sidi al-Tahir, as do Arnaud's notes in CAOM, 75 APOM 9/13. See also Ba 1980, and Traoré 1983. On Sidi al-Tahir, see Depont and Coppolani 1897: 431f.

27. I draw here from the most detailed version I heard on 21 January 1994.

28. The name of Hamallah's own mother was Assa – the way 'Aysha is pronounced in some of the region's vernaculars – Jallo. The many girls named after Assa Jallo are called Ba Jallo.

29. See 'Mahdi' in SEI.

30. Doucouré (1976: 44) refers to the 'Hamawiyya group' (Ar., *al-jama'a al-Hamawiyya*) forming in this way.

31. For instance, Sidi Muhammad Siby, the son of Sidi Abdallah mentioned above, who hailed from Nioro but lived in the Dar Salam neighbourhood of Bamako, claimed al-Akhdar had named him a *khalifa*. Siby never recognised Hamallah as his leader. Cf. Ba 1989: 205.

32. See ANM, 5E 19 (FA), Répertoire des réponses faites par les groupements musulmans à la circulaire arabe qui leur annonçait la révolte du grand chériff de la Mecque contre la Turquie, n.d., but, presumably 1916; cf. Harrison 1988: 121f.

33. See Ibn Mu'adh 1988 for an extensive list of *muqaddams* Hamallah named.

34. ANM, 4E 26–4 (FR), Rapport sur l'activité du Tidjanisme dans le cercle de Nema, 20 June 1930.

35. Some intellectuals associated with the Hamawiyya take great offence when the Sufi order is discussed in such terms.

36. See Ibn Mu'adh 1988: 235–6.

37. I have seen a copy of an Arabic text from the 1920s from a very prominent group

of religious specialists in Mauritania that states just this. I have been asked not to reveal the names of the authors of the text.

38. See also Kaba 1997 for a discussion of relations between Qadiris in Guinea and Hamallah.

39. They are listed in Ibn Mu'adh 1988: 236.

40. See ANS, 19G 23(108), Rapport, Capt. P.-J. André, 1923, and André 1924: 68.

41. On Ibn Mayaba, see Abun-Nasr 1965, Traoré 1983, and Ould Cheikh 2000.

42. See Ibn Mu'adh 1988 and especially page 28f where the author discusses al-Jilli and the notion of the Perfect Man.

43. See Soares and Hunwick 1996 for more extensive analysis of this poem. See Hamès 1982 for a poem in Pulaar.

44. On Ahmad al-Saghir, see Ibn Mu'adh 1988: 111, and al-Mahjubi 2001: 151ff. The poems in question are included in Ibn Mu'adh 1988: 111ff.

45. For some of his activities in the 1910s, see CAOM, PA 26/1/2, Journal de poste, Nioro du Sahel (1911–14). Some of Hamallah's followers apparently wrote poems insulting to Muhammad al-Mukhtar (Nicolas 1943). Muhammad al-Mukhtar is generally one of those singled out as an early opponent of Hamallah and often as the leader of the opposition. See, for example, Doucouré 1976.

46. ANM, 4E 32 (FR), Quest. relig., 1925.

47. On Fah, see CAOM, 75 APOM 8/11, Nioro, Notes sur quelques notables indigènes du cercle de Nioro, le marabout Fa O. Cheikh el Medi, July 1916, and Marty 1920: 222. On the Tinwajiyu, see Marty 1921: 401–22.

48. This is suggested in oral sources, as well as in archival materials. See CAOM, 75 APOM 8/11, Nioro, Notes sur quelques notables indigènes du c. de Nioro, December 1917; Archives, Nioro, 4E 2, Fiches de renseignements des personnages religieux, 1944; and Marty 1921: 401–22.

49. Three are listed in Ibn Mu'adh 1988: 233. See also CAOM, 75 APOM 8/11, Nioro, Notes sur les marabouts des tribus maures, 1915; cf. Marty 1921: 418–19.

50. This fraction of the Ahl Sidi Mahmud is the Idaw al-Hajj, among whom there were numerous *muqaddams* named by Hamallah, including some very prominent ones.

51. CAOM, 75 APOM 8/11, Nioro, Notes sur quelques notables indigènes du cercle de Nioro, le marabout Fa O. Cheikh el Medi, July 1916.

52. CAOM, Aff Pol carton 160, Soudan, Rapport Politique Annuel, 1923 and 1924.

53. This was apparent to the French before 1920. See Marty 1920: 221.

54. On the Aghlal, see Marty 1921: 365ff., and de Luze 1953.

55. See de Luze 1953, Nicolas 1943, and Gouilly 1948.

56. CAOM, Aff Pol carton 160, Soudan, Rapport Politique Annuel, 1923. See also ANM, 4E 19–2, Ségou, Rapport sur la politique musulmane, 1923.

57. See, for example, Rapport Descemet in Traoré 1983: 243, and Nicolas 1943: 45 who refers to Hamallah as 'the true instigator' of the conflicts. On the Ahl Sidi Mahmud conflicts, see Marty 1920: 221–2.

58. ANS, 15G 14(17), Tableau indiquant par tribus et fractions la population nomade ..., c. de Nioro, 7 February 1942.

59. See Rapport Descemet in Traoré 1983: 243.

60. ANM, 1E 36–4 (FR), Rapport Politique, 2d trim. 1924; Archives, Nioro, unclass. doc.; Rapport Descemet quoted in Traoré 1983: 243; CAOM, Aff Pol carton 160, Soudan, Rapport Politique, 1924.

61. See, for example, the narrative of Sidati, one of Hamallah's *muqaddams* from Nema, who stayed with Hamallah in Mederdra and then followed him to Côte d'Ivoire, in Mulay Muhammad (1986: 12–13).

62. CAOM, Aff Pol carton 160, Soudan, Rapport Politique, 1925.

63. ANM, 1E 36 (FR), Rapport Politique, c. de Nioro, 12 Jan. 1926.
64. CAOM, Aff Pol carton 160, Soudan, Rapport Politique, 1925.
65. Ibid.
66. Ibid.
67. In contrast, Shi'is are not unanimous in their view about Friday communal prayers. For the case of Iran where Friday communal prayers became obligatory after the creation of the Islamic Republic, see Fischer and Abedi (1990: 120–1).
68. On Muhammad Yahya al-Walati's (d. 1912) opinion (Ar., *fatwa*), see Boubrik 1999: 47.
69. Archives, Nioro, Extrait, Revue, 3d trim., illegible date but perhaps 1932.
70. One colonial administrator stated quite explicitly that the French did not permit separate Hamawi-run mosques. See Bertin 1955.
71. Archives, Nioro, Extrait, Revue, 3d trim., illegible date but perhaps 1932. The administrator pointed out that 'no allusion to the possibility of this request has been made by the interested parties'. I was unable to identify these interested parties.
72. CAOM, Aff Pol carton 160, Soudan, Rapport Politique Annuel, 1927.
73. This information is from some informants who visited Hamallah in Bamako in 1926. See also Nicolas 1943 who reports 6,000 people visiting Hamallah in Bamako.
74. See, for example, ANM, 4E 26–4 (FR), Rapport sur l'activité du Tidjanisme dans le c. de Nema, 20 June 1930.
75. ANM 4E 32 (FR), letter, n.d., signed EBOUE, n.d., but presumably on the eve of Hamallah's return to Nioro. See also d'Arbaumont 1941.
76. ANM, 4E 32 (FR), letter, signed EBOUE, n.d.
77. That Hamallah kept part of the *zawiya* closed after his return from exile in 1936 is noted by some in Nioro today. It was also known to the colonial administration. See ANM, 4E 26–4 (FR), Gov. Soudan to Comm. Nioro, Gao, etc., 24 September 1937.
78. ANS, 17G 60(17), Circulaire (confidential), Gov. Gen. AOF to Gov. Colonies AOF, 6 September 1937.
79. Later, colonial administrators would note that some in Mauritania had been abridging their prayers since the time of the French occupation. See, for example, d'Arbaumont 1941, and Gouilly 1952: 155.
80. CAOM, Aff Pol 2258/3, Circulaire, Gov. Gen. AOF to Lt-Gov. Colonies du Groupe and to Gov. Admin. de Dakar, 27 February 1937.
81. Gouilly 1952: 155 also makes this point.
82. Two of Doucouré's poems are published in Ibn Mu'adh 1988. On his opposition to Hamallah, see Ba 1989: 224–5, and Gouilly 1948.
83. Ibn Mu'adh 1988 also lists some of the other *muqaddams* who did not follow Hamallah in abridging their prayers.
84. For the legal arguments for abridged prayers made at the time in defence of Hamallah, see Mulay Muhammad 1986.
85. ANM, 4E 26–4 (FR), letter, Gov. Soudan to Comm. Nioro, Gao, etc., 24 September 1937.
86. ANM, 4E 26–4 (FR), Bulletin de Renseignements (confidential), Commandant Corrot, Nioro, 31 July 1937.
87. See Joly 1997 for an extended discussion of the reconciliation.
88. On Seydou Nourou Tall and his career, see Garcia 1994, 1997, Seesemann and Soares n.d., and Chapters 4 and 7 below.
89. CAOM, Aff Pol 539/6, Rapport Politique et Admin., AOF, 1937; ANS, 17G 377 (126), Renseignements (confidential), 27 December 1937.

90. Letter from Hamallah to Cerno Bokar Tall quoted in Brenner 1984:58.

91. ANM, 4E 26 (FR), Marabouts, personn. relig., Nara, 1930–43. Letter Gov. Soudan to Chef of Taleb Moktar, subdiv. Nara, Nema, 12 August 1937.

92. ANS, 17G 377 (126), Rapport de Tournée au Soudan, Gov. Gen. AOF, 15–27 December 1937.

93. Archives, Nioro, letter, Yacouba Sylla to Hamallah, 8 June 1939. See also Archives, Nioro, unclass. doc., 1937–9, and Nicolas 1943: 27.

94. These events are discussed in detail by Traoré 1983: 161–7. Cf. Rocaboy 1947a, 1947b, 1993.

95. See Traoré 1983, and Ba 1989. For a list of those executed, see Ibn Mu'adh 1988.

96. Archives, Nioro, Circulaire no. 1,100, Koulouba, 28 December 1942. This document refers to Hamallism as 'the principal danger'.

97. For a partial list of detainees from Nioro who died in exile, see Ba 1989: 233f.

98. CAOM, 14 mi 1835, ANS, 2G 42–3, Soudan, Rapport politique, 1942. A few of these people were able to remain in Nioro.

99. For some of the threats and actual sanctions, see, for example, ANM, 1E 36 (FR), Rapport tournée, Castex, Nioro, 21 June 1942; CAOM, 14 mi 1835, 2G 42–3, Soudan, Rapport politique, 1942; ANM, 2M 237 (FR), Nioro (1937–45).

100. ANS, 15G 43 (17), T.L. Gov. Soudan to Haussaire, Dakar, 10 January 1942. It is important to note there were earlier precedents in West Africa for the actions against Hamallah. There is, for example, the case of Maki, a grandson of Umar Tall, in Dinguiraye, Guinea. In 1899, while his father Agibu ruled in Macina in the Soudan, Maki was arrested. The French subsequently ordered the occupation and destruction of his residence, though not the mosque. See de Coutouly 1913. For even earlier precedents in North Africa, see Clancy-Smith 1994.

101. Archives, Nioro, letter (confidential), Gov. Gen. AOF to Gov. Soudan, 28 May 1946. See also CAOM, Aff Pol 2173/7, Confins soudano-mauritaniens, 1944.

102. This is also reported in some archival sources. See Joly 1993.

103. CAOM, 200 mi 1835, ANS 2G 42(2), Mauritanie, Rapport Politique, 1942; CAOM, Aff Pol 2258/3, Rapport Politique (Extraits), Mauritanie, 1944; ANS, 15G 43(17), Rapport sur la sit. pol. d'Ensemble du Soudan, February 1943; see also Lafeuille 1947; Gouilly 1952; and Traoré 1983: 191ff.

104. For renunciations by religious personalities in the circle of Nema, including Oualata, see ANM 4E 26–6 (FR), Notice sur trois notables du c. de Néma ..., n.d. The French role in these particular renunciations is not clear.

105. See ANM, 4E 1256 (ii), Note, Capitaine Cardaire, n.d., but presumably 1952 or 1953.

106. ANS, 15G 47(17), Soudan, Rapport Politique, Aug. 1946.

107. For the instructions to announce Hamallah's death, see ANM, 4E 1256 (ii), Circulaire, Gov. Gen. AOF to Gov., 7 June 1945. On the delay, see ANM, 4E 21 (FR), Circulaire (Secret), Gov. Gen. AOF to Gov. Colonies, 18 December 1944.

108. ANM, 4E 1256(ii), Admin. Nioro to Gov. Soudan, 24 February 1953.

109. Informants report that they gathered at the home of Dembu Nimaga in the Diakha neighbourhood of Nioro, while later others gathered at the home of Ahmad Wuld Sidi 'Uthman (d. 1956) near where Hamallah had lived. See also CAOM, Aff Pol 2258/3, Rapport de Mission sur la situation de l'Islam en AOF (3 April–31 July 1952), J. Beyriès.

110. ANM, 1E 36–24 (FR), Bull. de Renseignements, Nioro, 1st trim., 1949. See also Lafeuille 1947.
111. See CAOM, Aff Pol, 2258/3, Ministère de la France d'Outre-Mer, Dir. des Affaires Politiques, Note pour M. le Ministre, with the date given as 195–.
112. On this subject, see Moreau 1964, Traoré 1983, and especially Diallo 1997.
113. This is widely reported by people in Nioro, whether Hamawis or not. Although clearly many Hamawis supported RDA, this closeness between some Hamawis and RDA does not mean that the Hamawiyya was no longer a force. Cf. Alexandre 1970.
114. ANS, 15G 43(17), Soudan, Rapport situation politique, November–December, 1943, July–August, 1944.
115. Archives, Nioro, Admin. Nioro to Chef Terr. Soudan, 18 August 1958.
116. ANM, 1E 68–6 (FR), Revue Mensuelle des Evénements, Nioro, December 1957.
117. At least part of the library was held at IFAN in Dakar in the Fonds Hamallah.
118. For an extended discussion of Yacouba Sylla, see Traoré 1983, Savadogo 1998, 2000, and Hanretta 2003.
119. In contrast, Muhammadu's younger brother, Abu Bakr (a.k.a. Ibby) (d. 1992), who lived in neighbouring Aïoun (Mauritania) maintained close ties with Yacouba Sylla and his family.
120. See 'Interview de Cheikh Mohamedou Ould Cheikh Hamahoullah,' *Mauritanie Nouvelles*, 2–9 May 1994.
121. An obvious allusion to the *hadith*, '*Ru'ya* [visions] are from Allah, and *hulm* [dreams] are from Satan' included within al-Bukhari, *Ta'bir al-Ru'ya* and other collections of Hadith. See Wensinck 1927: 61.
122. The author of the letters, Dayf Wuld al-Bah of the Ahl Sidi Mahmud, has since died. His son is reported to live in Medina. On some of the meanings of 'amir', see 'Amir' in SEI.
123. See 'Gha'ib' in EI.
124. The request may have been from some in Nioro. See ANM, 4E 1256(ii), Admin. Nioro to Gov. Soudan, 24 February 1953. See also CAOM, Aff Pol 2260/9 letter (confidential), Min. France d'Outre-Mer to Haut Commiss., Gov. Gen. AOF, Dir. Gen. Interieur, Services des Affaires Politiques, 6 September 1950, and CAOM, Aff Pol 2259/1 Aff. Pol. Musulmanes, Rapport trim., 1st trim., 1951.
125. CAOM, Aff Pol, 2258/3, Ministère de la France d'Outre Mer, Paris, Note pour M. le Ministre, 195–.
126. ANM, 1E 36 (FR), Tel. letter, c. Nioro to Gov. Soudan, Rapport tournée Castex, 21 June 1942.
127. Personal communication with Mme Hélène Heckmann in 1994.
128. The most readily available of these are Ba 1980, Ba 1989, and Traoré 1983.

CHAPTER 4

1. Brenner 1984: 25–30; Robinson 2000: 151–3.
2. See ANM, 1E 212 (FA), letter, Admin. Bandiagara to Gov. Koulouba, 27 June 1907.
3. For some within the Tall family in the Kayes region, see ANM, 4E 23–2 (FR), Dossiers des personnages religieux, Kayes, 1943.
4. See, for example, Depont and Coppolani 1897: 418.
5. See Sall 1997 for a discussion of the career of Amadu Mukhtar Sakho.
6. He later died in detention during the repression of the 1940s.
7. ANS, 15G 54 (108), letter, Maki Agibu Tall to Gov. Gen. AOF, Dakar, 11 February 1926.

8. Cf. Ba 1989: 200–2 and Ba 1980: 65.
9. It is widely reported that Hamallah's mother was, at some point in her life, of servile-status.
10. Such a gift is called *hadaya* in the local vernaculars, a loan word from the Arabic (*hadiyya*; pl. *hadaya*). See Chapter 6.
11. CAOM, 14 mi 1835, 2G 42–3, Soudan, Rapport politique, 1942.
12. This is reminiscent of the request of the Sultan of Kano in present-day Nigeria to be buried near a particularly distinguished Muslim scholar. See Sanneh 1989: 197, and Al-Hajj 1968.
13. On the subject of Alfa Umar's tomb, see Adam 1903–4. It is important to note that no Futanke, even descendants of Umar Tall, had been buried within the fort in the past.
14. Although it was of course not unusual for members of the Muslim establishment to pray on behalf of France and for the French to ask them to do so, less is known about the kind of exchange of services discussed in this story.
15. This information comes from oral sources in Nioro.
16. ANM, 1E 2 (FR), Direction des Affaires Politiques, Revue Trim., 27 November 1950.
17. CAOM, Aff Pol 2158/3, Rapport de Mission sur la situation de l'Islam en AOF (3 April–31 July 1952), J. Beyriès.
18. See ANM, 4E 26–4 (FR), letter (confidential) Gov. Soudan to C. Nema, 18 August 1937.
19. 'Cerno' is the term used in Pulaar for Muslim religious leader.
20. See the undated account in Arabic of one of Seydou Nourou's visits to Niger, possibly in 1936, by Umar b. Muhammad, Umar Falke manuscript collection, doc. 1403, Northwestern University.
21. Seesemann and Soares n.d.
22. Some informants in Nioro say that Seydou Nourou arranged to meet Hamallah early during his first exile and only later became opposed to Hamallah. See also ANS 15G 54(108), letter, Maki Agibu Tall to Gov. Gen. AOF, 11 February 1926. In this letter, Maki Tall accuses Seydou Nourou of being sympathetic to Hamallah.
23. Some of these denunciations are mentioned in 'Oeuvres de Seydou Nourou Tall en AOF, 1923–1948,' ANS 19G 43(108). Gouilly 1948: 42ff. summarises some of them, and some of my informants present during some of his talks confirm these denunciations.
24. ANS, 2G 41–20, Soudan, rapport politique annuel, 1941.
25. In French, these schools are called *médersas*.
26. On Mahmud Ba, see Coureau 1952, Brenner 1991, 2001, and M. Kane 1997. See also Chapters 7 and 8 below.
27. On Ibrahima Niasse and his branch of the Tijaniyya, often called the Niassène or the Ibrahimiyya, see Froelich 1968, Paden 1973, Hiskett 1980, O. Kane 1997, and Seesemann and Soares n.d.
28. On his visits to the Soudan, particularly Ségou, see CAOM, Aff Pol 2258/2, Gouvernment Gen. de l'AOF, Service des Aff. Pol., Revue des Questions Musulmanes en AOF et en AOB[ritanniques], October 1952–September 1953, Dakar, October 1953; CAOM, Aff Pol 2259/4, l'Islam au Soudan, Rapports Trimestriels, 1954; and CARAN, 200 mi 2750, 2G 54(178), Soudan, Revue Trim., 3d trim., 1954.
29. On this subject, see CAOM, Aff Pol, 2260/1, (confidential) Note sur les questions islamiques communes aux Territoires français et britanniques d'Afrique Occidentale, November 1957.

30. On Seydou Nourou Tall's attempts to counter the influence of Niasse, see, for example, CAOM, Aff Pol 2259/1, Revue des Quest. Musul. en AOF, April 1955.

31. CAOM, Aff Pol 2260/9, Min. de la FOM, Dir. des Aff. Pol., Synthèse de Rens. Concernant les Activités des Communautés Islamiques de l'Afrique Noire au cours de l'année 1949.

32. In the 1960s, Ibrahima Niasse is reported to have been critical of other Tijanis in Senegal, specifically saying that the title of *khalifa* is not part of Islam (Behrman 1970: 71–2).

33. CAOM, Aff Pol 2261/3, Senegal: les Religions au Senegal, 1955; and CAOM, Aff Pol 2259/1, Revue des Quest. Musul. en AOF, April 1955.

34. I use here the orthography in French colonial documents. Transliterated from the Arabic, his name is Ibn Umar. On his career, see Seesemann and Soares n.d. Some of the relevant archival sources include: CAOM, Aff Pol 2259/1, Revue des Quest. Musul. en AOF, April 1955. On his trips to AOF, see CAOM, Aff Pol 2260/9, Min. de la FOM, Dir. des Aff. Pol., Synthèse de Rens. Concernant les Activités des Communautés Islamiques de l'Afrique Noire au cours de l'année 1949; CAOM, Aff Pol 2260/5, Synthèse des rens. concernant les Communautes Musulmanes de l'Union Française, 2d sem., 1948.

35. ANM, 1E 37–6, Revue des Evenements, 2d trim., c. de Nioro, 1955.

36. This was suggested as early as 1923. See CAOM, Aff Pol carton 160, Soudan, Rapport Politique, 1923.

37. CAOM, Aff Pol 2260/1, Notice Documentaire sur l'Islam en AOF, August 1940.

38. Hady's father and Seydou Nourou were 'brothers' as sons of two of Umar Tall's sons. For that reason, Hady and his brother Muntaga are Seydou Nourou's 'sons'.

39. Some of them are identified in a report by J. Beyriès. See CAOM, Aff Pol 2158/3, Rapport de Mission sur la situation de l'Islam en AOF (3 April–31 July 1952).

40. Interview with Madani Muntaga Tall, Dakar, May 1994. Muntaga is considered by many as the *khalifa* of the family of Umar Tall, a title he received from Seydou Nourou.

41. While some informants suggested that Seydou Nourou Tall had other representatives of equal rank, this has not been possible to verify.

42. There is some ambiguity about his title as well. His followers claim that Seydou Nourou Tall appointed him a *khalifa* as early as the 1950s.

43. See Chapters 5 and 6 below.

44. It was billed as such on the typed and photocopied programme in French for the January 1994 *ziyara* and the invitation in Arabic for the December 1994 *ziyara*.

45. In the broader region of western Mali but also in Bamako and Ségou as well as Boghé and Dakar. It is important to note that such ties are frequently reinforced through marriage alliances.

46. On the Tijanis of Médina Gounass, see Wane 1974, and Sow 1985–6. On Cerno Mansour Baro's activities in France, see Soares 2004a.

47. On the subject of changing Islamic education in contexts rather different from the one discussed here, see Eickelman 1985, and Messick 1993.

48. In the past several years, this has been changing. Until recently, there were only a handful of Tall from Nioro who ever completed more than a few years of formal French-language schooling, and these studies did not begin until the 1950s and 1960s, if not later. I am aware of only a few Tall family members from Nioro with an advanced education.

49. This is without mentioning Tall family members in Guinea, Senegal and Mauritania, all places where civil servants from the large Tall family are not uncommon.
50. On Murtada's help in the recruitment of soldiers before the First World War, see Marty 1920: 228–9.
51. This is the literal translation from various vernacular languages spoken in Mali. It is interesting to compare this perspective with what Behrman (1970: 148) reports for leading religious figures in Senegal, including Seydou Nourou Tall.
52. This is based on my observations and discussions with people in the town. It is not based on any kind of survey.

CHAPTER 5

1. Although some of these practices such as *tibb* and *du'a* might not always be categorised as secret, they are frequently thought of as such.
2. For example, Bledsoe and Robey 1986. Some notable exceptions to such an instrumentalist approach are Lambek 1990, 1993, Mommersteeg 1991, and Shaw 2002.
3. Cf. Stoller and Olkes 1987, and Olivier de Sardan 1992.
4. *Aandal balewal*, literally 'black knowledge', in Fulfulde.
5. See also Ibn Khaldun 1958, 3: 160 and, for an ethnographic example, Boddy 1989: 110 and n. 26.
6. In Chapter 7, I discuss some other practices, such as spirit possession, that are also subject to such criticism.
7. See Monteil 1924 for a discussion of the relationship of the non-Muslim Bambara rulers of Ségou to Islam and Muslims. See also Bravmann 1976, 1983.
8. On the subject of 'traditional' healers in Mali, see Brunet-Jailly 1993, and Diakité 1993.
9. See ANM, 1D 298, 299, 300 (FA), Inondation de la ville de Kayes, 1906.
10. He spoke in Hassaniyya and used the most commonly used word for Europeans, *nsara*, which literally means Christians.
11. For instance, I have been told by West Africans of Jacques Chirac's alleged visits to Senegalese *marabouts*. Some of his ties with African heads of states, such as Bongo of Gabon, have been widely reported in the media. Less reported have been the ties of such political leaders to *les grands marabouts*. Cf. Diallo 1988.
12. One man in his late seventies, who is neither from this lineage nor a member of a lineage of Muslim religious specialists, told me that the secrets were Islamic. It is entirely possible that in earlier periods such secrets were widely deemed Islamic.
13. This is also discussed by Doutté 1984 for North Africa.
14. This is similar to what Malinowski called the condition of the performer. See Malinowski 1925.
15. He used the word *leeki* in Fulfulde which means 'tree' as well as 'medicine'.
16. See Hunwick 1985.
17. Cf. al-Qayrawani 1975, and al-Nafrawi 1900, a commentary on this text. See also Owusu-Ansah 1991.
18. See ANM 1D 51-10 (FR), 'Les Toucouleurs Boundounkés', J. Bertin, Nioro, 1954.
19. In Bambara, *laturu* (divination), which may have been influenced by Islamic divination techniques as Brenner suggests was the case for Ifa. See Brenner 1985b, 2000.
20. This is similar to what Evans-Pritchard (1937) reported for the Azande.
21. In 1994, 500,000 FCFA.

22. For a discussion of geomancy in West Africa, see Brenner 1985b, 2000, and Shaw 2002.
23. I came to know this through discussions with Hamallah's son about the Fonds Hamallah at IFAN in Dakar.
24. Unclassified documents, Archives, Nioro.
25. I return to the history of this school in Chapter 7.
26. Because there was so much speculation about what happened, it was difficult to get much concrete information. Moreover, the sensitive nature of the subject made it impolitic to probe too deeply.
27. There is a wide range of other words used for different kinds of amulets. I have chosen not to use the word talisman (Ar., *tilsam*) for the simple reason that local people objected to its use for the kinds of *hijab* discussed here.
28. For a discussion of such objects in Muslim Africa, see el-Tom 1985, 1987; Hamès 1987, 1993, 1997b; Hamès and Epelboin 1993; and Abdalla 1981.
29. See Starrett 1995 for a discussion of protective objects in contemporary Egypt.
30. Details of this particular attack and its aftermath can be found in the Malian newspapers, *Les Echos*, 16 June 1992, and *Aurore*, 6 July 1992.
31. This is, of course, similar to the harassment and sometimes physical violence that some Tuaregs/Bidan/Arabs faced elsewhere in Mali, particularly in Bamako, where it received some press coverage.
32. This was reported in the print media. See Francis Kpatindé, 'Le plaidoire de M. Mountaga Tall,' *Jeune Afrique*, 13–19 March 1991, 12–13.
33. Ibid.
34. 'Abd al-Fattah al-Tukhi's *Manba'u usul al-raml*, 1956. On al-Tukhi, see Abdalla 1981.
35. Cf. Lory 1996 who discusses some of the reasons Muslim scholars have given for not using the esoteric sciences.
36. Interestingly enough, G. has married a woman from a local family of Muslim religious specialists, though he noted that his own status became a subject of debate during the marriage negotiations. His own father's extended family's marriage ties with one of the town's major religious leaders most likely played a role here.
37. It almost goes without saying that students and teachers of the Quran and jurisprudence do not share this view. From their perspective, what they are doing – attaining thorough knowledge of the Quran – is the absolute foundation of everything else. Moreover, they maintain that there are very few people who do know the Quran and jurisprudence thoroughly.
38. While this man consistently referred to these as 'names of God' in our conversations, some of the 'names' I was shown are reminiscent of some of the names on 'talismans' from Senegal analysed by Hamès and Epelboin (1993). Some seem to be written in a way that makes them nonsensical to the uninitiated.

CHAPTER 6

1. Cf. Weber 1978: 1,121f; Geertz 1968; Gellner 1969; Eickelman 1976; Cornell 1983, 1998; and Stone 1994. See also Dermenghem 1954.
2. It is useful to compare such 'popular' discourse with that found in some of the classical discussions of saints. Cf. al-Hujwiri 1936: 210–40.
3. Descendants of Umar Tall's family elsewhere in West Africa and beyond are involved in commercial activities. In 1994, for the first time, the Tall family in Nioro became directly involved in commerce in the town. A son of Cerno Hady opened an autoparts store in Nioro, an enterprise requiring a substantial amount of start-up capital unavailable to the average local merchant.

4. See MacLaughlin (1997) for a discussion of Islam and popular music in neighbouring Senegal.

5. The younger of the two men later explained to me in private that this is exactly what he meant.

6. On the Ahl Shaykh Sidiyya, see Marty 1916; Ould Cheikh 1991; Stewart 1973; and Robinson 2000.

7. Personal communication with Abdel Wedoud Ould Cheikh.

8. On the subject of pedagogical ties between teacher and student and the frequent reinforcement of such ties through marriage alliance, see Schmitz 1985.

9. In fact, I should note that after independence they were largely excluded from electoral politics in the town until the 1980s when the deputy to the National Assembly for Nioro was from the Kabalanke. Thus, their power was largely restricted to the religious and economic realms.

10. Again, the Tijani discourse on material wealth is relevant here.

11. There are, of course, other constraints associated with living in a city with its own larger and more diverse and competitive religious economy that I cannot discuss here.

12. Quoted in Johansen 1996: 163, 180–1.

13. As Miller 1995a points out, many social scientists who study commodities and consumption more generally use similar moralising discourses. See also Miller 1995b.

14. As Villalón shows in his recent study of a town in Senegal (1995).

15. For a discussion of such 'sacrifice' in a West African context, see Launay 1992.

16. The word is used in Bamanakan/Bambara, Hassaniyya, Pulaar/Fulfulde, Soninke, Jakhanke, Wolof, and in other languages spoken in West Africa. Its importance was discussed by some early colonial commentators, for example Poulet 1904.

17. See Ruxton 1916, and al-Qayrawani 1975.

18. Although Delafosse (1955) claimed that the word derived from the Arabic bara'a, meaning exculpation or settlement (of debt), this was not an etymology that any of my informants offered or found compelling. Some informants pointed out that the word did not appear to be of Arabic origin. As evidence, one person noted that in Fulfulde/Pulaar, the word did not belong to the same noun class usually reserved for words of foreign origin, including many words from Arabic.

19. It is interesting to note that this word sometimes has the meaning of gift or present. See Kazimirski 1860, 1: 13.

20. In this context, either one of the more conventional words for gift in the region's vernaculars (for example dokkal in Pulaar/Fulfulde) or a word with the sense of blessing (for example baraka) is used rather than hadaya.

21. This is not to suggest that they might not have received gifts called this in the past. Cf. Rançon 1894.

22. Eickelman (1976: 178) found similar practices in Morocco.

23. For the involvement of saints in the economy of Senegal, see the studies of the Mourides by Cruise O'Brien 1971, 1975, and Copans 1980. Although the involvement of members of the other Sufi orders in the economy in Senegal remains to be written, see Perry 1998.

24. Some of the changes are discussed by Lubeck 1986, and Watts 1996.

25. See Diallo 1988.

26. This is a process that Geertz (1979) identified in Morocco.

27. Elite followers are also more likely to have personalised photos of the religious leaders in which they even might pose with one of the leaders. These are also

prominently displayed in homes and in places of business.

28. See Comaroff 1994: 311, and Comaroff and Comaroff 2000 after Weller 2000 for a broader discussion of the development of 'fee-for-service' religions.

29. As indicated in Chapter 1, this is a subject discussed in some detail in written texts associated with the Tijaniyya Sufi order where people are instructed to choose a religious leader and not to frequent others.

30. The continuing importance of the Sufi orders in Senegal undoubtedly relates to differences in the colonial experience, particularly French colonial policies towards Muslims, as well as postcolonial state policies.

CHAPTER 7

1. On reformists in Mali, see Amselle 1977, 1985; Brenner 1993a, 2001; Cardaire 1954; Kaba 1974; Niezen 1987, 1990; and Warms 1992.

2. On the development of Salafi ideas and specifically anti-Sufism, see Sirriyeh 1999. On the influence of Salafi ideas on West African reformists, see Kaba 1974, and Brenner 2001.

3. See, for example, Cardaire 1954.

4. See ANM, 2D 64 (FR), Rapport de Mission en Mauritanie, December 1933–March 1934. See also Traoré 1983: 88 and Coulon 1988: 121.

5. See Kaba 1974.

6. On *la politique musulmane* during the 1950s, see Triaud 1997.

7. See, for example, Goichon 1950.

8. On this period, see Frémeaux 1991.

9. CAOM, Aff Pol 2158/3, Rapport de Mission sur la situation de l'Islam en AOF (3 April–31 July 1952), J. Beyriès.

10. See 'Kafir' in SEI.

11. According to some accounts, the well known reformist from AOF, Abd al-Rahman (d. 1957), who lived in the Hijaz, actively preached against the use of amulets, votive offerings, and animal sacrifices (Triaud 1986: 173), as well as against the Tijaniyya. See CAOM, Aff Pol 2259/1, L'Islam en AOF, Aff Pol Musulmanes, Rapport, 2nd & 3rd Trim. 1948). He had considerable contact with pilgrims and students from West Africa (Cardaire 1954: 80–1).

12. See Diané 1956, and Touré 1957.

13. There were some others whose perspectives might be called pro-French Muslim. For example, Ouane (1957) is critical of established religious leaders and practices in AOF, but argues against closer association or identification with the Arab world.

14. Ibn Mu'adh briefly mentions this (1988: 234).

15. CAOM, Aff Pol 2158/3, Rapport de Mission sur la situation de l'Islam en AOF (3 April–31 July 1952), J. Beyriès. Until his death in 1978, Wagué was a teacher at the school he ran in Barouéli that attracted students from far afield, including some from Nioro.

16. CAOM, Aff Pol 2158/3, Rapport de Mission sur la situation de l'Islam en AOF (3 April–31 July 1952), J. Beyriès. See also Le Grip 1953–4.

17. On the counter-reform movement, see Cardaire 1954, and Brenner 1991, 2001.

18. CAOM, Aff Pol 2259/4, handwritten note, Soudan, n.d.

19. On Mahmud Ba, see Coureau 1952, Brenner 1991, 2001, and M. Kane 1997.

20. ANM, 1E 37 (FR), Revue des Evenements, Nioro, 1956.

21. This is noted in the same report by Beyriès cited above.

22. On reformist objections to such sacrifices or prestations, see Launay 1992.

23. It is important to note that some West African Muslims, including some Tijanis, do pray with crossed arms. Ibrahima Niasse, who was based in Senegal,

popularised this manner of praying elsewhere in West Africa, particularly in northern Nigeria.

24. The first edition of this book dates from the 1950s. Although its stated purpose is to explain the five pillars of Islam in French, it is interesting to note that the only subject discussed in the book's prologue is the issue of praying with crossed arms.

25. Al-Akhdari's legal primer and the *Risala* of Ibn Abi Zayd al-Qayrawani (1975).

26. The one blacksmith has married endogamously.

27. Umar's (1993) discussion of anti-Sufism in northern Nigeria has influenced my argument here.

28. This is without mentioning some of the other tensions associated with return migration. Many note that most who go away for long periods of time and accumulate money have difficulties when they return to the town. Some point out that all long-term migrants – anti-Sufis or not – are invariably more individualistic and less inclined to help the broader community by sharing their wealth.

29. The following account draws from conversations with the man in question, as well as corroborating accounts by his friends and detractors.

30. On the development of *madrasas* in Mali, see Brenner 1991, 1993a, 2001; Sanankoua and Brenner 1991; and Cissé 1992.

31. He used the term *madrasa* but it is not clear whether the curriculum of this first school included a broad range of subjects like those in Bamako and elsewhere.

32. This is precisely what Coulon (1988) argues for reformists in Senegal.

33. See, for example, Park 2000 [1799], Raffenel 1856, and, from the colonial period, Chéron 1931.

34. See CAOM, 75 APOM 5/6, Robert Arnaud, Du commandement chez les Diawaras. Histoire d'une tribu guerrière du Soudan, 30 June 1918, 'Note sur une pratique fétichiste en usage chez les Diawara.' The rest of this paragraph draws from this source. See also Boyer 1953.

35. Cf. Boyer 1953.

36. On the *jiné don*, see Gibbal 1982; Malle 1985; and Soares 1999.

37. For a comparison of spirit possession and Sufi orders elsewhere in Africa, see Lewis 1986.

38. For example, meetings and ceremonies are generally only held with the permission of the head spirit medium(s).

39. See, for example, Diané 1956 where this is specifically discussed.

40. This is also discussed in Diané 1973. See also the discussion of this subject by Ibrahima Niasse in Froelich 1968.

41. For a discussion of some of the controversy surrounding Muslims visiting graves, see Johansen 1996.

CHAPTER 8

1. On the UCM in Soudan/Mali, see Kaba 1974 and Amselle 1985.

2. See, for example, Dramé 1986, and Cheick Sidya Diombana, 'La jeunesse et la foi en l'Islam', *La Roue*, 25 October–3 November 1993, p. 5.

3. I have written elsewhere about one of these religious leaders. See Soares 1996a, 1997, 1999. This is also without mentioning those religious leaders who come from neighbouring countries to visit Mali. See Chapter 4.

4. There is not space here to enter into a discussion of the complexities of trans-border trade and its legal and extra-legal regulation.

5. See 'Interview de Cheikh Mohamedou Ould Cheikh Hamahoullah,' *Mauritanie Nouvelles*, 2–9 May 1994.

6. I think it is inappropriate to reveal any more details about the matters discussed here.
7. Estimates of Mali's non-Muslim population range from 20 to 30 per cent, with a very small percentage of these non-Muslims said to be Christians. Indeed, probably less than 2 per cent of the population considers itself Christian, and the majority of Christians are affiliated with the Catholic church. Despite the presence of Protestant missionaries in the area since before 1920, Malian Protestants, including evangelicals, constitute a small fraction of the Christian population. Cf. Johnstone 1986.
8. I borrow the metaphor of saturation from Watts 1996: 276.
9. In this way, the public sphere in the Islamic world is much older than Eickelman and Anderson (1999) suggest.
10. For examples of such debates in the pre-colonial period, see Mahibou and Triaud 1983, and Hunwick 1996.
11. On these organisations in Senegal, see Gomez-Perez 1991, 1997, and Loimeier 1999. On new organisations in colonial Soudan and Mali, see Meillassoux 1968, and Brenner 2001.
12. See CAOM, Aff Pol 2259/1, L'Islam en AOF, Affaires Politiques Musulmanes, Rapport, 2nd & 3rd trim., 1948.
13. See CAOM, Aff Pol 2259/1, Aff Pol Musulmanes, Rapport Trim., 2nd trim., 1950.
14. CAOM, Aff Pol 2259/4, l'Islam au Soudan, Rapport Trim. 1954.
15. See, for example, CAOM, Aff Pol 2259/1, Aff Pol Musulmanes, Rapport Trim., 3rd trim., 1950.
16. See Amadou Hampaté Ba, 'Ramadan et Korité à Bamako', *Le Soudan Français*, n. 5, 1 August 1950, pp. 1–2; 'Le Ramadan à Bamako', *Le Soudan Français*, n. 188, 6 May 1954, p. 1; 'La fête du Ramadan à Bamako', *Le Soudan Français*, n. 192, 3 June 1954, p. 1; and 'La fête du Ramadan à Bamako', *Le Soudan Français*, n. 239–40, 19–26 May 1955, p. 1.
17. See Amadou Hampaté Ba, 'Tabaski et Oud-Hiyat à Bamako', *Le Soudan Français*, n. 9, 1 October 1950, pp. 1–2; Bemba Diarra, 'La Tabaski à Mopti ... et à Bafoulabé', *Le Soudan Français*, n. 201, 19 August 1954, p. 3; Coulibaly Koundou, 'Niono: Les fêtes de la Tabaski', *Le Soudan Français*, n. 203, 19 September 1954, p. 3.
18. See, for example, Gustave Mademba, 'Chronique religieuse: A propos de nos mariages musulmans', *Le Soudan Français*, n. 259, 6 October 1955, p. 2; Abdoul Wahab [Doucouré], 'Le Chant et la Musique vus de l'Islam', *Le Soudan Français*, n. 263, 3 November 1955, p. 1; 'Pèlerinage à la Mecque', *Le Soudan Français*, n. 99, 1 August 1952, p. 1; and 'Pèlerinage à la Mecque: Interview de M. Doucouré Abdoul Wahab', *Le Soudan Français*, n. 263, 3 November 1955, p. 4.
19. CARAN, 200 mi 2750, ANS 2G 54(178), Soudan, Rev. trim., 3d trim., 1954.
20. See 'Bamako reçoit le grand Chérif de Kankan', *Le Soudan Français*, n. 1, 1 June 1950, pp. 1–2.
21. See 'Conference religieuse', *Le Soudan Français*, n. 64, 23 November 1951, p. 1.
22. See, Doucouré Abdoul Wahab, 'Sources', *Le Soudan Français*, 11 July 1952, cited in Cardaire 1954: 155ff.
23. See, for example, M. Thiam, 'Conte africain: astuce d'un sage marabout', *Le Soudan Français*, n. 325, 29 March 1958, p. 3.
24. 'Pèlerinage à la Mecque: Interview de M. Doucouré Abdoul Wahab', *Le Soudan Français*, n. 263, 3 November 1955, p. 4.
25. See 'Pèlerinage à la Mecque: Interview de M. Demba Diallo, chef de Canton de

Diafarabé', *Le Soudan Français*, n. 261, 20 October 1955, p. 1. For a similar perspective, see Ouane 1957.

26. 'Radio-Soudan est né', *Le Soudan Français*, n. 290, 8 June 1957, p. 1.

27. See, for example, 'Programme des émissions de Radio-Soudan', *Le Soudan Français*, n. 311, 30 November 1957, p. 4, and 'Programme de Radio-Soudan', *Le Soudan Français*, n. 326, 12 April 1958, p. 3.

28. See Chailley 1962; Hodgkin and Morgenthau 1964.

29. Cf. Bowen 1993; Eickelman and Piscatori 1996; Fischer and Abedi 1990; and Eickelman and Anderson 1999.

30. See Brenner 1991, 1993a, 2001; Sanankoua and Brenner 1991; and Cissé 1992.

31. See Doumbia 1987. On the subject of West African migrants who send money home to finance the construction of mosques, see Quiminal 1991: 158f.

32. On the subject of the activities of Arab countries in Africa, see Oded 1987. On support from Arab countries to Mali, see Sanankoua 1991. On foreign-funded Islamic cultural centres in Mali, see Cissé 1992.

33. For a partial list of some of these new Islamic organisations, see Hock 1999.

34. *Témoignage afro-musulman*, 22 October 1991.

35. Mamadou Hachim Sow, 'Les islamistes préservent la paix', *Le Républicain*, 6 October 1993, p. 5.

36. *Le Politicien musulman*, n. 19, August 1993, p. 1.

37. In contrast, paid death announcements are regularly aired on Malian national radio.

38. See, for example, the coverage of a new Muslim 'religious sect' in central Mali, Kader Maïga, 'Secte religieuse à Macina: la menace des "Pieds nus"', *Le Républicain*, 17 July 1992, p. 6.

39. 'Islamisme', *Aurore*, 7 October 1993, 1. See also Nouhoum Keïta, 'A l'horizon: Activisme intégriste au Mali', *Le Démocrate*, 23 September 1993, p. 3.

40. See, for example, O. Bouaré, 'Grande mosquée de Bamako: la bourse des valeurs des escrocs', *Kabako*, 26 August 1999, n. 209.

41. One example from the period of my fieldwork is Modibo M. Konaté, 'Le carnet du musulman', *La Griffe*, 10 November 1993, p. 4.

42. Some of the texts are bilingual in Arabic and French. See, for example, Diané 1973. Books and pamphlets by one of Mali's most widely known scholars, Saad Oumar Touré (for example Touré n.d., 1993), have been available in shops in Bamako for even longer. A very limited number of pamphlets dealing with Islam are available in Bambara. For an extensive list of some of this literature, see Hunwick 2003a.

43. This statement is based on visits to bookshops and discussion with Malians since the 1990s and discussions with other researchers who have worked in Mali since the 1970s.

44. On the subject of sermons on cassette in neighbouring Côte d'Ivoire, see Launay 1997b.

45. The name in Arabic (*Ansar al-din*) is also transliterated into French as *Anesardine* or *Ane-Sardine* in some of the organisation's printed materials and in some newspaper coverage.

46. See S. Sidibé, 'Islam et société: prédicateurs', *L'Essor*, 25–6 December 1993, p. 4, and I. Traoré, 'Islam', *Le Républicain*, 11 December 1996, p. 4.

47. Indeed, the reformist from Nioro whose audio recordings denounce Sufi orders (see Chapter 7) are not widely diffused and generally not available for sale in the market.

48. In the 1990s, there was one video rental store in Nioro.

49. The original (unpirated) version of the video programme is *Is the Bible God's*

Word? Swaggart vs. Deedat Debate, Baton Rouge: Louisiana State University, 1986. If some of Deedat's writings (for example Deedat 1994) have been translated into French as early as 1990, they were not available in Bamako when I and others have checked for them on several occasions in the 1990s.

50. This statement is based on conversations with a number of people who were directly and indirectly involved in such exchanges between the state and religious leaders in this period.

51 See Traoré 1985.

52. This formulation draws on van der Veer's (1994) discussion of religious nationalism in India.

53. This is not to suggest in any way the existence of a particularistic Islam like the *Islam noir* of the colonial imagination.

54. According to Villalón (1995: 231), this is a way for certain groups in Senegal to show the state some of the limits to its power.

55. The debate about 'orthopraxy' in Islam is relevant here. Cf. Smith 1957; Asad 1986; and Eickelman 1989b.

56. My argument here is indebted to Bowen 1993 and Launay 1992.

57. These kinds of criticisms of Muslim religious leaders are not new. In fact, some criticised the celebrated Sufi Ahmad Ibn Idris for praying late. See O'Fahey 1990: 97.

BIBLIOGRAPHY

ARCHIVES AND OTHER COLLECTIONS

Archives, Cercle de Nioro du Sahel, Mali.

Archives Nationales du Mali (ANM), Koulouba, Mali.

Archives Nationales du Sénégal (ANS), Dakar, Senegal.

Centre des Archives d'Outre-Mer (CAOM), Archives Nationales, Aix-en-Provence, France.

Centre d'Accueil et de Recherche des Archives Nationales (CARAN), Paris, France.

Centre des Hautes Etudes Administratives sur l'Afrique et l'Asie Modernes (CHEAM), Paris, France.

WORKS CITED

'Les musulmans français et la guerre: adresses et témoignages de fidelité des chefs musulmans et des personnages religieux'. 1914. *Revue du Monde Musulman* 29.

'Le Salut au drapeau: témoignages de loyalisme des musulmans français'. 1915–16. *Revue du Monde Musulman* 33.

Abdalla, I. H. 1981. 'Islamic medicine and its influence on traditional Hausa practitioners in Northern Nigeria'. PhD dissertation, University of Wisconsin, Madison.

Abu-Lughod, L. 1989. 'Zones of theory in the anthropology of the Arab world', *Annual Review of Anthropology* 18, 267–306.

Abun-Nasr, J. M. 1965. *The Tijaniyya: A Sufi Order in the Modern World*. London: Oxford University Press.

Adam, M. G. 1903–4. 'Légendes historiques du pays de Nioro (Sahel)', *Révue Coloniale* 13, 81–98; 14, 232–48; 15, 354–72; 16, 485–96; 17, 602–20; 18, 734–44; 19, 117–24; 20, 233–48.

Akpo-Vaché, C. 1996. *L'AOF et la Seconde Guerre mondiale (septembre 1939–octobre 1945)*. Paris: Karthala.

Alexandre, P. 1970. 'A West African Islamic movement: Hamallism in French West Africa', in R. I. Rotberg and A. A. Mazrui (eds), *Protest and Power in Black Africa*. London: Oxford University Press.

Ali, A. (trans.). 1984. *Al-Qur'an*. Princeton: Princeton University Press.

Amselle, J.-L. 1977. *Les Négociants de la savane*. Paris: Anthropos.

Amselle, J.-L. 1985. 'Le Wahabisme à Bamako (1945–1985)', *Canadian Journal of African Studies* 19 (2), 345–57.

Amselle, J.-L. 1990. *Logiques métisses: Anthropologie de l'identité en Afrique et ailleurs.* Paris: Payot.

Anderson, B. 1991. *Imagined Communities.* New York: Verso.

André, P. J. 1922. *L'islam et les races,* 2 vols. Paris: P. Geuthner.

André, P. J. 1924. *L'islam noir.* Paris: P. Geuthner.

Antoun, R. T. 1989. *Muslim Preacher in the Modern World.* Princeton: Princeton University Press.

Appadurai, A. 1986. 'Introduction: commodities and the politics of value', in A. Appadurai (ed.), *The Social Life of Things: Commodities in Cultural Perspective.* Cambridge: Cambridge University Press.

Appadurai, A. 1996. *Modernity at Large: Cultural Dimensions of Globalization.* Minneapolis: University of Minnesota Press.

Arnaud, R. 1912. 'L'Islam et la politique musulmane française en Afrique occidentale française', *Bulletin du Comité de l'Afrique française, Renseignements Coloniaux* 3– 20; 115–27; 142–54.

Asad, T. 1986. 'The idea of an anthropology of Islam', Washington, DC: Georgetown University Center for Contemporary Arab Studies, Occasional Papers Series.

Asad, T. 1993. *Genealogies of Religion: Discipline and Reasons of Power in Christianity and Islam.* Baltimore: Johns Hopkins University Press.

Asad, T. 1999. 'Religion, nation-state, secularism', in P. van der Veer and H. Lehmann (eds), *Nation and Religion: Perspectives on Europe and Asia.* Princeton: Princeton University Press.

Austen, R. A. 1993. 'The moral economy of witchcraft: an essay in comparative history', in J. Comaroff and J. Comaroff (eds), *Modernity and Its Malcontents.* Chicago: University of Chicago Press.

Ba, A. 1989. *Histoire du Sahel Occidental Malien.* Bamako: Jamana.

Ba, A. H. 1980. *Vie et enseignement de Tierno Bokar.* Paris: Editions de Seuil.

Ba, A. H. and M. Cardaire. 1957. *Tierno Bokar, le sage de Bandiagara.* Paris: Présence africaine.

Ba, A. H. and J. Daget. 1962. *L'Empire peul du Macina.* Paris: Mouton.

Bagayogo, S. 1987. 'L'Etat au Mali: représentation, autonomie, et mode de fonctionnement', in E. Terray (ed.), *L'Etat contemporain en Afrique.* Paris: L'Harmattan.

Bailleul, Père C. 1981. *Petit Dictionnaire, Bambara-Français, Français-Bambara.* England: Avery Publishing Co.

Bathily, A. 1970. 'Mamadou Lamine Drame et la résistance anti-impérialiste dans le Haut-Sénégal (1885–1887)', *Notes africaines* 125, 20–32.

Bauberot, J. 1998. 'La laïcité française et ses mutations', *Social Compass* 45 (1), 175– 87.

Bazin, J. 1985. 'A chacun son Bambara', in J.-L. Amselle and E. M'Bokolo (eds), *Au coeur de l'ethnie: Ethnies, tribalisme et Etat en Afrique.* Paris: La Découverte.

Bazin, J. 1986. 'Retour aux choses-dieux', in C. Malamoud and J.-P. Vernant (eds), *Corps des dieux, Le Temps de la Réflexion* 7, 253–73.

Behrman, L. C. 1970. *Muslim Brotherhoods and Politics in Senegal.* Cambridge: Harvard University Press.

Beidelman, T. O. 1971. 'Nuer priests and prophets', in T. O. Beidelman (ed.), *The Translation of Culture: Essays to E. E. Evans-Pritchard.* London: Tavistock.

Bernus, E., P. Boilley, J. Clauzel and J.-L. Triaud (eds). 1993. *Nomades et commandements: Administration et sociétés nomades dans l'ancienne A.O.F.* Paris: Karthala.

Bertin, J. 1955. 'Les Toucouleurs Boundounkés du Soudan Français', CHEAM, Doc. 2491.

Bird, C. and M. Kendall. 1980. 'The Mande hero: text and context', in I. Karp and C. S. Bird (eds), *Theoretical Explorations in African Systems of Thought.* Bloomington: Indiana University Press.

Blanc, E. 1924. 'Contribution à l'étude des populations et de l'histoire du Sahel Soudanais', *Bulletin du Comité d'Etudes Historiques et Scientifiques de l'AOF* 7, 259–314.

Blank, J. 2001. *Mullahs on the Mainframe: Islam and Modernity among the Daudi Bohras.* Chicago: University of Chicago Press.

Bledsoe, C. H. and K. M. Robey. 1986. 'Arabic literacy and secrecy among the Mende of Sierra Leone', *Man* (n.s.) 21 (2), 202–26.

Boddy, J. 1989. *Wombs and Alien Spirits: Women, Men and the Zar Cult in Northern Sudan.* Madison: University of Wisconsin Press.

El Bokhari [al-Bukhari]. 1964. *L'Authentique tradition musulmane*, trans. G. H. Bousquet. Paris: Fasquelle.

Bonte, P. 1982. 'Tribus, factions, et Etat: Les conflits de succession dans l'émirat de l'Adrar', *Cahiers d'Etudes africaines* 22 (3–4), 489–516.

Boubrik, R. 1999. *Saints et société en Islam: La confrérie ouest-saharien Fâdiliyya.* Paris: CNRS Editions.

Bouche, D. 1968. *Les Villages de Liberté en Afrique noire française, 1887–1910.* Paris and The Hague: Mouton & Co.

Bourdieu, P. 1977. *Outline of a Theory of Practice*, trans. R. Nice. New York: Cambridge University Press.

Bourdieu, P. 1979. 'The disenchantment of the world', in P. Bourdieu, *Algeria 1960.* New York: Cambridge University Press.

Bourdieu, P. 1984. *Distinction: A Social Critique of the Judgement of Taste*, trans. R. Nice. Cambridge: Harvard University Press.

Bourgault, L. M. 1995. *Mass Media in Sub-Saharan Africa.* Bloomington: Indiana University Press.

Bowen, J. R. 1992. 'On scriptural essentialism and ritual variation: Muslim sacrifice in Sumatra and Morocco', *American Ethnologist* 19, 656–71.

Bowen, J. R. 1993. *Muslims through Discourse: Religion and Ritual in Gayo Society.* Princeton: Princeton University Press.

Boyer, G. 1953. *Un peuple de l'ouest soudanais: les Diawaras.* Dakar: IFAN.

Bravmann, R. A. 1976. *Islam and Tribal Art in Africa.* Cambridge: Cambridge University Press.

Bravmann, R. A. 1983. *African Islam.* Washington: Smithsonian.

Brenner, L. 1984. *West African Sufi: The Religious Heritage and Spiritual Search of Cerno Bokar Saalif Taal.* London: Hurst.

Brenner, L. 1985a. 'The "esoteric sciences" in West African Islam', in B. du Toit and I. H. Abdalla (eds), *African Healing Strategies.* Buffalo: Trado-Medic Books.

Brenner, L. 1985b. *Réflexions sur le savoir islamique en Afrique de l'Ouest.* Bordeaux: Centre d'Etude d'Afrique noire.

Brenner, L. 1988. 'Concepts of tariqa in West Africa: the case of the Qadiriyya', in D. B. Cruise O'Brien and C. Coulon (eds), *Charisma and Brotherhood in African Islam*. Oxford: Clarendon.

Brenner, L. 1991. 'Médersas au Mali: transformation d'une institution islamique', in B. Sanankoua and L. Brenner (eds), *L'enseignement islamique au Mali*. Bamako: Jamana.

Brenner, L. 1993a. 'Constructing Muslim identities in Mali', in L. Brenner (ed.), *Muslim Identity and Social Change in Sub-Saharan Africa*. Bloomington: Indiana University Press.

Brenner, L. 1993b. 'Representing power and powerlessness among West African Muslims', in J.-P. Chrétien (ed.), *L'invention religieuse en Afrique: Histoire et religion en Afrique noire*. Paris: Karthala and ACCT.

Brenner, L. 2000. 'Histories of religion in Africa', inaugural lecture, delivered on 25 March 1999, School of Oriental and African Studies, London: SOAS.

Brenner, L. 2001. *Controlling Knowledge: Religion, Power and Schooling in a West African Muslim Society*. Bloomington: Indiana University Press.

Brevié, J. 1923. *Islam contre 'naturisme' au Soudan français: essai de psychologie politique coloniale*. Paris: Ernest Leroux.

Brown, W. 1969. 'The Caliphate of Hamdullahi c. 1818–1864: a study in West African history and tradition'. PhD dissertation, University of Wisconsin, Madison.

Brunet-Jailly, J. (ed.). 1993. *Se soigner au Mali: Une contribution des sciences sociales*. Paris: Karthala and ORSTOM.

Calhoun, C. 1992. 'Introduction: Habermas and the public sphere', in C. Calhoun (ed.), *Habermas and the Public Sphere*. Cambridge: MIT Press.

Cardaire, M. 1954. *L'Islam et le terroir africain*. Koulouba: IFAN.

Casanova, J. 1994. *Public Religions in the Modern World*. Chicago: University of Chicago Press.

Cau, M. 1945. 'L'Islam au Sénégal', CHEAM, Doc. 949.

Chailley, M. 1962. 'Aspects de l'Islam au Mali', in M. Chailley et al. (eds), *Notes et études sur l'Islam en Afrique noire*. Paris: Peyronnet.

Chappelle, Cdt. 1948. 'L'expansion de l'Islam en Afrique Noire', CHEAM, Doc. 1290.

Chéron, G. 1931. 'Le Dyidé', *Journal de la Société des Africanistes* 1 (2), 285–9.

Chodkiewicz, M. 1986. *Le Sceau des saints: Prophétie et sainteté dans la doctrine d'Ibn Arabi*. Paris: Gallimard.

Cissé, S. 1992. *L'Enseignement islamique en Afrique noire*. Paris: L'Harmattan.

Clancy-Smith, J. A. 1994. *Rebel and Saint: Muslim Notables, Populist Protest, Colonial Encounters (Algeria and Tunisia, 1800–1904)*. Berkeley: University of California Press.

Clozel, F. 1913. 'Lettres de Korbous: politique musulmane au Soudan, pacification du Sahara soudanais', *Bulletin du Comité de l'Afrique française, Renseignements Coloniaux* 60–2; 106–9; 150–2; 182–5.

Comaroff, J. 1994. 'Defying disenchantment: reflections on ritual, power, and history', in C. F. Keyes, L. Kendall and H. Hardacre (eds), *Asian Visions of Authority*. Honolulu: University of Hawaii Press.

Comaroff, J. and J. L. Comaroff. 1991. *Of Revelation and Revolution*, vol. 1. Chicago: University of Chicago Press.

Comaroff, J. and J. L. Comaroff. 1993. 'Introduction', in J. Comaroff and J. Comaroff (eds), *Modernity and its Malcontents: Ritual and Power in Postcolonial Africa*. Chicago: University of Chicago Press.

Comaroff, J. and J. L. Comaroff. 1999. 'Occult economies and the violence of abstraction: notes from the South African postcolony', *American Ethnologist* 26 (2), 279–303.

Comaroff, J. and J. L. Comaroff. 2000. 'Millenial capitalism: first thoughts on a second coming', *Public Culture* 12 (2), 291–343.

Comaroff, J. and J. Comaroff. 1992. *Ethnography and the Historical Imagination*. Boulder: Westview Press.

Conklin, A. 1997. *A Mission to Civilize: The Republican Idea of Empire in France and West Africa, 1895–1930*. Stanford: Stanford University Press.

Copans, J. 1980. *Les marabouts de l'arachide: la Confrérie mouride et les paysans du Sénégal*. Paris, le Sycomore.

Cornell, V. 1983. 'The logic of analogy and the role of the Sufi shaykh in post-Marinid Morocco', *International Journal of Middle Eastern Studies* 15, 67–93.

Cornell, V. 1998. *Realm of the Saint: Power and Authority in Moroccan Sufism*. Austin: University of Texas Press.

Coulon, C. 1981. *Le marabout et le prince: Islam et pouvoir au Sénégal*. Paris: A. Pedone.

Coulon, C. 1988. *Les musulmans et le pouvoir en Afrique noire*, 2nd edn. Paris: Karthala.

Coureau, Lt. 1952. 'Caractères anciens et actuels du maraboutisme dans le Fouta Toro', CHEAM, Doc. 2102.

Crapanzano, V. 1973. *The Hamadsha*. Berkeley: University of California Press.

DNAFLA [Direction nationale d'alphabétisation fonctionnelle et de la linguistique appliquée]. 1979. *Lexique soninke-français*. Bamako: DNAFLA.

DNAFLA. 1993. *Lexique (fulfulde-français)*. Bamako: Ministère de l'Education Nationale.

Dannerlein, B. 2001. 'Legitimate bounds and bound legitimacy: the act of allegiance to the ruler (bai'a) in 19th-century Morocco', *Die Welt des Islams* 43 (3), 1–23.

d'Arbaumont, Lt. 1941. 'La Confrérie des Tidjania en Afrique française', CHEAM, Doc. 1411.

de Coutouly, F. 1913. 'Dinguiraye', *Bulletin du Comité de l'Afrique française, Renseignements Coloniaux* 7, 241–5.

Deedat, A. 1994. *The Choice, Islam and Christianity*. Delhi: Adam.

Delafosse, M. 1913. 'Traditions historiques et légendaires du Soudan occidental', *Bulletin du Comité de l'Afrique française, Renseignements Coloniaux* 8, 293–306; 9, 325–9; 10, 355–68.

Delafosse, M. 1917. 'De l'origine du mot "toubab"', *Annuaire et Mémoires du Comité d'Etudes Historiques et Scientifiques de l'Afrique Occidentale Française*, pp. 205–16.

Delafosse, M. 1955. *La Langue Mandingue et ses dialectes (Malinké, Bambara, Dioula)*, vol. 2. Paris: Imprimerie Nationale and Paul Geuthner.

de Lartigue, Lt. 1898a. 'Notice géographique sur la région du Sahel', *Bulletin du Comité de l'Afrique française, Renseignements Coloniaux* 5, 109–35.

de Lartigue, Lt. 1898b. 'Notice historique sur la région du Sahel', *Bulletin du Comité de l'Afrique française, Renseignements Coloniaux* 4, 69–101.

de Luze, C. 1953. 'La subdivision de Tamchakett en 1945', CHEAM, Doc. 2.169.

Denny, F. M. 1988. '"God's friends": the sanctity of persons in Islam', in R. Kieckhefer and G. D. Bond (eds), *Sainthood: Its Manifestations in World Religions*. Berkeley. University of California Press.

Depont, O. and X. Coppolani. 1897. *Les confréries religieuses musulmanes*. Algiers: Jourdan.

Dermenghem, E. 1954. *Le culte des saints dans l'islam maghrébin*. Paris: Gallimard.

Désiré-Vuillemin, G. 1962. *Contribution à l'histoire de la Mauritanie de 1900 à 1934*. Dakar: Editions Clairafrique.

Diaby, S. M. C. 1992. *Les textes fondamentaux de la IIIe République du Mali*. Bamako: n.p.

Diakité, D. 1993. 'Quelques maladies chez les Bamanan', in J. Brunet-Jailly (ed.), *Se soigner au Mali*. Paris: Karthala and ORSTOM.

Diallo, H. 1997. 'Moussa Aminou, le "mahdi" de Ouani', in D. Robinson and J.-L. Triaud (eds), *Le temps des marabouts*. Paris: Karthala.

Diallo, T. 1988. 'Pouvoir et marabouts en Afrique de l'Ouest', *Islam et sociétés au sud du Sahara* 2, 7–10.

Diané, El-Hadj K. 1956. *Le Coran: Lumière du Créateur*, vol. 1. Algiers: Imprimerie Guiauchain.

Diané, El-Hadj K. 1973. *Recueil des cinq piliers de l'Islam*, 4th edn, vol. 1. n.p.

Diawara, M. 1990. *La graine de la parole*. Stuttgart: Franz Steiner.

Dicko, S. O. 1999. *Hamallah: Le protégé de Dieu*. Bamako: Jamana.

Dieterlen, G. and D. Sylla. 1992. *L'empire du Ghana: Le Wagadou et les traditions de Yéréré*. Paris: Karthala and ARSAN.

Dirks, N. B. 1992. 'Introduction: colonialism and culture', in N. B. Dirks (ed.), *Colonialism and Culture*. Ann Arbor: University of Michigan Press.

Doucouré, C. T. 1976. *Al-Da'wa al-hamawiyya fi mirat al-tariqa al-ahmadiyya al-tijaniyya*. Dakar: Impricap.

Doumbia, F. 1987. 'Les mosquées à Bamako', *Jamana* 13, 31–5.

Doutté, E. 1984. *Magie et religion dans l'Afrique du Nord*. Paris: Adrien-Maisonneuve, Paul Geuthner.

Dramé, K. 1986. 'Réponse à la "Lettre de Mois de Carême"', *Jamana* 6, 5–6.

Dramé, T. 1988. 'Alfa Umar Kaba Jaxite, fondateur de Kabala, marabout et conseiller de Siixumaru Tal', *Islam et sociétés au sud du Sahara* 2, 114–21.

Dumont, L. 1980. 'World renunciation in Indian religions', in *Homo hierarchicus*, rev. edn. Chicago: University of Chicago Press.

Durkheim, E. 1961. *Moral Education: A Study in the Theory and Application of the Sociology of Education*. New York: Free Press.

Eickelman, D. F. 1976. *Moroccan Islam*. Austin: University of Texas Press.

Eickelman, D. F. 1982. 'The study of Islam in local contexts', *Contributions to Asian Studies* 17, 1–16.

Eickelman, D. F. 1985. *Knowledge and Power in Morocco*. Princeton: Princeton University Press.

Eickelman, D. F. 1987. 'Changing interpretations of Islamic movements', in W. R. Roff (ed.), *Islam and the Political Economy of Meaning*. Berkeley: University of California Press.

Eickelman, D. F. 1989a. 'National identity and religious discourse in contemporary Oman', *International Journal of Islamic and Arabic Studies* 6 (1), 1–20.

Eickelman, D. F. 1989b. *The Middle East: An Anthropological Approach*, 2nd edn. Englewood Cliffs: Prentice Hall.

Eickelman, D. F. and J. W. Anderson (eds). 1999. *New Media in the Muslim World: The Emerging Public Sphere*. Bloomington: Indiana University Press.

Eickelman, D. F. and J. Piscatori (eds). 1990. *Muslim Travellers*. Berkeley: University of California Press.

Eickelman, D. F. and J. Piscatori. 1996. *Muslim Politics*. Princeton: Princeton University Press.

Evans-Pritchard, E. E. 1937. *Witchcraft, Oracles and Magic among the Azande*. Oxford: Oxford University Press.

Evans-Pritchard, E. E. 1949. *The Sanusi of Cyrenaica*. Oxford: Clarendon Press.

Ewing, K. P. 1983. 'The politics of Sufism: redefining the saints of Pakistan', *Journal of Asian Studies* 42 (2), 251–68.

Ewing, K. P. 1997. *Arguing Sainthood: Modernity, Psychoanalysis, and Islam*. Durham: Duke University Press.

Fall, B. 1993. *Le travail forcé en Afrique Occidentale française (1900–1945)*. Paris: Karthala.

Fanon, F. 1967. *Black Skins, White Masks*. New York: Grove.

Fay, C. 1995. 'La démocratie au Mali, ou le pouvoir en pâture', *Cahiers d'Etudes africaines* 35 (1), 19–53.

Ferme, M. 2001. *The Underneath of Things*. Berkeley: University of California Press.

Fischer, M. M. J. and M. Abedi. 1990. *Debating Muslims*. Madison: University of Wisconsin Press.

Fisher, H. 1970. 'The early life and pilgrimage of al-Hajj Muhammad al-Amin the Soninke (d. 1887)', *Journal of African History* 11 (1), 51–69.

Foucault, M. 1978. *The History of Sexuality*, vol. 1, trans. R. Hurley. New York: Pantheon Books.

Fox, W. 1841. *A Brief History of the Wesleyan Missions on the Western Coast of Africa*. London: Aylott and Jones.

Frémeaux, J. 1991. *La France et l'Islam depuis 1789*. Paris: Presses Universitaires de France.

Froelich, J.-C. 1968. 'Visite à El-Hadji Ibrahima Niasse', *L'Afrique et l'Asie* 83–4, 37–41.

Gaffney, P. D. 1994. *The Prophet's Pulpit: Islamic Preaching in Contemporary Egypt*. Berkeley: University of California Press.

Garcia, S. 1994. 'El Hadj Seydou Nourou Tall, "Grand Marabout" tidjane; l'histoire d'une carrière (1868–1980)', mémoire de maîtrise, Université de Paris VII.

Garcia, S. 1997. 'Al-Hajj Seydou Nourou Tall, "grand marabout tijani"', in D. Robinson and J.-L. Triaud (eds), *Le temps des marabouts*. Paris: Karthala.

Geertz, C. 1968. *Islam Observed*. Chicago: University of Chicago Press.

Geertz, C. 1979. 'Suq: the bazaar economy in Sefrou', in C. Geertz et al. (eds), *Meaning and Order in Moroccan Society*. Cambridge: Cambridge University Press.

Gellner, E. 1963. 'Sanctity, puritanism, secularisation and nationalism in North Africa', *Archives de Sociologie des Religions* 15, 71–86.

Gellner, E. 1968. 'A pendulum swing theory of Islam', *Archives Marocaines de Sociologie*, 5–14.

Gellner, E. 1969. *Saints of the Atlas*. Chicago: University of Chicago Press.

Gellner, E. 1981. *Muslim Society*. Cambridge: Cambridge University Press.

Gellner, E. 1992. *Postmodernism, Reason, and Religion*. New York: Routledge.

Gellner, E. 1994. 'Foreword', in A. S. Ahmed and H. Donnan (eds), *Islam, Globalization and Postmodernity*. New York: Routledge.

Geschiere, P. 1997. *The Modernity of Witchcraft*. Charlottesville: University Press of Virginia.

Gibbal, J.-M. 1982. *Tambours d'eau*. Paris: Le Sycomore.

Gilsenan, M. D. 1973. *Saint and Sufi in Modern Egypt*. Oxford: Clarendon.

Gilsenan, M. D. 1982. *Recognizing Islam: Religion and Society in the Modern Arab World*. New York: Pantheon Books.

Gimaret, D. 1988. *Les noms divins en Islam: Exégèse lexicographique et théologique*. Paris: Editions du Cerf.

Goichon, A.-M. 1950. 'Le panislamisme d'hier et d'aujourd'hui', *L'Afrique et l'Asie* 9, 18–44.

Gomez, M. 1994. *Pragmatism in the Age of Jihad*. Cambridge: Cambridge University Press.

Gomez-Perez, M. 1991. 'Assocations islamiques à Dakar', *Islam et sociétés au sud du Sahara* 5, 5–19.

Gomez-Perez, M. 1997. 'Une histoire des associations islamiques sénégalaises (Saint-Louis, Dakar, Thiès): itinéraires, stratégies et prises de parole (1930–1993)'. Thèse de doctorat, Université de Paris VII.

Gouilly, A. 1948. 'Note sur le Hamallisme', Dakar, typescript.

Gouilly, A. 1952. *L'Islam dans l'Afrique Occidentale française*. Paris: Larose.

Graeber, D. 1996. 'Beads and money: notes toward a theory of wealth and power', *American Ethnologist* 23 (1), 4–24.

Gregory, C. A. 1982. *Gifts and Commodities*. London: Academic.

Gresh, A. 1983. 'L'Arabie saoudite en Afrique non arabe: puissance islamique ou relais de l'Occident?', *Politique africaine* 10, 55–74.

Guyer, J. I. 1993. 'Wealth in people and self-realization in equatorial Africa', *Man* (n.s.) 28, 243–65.

Habermas, J. 1989. *The Structural Transformation of the Public Sphere*, trans. T. Burger. Cambridge: MIT Press.

Al-Hajj, M. 1968. 'A seventeenth century chronicle on the origins and missionary activities of the Wangarawa', *Kano Studies* 1 (4), 7–16.

Hamès, C. 1980. 'Deux aspects du fondamentalisme islamique: Sa signification au Mali actuel et chez Ibn Taimiya', *Archives de sciences sociales des religions* 50 (2), 177–90.

Hamès, C. 1982. 'Un poème peul en l'honneur de Cheikh Hamallah', in J.-P. Digard (ed.), *Le cuisinier et le philosophe*. Paris: Maisonneuve et Larose.

Hamès, C. 1983. 'Cheick Hamallah ou qu'est-ce qu'une confrérie islamique (tariqa)', *Archives de sciences sociales des religions* 55 (1), 67–83.

Hamès, C. 1987. 'Taktub ou la magie de l'écriture islamique, textes Soninké à usage magique', *Arabica* 34, 305–25.

Hamès, C. 1993. 'Entre recette magique d'Al-Bûnî et prière islamique d'Al-Ghazâlî: textes talismaniques d'Afrique occidentale' in A. de Surgy (ed.), *Fétiches II: Puissance des objets, Charme des mots, Systèmes de pensée en Afrique noire* 12, 187–223.

Hamès, C. 1997a. 'Le premier exil de Shaikh Hamallah et la mémoire hamalliste

(Nioro-Mederdra, 1925)', in D. Robinson and J.-L. Triaud (eds), *Le temps des marabouts*. Paris: Karthala.

Hamès, C. 1997b. 'L'art talismanique en Islam d'Afrique Occidentale. Personnes, supports, procédés, transmission. Analyse anthropologique et islamologique d'un corpus de talismans à écritures'. Thèse de doctorat, l'Ecole pratique des hautes études, Paris.

Hamès, C. and A. Epelboin. 1993. 'Trois vêtements talismaniques provenant du Sénégal (décharge de Dakar-Pikine)', *Bulletin d'Etudes Orientales* 44, 217–41.

Hammoudi, A. 1997. *Master and Disciple: The Cultural Foundations of Moroccan Authoritarianism*. Chicago: University of Chicago Press.

Hanretta, S. 2003. 'Constructing a religious community in French West Africa: the Hamawi Sufis of Yacouba Sylla (Côte d'Ivoire)'. PhD dissertation, University of Wisconsin, Madison.

Hanson, J. H. 1989. 'Umarian Karta (Mali, West Africa) during the late nineteenth century'. PhD dissertation, Michigan State University.

Hanson, J. H. 1996. *Migration, Jihad, and Muslim Authority in West Africa*. Bloomington: Indiana University Press.

Hanson, J. H. and D. Robinson. 1991. *After the Jihad: The Reign of Ahmad al-Kabir in the Western Sudan*, African Historical Sources, 2. East Lansing: Michigan State University Press.

Happe, M. 1967. 'L'Islam au Sénégal dans le contexte politique', CHEAM, Doc. 4146.

Harmon, S. A. 1988. 'The expansion of Islam among the Bambara under French rule: 1890 to 1940'. PhD dissertation, University of California, Los Angeles.

Harrison, C. 1988. *France and Islam in West Africa, 1860–1960*. Cambridge: Cambridge University Press.

Harrison, C., M. Martin, and T. C. Ingawa. 1987. 'The establishment of colonial rule in West Africa, c. 1900–1914', in J. F. A. Ajayi and M. Crowder (eds), *History of West Africa*, 2nd edn, vol. 2. London: Longman.

Hefner, R. W. 2000. *Civil Islam. Muslims and Democratization in Indonesia*. Princeton: Princeton University Press.

Hirschkind, C. 2001. 'Religious reason and civic virtue: an Islamic counter-public', *Cultural Anthropology* 16, 3–34.

Hiskett, M. 1980. 'The "Community of Grace" and its opponents, the "Rejectors": a debate about theology and mysticism in Muslim West Africa with special reference to its Hausa expression', *African Language Studies* 17, 99–140.

Hiskett, M. 1984. *The Development of Islam in West Africa*. London and New York: Longman.

Hock, C. 1999. *Fliegen die Seelen der Heiligen? Muslimische Reform und staatliche Autorität in der Republik Mali seit 1960*. Berlin: Klaus Schwarz.

Hodgkin, T. and R. S. Morgenthau. 1964. 'Mali', in J. S. Coleman and C. G. Rosberg, Jr (eds), *Political Parties and National Integration in Tropical Africa*. Berkeley: University of California Press.

Hoffman, V. J. 1995. *Sufism, Mystics, and Saints in Modern Egypt*. Columbia: University of South Carolina Press.

Holy, L. 1991. *Religion and Custom in a Muslim Society*. Cambridge: Cambridge University Press.

Hourani, A. 1991. *A History of the Arab Peoples*. Cambridge: Harvard University Press.

Hrbek, I. 1979. 'The early period of Mahmadu Lamin's activities', in J. R. Willis (ed.), *Studies in West African Islamic History*, vol. 1. London: Frank Cass.

al-Hujwiri, 'Ali b. 'Uthman al-Jullabi. 1936. *Kashf al-Mahjub: The Oldest Persian Treatise on Sufism*, trans. R. A. Nicholson. London: Luzac & Co.

Hunter, T. 1977. 'The Jabi *Tarikhs*: their significance in West African Islam'. PhD dissertation, University of Chicago.

Huntington, S. 1996. *The Clash of Civilizations and the Remaking of World Order*. New York: Simon and Schuster.

Hunwick, J. O. 1985. *Shari'a in Songhay: The Replies of al-Maghili to the Questions of Askia al-Hajj Muhammad*. Oxford: Oxford University Press with the British Academy.

Hunwick, J. O. 1992. 'An introduction to the Tijani path: being an annotated translation of the chapter headings of the Kitab al-Rimah of al-Hajj Umar', *Islam et sociétés au sud du Sahara* 6, 17–32.

Hunwick, J. O. 1994. 'Sufism and the study of Islam in West Africa: the case of al-Hajj Umar', *Der Islam* 71, 308–28.

Hunwick, J. O. 1996. 'Secular power and religious authority in Muslim society: the case of Songhay', *Journal of African History* 37 (2), 175–94.

Hunwick, J. O. 2003a. *Arabic Literature of Africa, vol. IV: The Writings of Western Sudanic Africa*. Leiden: Brill.

Hunwick, J. O. 2003b. *Timbuktu and the Songhay Empire*. Leiden: Brill.

Ibn Khaldun. 1958. *The Muqaddimah: An Introduction to History*, 3 vols, trans. F. Rosenthal. New York: Pantheon Books.

Ibn Mu'adh, Sayyid Muhammad. 1988. *Al-Yaqut wa 'l-marjan fi hayat shaykhina himayat al-rahman*. Casablanca: Matba'at al-najah al-jadida.

Johansen, J. 1996. *Sufism and Islamic Reform in Egypt: The Battle for Islamic Tradition*. Oxford: Clarendon Press.

Johnstone, P. 1986. *Operation World*, 4th edn. Wayneboro, GA: STL Books and WEC Publications.

Joly, V. 1993. 'L'administration du Soudan français et les événements de 'Nioro-Assaba' (août 1940)', in E. Bernus et al. (eds), *Nomades et commandants*. Paris: Karthala.

Joly, V. 1997. 'La réconciliation de Nioro (septembre 1937): Un tournant dans la politique musulmane au Soudan français', in D. Robinson and J.-L. Triaud (eds), *Le temps des marabouts*. Paris: Karthala.

Kaba, L. 1974. *The Wahhabiyya: Islamic Reform and Politics in French West Africa*. Evanston: Northwestern University Press.

Kaba, L. 1997. 'Sheikh Mouhammad Chérif de Kankan: le devoir d'obéissance et la colonisation (1923–1955)', in D. Robinson and J.-L. Triaud (eds), *Le temps des marabouts*. Paris: Karthala.

Kane, M. M. 1987. 'A History of Futa Toro, 1890s–1920s: Senegal under colonial rule, the protectorate'. PhD dissertation, Michigan State University.

Kane, M. M. 1997. 'La vie et l'oeuvre d'Al Hajj Mahmoud Ba Diowol (1905–1978): du patre au patron de la "Revolution Al-Falah"', in D. Robinson and J.-L. Triaud (eds), *Le temps des marabouts*. Paris: Karthala.

Kane, O. 1997. 'Shaikh al-Islam Al-Hajj Ibrahim Niasse', in D. Robinson and J.-L. Triaud (eds), *Le temps des marabouts*. Paris: Karthala.

Kanya-Forstner, A. S. 1969. *The Conquest of the Western Sudan: A Study in French Military Imperialism*. Cambridge: Cambridge University Press.

Kazimirski, A. 1860. *Dictionnaire arabe-français*, 2 vols. Paris: Maisonneuve.

Kepel, G. 1986. *Muslim Extremism in Egypt: The Prophet and the Pharaoh*. Berkeley: University of California Press.

Kepel, G. 2002. *Jihad: The Trail of Political Islam*, trans. A. F. Roberts. Cambridge: Harvard University Press.

Klein, M. A. 1987. 'The demography of slavery in the Western Soudan during the late nineteenth century', in J. Gregory and D. Cordell (eds), *African Population and Capitalism*. Boulder: Westview.

Klein, M. A. 1998. *Slavery and Colonial Rule in French West Africa*. Cambridge: Cambridge University Press.

Kouanda, A. and B. Sawadogo. 1993 . 'Un moqaddem hammaliste au Yatenga au début du XXe siècle', in J.-P. Chrétien (ed.), *L'invention religieuse en Afrique: Histoire et religion en Afrique noire*. Paris: Karthala and ACCT.

Labouret, H. 1935. 'La sorcellerie au Soudan occidental', *Africa* 13, 462–72.

Lafeuille, R. 1947. 'Le Tidjanisme Onze Grains ou Hamallisme', CHEAM, Doc. 1189.

Lambek, M. 1990. 'Certain knowledge, contestable authority: power and practice on the Islamic periphery', *American Ethnologist* 17 (1), 23–40.

Lambek, M. 1993. *Knowledge and Practice in Mayotte: Local Discourses of Islam, Sorcery, and Spirit Possession*. Toronto: University of Toronto Press.

Lanrezac, H. C. 1905. 'Le Cercle de Nioro', *Bulletin de la Société de Géographie commerciale de Paris* 27, 227–61.

Last, M. 1988. 'Charisma and medicine in Northern Nigeria', in D. B. Cruise O'Brien and C. Coulon (eds), *Charisma and Brotherhood in African Islam*. Oxford: Clarendon.

Launay, R. 1982. *Traders without Trade: Responses to Change in Two Dyula Communities*. Cambridge: Cambridge University Press.

Launay, R. 1992. *Beyond the Stream: Islam and Society in a West Africa Town*. Berkeley: University of California Press.

Launay, R. 1996. 'La Trahison des Clercs? the "collaboration" of a Suwarian 'alim', in J. Hunwick and N. Lawler (eds), *The Cloth of Many Colored Silks: Papers on History and Society Ghanaian and Islamic in Honor of Ivor Wilks*. Evanston: Northwestern University Press.

Launay, R. 1997a. 'Des infidèles d'un autre type: Les réponses au pouvoir colonial dans une communauté musulmane de Côte d'Ivoire', in D. Robinson and J.-L. Triaud (eds), *Le temps des marabouts*. Paris: Karthala.

Launay, R. 1997b. 'Spirit media: the electronic media and Islam among the Dyula of northern Côte d'Ivoire', *Africa* 63 (3), 441–53.

Launay, R. 1998. 'Knowledgeable Muslims', *Reviews in Anthropology* 27 (4), 379–91.

Launay, R. and B. F Soares. 1999. 'The formation of an "Islamic sphere" in French colonial West Africa', *Economy and Society* 28 (4), 497–519.

Le Chatelier, A. 1899. *L'Islam dans l'Afrique Occidentale*. Paris: G. Steinheil.

Le Grip, A. 1953–4. 'Aspects de l'Islam en A.O.F.', *L'Afrique et l'Asie* 24, 6–20; 25, 43–61.

Levtzion, N. 1973. *Ancient Ghana and Mali*. London: Methuen.

Levtzion, N. 2000. 'Islam in the Bilad al-Sudan to 1800', in N. Levtzion and R. Pouwels (eds), *The History of Islam in Africa*. Athens and Oxford: Ohio University Press and James Currey.

Levtzion, N. and J. O. Voll (eds). 1987. *Eighteenth-century Renewal and Reform in Islam*. Syracuse: Syracuse University Press.

Lewis, I. M. 1986. *Religion in Context: Cults and Charisma*. Cambridge: Cambridge University Press.

Lewis, I. M, A. Al-Safi, and S. Hurreiz (eds). 1991. *Women's Medicine: The Zar-Bori Cult in Africa and Beyond*. Edinburgh: Edinburgh University Press for the International African Institute.

Loimeier, R. 1999. 'Political dimensions of the relationship between Sufi brotherhoods and the Islamic reform movement in Senegal', in F. de Jong and B. Radtke (eds), *Islamic Mysticism Contested*. Leiden: Brill.

Lory, P. 1996. 'Soufisme et sciences occultes', in A. Popovic and G. Veinstein (eds), *Les Voies d'Allah: Les ordres mystiques dans le monde musulman des origines à nos jours*. Paris: Fayard.

Lovejoy, P. 1983. *Transformations in Slavery*. Cambridge: Cambridge University Press.

Lubeck, P. 1986. *Islam and Urban Labour in Northern Nigeria*. Cambridge: Cambridge University Press.

Ly-Tall, M. 1991. *Un Islam militant en Afrique de l'ouest au XIXème siècle*. Paris: L'Harmattan.

Mahibou, S. M. and J.-L. Triaud. 1983. *Voilà ce qui est arrivé. Bayân mâ waqa'a d'al-Hâgg 'Umar al-Fûtî. Plaidoyer pour une guerre sainte en Afrique de l'Ouest*. Paris: CNRS.

al-Mahjubi, Abu Bakr b. Ahmad al-Mustafa. 2001. *Minah al-rabb al-ghafur fi dhikr ma ahmalahu sahib Fath al-Shakur*, ed. al-Hadi al-Mabruk al-Dali. Benghazi: Dar al-Kitab.

Malinowski, B. 1925. *Coral Gardens and their Magic*. New York: George Allen & Unwin.

Malle, Y. 1985. 'Le culte de possession en milieu bamanan: Le "Jiné-don" dans le district de Bamako: Etude clinique du "Jiné-bana"'. Mémoire, fin d'études, Ecole Normale Supérieure, Bamako.

Manchuelle, E. F. 1987. 'Background to Black African migration to France: the labor migrations of the Soninke, 1848–1987'. PhD dissertation, University of California, Santa Barbara.

Manchuelle, E. F. 1989. 'Slavery, emancipation and labour migration in West Africa: the case of the Soninke', *Journal of African History* 30, 89–106.

Manchuelle, E. F. 1997. *Willing Migrants: Soninke Labor Diasporas, 1848–1960*. Athens: Ohio University Press.

Martin, B. G. 1976. *Muslim Brotherhoods in Nineteenth-Century Africa*. Cambridge: Cambridge University Press.

Marty, M. E. and R. S. Appleby (eds). 1991. *Fundamentalisms Observed*. Chicago: University of Chicago Press.

Marty, P. 1915–16. 'L'Islam en Mauritanie et au Sénégal', *Revue du Monde Musulman* 31, 1–478

Marty, P. 1916. *Etudes sur l'Islam maure*. Paris: Ernest Leroux.

Marty, P. 1920. *Etudes sur l'Islam et les tribus du Soudan: La région de Kayes, le pays bambara, le Sahel de Nioro*, vol. 4. Paris: Ernest Leroux.

Marty, P. 1921. *Etudes sur l'Islam et les tribus du Soudan: Les tribus maures du Sahel et du Hodh*, vol. 3. Paris: Ernest Leroux.

Marty, P. 1927. 'Les Chroniques de Oualata et de Néma (Soudan français)', *Revue des Etudes Islamiques* 1 (3), 355–426; 1 (4), 531–75.

Masquelier, A. 2001. *Prayer Has Spoiled Everything: Possession, Power, and Identity in an Islamic Town of Niger*. Durham: Duke University Press.

El-Masri, F. H., R. A. Adeleye et al. 1966. 'Sifofin Shehu: an autobiography and character study of 'Uthman B. Fudi in verse', *Research Bulletin* (Centre of Arabic Documentation) 2 (1), 1–37.

Mbembe, A. 1992. 'Provisional notes on the postcolony', *Africa* 62 (1), 3–37.

MacLaughlin, F. 1997. 'Islam and popular music in Senegal', *Africa* 67, 560–81.

McNaughton, P. 1988. *The Mande Blacksmiths: Knowledge, Power, and Art in West Africa*. Bloomington: Indiana University Press.

Meillassoux, C. 1968. *Urbanization of an African Community: Voluntary Associations in Bamako*. Seattle: University of Washington Press.

Meillassoux, C. 1975. 'Etat et conditions des esclaves à Gumbu (Mali) au XIXe siècle', in C. Meillassoux (ed.), *L'esclavage en Afrique précoloniale*. Paris: Maspero.

Meillassoux, C. 1991. *The Anthropology of Slavery: The Womb of Iron and Gold*, trans. A. Dasnois. Chicago: University of Chicago Press.

Méniaud, J. 1931. *Pionniers du Soudan*, 2 vols. Paris: Société des publications modernes.

Messick, B. 1993. *The Calligraphic State: Textual Domination and History in a Muslim Society*. Berkeley: University of California Press.

Meyer, B. 1999. *Translating the Devil: Religion and Modernity among the Ewe of Ghana*. Edinburgh: Edinburgh University Press for the International African Institute.

Miller, D. 1995a. 'Consumption and commodities', *Annual Review of Anthropology* 24, 141–61.

Miller, D. 1995b. 'Introduction: anthropology, modernity and consumption', in D. Miller (ed.), *Worlds Apart*. New York: Routledge.

Miner, H. 1953. *The Primitive City of Timbuctoo*. Princeton: American Philosophical Society.

Mommersteeg, G. 1991. 'L'Education coranique au Mali: le pouvoir des mots sacrés', in B. Sanankoua and L. Brenner (eds), *L'enseignement islamique au Mali*. Bamako: Jamana.

Monteil, C. 1924. *Les Bambara de Ségou et du Kaarta*. Paris: Larose.

Monteil, V. 1980. *L'Islam noir*, 3rd edn. Paris: Editions du Seuil.

Moreau, P. 1938. *Les Indigènes d'A.O.F.: Leur condition politique et économique*. Paris: Domat-Montchrestien.

Moreau, R. L. 1964. 'Les marabouts de Dori', *Archives de sociologie des religions* 17, 113–34.

Morgenthau, R. S. 1964. *Political Parties in French Speaking West Africa*. London: Oxford University Press.

Mulay Muhammad b. Sidati. 1986. *Kitab qasr al-ta'ifa al-hamawiyya li-l-salat al-raba'iyya bahjat al-ashbah wa al-arwah*. Casablanca: Matba'at al-najah al-jadida.

Munn, N. 1986. *The Fame of Gawa*. Cambridge: Cambridge University Press.

Munson, H. 1993. *Religion and Power in Morocco*. New Haven: Yale University Press.

al-Nafrawi, Ahmad b. Ghunaym. 1900. *Al-Fawakih al-dawani*, vol. 2. Cairo.

Nicholson, R. A. 1921. *Studies in Islamic Mysticism*. Cambridge: Cambridge University Press.

Nicolas, F. 1943. 'Une mystique révolutionnaire socialo-religieuse: le Hamallisme ou Hamawisme (d'A.O.F.)', CHEAM, Doc. 1079.

Nietzsche, F. W. 1968. *The Will to Power*. London: Weidenfeld & Nicolson.

Niezen, R. 1987. 'Diverse styles of Islamic reform among the Songhay of Eastern Mali'. PhD thesis, University of Cambridge.

Niezen, R. 1990. 'The "Community of the Helpers of the Sunna": Islamic reform among the Songhay of Gao (Mali)', *Africa* 60 (3), 399–423.

Les noms les plus exaltés d'Allah (Soub-hana-wa-ta-Allah). n.d. No publisher.

Norris, H. T. 1986. *The Arab Conquest of the Western Sahara*. Harlow: Longman.

O'Brien, D. B. Cruise. 1967. 'Towards an "Islamic Policy" in French West Africa', *Journal of African History* 8 (2), 303–16.

O'Brien, D. B. Cruise. 1971. *The Mourides of Senegal*. Oxford: Clarendon Press.

O'Brien, D. B. Cruise. 1975. *Saints and Politicians*. Cambridge: Cambridge University Press.

O'Brien, D. B. Cruise and C. Coulon (eds). 1988. *Charisma and Brotherhood in African Islam*. Oxford: Clarendon Press.

O'Fahey, R. S. 1990. *Enigmatic Saint*. London: Hurst.

O'Fahey, R. S. and B. Radtke. 1993. 'Neo-Sufism reconsidered', *Der Islam* 70, 52–87.

Oded, A. 1987. 'The promotion of Islamic activities by Arab countries in Africa – contemporary trends', *Asian and African Studies* 21, 281–304.

Olivier de Sardan, J.-P. 1992. 'Occultism and the ethnographic "I": the exoticizing of magic from Durkheim to "postmodern" anthropology', *Critique of Anthropology* 12 (1), 5–25.

Oloruntimehin, B. O. 1971. 'Senegambia: Mahamadou Lamine', in M. Crowder (ed.), *West African Resistance*. London: Hutchinson.

Ouane, I.-M. 1957. *L'Islam et la civilisation française*. Paris: Les Presses Universelles.

Ould Abdellah, A. D. 2000. 'Le "passage au sud": Muhammad al-Hafiz et son héritage', in J.-L. Triaud and D. Robinson (eds), *La Tijâniyya*. Paris: Karthala.

Ould Cheikh, A. W. 1985. 'Nomadisme, islam et pouvoir politique dans la société maure précoloniale (XIeme siècle–XIXeme siècle): essai sur quelques aspects du tribalisme'. Thèse de doctorat, Université de Paris V.

Ould Cheikh, A. W. 1991. 'La tribu comme volonté et comme représentation: le facteur religieux dans l'organisation d'une tribu maure: les Awlad Abyayri', in P. Bonte et al. (eds), *Al-Ansâb: La quête des origines*. Paris: Editions de la M.S.H.

Ould Cheikh, A. W. 1993. 'L'évolution de l'esclavage dans la société maure', in E. Bernus et al. (eds), *Nomades et commandants*. Paris: Karthala.

Ould Cheikh, A. W. 2000. 'Les perles et le soufre: une polémique mauritanienne autour de la Tijaniyya (1830–1935)', in J.-L. Triaud and D. Robinson (eds), *La Tijâniyya*. Paris: Karthala.

Owusu-Ansah, D. 1991. *Islamic Talismanic Traditions in Nineteenth-Century Asante*. Lewiston: Edwin Mellen Press.

Paden, J. N. 1973. *Religion and Political Culture in Kano*. Berkeley: University of California Press.

Park, M. 2000 [1799]. *Travels in the Interior Districts of Africa*, ed. K. F. Marsters. Durham: Duke University Press.

Peletz, M. G. 2002. *Islamic Modern: Religious Courts and Cultural Politics in Malaysia*. Princeton: Princeton University Press.

Perry, D. 1998. 'The Patriarchs are Crying: discourses of authority and social change in rural Senegal'. PhD dissertation, Yale University.

Pollet, E. and G. Winter. 1971. *La Société Soninké (Dyahunu, Mali)*. Brussels: Editions de l'Institut de Sociologie de l'Université Libre de Bruxelles.

Poulet, G. 1904. *Les Maures de l'Afrique occidentale française*. Paris: A. Chalamel.

al-Qayrawani, Ibn Abi Zayd. 1975. *La Risâla ou Epître sur les éléments du dogme et de la loi de l'Islâm selon le rite mâlikite*, 6th edn, trans. L. Bercher. Algiers: Editions populaires de l'armée.

Quesnot, F. 1958a. 'Contribution à l'étude de l'Islam noir: evolution du tidjanisme sénégalais depuis 1922', CHEAM, Doc. 2865.

Quesnot, F. 1958b. 'Panorama de l'Islam au Sénégal' CHEAM, Doc. 3017.

Quiminal, C. 1991. *Gens d'ici et gens d'ailleurs: Migrations Soninké et transformations villageoises*. Paris: Christian Bourgois.

Radtke, B. and J. O'Kane. 1996. *The Concept of Sainthood in Early Islamic Mysticism*. Richmond: Curzon.

Raffenel, A. 1856. *Nouveau voyage dans le pays des Nègres*, vol 1. Paris: Napoléon Chaix.

Rançon, A. 1894. *Le Bondou: Etude de géographie et d'histoire soudaniennes de 1861 à nos jours*. Bordeaux: Imprimerie G. Gounouilhou.

Redfield, R. 1956. *Peasant Society and Culture*. Chicago: University of Chicago Press.

Riesebrodt, M. 1999. 'Charisma in Max Weber's sociology of religion', *Religion* 29, 1–14.

Roberts, R. L. 1987. *Warriors, Merchants, and Slaves: The State and the Economy in the Middle Niger Valley, 1700–1914*. Stanford: Stanford University Press.

Roberts, R. L. 1988. 'The end of slavery in the French Soudan, 1905–1914', in S. Miers and R. Roberts (eds), *The End of Slavery in Africa*. Madison: University of Wisconsin Press.

Roberts, R. L. and M. Klein. 1980. 'The Banamba slave exodus of 1905 and the decline of slavery in the Western Sudan', *Journal of African History* 21, 375–94.

Robinson, D. 1985. *The Holy War of Umar Tal*. Oxford: Clarendon Press.

Robinson, D. 1988. 'French "Islamic" policy and practice in nineteenth-century Senegal', *Journal of African History* 29, 415–35.

Robinson, D. 1997. 'The emerging pattern of cooperation between colonial authorities and Muslim societies in Senegal and Mauritania', in D. Robinson and J.-L. Triaud (eds), *Le temps des marabouts*. Paris: Karthala.

Robinson, D. 2000. *Paths of Accommodation: Muslim Societies and French Colonial Authorities in Senegal and Mauritania, 1880–1920*. Athens: Ohio University Press.

Robinson, D. and J.-L. Triaud (eds). 1997. *Le temps des marabouts: Itinéraires et stratégies islamiques en Afrique occidentale française v. 1880–1960*. Paris: Karthala.

Rocaboy, J. 1947a. 'L'Hamalisme', CHEAM, Doc. 1153.

Rocaboy, J. 1947b. 'Une confrérie du Sahel soudanais: le hamallisme', CHEAM, Doc. 988.

Rocaboy, J. 1993. 'Le cas hamalliste: les événements de Nioro-Assaba (août 1940)', in E. Bernus et al. (eds), *Nomades et commandements*. Paris: Karthala.

Rodinson, M. 1980. *La fascination de l'Islam*. Paris: Maspero.

Rosen, L. 1984. *Bargaining for Reality*. Chicago: University of Chicago Press.

Rowlands, M. and J.-P. Warnier. 1988. 'Sorcery, power and the modern state in Cameroon', *Man* (n.s.) 23 (1), 118–32.

Roy, O. 1994. *The Failure of Political Islam*, trans. C. Volk. Cambridge: Harvard University Press.

Ruxton, F. H. 1916. *Maliki Law*. London: Luzac.

Saad, E. 1983. *The Social History of Timbuktu: The Role of Muslim Scholars and Notables, 1400–1900*. Cambridge: Cambridge University Press.

Sahlins, M. 1992. 'The political economy of grandeur in Hawaii from 1820 to 1830', in E. Ohnuki-Tierney (ed.), *Culture through Time*. Stanford: Stanford University Press.

Sall, I.-A. 1997. 'Cerno Amadu Mukhtar Sakho, Qadi Supérieur de Boghe (1905–1934), Futa Toro', in D. Robinson and J.-L. Triaud (eds), *Le temps des marabouts*. Paris: Karthala.

Sall, I.-A. 1998. 'Mauritanie. Conquête et organisation administrative des territoires du sud (Gidimaxa, Fuuta Tooro et Waalo Barak). Rôle des aristocraties politiques et religieuses (1890–1945)'. Thèse de doctorat, Université de Paris VII.

Salvatore, A. 1997. *Islam and the Political Discourse of Modernity*. Reading: Ithaca Press.

Sanankoua, B. 1990. *Un empire peul au XIXe siècle*. Paris: Karthala and ACCT.

Sanankoua, B. 1991. 'L'enseignement islamique à la radio et à la télévision au Mali', in B. Sanankoua and L. Brenner (eds), *L'enseignement islamique au Mali*. Bamako: Jamana.

Sanankoua, B. and L. Brenner (eds). 1991. *L'enseignement islamique au Mali*. Bamako: Jamana.

Sanneh, L. 1989. *The Jakhanke Muslim Clerics: A Religious and Historical Study of Islam in Senegambia*. Lanham: University Press of America.

Sarr, D. and R. Roberts. 1991. 'The jurisdiction of Muslim tribunals in colonial Senegal, 1857–1932', in K. Mann and R. Roberts (eds), *Law in Colonial Africa*. Portsmouth: Heinemann.

Savadogo, B. 1998. 'Confréries et pouvoirs. La Tijaniyya Hamawiyya en Afrique Occidentale (Burkina Faso, Côte d'Ivoire, Mali, Niger): 1909–1965'. Thèse de doctorat, Université de Provence (Aix-Marseille I).

Savadogo, B. 2000. 'La communauté "Yacouba Sylla" et ses rapports avec la Tijâniyya hamawiyya', in J.-L. Triaud and D. Robinson (eds), *La Tijâniyya*. Paris: Karthala.

Schmitz, J. 1985. 'Autour d'al-Hajj Umar Taal: Guerre sainte et Tijaniyya en Afrique de l'Ouest', *Cahiers d'Etudes africaines* 25 (4), 555–65.

Seesemann, R. 1993. *Ahmadu Bamba und die Entstehung der Muridiyya*. Berlin: Klaus Schwarz.

Seesemann, R. and B. F. Soares. n.d. '"Being as good Muslims as Frenchmen": on Islam and colonial modernity in West Africa', in J. H. Hanson and R. van Dijk (eds), *Religious Modernities in West Africa*. Bloomington: Indiana University Press (in press).

Shaw, R. 2002. *Memories of the Slave Trade*. Chicago: University of Chicago Press.

Shereikis, R. 2001. 'From law to custom: the shifting legal status of Muslim *originaires* in Kayes and Medine, 1903–13', *Journal of African History* 42, 261–83.

Shereikis, R. 2003. 'Customized courts: French colonial legal institutions in Kayes, French Soudan, c. 1880–c. 1913'. PhD dissertation, Northwestern University.

Sirriyeh, E. 1999. *Sufis and Anti-Sufis: The Defense, Rethinking and Rejection of Sufism in the Modern World*. Richmond: Curzon.

Smith, W. C. 1957. *Islam in Modern History*. Princeton: Princeton University Press.

Soares, B. F. 1996a. 'A contemporary Malian shaykh', *Islam et Sociétés au Sud du Sahara* 10, 145–53.

Soares, B. F. 1996b. 'The prayer economy in a Malian town', *Cahiers d'Etudes africaines* 36 (4), 739–53.

Soares, B. F. 1997. 'The Fulbe shaykh and the Bambara "pagans": contemporary campaigns to spread Islam in Mali', in M. de Bruijn and H. van Dijk (eds), *Peuls et Mandingues: dialectiques des constructions identitaires*. Paris: Karthala.

Soares, B. F. 1999. 'Muslim proselytization as purification: religious pluralism and conflict in contemporary Mali', in A.A. An-Na'im (ed.), *Proselytization and Communal Self-Determination in Africa*, Maryknoll: Orbis.

Soares, B. F. 2000. 'Notes on the anthropological study of Islam and Muslim societies in Africa', *Culture & Religion* 1 (2), 277–85.

Soares, B. F. 2003. 'A warning about imminent calamity in colonial French West Africa: the chain letter as historical source', *Sudanic Africa: A Journal of Historical Sources* 14.

Soares, B. F. 2004a. 'An African Muslim saint and his followers in France', *Journal of Ethnic and Migration Studies* 30 (5).

Soares, B. F. 2004b. 'Islam and public piety in Mali', in A. Salvatore and D. F. Eickelman (eds), *Public Islam and the Common Good*. Leiden: Brill.

Soares, B. F. 2004c. 'Muslim saints in the age of neoliberalism', in B. Weiss (ed.), *Producing African Futures: Ritual and Reproduction in a Neoliberal Age*. Leiden: Brill.

Soares, B. and J. Hunwick. 1996. 'The shaykh as the locus of divine self-disclosure: a poem in praise of Shaykh Hamahu'llah', *Sudanic Africa: A Journal of Historical Sources* 7, 97–112.

Sow, D. 1985–6. 'Contribution à l'étude de l'islam en Afrique. La communauté Tijani de Madiina Gunaas'. Mémoire de maîtrise, Université de Nouakchott, Mauritania.

Starrett, G. 1995. 'The political economy of religious commodities in Cairo', *American Anthropologist* 97 (1), 51–68.

Starrett, G. 1997. 'The anthropology of Islam', in S. D. Glazier (ed.), *The Anthropology of Religion: A Handbook*. Westport: Greenwood Press.

Starrett, G. 1998. *Putting Islam to Work: Education, Politics, and Religious Transformation in Egypt*. Berkeley: University of California Press

Stewart, C. C. with E. K. Stewart. 1973. *Islam and Social Order in Mauritania*. Oxford: Oxford University Press.

Stoller, P. 1989. *Fusion of the Worlds: An Ethnography of Possession among the Songhay of Niger*. Chicago: University of Chicago Press.

Stoller, P. and C. Olkes. 1987. *In Sorcery's Shadow*. Chicago: University of Chicago Press.

Stone, D. 1994. 'Aspects du paysage religieux: marabouts et confréries', *Politique africaine* 55, 52–6.

Suret-Canale, J. 1971. *French Colonialism in Tropical Africa, 1900–1945*, trans. T. Gottheiner. London: Hurst.

Taine-Cheikh, C. 1990. *Lexique Français-Hassaniyya (Dialecte arabe de Mauritanie)*. Nouakchott: Centre Culturel Français A. de Saint-Exupéry & Institut Mauritanien de Recherche Scientifique.

Tall, C. A. 1995. *Niche des secrets: Recueil d'arcanes mystiques dans la tradition soufie (islamique)*, 2nd edn. Dakar: n.p.

Tambiah, S. J. 1984. *The Buddhist Saints of the Forests and the Cult of the Amulets*. Cambridge: Cambridge University Press.

el-Tom, A. O. 1985. 'Drinking the Koran: the meaning of Koranic verses in Berti erasure', *Africa* 55 (4), 414–31.

el-Tom, A. O. 1987. 'Berti Qur'anic amulets', *Journal of Religion in Africa* 17 (3), 224–44.

Touré, C. 1957. *Afin que tu deviennes un croyant*. Dakar: Imprimerie Diop.

Touré, El Hadj Saad Oumar Saïd. n.d. *Les Invocations*. Tunis: Imprimerie al-Manar.

Touré, El Hadj Saad Oumar Saïd. 1993. *Sauvegarde des élèves des médersahs des étudiants et toute notre jeunesse musulmane contre les tentatives de devoiement des hommes des églises chretiennes*. Casablanca: Dar Errachad El Haditha.

Traoré, A. 1983. *Islam et colonisation en Afrique: Cheick Hamahoullah, homme de foi et résistant*. Paris: Maisonneuve et Larose.

Traoré, M. 1985. 'Lettre de mois de carême', *Jamana* 4.

Triaud, J.-L. 1974. 'La question musulmane en Côte d'Ivoire (1893–1939)', *Revue française d'histoire d'Outre-Mer* 61 (225), 542–71.

Triaud, J.-L. 1986. 'Abd al-Rahman l'Africain (1908–1957), pionneur et précurseur du wahhabisme au Mali', in O. Carré and P. Dumont (eds), *Radicalismes islamiques*, vol 2. Paris: L'Harmattan.

Triaud, J.-L. 1992. 'L'Islam sous le régime colonial', in C. Coquery-Vidrovitch (ed.), *L'Afrique occidentale au temps des Français (colonisateur et colonisés, c. 1860–1960)*. Paris: Editions la Découverte.

Triaud, J.-L. 1997. 'Le crepuscule des "Affaires Musulmanes" en A.O.F. (1950–1956)', in D. Robinson and J.-L. Triaud (eds), *Le temps des marabouts*. Paris: Karthala.

al-Tukhi, Abd al-Fattah al-Sayyid 'Abduh. 1956. *Manba' usul al-raml*. Cairo: Maktabat wa-Matba'at Muhammad 'Ali Subayh.

Turner, B. S. 1974. *Weber and Islam*. London: Routledge & Kegan Paul.

Turner, V. W. 1973. 'The center out there: pilgrim's goal', *History of Religions* 12, 191–230.

Tyam, M. A. 1935. *La vie d'El Hadj Omar: Qacida en poular*, trans. H. Gaden. Paris: Institut d'ethnologie.

Umar, M. S. 1993. 'Changing Islamic identity in Nigeria from the 1960s to the 1980s: from Sufism to anti-Sufism', in L. Brenner (ed.), *Muslim Identity and Social Change in Sub-Saharan Africa*. Bloomington: Indiana University Press.

Umar b. Sa'id al-Futi [Tall] n.d. *Rimah hizb al-rahim 'ala nuhur hizb al-rajim*, published in the margins of Ali Harazim, *Jawahir al-Ma'ani*. Beirut: Dar al-Jil.

van der Veer, P. 1994. *Religious Nationalism: Hindus and Muslims in India*. Berkeley: University of California Press.

Villalón, L. A. 1995. *Islamic Society and State Power in Senegal: Disciples and Citizens in Fatick*. Cambridge: Cambridge University Press.

Wane, Y. 1969. *Les Toucouleurs du Fouta Tooro (Sénégal)*. Dakar: IFAN.

Wane, Y. 1974. 'Ceerno Muhamadu Sayid Baa ou le soufisme intégral de Madiina Gunaas (Sénégal)', *Cahiers d'Etudes africaines* 14 (4), 671–98.

Warms, R. L. 1992. 'Merchants, Muslims, and the Wahhabiyya: the elaboration of Islamic identity in Sikasso, Mali', *Canadian Journal of African Studies* 26 (3), 485–507.

Warner, M. 2002. *Publics and Counterpublics*. New York: Zone Books.

Watts, M. 1996. 'Islamic modernities? Citizenship, civil society and Islamism in a Nigerian city', *Public Culture* 8(2), 251–89.

Weber, M. 1978. *Economy and Society*, 2 vols. Berkeley: University of California Press.

Weller, R. P. 2000. 'Living at the edge: religion, capitalism, and the end of the nation-state in Taiwan', *Public Culture* 12 (2), 477–98.

Wensinck, A. J. 1927. *A Handbook of Early Muhammadan Tradition*. Leiden: Brill.

Werbner, P. J. 1998. '*Langar*: pilgrimage, sacred exchange and perpetual sacrifice in a Sufi saint's lodge', in P. J. Werbner and H. Basu (eds), *Embodying Charisma*. New York: Routledge.

Werbner, P. J. 2003. *Pilgrims of Love*. London: Hurst.

Werbner, P. J. and H. Basu (eds). 1998. *Embodying Charisma: Modernity, Locality and the Performance of Emotion in Sufi Cults*. New York: Routledge.

Wilks, I. 1968. 'The transmission of Islamic learning in the Western Sudan', in J. R. Goody (ed.), *Literacy in Traditional Societies*. Cambridge: Cambridge University Press.

Williams, E. 1988. 'Ethnology as myth: a century of writing on the Peuls of West Africa', *Journal of the History of the Behavioral Sciences* 24, 363–77.

Willis, J. R. 1976. 'The Western Sudan from the Moroccan invasion (1591) to the death of al-Mukhtar al-Kunti (1811)' in J. F. Ade Ajayi and M. Crowder (eds), *History of West Africa*. Vol. I. New York: Columbia University Press.

Willis, J. R. 1978. 'The Torodbe clerisy: a social view', *Journal of African History* 19 (2), 195–212.

Willis, J. R. 1989. *In the Path of Allah: The Passion of al-Hajj Umar*. London: Frank Cass.

el-Zein, A. H. M. 1977. 'Beyond ideology and theology: the search for an anthropology of Islam', *Annual Review of Anthropology* 6, 227–54.

Zubaida, S. 1995. 'Is there a Muslim society? Ernest Gellner's sociology of Islam', *Economy and Society* 24 (2), 151–88.

NEWSPAPERS AND PERIODICALS

Aurore (Bamako)
Le Démocrate (Bamako)
Les Echos (Bamako)
L'Essor (Bamako)
La Griffe (Bamako)
L'Indépendant (Bamako)
Jeune Afrique (Paris)
Kabako (Bamako)
Mauritanie Nouvelles (Nouakchott)
Le Politicien musulman (Bamako)
Le Républicain (Bamako)
La Roue (Bamako)
Le Soudan Français (Bamako)
Témoignage afro-musulman (Ségou)

INDEX